Gender in Communication

Second Edition

This book honors our mothers:
Victoria DeFrancisco Leto (1924–2004)
Maj. Helen Mary Finks Palczewski (1921–1999)
Mary Lu Dick (1956–)

Gender in Communication

A Critical Introduction

Victoria Pruin DeFrancisco
University of Northern Iowa

Catherine Helen Palczewski
University of Northern Iowa

with Danielle Dick McGeough
University of Northern Iowa

⑤SAGE

Los Angeles | London | New Delhi
Singapore | Washington DC

Los Angeles | London | New Delhi
Singapore | Washington DC

FOR INFORMATION:

SAGE Publications, Inc.
2455 Teller Road
Thousand Oaks, California 91320
E-mail: order@sagepub.com

SAGE Publications Ltd.
1 Oliver's Yard
55 City Road
London EC1Y 1SP
United Kingdom

SAGE Publications India Pvt. Ltd.
B 1/I 1 Mohan Cooperative Industrial Area
Mathura Road, New Delhi 110 044
India

SAGE Publications Asia-Pacific Pte. Ltd.
3 Church Street
#10-04 Samsung Hub
Singapore 049483

Acquisitions Editor: Matthew Byrnie
Editorial Intern: Gabrielle Piccinnini
Production Editor: Stephanie Palermini
Copy Editor: Mark Bast
Typesetter: C&M Digitals (P) Ltd.
Proofreader: Ellen Howard
Indexer: Maria Sosnowski
Cover Designer: Glenn Vogel
Marketing Manager: Liz Thornton

Printed in the United States of America

Library of Congress Cataloging-in-Publication Data

DeFrancisco, Victoria L. (Victoria Leto)
[Communicating gender diversity]

Gender in communication : a critical introduction / Victoria Pruin DeFrancisco, University of Northern Iowa, Catherine Helen Palczewski, University of Northern Iowa.

pages cm
Revision of the author's Communicating gender diversity : a critical approach, published in 2007.
Includes bibliographical references and index.

ISBN 978-1-4522-2009-3 (pbk. : alk. paper)

1. Sex role. 2. Gender identity. 3. Communication—Social aspects. 4. Communication—Sex differences. 5. Sexism in language. I. Palczewski, Catherine Helen. II. Title.

HQ1075.D43 2014
305.3—dc23   2013009320

This book is printed on acid-free paper.

13 14 15 16 17 10 9 8 7 6 5 4 3 2 1

Brief Contents

Detailed Contents

Preface

Gender in communication is a recurrent topic of discussion. You can watch television almost any day of the week and hear some version of the following: A woman complains that her husband never listens to her, then another person complains that the women she or he works with gossip and are not to be trusted; finally, audience members or experts diagnose these anecdotal experiences as examples of common "gender communication problems." Given most people's ability to generate such a seemingly obvious explanation, you may wonder whether you even need a course on gender in communication.

Research suggests, however, that women and men alike use gossip to build group solidarity, but society usually does not derogatively label men's talk as gossip (Coates, 1996; Pilkington, 1998). Similarly, researchers suggest that differences in listening are more likely influenced by socialization than by biology (Johnson, Weaver, Watson, & Barker, 2000). More than actual differences in communication patterns, it is perceptions and expectations of people's behaviors that are gendered. In *Same Difference: How Gender Myths Are Hurting Our Relationships, Our Children, and Our Jobs* (2004), psychologist Rosalind Barnett and journalist Caryl Rivers critique social myths of gender differences. They argue that the predominant cultural belief in gender differences has created a self-fulfilling prophecy in which people's beliefs actually create the differences.

From where do these flawed popular beliefs come? If you are like many, you have heard that women and men cannot communicate with one another; they speak different languages. John Gray's *Men Are From Mars, Women Are From Venus* (1992) made this assumption popular. In this and his subsequent self-help books, speeches, films, and website, Gray suggests gender differences in communication are so vast, women and men might as well have come from different planets.

Is there any reason Gray should have the influence and reach he does? Gray's degree is from an unaccredited mail order company, and he has never published in a peer-reviewed research journal. Scholars criticize Gray's book because it is not research based, drawing only on his perceptions and reinforcing stereotypical assumptions (DeFrancisco & O'Connor, 1995; Guerrero, 2012; Hyde, 2005; Wood, 2002). Despite this, his message sells. His website notes that he has sold over 50 million copies of his books in 50 languages (Gray, 2012). Gender communication scholar Kathryn Dindia (2006) rightly points out that if he argued women and men were more similar than different, his publications would not sell: "Not only does sex sell, but sex differences sell" (p. 13).

If men and women are different, are "opposite" sexes, and their differences lead to disagreements, then it is not too far of a leap to conclude women and men have little in common and are in constant conflict—at war with one another. The video game *Gender Wars* embraces this idea as it proclaims "the final battle of the sexes" has been declared. A review of the game explains the contours of this war:

> Have you ever had a problem with the opposite sex? If you're a woman, maybe you're sick and tired of men leaving the toilet seat up. Men may be annoyed by women who seem overly emotional. There is a solution. Complete eradication of one sex or the other. In Gender Wars, getting started is simple: Pick a sex, form a squad (from 1–4 members), and use 10 various weapons to wipe the opposite sex off the face of the earth. . . . Brute force missions call for very aggressive and accurate soldiers armed with the most destructive weapons available. Stealth missions are just the opposite, with quick movement and light armament taking the day. Enemies are always around. (Bosher, 1996, par. 1)

What do you notice in this description? It encourages a binary listing of complaints about another sex: for example, men are inconsiderate and women are emotional. Its description of two opposite war strategies—"brute force" versus "stealth"—strongly parallels stereotypes of masculinity as aggressive and femininity as sneaky. Furthermore, the war is universal—all women fight men and all men fight women. This video game provides a frightening description of stereotypical gender differences at the expense of pitting women and men against each other, portraying them as enemies who will never peacefully coexist, and it assumes the world is heterosexual.

Popular culture abounds with references to gender war, a war between the sexes, or even "the bloody gender wars" as described in an issue of *Psychology Today* (White & Tyson-Rawson, 1996, p. 74). Lest you think the war metaphor refers only to video games and popular culture, news media use "gender war" to frame stories about health, education, business, marriage, sexuality, child care, brain structure, military, war, sexual harassment, athletics, computer use, emotions, acting, toilet seat norms, computer marketing, clothing, and even camping equipment.

A Google search for "gender war" generated more than 225,000,000 hits. In a LexisNexis search, the phrase appeared 235 times during 2012 in major world publications. The term also is exploding on social media such as Twitter and Facebook. Bing Videos has 16,800 links under the label "gender war," including entries on YouTube. Gender is portrayed as an inevitable war to prove which sex is superior.

"Gender war" is a structural metaphor (Lakoff & Johnson, 1980), meaning that the phrase structures one concept in terms of another: gender relations = war. Structural metaphors are extended by a series of additional metaphors, as in "the latest skirmish in the war between the sexes" (Blustain, 2000, p. 42). If one thinks of gender and sex relations as a constant battle, with casualties, assigned sides, enemies, and weapons, the ultimate goals of surrender or annihilation become evident. The war metaphor normalizes the idea that relations between the sexes are a perpetual conflict.

The war metaphor is not a coincidence. The attention it draws helps to police female and male behavior by reinforcing differences between, and ignoring diversity among, them. The assumption is there are two very different views of reality, with conflicting sides assigned at birth. As in actual wartime, both sides use propaganda to demonize the enemy. Thus, women often are demonized as being relationally demanding, emotionally unstable, and needy. Men are often demonized as being withdrawn, unemotional, and uncontrollably aggressive. Those who do not fit on one side or the other simply do not exist.

Although it is true that people tend to laugh at the gender war metaphor, poking fun at women and men, this humor is part of the metaphor's power. Humor helps to popularize the metaphor of gender war, and its seemingly innocuous character helps it remain popular. But humor is harmful because it can trivialize real issues, such as bullying, sexual harassment, homophobia, domestic violence, and rape, all of which have a detrimental effect on many women, men, and children. Further, the humor is based on cultural stereotypes, not the complex, diverse, real ways individuals and cultures do gender in their daily lives.

After decades of studying gender in communication, we have concluded that gender diversity, rather than gender war, is a more useful lens through which to examine gender in communication. The gender war metaphor has resulted in an underrecognition of the diversity among women, among men, and among all people. This textbook represents our best effort to be critical reviewers of existing knowledge on the topic of gender in communication. It represents our attempt to make sense of the material we felt was most important to share. It is our attempt to end the war (metaphor).

Organization of the Book

The book is divided in two parts. "Part I: Foundations" includes five chapters that describe the fundamentals of studying gender in communication: definitions and explanations of key terms, alternative theoretical approaches, gender in conversation, gendered bodies, and language. These chapters provide a foundational vocabulary that enables people to study gender in communication with more subtlety and nuance. "Part II: Institutions" includes an introductory chapter to explain a focus on social institutions, followed by five chapters on the institutions that make most evident the intersections of gender and communication: family, education, work, religion, and media. Each chapter examines how individuals experience and enact gender within the institution and how institutional structures and predominant ideology influence the experience and performance of gender. The concluding chapter highlights links among the preceding chapters and presents visions for future study.

Core Principles

Because gender is a constantly evolving concept, in terms of individuals' gender identity development, the larger culture's predominant notions about gender, and the continued progression of research in the field, absolute claims are not possible and would be irresponsible. Instead, our intent is to better equip readers with tools they can use to examine and make sense of gender in communication. As such, this book is not simply a review of communication research but rather an attempt to place the research in the context of larger theoretical, social, and political issues that influence, and are influenced by, gender in communication. We have attempted to write this book as an extended conversation in which we interact with research and popular discussions of gender in communication that have most excited our own scholarly imaginations.

To summarize our approach to gender in communication, we say this: We study the variety of ways in which communication of and about gender and sex enables and constrains people's identities. We believe that people are social actors and create meaning through their symbolic interactions. Thus, our emphasis is not on how gender influences communication but on how communication constitutes gender. We believe people are capable of being self-reflexive about communication processes and creative in generating new ways to play with symbols.

To study how people construct, perform, and change gender and what factors influence these performances, we draw on seven principles:

1. *Intersectionality.* You cannot study gender or sex in isolation. How a particularly sexed body performs gender always intersects with other identity ingredients, including race, ethnicity, social class, age, sexual orientation, physical ability, and more. People are who they are and act the way they act not just because of their sex or gender. People are wonderfully complex and form their gendered identities at an intersection of influences from multiple identity ingredients. Thus, to more accurately study gender, we study gendered lives in the context of other social identities.

2. *Interdisciplinarity.* We seek to fuse and balance social scientific, humanistic, and critical methods. Thus, we cite quantitative, qualitative, rhetorical, and critical studies. As coauthors, we have the benefit of drawing on three fields of communication studies that often operate independent of each other but that we believe are inextricably linked: rhetoric, social science, and performance studies. Palczewski, trained as a rhetorical scholar, was a college debate coach for 15 years and studies political controversies and social protest. DeFrancisco, trained as a social scientist, uses qualitative research methods to study how gender and related inequalities and acts of resistance are constructed through interpersonal relationships and individuals' identities. Dick McGeough, trained in performance studies and qualitative methods, uses creative approaches to explore scholarly questions. Most texts on gender in communication focus on social science studies of gendered interpersonal interactions and, thus, fail to recognize how broader, public discourse can influence gender.

Not only do we bridge methodological chasms within our own discipline, but we do so among disciplines. We purposely reviewed each topic from multiple disciplinary and activist perspectives. Throughout the text, we honor the contributions of black womanist theory, we celebrate the challenges offered by third-wave feminisms, we gratefully include lessons taught by queer theory, we integrate the insights of men's studies scholars, and we happily navigate the tensions between global and postmodern feminisms. The result is a richer, fuller understanding of the topic that stretches the boundaries of what is commonly considered relevant for a communication text.

We do not present research consistent with our view only. People learn most by stepping outside their academic or personal comfort zones to consider other perspectives. We value engaged and vital disagreement because we believe readers are able to glean more from our presentation of substantiated arguments than they could if we presented the research as if it were all consistent and value free. We will express our views of the material, and we hope this encourages you to do the same. Know up front that we believe agreement is neither a necessary nor a preferred requirement for learning from this book, and disagreement is not a sign of disrespect.

3. *Gender diversity, not sex differences.* We do not subscribe to typical conceptualizations of gender as a form of difference. Instead, we problematize the differences view by showing how it ignores power, reinforces stereotypes, fails to account for intersectional identities, and is inconsistent with statistical analyses demonstrating that sex does not consistently account for differences in communication. However, our rejection of the differences approach does not mean that we deny differences exist. Instead, we seek to recognize differences within genders as a result of intersectionality. We reject binary ways of thinking. We embrace a gender diversity approach. Research embracing this approach continues to grow, and we make a concerted effort to recognize femininities and masculinities and complex mixtures of them.

4. *Gender is performed.* Gender is something a person *does,* not something a person *is.* Gender is not something located within individuals; it is a social construct that institutions and individuals maintain (and occasionally challenge). Thus, we examine the microlevel (how an individual might perform gender) and the macrolevel (how social understandings of gender are performed on individuals).

5. *Masculinity.* The study of gender is not exclusively the study of women. However, the study of gender has traditionally been considered a "women's issue," hence researchers and textbooks often have focused almost exclusively on women and femininities, underemphasizing men and masculinities. Thanks to the recent growth in men's studies, we have at our disposal a rich literature base that considers gender and masculinity. In this textbook, we make a concerted effort to include masculinities.

6. *Violence.* To study gender in lived experiences means to study the darker side of gender: oppression and violence. In this textbook, we do not shy away from this

uncomfortable reality. Ours is not a narrative that says, "We are all just different, and isn't that nice?" To tell the whole story one must go deeper, making visible connections to the realities of gendered violence. This does not mean we are bashing men or that we presume all men have the potential to be violent and all women are victims. Rather, we recognize violence as systemic. That is, who can be violent and who can be a victim and who can be viewed as violent and who can be viewed as a victim are all part of a socially constructed system to maintain differences and inequalities. Gendered violence includes domestic abuse, rape, violence against LGBTQ people, street trafficking, and cyberbullying.

In each chapter, we make visible the connections between presumably innocent gendered practices and a range of specific social injustices connected to the topic of discussion. By linking gendered practices to more overt forms of gendered violence, we move beyond superficial generalizations about gender differences and make visible the struggles many people face in their unique cultural contexts.

7. *Emancipation.* Even as we recognize how gendered norms are linked to gendered violence, we also seek to make visible the emancipatory potential of gendered practice. To focus only on the negative would be to reinforce stereotypes and ignore the active ways people take on gendered norms to create spaces for diverse individual and group choices. Gender identity need not be oppressive and limiting. We offer examples of how diverse groups of people have created strategies to free themselves of stereotypical gender restrictions and other cultural expectations.

In writing this book we engage in intellectual activism. *Intellectual* and *activism* often are perceived as opposites, polarized along the lines of theory and action—but we see them as inextricably involved in the creation of a world that is more welcoming of people who diverge from expected sex roles and gender norms.

We do not shy away from complex and controversial subjects. We reject the sex binary of male and female, instead recognizing the existence of intersex and transgender people. We reject the binary-differences approach to studying gender as masculine *or* feminine, instead finding people to be wonderfully diverse and competent at adjusting their behavior according to situational needs. We reject the false assumption that the norm is to be cisgender (meaning one's sex and gender are consistent according to social dictates), instead recognizing most people are far more complex. We reject heteronormativity, instead seeing heterosexuality, homosexuality, bisexuality, and queer sexualities as equally valid sexual orientations.

New to This Edition

The second edition of this textbook is revised and updated to make it more accessible to undergraduate students while still challenging them. Graduate students will still find it a strong critical introduction to the study of gender in communication. The chapters have been significantly rewritten to reflect major shifts in the state of knowledge. The changes in this second edition are so extensive, they warranted a new title for the book: *Gender in Communication: A Critical Introduction.*

We hope our second edition challenges the way in which readers think about gender and sex, as well as how gender and sex intersect with race, class, sexual orientation, and nationality. Instead of providing simplistic answers, we hope we provide guidance on how to ask good questions. We also hope this book will inspire researchers to contribute to the study of gender in communication, further stretching the boundaries of culturally gendered perceptions.

Acknowledgments

This book could not have been written without the assistance of our colleagues. People too numerous to list have helped us as we wrote this book, but a few deserve special note for the extra time they spent sharing resources, reading chapters, and providing invaluable research assistance. The chapters would not have been as grounded in current scholarship, and the examples would not have been as rich, had it not been for the excellent contributions of graduate research assistants over the years: Derk Babbitt, Ruth Beerman, Kiranjeet Dhillon, Danelle Frisbie, Tristin Johnson, Danielle Dick McGeough, Emily Paskewitz, and Eric Short. Colleagues, students, friends, and staff served as resources, offering ideas, examples, and other support: Rob Asen, Judith Baxter, Harry Brod, Dan Brouwer, Patrice Buzznell, April Chatham-Carpenter, Jeanne Cook, Valeria Fabj, Jennifer Farrell, Patricia Fazio, John Fritch, Kelsey Harr-Lagin, Diana Jones-Harris, Karen Mitchell, Amymarie Moser, Harrison Postler, Jennifer Potter, Alimatul Qibtiyah, Martha Reineke, Mary Beth Stalp, Donna Uhlenhopp, Leah White, and Nikki Zumbach Harken. We recognize that no book is created in isolation. We thank Julia Wood (*Gendered Lives*), Diana Ivy and Phil Backlund (*GenderSpeak*), and Karlyn Kohrs Campbell (*Man Cannot Speak for Her*) for helping pave the way in gender/sex in communication textbooks, as well as scholars whose work has informed the development of our own gendered lenses: Judith Butler, Patricia Hill Collins, Celeste Condit, bell hooks, Cheris Kramarae, Judy Pearson, Dale Spender, and Anita Taylor. We thank our life partners, Arnie Madsen, David Pruin, and Ryan McGeough, for honoring our work.

We give special thanks and authorial recognition to Danielle Dick McGeough, a former student and present colleague, for her invaluable assistance with completing the revisions. As a teacher who used this text in classes at other universities, her insights guided many of our early revisions. And when we needed another set of eyes to complete final edits, hers were ready. We truly can say that were it not for Danielle, the second edition would not have been completed. The order of author names, DeFrancisco then Palczewski, is alphabetical. Palczewski deserves special recognition for her diligence in leading us to the completion of this second edition.

We thank the Sage staff. Our Sage editor, Matthew Byrnie, advocated for this second edition. We also want to thank the skilled Sage professionals who worked with us through the final stages of the publication process: Gabrielle Piccinnini (editorial intern), Stephanie Palermini (production editor), and Mark Bast (copy editor). Support for the development of this book was provided in part by the

University of Northern Iowa's Graduate College, the College of Humanities and Fine Arts, the Department of Communication Studies, and the Women's and Gender Studies Program.

Sage Publications gratefully acknowledges the following reviewers:

Cynthia Berryman-Fink, University of Cincinnati; Derek T. Buescher, University of Puget Sound; Sandra L. Faulkner, Syracuse University; Lisa A. Flores, University of Colorado Boulder Jeffrey Dale Hobbs, University of Texas at Tyler; Charlotte Kr2.kke, University of Southern Denmark; D. K. London, Merrimack College; Linda Manning, Christopher Newport University; M. Chad McBride, Creighton University; Elizabeth Natalle, University of North Carolina, Greensboro; Narissra Punyanunt-Carter, Texas Tech University; Leah Stewart, Rutgers University; and Lynn H. Turner, Marquette University.

PART I

Foundations

CHAPTER 1

Developing a Critical Gender/Sex Lens

Gender, the behaviors and appearances society dictates a body of a particular sex should perform, structures people's understanding of themselves and each other. Communication is the process by which this happens. Whether expressed through a person's communication or in how others interpret and talk about the person, gender is "always lurking" in interactions (Deutsch, 2007, p. 116). Gender is present in an individual's gender performance and in other messages that create, sustain, or challenge gender expectations. To illustrate this, consider an example from popular culture: the seemingly innocent custom of assigning infants pink or blue based on the baby's biological sex.

- When parents announce the birth of a child, what is the first question asked? "Is it a boy or girl?" or "Is the baby healthy? Is the baby eating and sleeping well? Is the birth mother okay?"
- What do birth celebration cards look like? We found two main choices: pink or blue, and the pink cards are decorated with flowers and docile girls while the blue cards are decorated with animals or transportation vehicles (planes, trains, automobiles, and ships) and active boys (see Figure 1.1).
- What mistake tends to cause people the most embarrassment when complimenting new parents on the birth of their child? What happens if you say, upon seeing a baby boy, "Isn't she pretty" instead of "He is so big"? Or, what happens if you say, upon seeing a baby girl, "Wow, what a bruiser" instead of "She is so cute"?
- How do parents react if another person misidentifies the sex of their newborn? In order to avoid mistaken sex identification, what do many new parents tend to do? They dress their child in pink if she is a girl or blue if he is a boy so no one will mistake the baby's sex.

Figure 1.1   Baby Girl Celebration Card (left) and Baby Boy Celebration Card (right)

Sources: Flickr/Ecooper99 and Flickr/Nayana Sondi

The point is, at the moment of birth (if not before if sex identification happens in vitro), people differentiate children on the basis of sex and begin to impose gendered expectations on them with clothing, activities, and interactions (Zosuls, Miller, Ruble, Martin, & Fabes, 2011).

In case you think pink and blue color designations have been practiced forever or exist across cultures, consider this:

- Color segregation on the basis of sex is primarily a U.S. and Western European custom, although Western commercialization is spreading it globally.
- Dresses were commonly worn by *all* infants until the early 1900s when, suddenly, dresses were seen as feminizing boys.
- Sex-based color assignments did not appear until the early 1900s, and initially the colors were reversed. When first assigned, the generally accepted rule was pink for the boy and blue for the girl. Pink was thought to be a more decisive and stronger color while blue was seen as delicate and dainty (*Ladies Home Journal*, June 1918, as cited in Frassanito & Pettorini, 2008).
- The colors assigned to babies did not switch until the 1950s. No one is sure why.
- The stipulation that pink is for girls and blue is for boys came from advice books and magazines targeted at White, upper-class people in the United States.
- Although sex-segregated colors lessened in the 1970s, by the 1980s their dominance returned, as is evidenced by the fuchsia pink and cobalt blue aisles of toys at major retailers (McCormick, 2011; Paoletti, 2012).

If you look at babies dressed in blue or pink, and do not ask critical questions, you may see an unremarkable cultural practice. But if you look at the practice through a *critical* gendered lens, you might begin to ask some questions, like the following: Why do we need to assign sex to infants? Why is it so important that sex identification is accurate? What does it mean that pink is seen as passive and blue is seen as strong? Why does it seem that a cultural choice is made to appear as a biological necessity? If you apply a critical gendered lens to the custom of pink and blue, what can you begin to learn about gender in communication?

Obviously, the colors are not biologically caused or universally gendered the same way. The color designations result from the communication practices of specific time periods in commercialized cultures and a particular set of political beliefs about consistent differences between women and men. Further, the color designations indicate how people have become conditioned to differentiate between sexes and genders. Although babies may now wear green, yellow, and purple, few parents are daring enough to dress a boy baby in pink or a girl baby in blue. The symbols people use to describe the sexes (pink or blue, pretty or strong), and the way they interact with others on the basis of their sex, matter.

Ultimately, this example reveals that gender is communicated in a variety of forms, even those as mundane as greeting cards. Communication scholar Bren Murphy (1994) makes this clear in her analysis of holiday cards targeted at children when she notes they are "part of a social discourse that constructs everyday gender patterns and perceptions" (p. 29). A variety of cultural texts "construct our understandings of gender and gendered relationships" (Keith, 2009, p. iv). Thus, to study gender in communication, you need to study not only how gendered bodies communicate but also how gender is constructed through communication in cultural texts.

Tellingly, many people do not know how to talk to or about a person without first categorizing that person as female or male. *Saturday Night Live* captured this in its classic recurring 1990s sketch "It's Pat," in which Julia Sweeney plays a character whose sex no one can identify (see Figure 1.2).

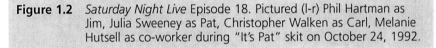

Figure 1.2 *Saturday Night Live* Episode 18. Pictured (l-r) Phil Hartman as Jim, Julia Sweeney as Pat, Christopher Walken as Carl, Melanie Hutsell as co-worker during "It's Pat" skit on October 24, 1992.

Source: Photo by Norman Ng/NBC/NBCU. Photo Bank via Getty Images.

In the "Pat" sketches, the other characters bumble with what topics to raise, what pronouns to use, and how to avoid offending Pat. The sketch revealed a great deal about gender and sex stereotypes and expectations and people's discomfort with uncertainty. Often, people determine a person's sex by the way a person performs gender: how that person dresses, acts, talks, moves, and interacts, but Pat's behavior did not follow gender stereotypes. As the Pat sketch illustrates, the social constructions of gender and sex make a difference in how people communicate with each other.

To say that most gender and sex differences are socially constructed rather than biological does not mean that no differences exist or that perceived differences do not matter. In fact, our argument throughout this textbook is that a range of differences exists and needs to be interrogated. We celebrate that human beings are wonderfully diverse. But to limit one's understanding of diverse human communication to only two choices, feminine or masculine, reinforces stereotypes. Still, that is often how people think about gender in communication—as a description of the differences between how women and men communicate. If you start from the assumption that women and men communicate differently, then you tend to see only differences between them, rather than the more common similarities (Dindia, 2006).

More than actual differences in communication patterns, cultural and individual *perceptions* of women's and men's behaviors are gendered. People see baby girls and baby boys as different because people code them that way; girls are pink, sweet, and pretty, and boys are blue, agile, and burly. This leads people to interact differently with babies, coddling ones they think are girls and playing more roughly with ones they think are boys (Frisch, 1977; Rubinstein, 2001). That is how emphasizing sex differences can be harmful. It reinforces separate expectations about how women and men should behave. In doing so, it restricts what is considered acceptable behavior for all people, and it puts rigid limitations on children's potentials. In *The Truth About Girls and Boys: Challenging Toxic Stereotypes About Our Children* (2011), journalist Caryl Rivers and psychologist Rosalind Barnett argue that gendered social myths are growing out of control, supported by popular media and consumer demand. As a result, a new type of mythical biological determinism is emerging supported by questionable data that humans are born with "brains in pink and blue" (p. 10). This social myth creates a self-fulfilling prophecy in which parents and teachers contribute to maintaining assumptions of sex-based gender differences. Instead, "Human beings have multiple intelligences that defy simple gender pigeonholes. Unfortunately, the real (and complex) story line is generally missing from the popular media. It is buried in scholarly peer-reviewed journals and articles that seldom see the light of day" (p. 2).

Although the predominant culture continues to assume that women and men are different, and therefore communicate in different ways, actual research does not support such a clear distinction (e.g., Anderson & Leaper, 1998; Burleson & Kunkel, 2006; Edwards & Hamilton, 2004; Holmstrom, 2009). Research suggests that gendered behavior variances *among* women and *among* men are actually greater than those *between* women and men (Burleson & Kunkel, 2006; Dindia, 2006; Hyde, 2005, 2007; Mare & Waldron, 2006). Many other factors affect behavior, such as social roles, ethnicity, individual differences, and purpose of the interaction (Aries, 2006; Deutsch, 2007). The focus exclusively on sex differences is too simplistic. Consider the following question: Do all women around the world and across ethnic groups and generations communicate the same way? Do all men?

There are some reasons why people might believe in universal sex and gender differences. For starters, sex is a primary way in which people categorize themselves and others, and people have a great deal invested in maintaining these categories. Society expects everyone to be heterosexual unless proven otherwise. Early on, girls and boys are encouraged to see each other as the "opposite" sex and to vie for the other's attention. Heterosexual dating is a primary means to popularity for many in U.S. middle and high schools. And heterosexual weddings are the ultimate heterosexual social ritual (Ingraham, 2008), so much so that some states have amended their constitutions to bar marriage among gays and lesbians.

The continued cultural insistence on differences despite a massive amount of research that disconfirms this view is *political*. Subscribing to a differences perspective helps maintain the status quo, and in that status quo particular groups are privileged (heterosexuals, men, Whites) while others are marginalized and subordinated. This is not to blame individual White men or individual heterosexuals for power differentials but to recognize all people are complicit in the process when they fail to question it. Linguist Mary Crawford (1995) explains that if communication problems were due solely to gender differences and not to group power or status, women and men could borrow each other's styles of communicating with similar effectiveness. In reality, what style works depends on the situation, the social status of the speaker, and the power relations between the speaker and listener. The same communication styles do not perform equally for all people. A woman who adopts a more assertive style may be labeled with the "B" word. A man who adopts a caring collaborative style may be labeled with the "F" word.

Another related answer to why the culture continues to embrace (empirically disproved) gender and sex differences is that it sells. Sex, differences, and conquest sell. If you are not sure about that, check out the ways in which retail sellers target specific sexes in toy aisles, cosmetics, wedding planning, sports, music, and gaming.

In this book, we summarize current research on gender in communication and equip you with critical analytical tools to develop your own informed opinions about that research, society's gender expectations, and prevailing cultural views. To accomplish this, it is necessary to understand how predominant cultural views about gender and sex create a gendered lens through which people view reality. This lens can become so embedded that people do not realize how it limits their perceptions of reality. We hope to help you construct a more *critical* gendered lens by providing analytic tools with which you can examine common assumptions about gender, sex, and communication. We hope to show how communication in and about the institutions of family, education, work, religion, and media construct and maintain gender and how communication about gender can transform understandings of it. The following concepts make clear why a focus on differences between women and men as homogeneous groups is impossible and, in fact, produces inaccurate descriptions of human communication.

Vocabulary for a Critical Gendered Lens

A precise vocabulary is needed to develop a critical gendered lens: intersectionality, communication, and systemic violence. Together the concepts provide a more realistic understanding of gendered cultural identity and how one does gendered identity work through communication. Ultimately, to understand gender in communication, one needs to understand identity and the role gender plays in its formation and maintenance.

Generally speaking, the term **identity** refers to how people see themselves as individuals and as members of groups *and* how others see them as individuals and as members of groups. Identity includes concepts such as personality; the multiple group identities one holds—for example, gender, sex, race, class, sexuality, nationality; and contextual role identities—for example, friend, lover, student, supervisor. A person's identity has multiple interacting, and sometimes contradicting, facets (Krølokke & Sørensen, 2006; Tracy, 2002). For example, the social expectations of a person who identifies as a man may seem to contradict with the role that person plays as a teacher or day care provider. The boxes on surveys that ask people to identify as male *or* female (or as White *or* African American, Hispanic American, Asian American, Native American) force people to choose, privileging one part of their identity and ignoring the reality of transgender, biracial, or multiethnic identities.

Although people may prefer to box others into set categories, from a communication perspective, identity is not fixed and unchanging. Rather it is constantly negotiated through intrapersonal, interpersonal, and public communication circulating in mass media and popular culture. Consider, for example, how your identity has changed since entering college, leaving home, or traveling abroad. This does not mean that people can change their identities on a whim. Although identity is in constant flux, it is perceived as stable. As such, individuals and groups have some control over their identity construction, but much of the predominant cultural assumptions extend beyond one's awareness or control (Butler, 2004; Tracy, 2002). Thus, identity includes political nuances imposed on individuals and groups. As we unpack components of identity, you will find that we have not provided simple dictionary definitions for these terms but rather indicate why these concepts deserve critical analysis and must be discussed in relationship to each other.

Intersectionality

Writing a book that focuses only on gender in communication would merely serve to reinforce stereotypes. In reality, it is impossible to separate out the influence of gender from other contributors to one's identity. Race, class, sex, sexual orientation, citizenship status, religion, and gender all intersect to form a person's identity. So, before you can understand gender in communication, you first need to understand that a person's gender identity, and how gender identity is performed, is not separable from the person's race, class, sex, sexual orientation, citizenship status, or religion.

Legal scholar and critical race feminist Adrien Wing (1997) explains the theory of **intersectionality** as the idea that identity is "multiplicative" rather than additive (p. 30), as contrasted in Figure 1.3.

Figure 1.3 Additive Versus Multiplicative Conceptions of Identity

The additive approach:

1 (race/ethnicity) + 1 (sex) + 1 (gender) + 1 (class) + 1 (sexual orientation) ≠1 person

The multiplicative approach:

1 (race/ethnicity) × 1 (sex) × 1 (gender) × 1 (class) × 1 (sexual orientation) = 1 person

Instead of understanding identity as the addition of one independent element to another and another, identity makes more sense if you think of each element as inextricably linked with the others. An intersectional approach to identity in general, and gender identity in particular, makes clear that all facets of identity are integral, interlocking parts of a whole.

African American women were the first to make this point clear. Freed Black woman Sojourner Truth delivered her famous "Aren't I a Woman" speech at the 1851 Women's Rights Convention. In it, she challenged society in general, and White woman suffrage advocates in particular, to recognize that Black women were, indeed, women:

> That man over there says that women need to be helped into carriages, and lifted over ditches, and to have the best place everywhere. Nobody ever helps me into carriages, or over mud-puddles, or gives me any best place. And aren't I a woman? Look at me! Look at my arm. I have plowed and planted and gathered into barns, and no man could head me. And aren't I a woman? I could work as much and eat as much as a man—when I could get it—and bear the lash as well. And aren't I a woman? I have borne thirteen children, and seen them most all sold off into slavery, and when I cried out with a mother's grief, none but Jesus heard me! And aren't I a woman? (Truth, 1851, par. 2)

Truth's experiences cannot be fully explained by focusing on her sex or gender alone. As a Black woman living during slavery, Whites did not perceive her to be capable of attaining the full attributes of femininity expected of wealthy White women. Yet, she was a woman. Truth clarifies that when people see or hear popular portrayals of gender (women are feminine, men are masculine), the unspoken norm is that these are White, middle-class, heterosexual women and men. This fails to include the ways in which African American, Asian, Hispanic, Native American, LGBTQ (lesbian, gay, bisexual, transgendered, and queer), and others experience gender as part of simultaneous oppressions tied to race, ethnicity, class, sexual orientation, citizenship, religion, and more. Kimberlé Crenshaw (1989), a lawyer and legal scholar, was the first to use the word *intersectionality* to describe how the oppression faced by Black women was greater than the sum of oppression from race and sex combined.

Author Audre Lorde (1984) offers a description of how an intersectional approach is necessary to fully understand and accept your own identity:

> As a Black lesbian feminist comfortable with the many different ingredients of my identity, and a woman committed to racial and sexual freedom from oppression, I find I am constantly being encouraged to pluck out some one aspect of myself and present that as the meaningful whole, eclipsing or denying the other parts of self. But this is a destructive and fragmenting way to live. My fullest concentration of energy is available to me only when I integrate all the parts of who I am, openly, allowing power from particular sources of my living to flow back and forth freely through all my different selves, without the restrictions of externally imposed definition. Only then can I bring myself and my energies as a whole to the service of those struggles which I embrace as a part of my living. (p. 120)

Lorde's use of the metaphor *ingredients* is useful when explaining intersectionality. For example, a cake is an object with ingredients such as flour, eggs, oil, sugar, and milk that can exist separately from each other, but once combined each element influences the others. Even though the cake contains all the ingredients, none are recognizable in their separate forms. A cake is not just flour and eggs and sugar and oil and milk. A cake is a cake only when the ingredients are so fused together that they cannot be separated again. Like a cake, human identity is the result of a fascinating alchemic process in which ingredients are fused in such a way that each is influenced by the others, to the point where you cannot extricate the flour from the cake once it is baked. The flour is not simply flour (and gender is not simple gender) once fused with other ingredients.

Given the way ingredients of identity interact, this means one cannot understand how a person does gender unless one also considers how that person's gender, sex, sexual orientation, race, national identity, and socioeconomic class interact to demand a particular gender performance. Researchers who take only gender into account do not recognize that identity actually occurs as a complex, synergistic, infused whole that becomes something completely different when parts are ignored, forgotten, and unnamed (Collins, 1998).

Gender and Sex, Gender/Sex

If you have ever filled out a survey, you likely have been asked about your gender and then given the options of male and female. Often, the words *sex* and *gender* are used interchangeably, even though they refer to two analytically distinct things. Sex refers to biological designations (e.g., female, male), while *gender* refers to the cultural designations of feminine and masculine. Why are they often used interchangeably, and what, if any, distinctions do they hold?

Before the 1970s, most people assumed people's sex determined their behavior; no concept of gender as distinct from sex existed. In the late 1970s, researchers began using the term *gender* as distinct from *sex* to identify attributes of women and men (Unger, 1979). They used *gender* to refer to one's self-identity—that is, the degree to which a person associates herself or himself with what society has prescribed as feminine or masculine. You can probably brainstorm presumed and expected gender-specific stereotypical attributes yourself: Expected feminine attributes are to be emotional, a caretaker, sensitive, compassionate, revealingly dressed; expected masculine attributes are to be rational, independent, tough, aggressive, comfortably dressed (Coates, 2004; Eagly & Koenig, 2006; Eliot, 2009a; Lorber & Moore, 2007). Thus, when researchers embraced the concept of gender, sex and gender were seen as distinct. In other words, one's sex did not determine one's gender.

This understanding of gender recognized variances in human identity as on a continuum, rather than as two *binary* or opposite categories where one is *either* male/masculine *or* female/feminine. The continuum helps make visible that instead of two independent categories, there are degrees of gender (see Figure 1.4).

Figure 1.4 Gender Continuum

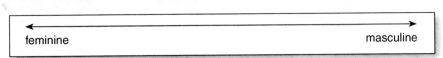

One could be more masculine (and less feminine) or more feminine (and less masculine). Because researchers saw gender as socially prescribed rather than biologically caused, they assumed that people identify to varying degrees with masculinity *and* femininity, rather than just one *or* the other. This was heralded as an important breakthrough for research and for human rights. No longer were authors saying all men acted one way and all women another, based solely on their biological sex.

Further developing this idea, psychologist Sandra Bem (1974) coined the term **androgyny** by combining two Greek words: *andros* meaning "male" and *gyne* meaning "female." Bem developed a questionnaire called the Sex-Role Inventory (SRI) to identify a person's gender orientation on a continuum from highly feminine to highly masculine, androgynous (high in both), or undifferentiated (low in both masculine and feminine traits). Persons who are androgynous are said to have more behavioral flexibility. Instead of seeing masculinity and femininity as in a zero-sum tradeoff on a continuum, Bem believed one could exhibit characteristics of both (see Figure 1.5).

Thinking back to the *SNL* Pat character, one can see further confusion about language. Although the sketch referred to Pat as androgynous, in reality Pat was more likely undifferentiated given Pat exhibited low identifications with masculinity and femininity.

Although focusing on gender instead of sex was meant to be a step away from overgeneralizing women's and men's identities, masculinity and femininity are

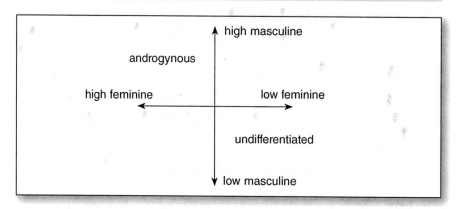

Figure 1.5 Gender Diversity

still stereotypes, prescribing how women and men are supposed to behave (Crawford & Fox, 2007). Even researchers who use the Bem SRI are still limiting descriptions of persons according to the two stereotypic concepts of masculinity and femininity. The limitation of androgyny is that it merely collapses the two gender stereotypes together and thus, inadvertently, helps to maintain them. Because of this criticism, in recent uses of the SRI, researchers have dropped the terms *masculine* and *feminine*, relying instead on measures of dominance, nurturance, orientation toward self versus others, and so forth, but the stereotypical inferences are still present. The conclusion? There is no ideal social science means to study gender identity.

To add to this problem, researchers and popular media often do not use the concept of gender correctly or consistently (Muehlenhard & Peterson, 2011). If you read published research, you will find that many claim to have found gender differences or similarities, when in actuality they never asked for or assessed the participants' self-identities of gender. They merely asked participants to label themselves as biologically female or male and then assumed that by studying females, they could determine what was feminine and that by studying males, they could determine what was masculine.

Further complicating the distinction between sex (as biologically given) and gender (as socially constructed) is that even biological attributes are socially constructed. The only way a person can come to understand anything, even biology, is through one's language and through cultural experience (Butler, 1993a).

One's understanding of the body and its relationship to identity is always mediated by the words each person uses to talk about the body; therefore, one can never comprehend a biological entity without the meanings language attaches to it. In the words of Judith Butler (1993a), a professor of rhetoric and comparative literature, "There is no reference to a pure body which is not at the same time a further formation of that body" (p. 10). People's perceptions limit their abilities to comprehend. Thus, sex is as much a cultural creation as gender, and bodies have no meaning separate from the meaning language gives them. The argument that people's biological sex is influenced by communication is not to deny the existence of a material body "but to insist that our apprehension of it, our understanding of it, is necessarily mediated by the *con*texts in which we speak" (Price & Shildrick, 1999, p. 7; italics in original).

In addition, social constructions can be very difficult to change. Butler (2004) argues that sex is as socially constructed as gender and that gender is often as immutable as sex, given how social institutions and language constantly reiterate and reinscribe it. One of the primary ways sex and gender discipline bodies is through the enshrinement of **binary** views (meaning you have only one choice or another) of one's sex, gender, and sexuality. Perhaps this is why some youth today are choosing to label themselves as **genderqueer**. The label is used to "defy all categories of culturally defined gender"; it is "gender free" or "gender neutral," claiming an identity "outside gender" (Ehrensaft, 2011, p. 531).

Ultimately, the approach we take to gender and sex urges you to see gender and sex as something you do, not something you are. If gender is something that is done, it can be done in a wide variety of ways.

That being said, gender is not something that belongs to an individual but is done by people interacting in accordance with institutional and cultural demands. It is a performance. Accordingly, we want to recognize that people experience their gender and sex together, and sex and gender are both socially constructed and difficult to change. By using the term **gender/sex** in this textbook, we emphasize the interrelation between the concepts of gender and sex. We make this choice to reference gender/sex consciously aware of the history and related arguments regarding the two terms. When we discuss gender in communication, we always discuss sex in communication because communication that is about gender, that is influenced by gender, and that differentiates gender also always is about sex, is influenced by sex, and differentiates sex.

Transgender and Intersex

Transgender or "transgenderism is a contested umbrella term used to describe individuals whose gender expression and behavior do not match the usual expectations associated with the male-female binary system" (Gherovici, 2010, p. xiii). A transgender person is one who overtly challenges the linkage of gender with sex. Transgender people include those who identify as transmen (born females who identify as men) and transwomen (born males who identify as women), choose to take hormones, have surgical sexual organ changes (also called transsexuals), and identify as genderqueer. *Transgender* should be used as an adjective modifying a person's identity. It is not a noun, meaning it is not a static identity but one that suggests process or transition is key to the identity (GLAAD, n.d.).

When the predominant culture names the sex of a body female *or* male (and nothing else), the culture has already engaged in an act of communication that has "normative force" as it recognizes some parts of a person but not all (Butler, 1993a, p. 11). Even as the body is referenced, a particular formation occurs—a formation of the body as *either* female *or* male. Butler identifies the binary linguistic framing of bodies as an act of power because it refuses to recognize the existence of transgender and intersex persons. The reality, however, is that many bodies do not fit the binary of female *or* male.

The way the language of the sex/gender binary constructs sex and gender is found in the cultural policing of transgender persons. Until 2012, the standard diagnostic manual used by U.S. mental health practitioners identified persons who desire to be "another sex" or participate in the pastimes of the "other sex" as having a disorder (American Psychiatric Association, 2000, pp. 576–577). Gender identity disorder was the label given to this "dysfunction." It was also used for individuals with homosexual or bisexual tendencies, and some practitioners attempted to alter the individuals' gender identities. However, psychotherapy rarely changes gender identity (Gherovici, 2010; Reis, 2009; Unger & Crawford, 1992). Intersex and transgender activists raised the question of how medical professionals can ascertain a person's "real" gender/sex identity. They argued that gender should be a matter of personal choice (Schilt, 2011). As a result of this activism, the American Psychiatric Association decided in 2012 to change its diagnostic manual so that it no longer refers to gender identity disorder but instead to gender dysphoria (Lennard, 2012).

Intersex refers to a person who has ambiguous sex features at birth, meaning the person has both female and male sex characteristics (genitalia, chromosomes). Lest you think this is an extraordinarily rare medical phenomenon, from 1,000 to 15,000 intersex babies are born a year in the United States (Greenberg, 2012, p. 7). In a study that reviewed medical literature from 1955 to 2000, the authors concluded that intersex babies may account for as many as 2% of live births (Blackless et al., 2000). Despite this, the way U.S. society talks about and legislates sex constantly reinforces the idea that there are only two distinct sexes (and that one's sex determines one's gender). Law professor Julie Greenberg (1999) explains how this works:

> Implicit in legislation utilizing the terms "sex" and "gender" are the assumptions that only two biological sexes exist and that all people fit neatly into either the category male or female. In other words, despite medical and anthropological studies to the contrary, the law presumes a binary sex and gender model. The law ignores the millions of people who are intersexed. A binary sex paradigm does not reflect reality. Instead, sex and gender range across a spectrum. Male and female occupy the two ends of the poles, and a number of intersexed conditions exist between the two poles. (p. 275)

An explicit example of authorities imposing sex binaries is what was done to infants born with both female and male sex organs or with sex organs typically associated with one sex and chromosomes typically associated with another. An infant born with ambiguous genitalia was considered a "medical emergency" (Fausto-Sterling, 2000, p. 45), and in European countries parents were told to decide within the child's first day of life if the baby will be male or female, until new policies were proposed in 2005 (Pasterski, Prentice, & Hughes, 2010). The rate of infant genital surgery is still high, and there is a continued tendency to surgically alter infants' genitals to female because the vagina is easier to construct surgically. Butler (2004) points out that this practice tells us how narrowly defined "normal" is in society, and the failure to recognize that intersex persons are part of the human continuum prevents them from being treated with respect.

As early as 1993, developmental geneticist Anne Fausto-Sterling argued that people should recognize at least five sexes, with an infinite range in between:

> [I]f the state and legal system have an interest in maintaining a two-party sexual system, they are in defiance of nature. For biologically speaking, there are many gradations running from female to male; and depending on how one calls the shots, one can argue that along that spectrum lie at least five sexes [female, ferm, herm, merm, male]—and perhaps even more. (p. 21)

If the language allows only two sexes to exist, then only two will be seen and any body that does not fit into the two sexes will be forcibly, surgically altered to fit. Similarly, if one's gender did not fit with one's sex, then one was labeled as having a disorder. Language has structured the reality of sex and gender in such a way that the grand diversity of human existence is stifled.

To summarize, researchers in the field of communication studies began by focusing on sex, visualizing it as a binary. They progressed to using the term *gender*, as two culturally imposed opposite identities located on one continuum. This approach was nuanced to recognize gender as not necessarily a zero-sum game; androgynous people could have many characteristics of both masculinity and femininity. This allowed the recognition of more variances of behavior and identity (Slesaransky-Poe & García, 2009). Now researchers are moving toward a much more diverse, realistic portrayal of gender and sex, thanks to the knowledge of people who are transgender or intersex.

Increased awareness of transgender and intersex people across cultures is rapidly and dramatically changing the way researchers think about the concepts of gender and sex. Transgender and intersex persons challenge the gender/sex binary (Gherovici, 2010). People who cross the culturally constructed sex and gender lines reveal **gender fluidity**; they are not limited to the two binary (either/or) options but are recognized as part of a world of gender diversity (Malpas & Lev, 2011). Gender fluidity is not necessarily about wanting to be the other sex but is more about not being bound to the binary (Ehrensaft, 2011).

Sexuality

Gender, sex, transgender, and intersex often are incorrectly confused with sexual orientation. People tend to assume that a feminine man is gay, a masculine woman is a lesbian, and transgender and intersex people are not heterosexual. However, neither one's gender nor sex determines one's sexual orientation.

Sexual orientation refers to whether one is physically and romantically attracted to or has sex with persons of the same sex, the other sex, or both. You might notice that sexual orientation depends on a sex binary (same or other); if there are five sexes, which is the "other" sex? Again, the sex/gender binary plays a role in limiting human understanding, in this case, an understanding of sexuality.

Even before children understand sexuality, they bully other children who do not perform the gender society has attached to their sex, and those children are bullied in a way that calls their sexuality into question. Girls are teased for being tomboys and called dykes; boys are teased for being effeminate and called fags. Notice that the bullying says more about the bully than the recipient. Children learn early to police gender and sexual orientation (Eliot, 2009a; McGuffey & Rich, 2003).

This conflation of gender/sex and sexual orientation is an example of the power of identity oppressions working together. In U.S. culture, the worst thing a male can be called is a woman or fag. Based on social stereotypes, gays are assumed to be effeminate, lesbians are assumed to be masculine, and bisexuals are often ignored by all groups or labeled confused. But sexual orientation is not the same as gender or sex. Although the term *gay* is often used generically to refer to anyone who is not heterosexual, it identifies males who are homosexual; *lesbian* refers to women who are homosexual, and *bisexual* refers to males or females who are attracted to both women *and* men.

However, sexuality is more than attraction orientation. It is what one does when one is sexual. The term **queer** is used by heterosexuals and LGBTQ folks who reject heteronormative restrictions. **Heteronormativity** describes how social institutions and policies reinforce the presumption that people are heterosexual and that gender and sex are natural binaries (Kitzinger, 2005).

Our goal is to make clear that sex, gender, transgender, and intersex are distinct from sexual orientation, even though the predominant culture conflates them. The way culture communicates about sexual orientation constructs and maintains not only differences but maintains heterosexuality as the norm (Rich, 1980). Persons who are discriminated against because of their sexual orientation are being oppressed because they are perceived as sexual deviants. Sociologist Gayle Rubin (1984) states, "The system of sexual oppression cuts across other modes of social inequality" such as racial, class, ethnic or gendered inequality "sorting out individuals and groups according to its own intrinsic dynamics. It is not reducible" (p. 293). Conversely, discussions of gender and sex are intricately tied to sexual orientation and sexuality. They are not separable. In the study of gender/sex, people must recognize the role of heteronormativity and sexual identity.

Race and Ethnicity

Like gender/sex, race is a primary social category used to identify people, even though scientists have known for some time that race is not an accurate means by which to categorize human beings in terms of ancestry or genetics (Blakey, 1999; Long & Kittles, 2003; "Race," 2011). Yet, in daily life and popular culture, people still assume they can identify a person's race by examining a few physical traits, such as skin color, hair texture, eye color, and the shape of eyes and nose. When scientists look at these physical traits, they find no consistent identifiers shared within a group of people. Furthermore, there are more genetic variations *within* groups of people than *between* them (Tobin & Dusheck, 1998). Skin color, for example, can vary greatly whether in a family or racial group. The huge variances within a group of people mean, for example, that persons who are labeled White can have darker skins than some persons who are labeled Black.

Why does society hold on to this false assumption that race is a legitimate category? The same reasons popular culture continues to cling to the assumption of two binary genders/sexes. Believing in such differences is easy and it benefits those in power. We use the term *race* to recognize that many people self-identify with a particular race and take great pride in their racial identity.

Race, like gender/sex, has a socially constructed meaning that has real consequences. Sociologist Estelle Disch (2009) explains why and how we use the term in this book:

> The term race is itself so problematic that many scholars regularly put the word in quotation marks to remind readers that it is a social construction rather than a valid biological category. Genetically, there is currently no such thing as "race" and the category makes little or no sense from a scientific standpoint. What is essential, of course, is the meaning that people in various cultural contexts attribute to differences in skin color or other physical characteristics. (p. 22)

To illustrate, consider that Germans, Irish, Italians, and Russians are now considered White in the United States, but after the great migration of the early 1900s up to the 1960s, they were considered "colored or other" (Foner & Fredrickson, 2005). Consequently, we cannot offer a precise definition of race in this text. At its simplest, race is how groups of people are socially categorized.

Ethnicity, too, is a contested term; identifying one's ethnic origins is not as clear as researchers once thought, given the increasingly transnational world and how cultural labels are subject to change. **Ethnicity** is a term commonly used to refer to a group of people who share a cultural history, even though they may no longer live in the same geographic area (Zack, 1998). They may share values, a language, and a way of life. It is often used incorrectly when, for example, people in the United States assume all immigrants from South and Central America share a Mexican ethnic identity. In reality, immigrants in the United States are not all from Mexico. They are Guatemalan, Salvadoran, Nicaraguan—to name a few—and have diverse ethnicities. As is true in the United States, within these countries there are indigenous people as well as people who migrated from Europe and many other parts of the world. Many from Spain, for example, would pass as White in the United States, and certainly not all immigrants are from poor social classes.

One way to more clearly see the power of arbitrary social group constructions is to consider what one knows about White identity. Whiteness is a racial and ethnic category even if society typically does not recognize it as such. The central position of Whiteness in predominant culture allows it to be normalized to the extent that it almost disappears; it is deraced and nonethnic. Many who identify as White do not even realize it is a category. They can readily list stereotypes of other races of peoples, such as the expectation that Asians should be smart and that

African Americans should be good at sports, but they have difficulty naming a quality that applies to their race (Nakayama & Krizek, 1999).

When race is conceptualized as natural rather than as culturally created, the power of this category is hidden (Kivel, 2002). In particular, it is important to recognize Whiteness in the study of gender because, if one does not, race remains a concern only for those considered non-White, and gender, when studied alone, remains implicitly an identity owned solely by Whites. What is important to remember is that, like gender/sex, when society constructs arbitrary racial and ethnic categories, these categories are rarely different and equal. Rather, race and ethnicity have been used as tools of social oppression.

Throughout this book, we capitalize *Black* and *White* to clarify that we are referring to racial categories and the politics of skin color rather than to hues on the color wheel. Authors often use other terms, such as *Northern European* and *Euramerican* to refer to Whites and *African Americans* to refer to Blacks. We, too, use the more specific *African American* where relevant or when used by an author we are quoting, but we feel that *Northern European* does not clearly differentiate Whites, because Blacks can also be born in Northern Europe.

National Identity

National identity refers to a person's immigration status, citizenship, and country allegiance. Interdisciplinary feminist scholars and global human rights activists were the first to explore how national cultural identities are gendered/sexed and how citizens tend to experience their national rights differently based on gender/sex (Enloe, 1989; Moghadam, 1994; Yuval-Davis, 1997, 2003). International studies scholar Tamar Mayer (2000) posits that "control over access to the benefits of belonging to the nation is virtually always gendered" and that "the ability to define the nation lies mainly with men" (p. 2). So, the feeling of belonging to a nation and the privileges and oppressions contained therein are gendered/sexed in unique ways according to cultural norms, histories of religion, ethnic and class conflicts, economics, and much more. National identity changes according to how current political leaders wish to draw geographic boundaries, as happened after the 1990s fall of the former Eastern Bloc communist countries in Europe.

Gender/sex issues happening around the world *are* extremely relevant to any study of gender in communication. Placing the study of gender in the context of national identity prevents an overgeneralized gender differences approach that assumes universal differences between women and men or, worse yet, assumes that research primarily conducted in the United States represents gendered lives around the world. Gender and ethnic studies scholar Nira Yuval-Davis (1999) explains, "Essentialist notions of difference . . . are very different from the notions of difference promoted by those of us who believe in the importance of incorporating notions of difference into democracy. In the first case notions of difference replace notions of equality—in the second case they encompass it" (p. 131). Recognizing national identities is an important part of creating a gender diversity approach to the study of gender/sex in communication.

When national identity is included in the study of gender/sex, the focus has usually been on citizens of economically disadvantaged countries. The influence of the United States as a nation has not been a primary focus in gender/sex in communication research. Instead, most of the research has focused on the one-to-one relationship level, as if it existed independently of national identity. Yet, the U.S. national identity and its economic power have had a profound influence not only on carving out gender identities in the United States but worldwide. Gender/sex and national identity are related, not just for persons in economically disadvantaged countries, or in countries with more visible internal violence, but for U.S. citizens as well (Mayer, 2000; Mohanty, 2003).

Socioeconomic Class

In the United States, **socioeconomic class** refers to the social position people enjoy as a result of their income, education, occupation, and place of residence. Just as race and nationality intersect with gender/sex, so too does class. The expectations of how gender should be performed are influenced by the class to which a person belongs. When children from poorer economic backgrounds are told to act like a lady or a gentleman, the underlying message is usually about class. They are being told to act like a particular type of gender/sex, one that knows the upper-class gentile norms of politeness and identity performance. The message goes even further when children of color receive this message. They are being told to act like White upper class people do. This does not mean poor children or children of color cannot be gentlemen and ladies; it simply means that these terms carry with them class-prescribed expectations of gendered/sexed behaviors and that White upper-class people have controlled the definition of these expectations.

Perhaps because social class is difficult to define, the field of communication studies has been slow to examine the ways in which it may affect communication in the United States. Yet it is clear class often determines how much leeway one is allowed in gender performance, often with the most restrictive gender expectations for the upper class. For example, historian Glenna R. Matthews (1992) explains how working-class women were able to enter the public realm as labor activists more easily than upper-class women in the 1930s because they were already present in the economic sphere. Economic necessity required them to work and, hence, to violate the social demands of the time requiring that wealthy White women remain domestic. Being politically active presented no unique violation of gender/sex expectations for the working-class women. As a result, the history of labor activism is full of women leaders: Mary Harris "Mother" Jones (Tonn, 1996), Emma Goldman (Kowal, 1996; Solomon, 1987), Voltairine de Cleyre (Palczewski, 1995), and Lucy Parsons (Horwitz, 1998).

Class affects how gender is performed and how gender/sex is perceived. Men of lower classes face the stereotype that they are less intelligent, immoral, and prone to criminality. Women of lower classes are stereotyped as sexually promiscuous, easily duped, and dependent on state assistance. This discrimination and related stereotypes help maintain oppression (Ehrenreich, 1990), which can be multiplied by oppressions due to racism and sexism.

Intersectionality Conclusion

An intersectional approach has many implications for the study of gender. First, an intersectional approach prevents scholars from falling into a specific type of generalization called essentialism. **Essentialism** is the presumption that all members of a group are alike because they have one quality in common, such as when one assumes all *men's* communication will be alike because the individuals are all men, or *Black women's* communication will all be alike, or all *LGBTQ* communication will be alike. Author Angela Harris (1997) advocates the avoidance of essentialism, explaining that "fragmentation of identity and essentialism go hand in hand" (p. 11). If researchers study only the fragment of a person called *gender* or *sex*, they reduce a person's complex identity to one dimension. Sexuality, race, nationality, and class also must be considered.

Second, intersectionality recognizes that assumptions about gender, sexual orientation, race, nationality, and class do exist and influence the way individuals view the world. It recognizes the social realities and inequalities they produce (Jordan-Zachery, 2007). Thus, the study of gender is not about the quirks of personality but is about the way broad social patterns privilege some people and disadvantage others. Intersectional identity theory makes clear how oppressions of groups interrelate. Consequently, it clarifies what must be included in efforts toward social justice. Just as any analysis of gender in communication is incomplete without taking one's intersectional identity into account, so, too, is any analysis of the cultural tools used in power and privilege (Davis, 2008). Educator-consultant Heather Hackman (2012) explains that one cannot accomplish social justice by addressing one form of oppression in isolation. Oppressions are not independent. A part of the power of oppressions is the ways they intersect, supporting each other.

Third, intersectionality recognizes that all people are labeled with and internalize multiple group identities: "It is not just the marginalized who have a gender, race, and so on" (Harding, 1995, p. 121). Whiteness is part of identity, as is heterosexuality and being a man. People do not always recognize these ingredients because they are considered the norm. So, even as intersectionality enables the understanding of complex forms of subordination, it also makes visible how dominant groups have a race, sex, gender, and class. This does not mean, however, that intersectionality is an endorsement of identity politics or the uncritical acceptance of the current socially acceptable label for a group. Intersectionality should make visible how essentializing, stereotyping, and the ignoring of multiple group identities is accomplished (Crenshaw, 1989).

In sum, intersectionality renders a more complex, realistic portrayal of individuals' gendered/sexed experiences. Sociologist Leslie McCall (2005) terms it the "intracategorical approach to complexity" that "seeks to complicate and use [identity categories] in a more critical way" (p. 1780). Like McCall (2005), in this text we seek to "focus on the process by which [categories of identity] are produced, experienced, reproduced, and resisted in everyday life" (p. 1783). As you begin to explore your own intersectional identity, the list of ingredients making up your identity can be quite lengthy, including religious or faith affiliation, age, physical and mental abilities, immigration status, marriage status, and region of country. We begin here by unpacking the most commonly noted group identifiers for our study of gender in communication: gender, sex, sexuality, race, ethnicity, national identity, and socioeconomic class. Keep in mind that all of these are social constructions that influence one's perceptions. They are not innate, permanent, or universal categories.

Our attention to the intersectionality of identities and oppressions is meant to highlight the way cultural identities and inequalities are embedded in political systems and social structures, not only in people. Philosopher Sandra Harding (1995) explains that sexual and racial inequalities "are not *caused* by prejudice—by individual bad attitudes and false beliefs." In fact, she believes that focusing on "prejudice as the cause of racial (or gender, class, or sexual) inequality tends to lodge responsibility for racism on already economically disadvantaged whites who might hold these beliefs." It keeps the focus on individuals rather than on the larger culture in which their attitudes were created. Clearly, prejudice does contribute to racism, sexism, and other forms of inequity, but Harding argues that people should view inequalities as "fundamentally a political relationship" that manifests itself through cultural strategies or norms that privilege some groups over others (p. 122).

Communication

Communication constructs, maintains, and changes gender/sex. It is how group and individual differences and inequalities are created and sustained. Fortunately, because of its dynamic nature, communication also makes social change possible. For these reasons, it is particularly beneficial to focus on communication when examining gender.

We define **communication** broadly as a meaning-making process, consistent with a social construction perspective (Gergen, 1994). People are not passive receivers of meanings but are actively engaged in the meaning-making process. As the title of this book suggests, one of those meanings being continually constructed through and *in* communication is gender (Taylor, personal correspondence, January 2003). For us, communication is an action (not a reflex). Given gender is communicated, it, too, is an action or something people do.

If we had to summarize the thesis of this entire book in one sentence, it would be this: Communication creates gender, gender does not create communication. Instead of examining how gender influences communication, we explore how communication constrains, perpetuates, stimulates, ignores, and changes gender (Rakow, 1986). We hope to spotlight the profound role communication plays in the construction of gender/sex identities.

Putting communication first, as the constructor of gender/sex identity, offers important benefits. First, it reminds one that individual gender identities and cultural assumptions about gender change over time. Second, it clarifies that gender does not simply exist on the individual level. Rather, gender is a cultural *system* or *structure* of meaning constructed through interactions that govern access to power and resources (Crawford, 1995). Third, it reveals that individuals play an active role in maintaining and/or changing gender constructions.

A communication approach helps prevent essentializing gender as two universal binaries because it treats gender as a verb, not a noun. Gender is a process, not a thing or a universal product. Accordingly, in this book we examine how people "do" (West & Zimmerman, 1987) or "perform" (Butler, 1990a) gender. Gender emerges in the seemingly apolitical, routinized daily behaviors one enacts in conscious and less-than-conscious ways. This, however, does not mean that one's performance is without gendered intent or goals. Communication is goal driven. Through repeated stylizations such as gender performance, the communication may become automatic, but it is no less strategic (Brown & Levinson, 1978; Kellerman, 1992). The word *strategic* is used in its broadest sense to refer to how people use components of communication in an attempt to accomplish their multiple, simultaneous interactional goals.

Our reference to a cultural *system* and *structure* highlights the point that communication never happens in a void. It always takes place in multiple contexts, including physical, relational, cultural, and temporal. Cultural systems and values play major roles in constructing meanings. Studying gender as a cultural system or structure makes visible how gender is constructed on at least three communication levels covered in this textbook: individual, interpersonal, and societal (Crawford, 1995).

At the individual or intrapersonal communication level, a person develops personal gendered identities. At the interpersonal communication level, people influence each other's gender identities. At the societal level, social institutions contribute to the construction of gender/sex—both by imposing gender expectations and by liberating persons from them. This is why we dedicate the second half of the textbook to a close analysis of the ways in which family, education, work, religion, and media contribute to the construction of gender/sex.

Individuals do not experience these communication levels one at a time. Rather, they occur simultaneously. For example, rape is an attack on the individual, but it happens in an interpersonal context, and the reason for the sexual assault, the meaning it is given, and even the laws that define the attack as a crime are gendered. (Note, for example, that not until 2012 did the FBI definition of rape recognize the possibility that men could be raped.) Rape is a crime of gendered and sexual power and domination. It is not a coincidence that women as a group have historically been the most frequent victims of rape, that men as a group have historically been the most frequent aggressors, and that when individual men are the victims, they are emasculated intrapersonally, interpersonally, and culturally. A phrase from the 1960s U.S. women's movement makes the three levels of gender in communication clear: "The personal is political." This maxim explains that what happens to people on a *personal* level is inherently tied to social norms supported by *political* social structures, such as norms about masculinity and femininity.

In order to study communication about gender, it is essential to understand rhetoric. Communication scholars Catherine Palczewski, Richard Ice, and John Fritch (2012) define **rhetoric** as the use of symbolic action by human beings to share ideas, enabling them to work together to make decisions about matters of common concern and to construct social reality. Rhetoric is the means by which people make meaning of and affect the world in which they live. . . . Rhetoric can enlighten and confuse, reveal and hide. (p. 5)

In the study of gender/sex, rhetorical analyses enable close examination of how gender/sex is socially constructed, how the social reality of gender/sex is created, maintained, and changed. Ultimately, we use rhetorical research here to help you understand how public rhetoric about gender/sex influences how individuals express their gender/sex and the cultural expectations for those expressions (Sloop, 2004).

The most comprehensive way to study gender in communication is to study all three of these levels—individual, interpersonal, and societal or public. Doing so makes it easier to recognize how the gender/sex norms that influence individual and interpersonal communication also influence the range of rhetorical choices available to people in public contexts. Similarly, the way politicians or popular culture stars communicate in public contexts may influence one's expectations of how people will interact in daily life. In this text, we examine how communication contexts create, maintain, and change gender/sex in people's lives.

Systemic Gendered Violence

You cannot adequately study gender in communication without addressing its dark side: violence. We use the term *violence* to include intimidation, emotional abuse, verbal abuse, physical abuse, sexual assault, and murder. There is a range of violent relationships, and violence is gendered/sexed (Johnson, 2006).

Around the world, violence disproportionately affects one sex: women. According to the United Nations,

> Violence against women and girls is one of the world's most widespread human right violations. It cuts across the boundaries of age, race, culture, wealth and geography. And it happens everywhere: at home and at work, on the streets and in schools, during times of peace and conflict. Up to 70 percent of women and girls will be beaten, coerced into sex or otherwise abused in their lifetime. ("UN Trust Fund," 2011, par. 1)

Women and girls, as a result of living in systems that devalue them, face violence as a result of their sex.

In addition to violence being sexed, it also is gendered. Gendered violence extends beyond a description of which sex is most often the victim and which sex the perpetrator. The reality is that regardless of the sex of the victim, masculine men tend to be the perpetrators of violence. Typically, those targeted for violence tend to be gendered feminine (or at least not masculine). The term *systemic gendered violence* makes clear that across cultures, perceptions of violence, perpetrators, and victims are gendered.

Gendered/sexed violence is institutionalized. Systems or social structures maintain the notion that being violent, whether in the case of war or seemingly benign verbal bullying, is a legitimate part of heterosexual masculinity—so much so that violence becomes a normalized, accepted behavior for men. Predominant expectations of masculinity tend to enable men to dominate other men, women, children, animals, and their environment. Men's studies scholar Harry Brod (1987) explains,

> Whether learned in gangs, sports, the military, at the hands (often literally) of older males, or in simple acceptance that "boys will be boys" when they fight, attitudes are conveyed to young males ranging from tolerance to approval of violence as an appropriate vehicle for conflict resolution, perhaps even the most manly means of conflict negation. From this perspective, violent men are not deviants or *non*conformists; they are *over*conformists, men who have responded all too fully to a particular aspect of male socialization. (p. 51)

If violence is equated with proving one's masculinity, it becomes difficult for young men, in particular, to be nonconformists, nonviolent, and maintain their masculinity. Worse yet, society struggles to recognize boys and men as victims of psychological or physical abuse by other men, let alone by women. It is as if men who do become victims are emasculated. Furthermore, when women are violent, as in suicide bombers or murdering their spouses or children, society struggles to recognize the acts as violence. They are typically explained as acts of self-defense (Johnson, 2006; Stuart et al., 2006), acts of martyrdom, or a form of mental desperation. They are viewed as unusual or unnatural acts for women.

Such stereotypical explanations for women's and men's violent behaviors hearken back to the discussion of essentialized gender differences. Gendered violence cannot simply be explained by examining individual women's and men's violent behaviors. Placing blame only on individual men ignores the social structures that enable and even encourage such behavior. Women and men are taught from an early age to view men's violence as the natural effect of testosterone. But if it were the hormone that causes aggression, all people with higher levels of testosterone would be violent, and they are not. In actuality, men are socialized to act aggressive in order to become men. There is a hierarchy of masculinity, and those at the bottom due to factors such as body size, racism, sexual orientation, or classism must work harder to prove their masculinity (Kimmel, 2012b).

Countless social practices contribute to a culture that normalizes the violence committed by many men against many women, men, feminine people, people perceived as homosexual, and children. These practices include the seemingly innocent standard that girls and women should be more polite, ladylike, and willing to smile and that they should take sexist remarks, street calls, and whistles as innocent jokes or flattery whether they like it or not (Kramarae, 1992). Those who speak up risk criticism or physical retaliation. Such gendered social practices also include the expectation that all men should be aggressive, sexually active, and unemotional or risk abuse of some kind.

Sociologist Charlene Muehlenhard and associates point out that social pressures can be coercive and that the communication of *coercion* is violence. People who are coerced feel they have no choice but to comply, such as when married persons and young teens have sexual relations even though they do not want to or are ambivalent (Muehlenhard, Goggins, Jones, & Satterfield, 1991; Muehlenhard & Peterson, 2005).

Feminist communication scholars Cheris Kramarae (1992) and Elizabeth Arveda Kissling (1991) offer the concept of a **violence continuum** as a tool to conceptualize the relationships between coercive gendered norms and violence. They suggest viewing all forms of such gendered/sexed practices and the degree of violence within each of them on a continuum. By locating seemingly innocent gendered norms (e.g., men should be virile, women should play hard-to-get) on a common line with more overt forms of violence (e.g., rape, physical abuse), the observer is better able to see how social practices create a culture in which gendered/sexed violence becomes normalized. The violence continuum reveals that violence can be overt or covert; intentional or unintentional; and verbal, emotional, or physical. The connections among all forms of violence expose that the responsibility for violence lies not just in the individual violator but in all who maintain the cultural ideology and structure.

Conclusion

This chapter demonstrates why a gender diversity approach is necessary. Gender as an identity ingredient does not exist in isolation from other ingredients, nor does it exist in isolation from social pressures and structures that maintain it. Anthropologist Nancy Henley and communication scholar Cheris Kramarae (1991) explain that "cultural difference does not exist within a political vacuum; rather, the strength of difference, the types of difference, the values applied to different forms, the dominance of certain forms—all are shaped by the context " (p. 40). When two people communicate, there are never just two parties present in the interaction but multiple social groups (race, class, and gender) are represented, each with varying degrees of privilege and oppression.

We seek to study gender/sex in communication in a more dynamic way that allows for multidimensional, simultaneous, and intersecting influences. We seek to recognize the political nature of gender/sex in communication. Given people's intersectional identity, it makes sense that there are far more than two gendered styles of communication. Studying gender diversity in communication calls for an analysis of more than just masculine and feminine styles of communication. In order to investigate gender diversity in communication, we have provided a vocabulary of key concepts we use throughout the rest of this textbook.

In many ways, this textbook is a "how to" book. It explains *how* to study gender/sex more than it explains what already has been discovered in gender/sex research (although we'll do a good bit of that as well). Given that researchers' understandings and people's performances of gender/sex continually evolve, it is more important to know how to read, hear, understand, and critique gender in communication than it is to know what has already been discovered. Our goal is not to tell you the way things are, for the state of knowledge changes. Instead, our goal is to teach *how* to see *why* things are the way they are. That way, you can consciously choose to embrace that which is liberatory and work against that which denies the full measure of your wonderfully unique, distinct, and idiosyncratic humanity.

KEY CONCEPTS

androgyny 11	genderqueer 13	race 17
binary 13	gender/sex 13	rhetoric 22
communication 21	heteronormativity 16	sex 10
essentialism 20	identity 8	sexual orientation 15
ethnicity 17	intersectionality 9	socioeconomic class 19
gender 3	intersex 14	transgender 13
gender fluidity 15	queer 16	violence continuum 25

DISCUSSION QUESTIONS

1. What do the authors mean by a "critical gendered lens"? Why does this seem useful to the study of gender in communication?

2. Identify five key ingredients that make up your intersectional identity. Reflect on how they interact with each other, creating your gender identity.

3. What does it mean to "do gender"? In what ways is the study of communication central to the study of gender?

4. In your own life, you do gender. Think of examples where you were rewarded for gendered behavior appropriate to your sex or punished for gendered behavior that did not fit your sex. How did this affect how you do gender?

CHAPTER 2

Theories of Gender/Sex

Although people often think of theory as an abstraction far removed from day-to-day living, theories, especially those about gender/sex, constantly circulate through public and interpersonal discussions. For example, in April 2011, controversy erupted about an e-mail advertisement showing J. Crew president and creative director Jenna Lyons with her son, whose toenails are painted neon pink. The advertisement about how to be stylish during weekends includes a quotation indicating how happy Jenna is to have a son whose favorite color is pink (see Figure 2.1).

Figure 2.1 April 2011 J. Crew E-mail Advertisement

Media reactions appeared on all the major news networks and across the Internet. Responses ranged from Jon Stewart on *The Daily Show* calling the controversy "Toemageddon" to the following:

> "[I]t may be fun and games now, Jenna, but at least put some money aside for psychotherapy for the kid—and maybe a little for others who'll be affected by your 'innocent' pleasure.... [A]lmost nothing is now honored as real and true.... [T]his includes the truth that ... it is unwise to encourage little boys to playact like little girls.... [E]ncouraging the choosing of gender identity, rather than suggesting our children become comfortable with the ones that they got at birth, can throw our species into real psychological turmoil."

Dr. Keith Ablow, psychiatrist and
Fox News contributor

> The J. Crew ad is a "marketing piece that features blatant propaganda celebrating transgendered children."

Erin R. Brown, Culture and Media Institute

> "I can say with 100 percent certainty that a mother painting her children's toe nails pink does not cause transgenderism or homosexuality."

Dr. Jack Drescher, psychiatrist
(as cited in S. D. James, 2011)

Embedded within these statements are theories about where a person's gender/ sex comes from and whether it is acceptable for a person (even a 5-year-old) to engage in actions that violate the norms of gender socially assigned to the person's sex. Dr. Ablow's declaration that psychotherapy will be needed is premised on a theory that children's early experiences may be suppressed in their unconscious and that this particular experience will cause harm requiring therapy. He also asserts that the natural "truth" about one's gender identity is "got at birth," and it is harmful for parents to manipulate it through social interactions. In contrast, Dr. Drescher argues that a single gender nonnormative action will not cause a change in gender/sex or sexual orientation. In other words, to completely understand the controversy, one has to be aware of the different underlying theories at work to explain formative influences on gender/sex.

In this chapter, we examine theories on the development of gender/sex. Researchers use these theories to attempt to explain where gender comes from. They generally identify one of three influences as central: biological, psychological, or cultural. **Biological theories** define gender as biologically tied to sex, and distinctive hormones, brain structures, and genitalia typify each sex. **Psychological theories** emphasize the internal psychological processes triggered by early childhood experiences with one's body and interpersonal interactions with primary caregivers and close contacts. **Critical/cultural theories** emphasize the role broad cultural institutions and norms play in the construction and maintenance of gender.

Any research done on gender in communication is premised on some set of theoretical assumptions. Theories guide what questions researchers ask. For example, research that begins with a question about *how* men and women communicate differently makes sense only if one believes that men and women are biologically different. If you resist the biological approach, then you might instead ask: *Do* men and women communicate differently? or How do diverse people communicate? In many ways, research that begins with the assumption that differences exist reinforces those very differences by not asking questions about similarities or whether the differences might be a result of some other variable, such as social power, rather than sex. The research question posed directs the type of research methods used and, consequently, what academics come to call knowledge about gender in communication.

Two basic worldviews explain how knowledge is constructed: objective (or positivist) and interpretive. Researchers using an **objective** (or scientific) worldview see truth as existing prior to researchers' efforts and thus as discoverable. The goal of using a theory is to explain and predict behaviors; research methods are used to focus on controlling possible subjective influences by using laboratory experiments and surveys. Researchers seek to make larger generalizations through the use of statistical analyses where truths are generated based on laws of probability or statistics. An objective worldview is most prevalent in the physical sciences and was adopted by researchers who first developed the social sciences. However, its theoretical prevalence spread far beyond the scientific domain. People often assume their view of the world is objective and others are biased.

Researchers using an **interpretive** (or humanistic) worldview see knowledge as subjective and recognize that people play an active role in the creation of what they come to see as truth. The goal of using theory is to describe and understand the perceptions of the people in a study. Thus, researchers in this worldview use qualitative research methods (such as in-depth interviews, ethnography, analysis of conversations, textual criticism, and field observation) to better reveal the unique influences of context. This view is most used in the interpretive social sciences and humanities.

Not all interpretive views are the same, however. Within humanistic approaches, one also finds theories of *critical/cultural studies* that emphasize that because knowledge is subjective and political, researchers do not leave their personal values at the library or laboratory door. Knowledge is constructed in the context of predominant cultural ideology and beliefs. Research results become accepted as facts often because they fit predominant cultural beliefs.

Although we describe the two predominant approaches as distinct, they are not as independent as they might seem. Increasingly researchers are realizing the value of combining approaches. In fact, one could understand the theories, and their relationship to methods of researching gender, by considering them as a continuum:

Figure 2.2   Theoretical Worldviews

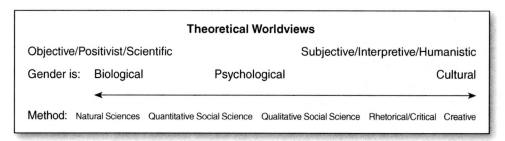

Based on the worldviews of knowledge construction, researchers have studied gender from a biological (scientific worldview), psychological (scientific or interpretive social scientific worldview), and cultural (interpretive and/or critical humanistic worldview) perspective. As the continuum suggests, the research methods shift accordingly, from being highly quantitative, to being more qualitative and interpretive, and finally to a humanistic approach to learning through critical interpretation or creative expression.

We should caution that the research methods and worldviews are not always distinct in actual practice, as it is difficult to separate the three influences (biological, social, and symbolic) from one another (Caplan & Caplan, 1999; Fausto-Sterling, 1992). Some gender phenomena do seem strongly influenced by psychological gender/sex roles, some by broader social influences and institutions, and some by biology. However, even if researchers find that a particular gender attribute is influenced by biology, this does not mean they know if the biology alone caused the attribute or how to value that gender attribute. This is also true for research gathered from psychological or cultural studies. Data are just data until people imbue them with meaning.

In this chapter, we review biological (natural science), psychological (social scientific) and critical/cultural (humanistic) theories of gender/sex. By the end of the chapter, whenever you hear a statement about gender/sex in communication, or read research about it, you should be able to identify the theoretical assumptions supporting that research or statement.

Biological Theories

Biological theories of gender/sex show up everywhere, including in popular culture. An October 6, 2011, *Grey's Anatomy* episode, titled "What Is It About Men," opened with the male doctors in the show offering the following declarative statements:

There are distinct differences between male and female brains. Female brains have a larger hippocampus, which usually makes them better at retention and memory. Male brains have a bigger parietal cortex, which helps when fending off an attack. Male brains confront challenges differently than female brains. Women are hard-wired to communicate with language, detail, empathy. Men—not so much. It doesn't mean we are any less capable of emotion. We can talk about our feelings. It is just that most of the time, we'd really rather not. (McKee, 2011)

Research, theories, religious doctrine, or popular literature that describe the feminine/masculine gender binary as "hard-wired," and place an emphasis on "differences between male and female brains," rely on biological explanations for gender. This does not mean that the researcher completely denies any psychological or cultural influences on gender but that the researcher attributes *primary* causation to genetics, and the assumption of two "opposite" sexes leads to an emphasis on two "opposite" genders (Fausto-Sterling, 1992; Tavris, 1992). Most of this research focuses on two areas of difference: chromosomes (which in turn produce hormones and genitalia) and brain development. As we review this research, you will note that it is far more complex, contradictory, and unsettled than the *Grey's Anatomy* characters would have you believe.

Chromosomes (Hormones and Genitalia)

One determinant of the sex of a fetus is its chromosomes (usually XX for female and XY for male). We say *one* determinant because, although discussions of sex do not usually recognize other variations, some people have sex chromosome combinations of XO, XXX, XXY, or XYY. The presence of intersex persons proves there are more than two sexes.

Something you rarely hear about is how males' and females' chromosomes are more alike than different. Males and females share 22 of 23 of the pairs of chromosomes in humans. Furthermore, a fetus's sex is undifferentiated through the sixth week of gestation; anatomically and hormonally all fetuses are alike (Carroll, 2005; Strong, DeVault, & Sayad, 1999). The genes present in the chromosomes begin to induce gonadal (or reproductive gland) differences in about the sixth or seventh week, leading to hormonal and anatomical differences between the sexes.

Anatomical differences linked to the X and Y chromosomes have long played a central role in explaining gender/sex identity. People from every walk of life— from artists, journalists, and historians to religious leaders—have heralded the penis as an outward sign of men's virility and right to assert their strength over others. The virile penis has become an essential characteristic of masculinity. Communication studies scholar Diana Ivy (2011) suggests that the more obvious, external nature of males' sex organs makes the strength of it more overt than females' less overt sex organs: "The social interpretations of women's sexual organs identify them as reactors, receivers, followers, and beneficiaries of men's decisions" (p. 49).

Granted, male and female genitalia are distinct, but what the penis (and clitoris) means is socially constructed. As the earlier discussion of the penis makes clear, power has been linked to it, at least in part, because of its visible size in comparison to the clitoris. But that size assessment is open to contest. Pulitzer Prize–winning science author Natalie Angier (1999) notes, "The clitoris is simply a bundle of nerves: 8,000 nerve fibers, to be precise. That's a higher concentration of nerve fibers than is found anywhere else on the body, including the fingertips, lips, and tongue, and it is twice the number in the penis" (pp. 63–64). So, is a woman's clitoris smaller than a man's penis? In terms of external exposed tissue, yes. But in terms of its function as a pleasure organ, is the clitoris smaller? Not if you measure size by the number of nerve endings. The meaning of sexual organs is socially constructed.

Not surprisingly, reproductive functions tied to genitalia also commonly influence conceptions of gender/sex; it seems as though she who gives birth must also give care. Ivy (2011) argues, "The reproductive capabilities of men and women have more profound social translations than any other biological property or function" (p. 50). The fact that women bear children has led them to be expected to do nurturing and caregiving. Men's provision of sperm to the egg in order to create an embryo is seen as virile and in control, consistent with expectations to be assertive and self-protective. To demonstrate how much reproduction affects gender expectations, Ivy suggests that traditional gender roles likely would not have been the same had the reproductive process been reversed.

Testosterone tends to occur in larger proportions in males, and estrogen tends to occur in larger proportions in females. However, both hormones appear in both male and female bodies. This often is forgotten. Biology professor Anne Fausto-Sterling (2000), after reviewing a year of articles in major newspapers, noted that "despite the fact that both hormones seem to pop up in all types of bodies, producing all sorts of different effects, many reporters and researchers continue to consider estrogen the female hormone and testosterone the male hormone" (p. 179). She urges people to remember, when thinking about hormones, "social belief systems weave themselves into the daily practice of science in ways that are often invisible to the working scientist" (p. 194). The question is, How do hormones interact with all people's bodies? Not, How do hormones determine sex?

Testosterone appears to be related to aggression and risk taking (Archer, 2006; Hermans, Ramsey, & van Honk, 2008; McAndrew, 2009). Although many think there is a simple relationship wherein testosterone induces violent and aggressive behavior, the reality is much more complicated. Research makes clear that situational factors strongly influence how testosterone affects behavior. In their book, *Heroes, Rogues, & Lovers: Testosterone and Behavior*, social psychologist James Dabbs and Mary Dabbs (2001) review over two decades of research indicating that in certain circumstances (usually those relating to competition for social dominance), testosterone tends to motivate rebellious, aggressive, delinquent, and violent behavior. Under other conditions (where a person is in a protective position like a firefighter), testosterone tends to motivate altruistic and prosocial heroic behaviors. In other words, the social situation influences testosterone's effects. There is no simple biological cause but a complex interplay of biology and culture. Quite simply, testosterone does not determine one's gender or one's behavior.

Brain Development

Research about whether men's and women's brains differ has been conducted for well over a century. In the 1900s, scientists argued that because women's brains were smaller, women were intellectually inferior. The fact that this would also mean that smaller men were intellectually inferior to larger men did not seem to register (Boddice, 2011). The debate about brain difference was reignited in 2005 when then Harvard president Lawrence Summers, in a speech about diversifying the science and engineering workforce, offered the explanation that women were underrepresented because of "different availability of aptitude at the high end" (par. 2). Embedded in Summers's statement is a biological theory of gender/sex differences in development.

In the last decade, investigators have found functional, chemical, and structural variations between men's and women's brains. Thus, you can see why Summers might have felt comfortable making that statement. However, before we detail this research, we want to offer a few caveats—caveats Summers might have been wise to consider.

First, the existence of structural differences does not mean they are biologically caused. The plasticity of the brain (the fact the brain changes depending on a person's experiences over a lifetime) means little can be inferred from the identification of differences (Vidal, 2011). Psychologist Cordelia Fine (2010) explains the idea of "brain development as a gene-directed process of adding new circuitry" that dominates the popular press is just plain wrong. The most recent research makes clear how "our brains . . . are changed by our behavior, our thinking, our social world" (pp. 176–177; see also Hyde, 2007). Differences are not inherent and structural based on sex but are caused by experiences over a lifetime.

The London Cabbie Experiment

Maguire, Eleanor A., Gadian, David G., Johnsrude, Ingrid S., Good, Catriona D., Ashburner, John, Frackowiak, Richard S. J., & Frith, Christopher D. (2000, April 11). Navigation-related structural change in the hippocampi of taxi drivers. *Proceedings of the National Academy of Sciences, 97*(8), 4398–4403.

Subjects: MRIs of the brains of London taxi drivers were compared to a control group of people who did not have extensive navigation experiences.

Findings: The taxi drivers' posterior hippocampi were significantly larger than the control subjects', and hippocampal volume correlated with the amount of time spent as a taxi driver, meaning the longer one was a taxi driver, the larger the posterior hippocampi, which stores a spatial representation of the environment.

Conclusion: "There is a capacity for local plastic change in the structure of the healthy adult human brain in response to environmental demands" (p. 4398).

Second, discussing sex differences in a way that emphasizes them can create a self-fulfilling prophecy. **Stereotype threat** occurs when a group is informed of a stereotype and then the group's performance is affected by the stereotype. In a study of performance in an upper-level university math course, one class was given a test under normal circumstances and another group was told that "this mathematics test has not shown any gender differences in performance or mathematics ability" to nullify the stereotype that males perform better than females in math (Good, Aronson, & Harder, 2008). In the first case, women and men performed equally well. In the second, women not only performed as well as the men in the class, but their performance "was raised significantly to surpass that of the men in the course" (p. 17). The study concludes, "Even among the most highly qualified and persistent women in college mathematics, stereotype threat suppresses test performance" (p. 17). When Summers mentioned sex differences in the sciences, he actually may have helped cause or maintain them. Thus, we want to be very clear: We will note the differences in brain structure, but there is *no* evidence they actually affect performance.

Scientists have examined brain structure to identify sex (and then infer gender) differences. Men's brains do tend to be larger than women's by about 100 grams (Ankney, 1992), but brain size is relative to body size, and men tend to be larger than women. In addition, debate continues over whether brain size and IQ are related (Peters, 1995; Rushton & Ankney, 2009).

Some argue that women tend to be better at using both sides of the brain because the corpus callosum, which bridges the two hemispheres, tends to be larger in women. This has been used to explain many women's tendency toward stronger language skills, the ability to identify others' emotions more quickly (Begley & Murr, 1995), and the ability to use both hemispheres for listening. However, neurons travel quickly across the two hemispheres regardless of the size of the corpus callosum. Psychologist David G. Myers (2004) cautions against assuming that people use only one hemisphere for individual tasks. Instead, they almost always use both hemispheres because there is a constant exchange of information. Social psychologist Carol Tavris (1992) explains, "The two hemispheres of the brain do have different specialties, but it is far too simple-minded (so to speak) to assume that human abilities clump up in opposing bunches" (p. 49). The two hemispheres have the ability to compensate for each other and to cooperate. For example, if one hemisphere is damaged, the other hemisphere takes over its tasks. This demonstrates that both sides have the neurological ability to perform the other side's tasks. Even though this plasticity decreases with age, the two hemispheres are interdependent (Myers, 2004).

Researchers have found more consistent links between sex differences and responses to mental disorders, stress, hormones, and memory (Cahill, 2005). These findings have raised awareness that research and medical treatment procedures performed on men cannot be generalized to all women or even to all men. Additionally, the National Academy of Sciences reports that sexual orientation may be influenced by brain differences. A band of fibers called the anterior commissure, which connects brain hemispheres, tends to be larger in gay men than in heterosexual women and men (Elias, 1992). Other researchers have found that twins raised apart tend to have the same sexual orientation (Whitam, Diamond, & Martin, 1993), and lesbians are consistently different from heterosexual women in self-reported sexual orientations across cultures (Whitam, Daskalos, Sobolewski, & Padilla, 1998). Yet, researchers do not know whether the fiber band's size is affected by use and whether it can change. In addition, cognitive researcher William Byne (2005) points out that quantitative size differences in brain structure alone cannot tell about qualitative differences in sexual orientation.

Although some evidence of biological influences exists, the links to gender are not as simple as some might think. Ultimately, biology alone cannot determine gender identities, and it certainly cannot predict gendered communication. Otherwise, all women and all men in all cultures and all countries across the world would express masculine and feminine gender in identical ways. Biological links to gender are probably more realistically described as influences rather than as sole or direct causes (Reiss, 2000).

In fact, when researchers refuse to start from the assumption that the sexes differ, and instead sort people based on gender, interesting results emerge. Researchers at the University of Iowa studied the relationship among sex, gender, and social cognition. Given studies have found women are more adept than men at social perception and the interpretation of nonverbal social cues, the researchers wondered whether the brain might give some clue as to why. They studied 30 men and 30 women matched for age and IQ. The researchers used a magnetic resonance imaging (MRI) scan to measure gray matter volume and surface area of the ventral frontal cortex (VFC). However, instead of just comparing people based on sex (comparing men to women), they sought to compare people based on gender (as determined by the answers to the Personal Attributes Questionnaire, the PAQ, a scale of femininity and masculinity). They found "identification with more feminine traits on the PAQ correlated with greater SG [straight gyrus] gray matter volume and surface area. In addition, higher degrees of femininity correlated with better performance on the IPT [Interpersonal Perception Test]" (Wood, Heitmiller, Andreasen, & Nopoulos, 2008, p. 534).

This begs the question, Why is the SG larger in adult women? So, the researchers did a second study to look at 37 girl and 37 boy children to see if the size difference was innate (meaning programmed from birth). They found the SG was actually *larger* in boys, yet the same test of interpersonal awareness showed that skill in this area correlated to a smaller SG (Wood, Murko, & Nopoulos, 2008). In commentary on these studies, neuroscience professor Lise Eliot (2009b) explains,

> This finding—that brain structure correlates as well or better with psychological "gender" than with simple biological "sex"—is crucial to keep in mind when considering any comparisons of male and female brains. Yes, men and women are psychologically different and yes, neuroscientists are uncovering many differences in brain anatomy and physiology which seem to explain our behavioral differences. But just because a difference is biological doesn't mean it is "hard-wired." Individuals' gender traits—their preference for masculine or feminine clothes, careers, hobbies and interpersonal styles—are inevitably shaped more by rearing and experience than is their biological sex. Likewise, their brains, which are ultimately producing all this masculine or feminine behavior, must be molded—at least to some degree—by the sum of their experiences as a boy or girl. (par. 10)

The studies by Wood and her colleagues are important because theirs are some of the very few studies that do not look solely for sex differences.

Biological Theories Conclusion

Biological theories should be approached with some skepticism. If something is presented as caused by biology, this creates the impression it is unchangeable. If something is natural, then nothing can be done about it. **Biological determinism**—the idea that biology (sex) determines gender differences—means that inequalities are natural and, hence, cannot be changed by social action. Biologist Fausto-Sterling (2000) urges us to never "lose sight of the fact that our debates about the body's biology are always simultaneously moral, ethical, and political debates about social and political equality and the possibilities for change. Nothing less is at stake" (p. 255).

Psychological Theories

When you read research, theory, or popular material that assumes gender is an innate part of one's personality, the authors are likely drawing from the field of psychology. They do not necessarily claim that biology and culture have no influence, but most focus on how one's identity becomes gendered through early childhood experiences, as when Ablow warned of the "psychological turmoil" caused by a young boy having his toenails painted in the J. Crew advertisement. In fact, some argue that a child's gender identity is generally set as early as 1 to 3 years of age (A. Campbell, 1993). Although psychological theories vary, they focus on linking one's sex to gendered personalities via the influences of close relationships. Later theories also recognize the influences of culture in developing one's gender.

Psychoanalysis and Psychoanalytic Feminism

Psychoanalytic theories call attention to how unconscious thoughts and memories influence a person's identity, actions, and beliefs. Thus, to truly understand why a human being is the way that person is, psychoanalysis demands attention to the person's past. In terms of gender, this means that "early bodily and emotional experience in infancy and early childhood" are central elements forming the unconscious ways people do gender (Minsky, 1998, p. 6).

Sigmund Freud originated psychoanalysis as a psychological treatment technique. Central to psychoanalysis was the study of gender and sex identity formation. Freud (1975) theorized that children develop gender identity personalities based on their perceptions of sex differences in biological genitalia. He theorized that until age 4, sex difference is irrelevant to the child. At around 3 to 4 years of age, "the sexual life of children usually emerges in a form accessible to observation" when they enter the phallic stage during which they become aware of their genitals (pp. 42–43). From the phallic stage till puberty (the genital stage), Freud argued children see themselves in terms of having, or not having, a penis. While little boys initially assume everyone has a penis like theirs, Freud argued that little girls recognize their genitals are different and "are overcome by envy for the penis—an envy culminating in the wish . . . to be boys themselves" (p. 61). When boys do notice girls lack a penis, they experience "castration complex" wherein they recognize the possibility that the penis can be removed, and they begin to fear castration as punishment (p. 61). In Freud's view, for girls to develop normally, they must turn to a development of heterosexuality and maternality, or association with their mother, to compensate for their failed masculinity. For boys to develop normally, they must ultimately identify with their father. According to Freud's original theory, boys who do not make a complete break in their dependence on their mothers will not become fully masculine (Brannon, 2011). Thus, successful gender and sexual development in girls and boys is marked by their willingness to identify with the parent of their sex (instead of seeing that parent as competition for the affections of the other parent).

Much of Freud's work has been criticized for reflecting a masculine bias and a misunderstanding of women's psyche. A contemporary of Freud, Karen Horney, initiated the criticism. She argued that for girls, penis envy did not represent a literal envy for the physical penis but rather represented a symbolic envy for the social power and prestige men and boys experienced. In addition, she argued that men experienced "womb envy," in which men sought social and material accomplishments to compensate for their inability to give birth. She wrote, "From the biological point of view woman has . . . in the capacity for motherhood, a quite indisputable and by no means negligible physiological superiority. This is most clearly reflected in the unconscious of the male psyche in the boy's intense envy of motherhood" (Horney, 1967, pp. 60–61).

In addition to the near universal rejection of the theory that all women experience "penis envy" (Tavris, 1992), Freudian psychoanalysis is criticized because it essentializes gender/sex when it dictates only two sex-based paths for successful gender identity development (Bell, 2004). The reality is children respond to gender identity in highly idiosyncratic and individual ways. Further, Freud's early theory recognized only heterosexual identities, not homosexual or bisexual ones, and did not consider cross-cultural variations.

Although many rightly critique Freud's work, his attention to the unconscious and the role of early experiences in gender identity formation were revolutionary. For feminists, Freud helped make clear that gender was not biologically determined but was influenced and formed by social experiences. One could understand gender from a psychoanalytic perspective by focusing on the way adults impose gender/sex norms on infants and, in the process, structure the human mind. Psychoanalysis generated multiple strands of psychoanalytic feminism (e.g., interpersonal psychoanalytic feminism [Gilligan, 1982], Lacanian theory [Lacan, 1998]). One strand, object relations theory, is particularly relevant to the discussion here.

In object relations theory, feminist psychologist Nancy Chodorow (1978) built on Freud by arguing that the mind (and gender identity) is formed in childhood, not in response to children discovering their genitalia but rather by the relationships children have with others—particularly their primary caregivers, who tended to be women. According to Chodorow, because the mother is a gendered person herself, she interacts with boy and girl children according to her gender, forming distinct relationships. At the same time, each child experiences internal conflict in trying to construct a separate identity from the mother. Because the mother and daughter are overtly similar, the daughter resolves her conflict by identifying with the mother and thus emulates a feminine gender identity. The girl develops intimacy and relationship as a primary part of who she is. According to Chodorow, the mother tends to treat a boy child differently from a girl child. The mother encourages independence in the boy earlier than in the girl and is less intimate in her talk with the boy. The boy child also recognizes that he is not like his mother in basic ways. To resolve his internal conflict, the boy must reject the mother as a part of his independent identity development. The boy develops an orientation toward independence and activity as a primary part of who he is and thus finds relationships potentially smothering.

Object relations and other strands of feminist psychoanalysis agree with Freud that all gender identity meanings, conscious and unconscious, have their origins in early bodily and emotional experiences and the fantasies associated with them (Minsky, 1998). They also suggest gender is influenced by one's sex identity and vice versa. Persons do not experience these in isolation but rather as related parts of the self (Bell, 2004). However, this does not mean that sex *causes* gender. Psychoanalytic theorists since Freud have emphasized the role of culture in gender development. By combining the influences of culture and the unconscious self, theorists are better able to explain why some individuals do not conform to cultural pressures of gender/sex expectations; why gender, sex, and sexuality are more fluid and diverse than cultural stereotypes suggest; and how race, class, and culture create multiple variations of gender, sex, and sexuality (Bell, 2004). Social learning and cognitive development theorists offer examples of these.

Social Learning

Social learning theory posits gender is a learned behavior, learned by observing, analyzing, and modeling others. When gender behavior is modeled correctly, meaning it is consistent with sex identity, it is rewarded; if done incorrectly, it is punished. Particularly with children, this process of modeling, reinforcement, and punishment shapes gender/sex identities. Originally developed by Walter Mischel (1966) and later modified by Albert Bandura (2002; Bandura & Walters, 1963), this theory examines the socialization process whereby children internalize many identity ingredients and norms of behavior, not just gender. The theory portrays socialization as a passive process in which children learn by observing and imitating others and by being rewarded for these behaviors. When children are positively rewarded for mimicking preferred behaviors, the behaviors attached to prescribed social roles become internalized habits (Addis, Mansfield, & Syzdek, 2010). According to this approach, young girls tend to be rewarded for being polite, neat, emotionally expressive, and well behaved. Young boys tend to be rewarded for being independent, emotionally controlled, and physically active. Thus, girls tend to develop feminine qualities, and boys tend to develop masculine qualities.

As with object relations theory, in the initial research on social learning theory, the parents' and/or primary caregivers' behaviors were considered most influential. However, more recent uses of social learning theory have highlighted two things. First, observational learning occurs not only in relation to immediate family but also through media sources such as video games (Wohn, 2011), meaning social learning theory can be used to explain interpersonal family communication and mediated communication. Second, social learning is situational, meaning a single way to do gender is not enforced. Instead, a variety of ways to do gender in different situations are rewarded.

Understanding the role media play in social learning is necessary. For example, given most people do not directly observe others' sexual activity, social learning theory recognizes people can learn from, and model, mediated gender performances. This also demonstrates why "increased exposure to media is associated with more sexually permissive behaviors and attitudes" (Petersen & Hyde, 2010, p. 23). Given that sex scenes on television doubled from 1998 to 2003, and that they increased most dramatically in depicting sexually permissive women, based on social learning theory, researchers predicted that women would report engaging in more sexual behaviors. These predictions proved true (Petersen & Hyde, 2010). Mediated communication practices contribute to the formation of gendered expression.

Recent research on social learning also encourages scholars to recognize that learning is far more situational than previously thought. The same action might be rewarded by one group in one setting but punished by a different group in a different setting. Psychologists Addis, Mansfield, and Syzdek (2010) explain:

> Social learning is situated learning; particular actions are followed by particular consequences in specific contexts. Young boys, for example, often learn that expressing soft vulnerable emotions like sadness will be followed by punishment and other forms of ridicule, particularly when this behavior occurs in the context of other dominant males. These same consequences may be less likely to occur among close confidants, or around one's mother versus one's father. Over time, what emerge are relatively differentiated or discriminated repertoires of activity that are highly sensitive to context. (p. 80)

As a result of their research, these psychology professors argue that researchers and theorists should "embrace the contextual nature of gendered social learning" and "avoid metaphors that locate gender as an internal property of individuals" (p. 83). Again, gender is something one does, not something one has.

Social learning theory fares better than the psychoanalytic approaches in its ability to help explain communication influences and because it is much easier to directly observe and test. However, it has not stimulated much subsequent theory development, it still tends to dichotomize gender/sex, and it cannot explain why some boys and girls do not conform to social expectations.

Cognitive Development

Those who use **cognitive development** theory seek to explain human behavior by understanding the development of identity as a process that goes through stages (Piaget, 1965). Like psychoanalysis, cognitive development explains gender identity development as a mental process. Like social learning, it notes that children will behave according to social norms of gender. Cognitive development theory is different from social learning theory however, because the assumed motive for learning gender is not a desire to mimic and attain rewards from others but a desire for self-development and competency. Unlike social learning theory, this approach recognizes the more active role children play in developing their own gender identities (Vygotsky, 1978). Children develop cognitive categories (what researchers call schemas) in relation to gender and organize the information they receive from observations around those categories. In social learning theory, children learn behaviors and then mimic them. In cognitive development theory, children first adopt a gender identity and then perform behaviors consistent with it. For example, when young boys say they cannot play with a doll because it is a girl's toy, they are categorizing behaviors and objects using a gender schema, and depending on where something fits in the schema, they decide whether or not they can do it. Researchers have used this theory to argue cognitive abilities are gender linked.

Psychologist Lawrence Kohlberg (1966) argued cognitive development and moral reasoning are a process of increasingly complex thinking, from basic concrete, extreme views, such as "only boys can play football" or "only girls can play with dolls," to less stereotypical understandings. Based on his research in an all-boys school, he concluded only boys can advance to the highest stage of moral reasoning. He argued that it is necessary for boys to do so because this is where they realize they must and can separate their identities from their mothers' as primary caregivers. According to Kohlberg, girls do not advance to this stage because they cannot separate themselves from their mothers' identities.

Although cognitive development theory has generated a great deal of research because it is more easily observable, earlier gender applications regarding morality such as Kohlberg's have been rejected. First, researchers in cross-cultural studies point out that defining the highest morality as individualistic is reflective of Western cultural values and does not adequately account for Chinese, South African Blacks, and other cultures that place more value on collectivism (Chow & Ding, 2002; Ferns, 2000). Second, research on actual cognitive development does not report significant differences based on sex. In one study, 788 monolingual children (350 boys, 438 girls) ages 5 to 16 years from Mexico and Colombia were studied. The result suggests that "[sex] differences in language and other cognitive abilities are usually nonsignificant or very small" (Ardila, Rosselli, Matute, & Inozemtseva, 2011, p. 989). In fact, the research found "the existence of a larger number of gender similarities than gender differences" that supports the assumption that gender differences during cognitive development are minimal, appear in only a small number of tests, and account for only a low percentage of the score variance. It is likely, therefore, that certain cultural factors may be responsible for at least some of the gender differences that appeared in test scores (Ardila et al., 2011, p. 989).

Third, feminist researchers point to inherent sexism in Kohlberg's research. Like Freud, Kohlberg defined femininity as an absence of desired masculine qualities. Most of Kohlberg's research was based on the study of White males, using male actors in moral dilemma tests. Feminist psychologist Carol Gilligan (1982), in her studies of predominantly White young women and men, found that by not rejecting their mothers, the girls tended to gain a sense of identity *through* relationships, whereas the boys who differentiated themselves from their mothers tended to gain a sense of identity *outside* relationships. In both cases, the children's choices seemed influenced by cultural and parental gender expectations. She further argued that from these different orientations, people may form different but equally valid moral codes. Women's expected gendered morality is defined as an ethic of responsibility/relationship and men's expected gendered morality as an ethic of individual rights. Gilligan helped raise awareness that feminine attributes can be positive and that research on male adolescents cannot be generalized to females.

Feminists have since criticized Gilligan's theory for continuing to essentialize the two sexes as having two opposing moral orientations. What cognitive development theorists seem to agree on is that children pass through phases of gender identity development by ages 3 to 6 and form what is called a gender constancy, or gender identity, that is less likely to change (Dubois, Serbin, & Derbyshire, 1998). After that point, children actively seek role models and information from peers, popular culture, siblings, and elsewhere to know how to perform their gender competently.

Psychological Theories Conclusion

Psychological approaches suggest that gender identity is not naturally set at birth but instead developed through early childhood interaction. In general, the psychological approaches we reviewed presume that all children are raised in Western, two-parent, heterosexual, nuclear, bourgeois families. Cultural complexities have led many to question the existence of psychological differences between women and men. Psychologist Janet Hyde (2005) conducted a review of 46 meta-analyses on gender and psychology research. She concludes that there is no foundation for the continued belief in prominent psychological gender differences: "The gender similarities hypothesis holds that males and females are similar on most, but not all, psychological variables. That is, men and women, as well as boys and girls, are more alike than they are different" (p. 581).

Critical/Cultural Theories

Writing in 1949, French philosopher Simone de Beauvoir questioned the way the natural and social sciences had depicted womanhood as mysterious in justifying women's inferiority. She argued that even these supposedly objective sciences were biased in the presumption of women's inferiority to men and, in turn, reinforced that bias and justified patriarchy (the institutionalized maintenance of male privilege). Although Beauvoir recognized biological differences exist, she challenged the social value attached to those differences. To make clear the cultural, and not innate biological or inherent psychological, causes of gender, Beauvoir (2011) declared,

> One is not born, but rather becomes, woman. No biological, psychic, or economic destiny defines the figure that the human female takes on in society; it is civilization as a whole that elaborates [what] is called feminine. Only the mediation of another can constitute an individual as an *Other.* (p. 283)

Although the social inequality between the sexes had been questioned for decades, if not centuries, Beauvoir's book marked a turning point in the critical analysis of the cultural foundations of gender. The *Stanford Encyclopedia of Philosophy* declares, "Beauvoir's *The Second Sex* gave us the vocabulary for analyzing the social constructions of femininity and the structure for critiquing these constructions" ("Simone de Beauvoir," 2010, part 6, par. 6). If one is to fully understand where gender/sex comes from, then critical attention to cultural constructions of gender/sex is necessary.

In many ways, the emphasis on gender as something a person *does* and not something a person *is* emerges from this perspective. Instead of understanding gender as something a person is born with, or as an innate component of a person's psychological identity, a critical/cultural approach calls for people to understand gender as something that is done—by individuals, groups, and institutions. Gender cannot be understood by examining a single individual's biology or psychology. Instead, the broader situations in which an individual lives—the social meanings embedded within communication—must be studied. West and Zimmerman (1987), the scholars who wrote the germinal essay "Doing Gender," explain,

> Doing gender involves a complex of socially guided perceptual, interactional, and micropolitical activities that cast particular pursuits as expressions of masculine and feminine "natures."

> When we view gender as an accomplishment . . . our attention shifts from matters internal to the individual and focuses on interactional and, ultimately, institutional arenas. In one sense, of course, it is individuals who "do" gender. But it is a situated doing, carried out in the virtual or real presence of others who are presumed to be oriented to its production. Rather than as a property of individuals, we conceive of gender as an emergent feature of social situations: both as an outcome of and a rationale for various social arrangements and as a means of legitimating one of the most fundamental divisions of society. (p. 126)

Thus, to study gender, one needs to be critical of how it is culturally and socially constructed. One's gendered lens should focus not just on an individual doing gender but also on how social interactions and institutions do gender by gendering people and practices (see also West & Zimmerman, 2009).

A range of critical/cultural approaches to gender/sex exist, including postmodernism, deconstructionism, poststructuralism, postcolonialism, queer theory, and cultural studies. In what follows, we outline some of the common assumptions these approaches share and then focus on two of them to give a better sense of how critical/cultural approaches explain how gender/sex comes to be.

Critical/cultural approaches to gender/sex theorize that one can never understand gender and sex unless one studies broad cultural systems that sustain power differences, and this requires heightened attention to the way communication constructs gender and sex. Critical/cultural approaches make clear that communication is not merely a means by which culture is transmitted (say, from parent to child) and instead describe communication as the process by which culture as a social reality is constructed, maintained, and altered. Thus, sex and gender, themselves, are not considered preexisting categories that structure research, but *how* gender and sex have been formed as categories becomes the focus of research. Critical/cultural approaches challenge theories that argue women and men are merely, and always, different as unrealistic and counterproductive. Differences are never neutral; instead, differences go hand in hand with inequalities. Thus, critical/cultural approaches share assumptions that encourage those who study gender to recognize culture is a human construction (constructed via communication and symbols) that contains systems of hierarchy and power differentials.

Shared Assumptions

1. *The social reality of culture is communicatively constructed.* **Culture** is "learned patterns of behavior and attitudes shared by a group of people" (Martin & Nakayama, 2004, p. 3). These patterns and attitudes can be found in conceptions of knowledge, experiences, beliefs, values, attitudes, meanings, hierarchies, religions, time, social roles, worldviews, land, and even the material possessions or artifacts acquired by a group of people. The primary function of culture is to create shared meanings, collective worldviews, and a group identity. Through these characteristics, cultures also serve to help reduce uncertainty by socializing their members to behave in prescribed ways. Cultures exist on many levels: in families, neighborhoods, towns and cities, ethnic and racial groups, religious groups, regions of a country, and nations.

Within a given culture, predominant views and groups exist. And if one group is predominant, then others are subordinated. Intercultural communication researchers Judith Martin and Thomas Nakayama (2004) argue that cultures are by nature "contested zones" (p. 58), meaning multiple power inequalities exist within a given culture, including inequalities relating to gender/sex. To identify these cultural inequalities, critical/cultural critics examine the systems of hierarchy at play in a culture.

Social reality is reality as understood through the symbols humans use to represent it. Social reality is created as people name objects, actions, and each other.

Although a material world from which human beings receive sensory data exists, people do not know how to interact with that world until their sensory data is given meaning through symbolic action. Human beings' only access to reality is through their symbols. Imagine if you had to find a way to communicate your gender to the world, but you could not use any form of communication. You could not speak, wear clothes (which carry with them symbolic messages), or move. How would others know your gender? Linguist Mary Crawford (1995) explains that gender is a social construct:

> a system of meaning that organizes interactions and governs access to power and resources. From this view, gender is not an attribute of individuals but a way of making sense of transactions. Gender exists not in persons but in transactions; it is conceptualized as a verb, not a noun. (p. 12)

For critical/cultural theorists, gender is something one does, not something one is, *and* gender is something that is socially created, not biologically or individually created.

The centrality of communication to social reality is explained by communication scholar Barry Brummett (1976), who argues "[e]xperience is sensation plus *meaning*" and "*reality is meaning*" (pp. 28, 29). All symbolic action participates in the creation of meaning. The power of symbols to make meaning explains why communication scholars note a distinction between reality and *social* reality. Critical/cultural theorists emphasize the power of discourse to shape social reality and study the processes by which this is accomplished.

In terms of gender/sex, this means there really is no biological entity that humans can access without socially constructing it in some way. Critical/cultural scholars emphasize the role communication plays in forming people's understandings of the world. Even the seemingly simple terms of *female* and *male* illustrate the power of communication to create (and maintain and change) social reality. As long as these were the only terms available to refer to the human body, bodies were forcibly fit—through sex assignment surgery at birth—into one of those binary categories. Until the language for intersex emerged, bodies could only be one of two things.

2. *Categories such as sex, gender, sexuality, and race themselves become the focus of criticism.* Because reality is socially constructed, critical/cultural theorists do not take for granted that sex (male, female), gender (masculine, feminine), sexuality (heterosexuality, homosexuality), race (Black, White), and other categories are objective designations. Categories are not neutral designations of "the way things are" but are how people structure what is. Philosopher Judith Butler (1992) explains how the critical/cultural theory of poststructuralism highlights how "power pervades the very conceptual apparatus" that people use to understand the world and themselves (p. 6).

Critical/cultural theorists note how the categories just listed tend to be mutually exclusive binaries (if you are *either* male *or* female, then intersex people do not exist; if you are *either* Black *or* White, then multiracial people do not exist). The categories determine whose lives are recognizable and intelligible—which people exist socially. Thus, instead of starting from the assumption that males and females indicate the two sexes that exist, a critical/cultural theorist would question and investigate how those categories were created, who those categories benefit, and how the categories are placed in a hierarchical relation to each other.

3. *One cannot study gender/sex unless one also studies systems of hierarchy.* Systems of hierarchy refer to the cultural patterns and institutional structures that maintain inequality between groups. Critical/cultural scholars emphasize the broad cultural patterns at play to highlight that gender/sex is not simply located within individuals but is sustained throughout the culture, in its symbol systems, institutions, and rituals. In other words, gender is not something you were born with or learned only from interactions with your parents. The range of gendered practices across cultures around the globe makes clear that gender is not innate or biologically determined. Saying that you learned gender from only your parents begs the question: Where did your parents learn gender? Gender/sex, together with race, class, sexual orientation, and other cultural identities, lives in the ideology, norms, laws, worldview, traditions, popular culture, and social institutions that sustain a culture. Critical/cultural approaches argue that you cannot understand gender only by studying individuals' performance of it. Instead, one must study the systems of hierarchy that privilege some sexes over others and some performances of gender over others.

Critical/cultural scholars make clear that the issue is not only whether one person exerts power over another. Instead, one needs to critique systems. Systems of hierarchy, embedded within social, economic, and political institutions, explain the existence of racial and gender/sex inequality; biology and personal bias are not the central foundations of inequality. Racism, sexism, homophobia, and other biases

> are not *caused* by prejudice—by individual bad attitudes and false beliefs. The tendency to see prejudice as the cause of racial (or gender, class, or sexual) inequality tends to lodge responsibility for racism on already economically disadvantaged whites. . . . Racism is enacted in many different ways, and overt individual prejudice is just one of them. (Harding, 1995, p. 122, italics in original)

Critical/cultural scholars understand discrimination as a system of hierarchy, "fundamentally a political relationship, a strategy that" as a system, gives social, economic, political, psychological, and social privileges to one group and denies them to another (p. 122).

Privileges are unearned freedoms or opportunities. Often, privileges are unconscious and unmarked. They are socialized through cultural hegemony, which makes them easy to deny and more resistant to change. When violence prevention educator Jackson Katz (2003) asks men in his workshops what they do to prepare to walk alone on campus at night, most of them respond with an unknowing stare. When he asks women this question, they readily offer several strategies they use to keep safe, such as phoning roommates ahead to tell them they are leaving, carrying their keys pointed out between their fingers as a weapon against would-be attackers, or looking in their cars before they open the doors. Gay, lesbian, bisexual, and transgendered persons often try to pass as straight to avoid possible verbal or physical violence. Heterosexuals usually do not have to consider such acts.

4. *Oppositional critical views are necessary to critique hegemonic norms.* Hegemony designates the systems of hierarchy maintained by the predominant social group's ideology (Gramsci, Rosenthal, & Rosengarten, 1993). Philosopher Rosemary Hennessy (1995) explains that hegemony is not a form of power that controls through overt violence. Rather, it controls subtly by determining what makes sense: "Hegemony is the process whereby the interests of a ruling group come to dominate by establishing the common sense, that is, those values, beliefs, and knowledges that go without saying" (pp. 145–146). People willingly belong to cultures for the protection and order those cultures provide, even though predominant cultural ideology may control them in some ways. By following society's norms of behavior, members uphold the culture's ideology.

When analysts of gender talk about **patriarchy**, they are not talking about the domination of one man over one woman but are talking about a hierarchical system that exercises hegemonic control wherein men are privileged over women, and some men are privileged over men, and in which even some of those who are subordinate in the hierarchy accept it because such an ordering appears to make sense.

To explain how patriarchy operates, sociologist R. W. Connell introduced the concept of hegemonic masculinity. Connell noted there is not one single way to perform masculinity; instead, a range of masculinities exists. But not all forms of masculinity are equal; some forms of masculinity are privileged (White, upper-class, wage-earning, heterosexual, athletic) over other forms, and masculinity is privileged over femininity. Although Connell recognized that a plurality of masculinities exists, the focus was on the normative form of masculinity, the type that has been the most honored way to be a man, even if it is not the type that is most prevalent (the norm). Hegemonic masculinity does not require all men to engage in overt toxic practices, but it does encourage men to remain silent to protect their own masculinity when others commit such practices. In doing so, they become complicit in the violence (Katz, 2003). Thus, hegemonic masculinity constitutes a "pattern of practices . . . that allowed men's dominance over women to continue" (Connell & Messerschmidt, 2005, p. 832).

Therefore, to understand gender, critical/cultural approaches insist that power, in the form of hegemonic systems of hierarchy, must be analyzed as well. Power is a social phenomenon. People have power in relationship to others. Social power is embedded in the communicative negotiations of gender/sex, race, class, sexual orientation, and other identities. For each of these social groups, multiple differences are socially created, and differences are rarely constructed equally. Rather, the groups that have more say about the construction are privileged over others.

Power can simply mean "the ability to get things done" (Kramarae & Treichler, 1992, p. 351). It is not an innately evil concept. However, feminist theorists make an important distinction between "power to" and "power over" (Freeman & Bourque, 2001, pp. 10–11). *Power to* is the ability to get things done that do not infringe on others' rights and may actually lead to the emancipation of others. *Power over* refers to coercive misuses of power. If one is in a position of power over others, then one can dominate and coerce others and in the process subordinate or oppress them. If one lacks power over, one is more likely to be in a subordinate position. The interesting point is that to respond to any instance of power over, or to get out of a situation in which one is subordinated by those who have power over, one needs power to.

Power can exist at the interpersonal level in one's ability to control or dominate others in the negotiation of personal or professional relationships (Weber, 1947). However, power also is systemic. It exists at multiple levels in society at one time. It can exist at the larger institutional level (as when the institution of family privileges the nuclear family over other forms), in power differences ascribed according to social categories that oppress some groups to benefit other groups, and in the general hegemonic relations the dominant culture has with individuals (Foucault, 1980).

To see hegemony at work, one needs to be critical of taken-for-granted cultural norms, to take what media scholar Stuart Hall (1993) identifies as an oppositional, or counterhegemonic, reading of cultural texts (pp. 98–102). Instead of *"operating inside the dominant code"* (p. 102, italics in original), an oppositional reading challenges the social meanings. Thus, one finds critical/cultural scholars critiquing the way blood donation, as "a performative act of civic engagement," constructs sex, sexuality, and citizenship in a way that disempowers gay men (Bennett, 2008, p. 23); how *Knocked Up, Juno,* and *Waitress,* three 2007 films that all center around a White pregnant woman, "reframe unplanned pregnancy as women's liberation" and present a model of family that serves only the needs of White, economically privileged women (Hoerl & Kelly, 2010, p. 362); and how media stories about Black male athletes accused of domestic violence construct understandings of them as "naturally aggressive due to their sporting background and black rage" and, in the process, reinforce hegemonic White masculinity (Enck-Wanzer, 2009, p. 1).

Critical/cultural approaches focus on hierarchy, hegemony, power, and privilege. They also emphasize the role that communication plays in the social construction of reality. Communication is more than a means to transmit information. When people communicate, they participate in the construction of social reality. By saying that people construct social reality, we not mean things and people do not preexist human symbolic action. Instead, the meaning people ascribe to the things in their world is not predetermined but is created in communicative interactions. Although people may know things exist apart from their symbol systems, they cannot know what those things mean, or how they are to react to them, except through the symbol system. Thus, reality is constructed, meaning it is made (not given), and social, meaning it is created interactively. In terms of gender/sex, critical/cultural approaches examine gender as a social construction, communicatively constituted, and ask how a particular construction of gender and sex privileges some and disempowers others.

Multiracial and Global Feminisms

Scholars and activists studying gender/sex through the lens of *global feminist theory* and *multiracial feminist theory* have crystallized the reasons that gender/sex must be studied from a critical/cultural perspective. They note how the category of woman often has represented the concerns of White, economically privileged women from Western countries and, as a result, has reinforced hierarchies that emphasize the concerns of the privileged. Their position is that no singular gendered experience defines women or men, and the norms of one culture should not be imposed on another in an attempt to improve women's and children's human rights. Law professor Isabelle Gunning (1997) puts the challenge this way: Instead of being "arrogant perceivers" of the world who judge other cultures based on the **ethnocentric** view of their own culture as the norm, people should strive to be "world travelers" (p. 352). To be world travelers means to be ethnographers, to try to view other cultures from their members' perspectives rather than one's own. To be world travelers also means to recognize the interconnections between cultures. This requires not only observing the other culture but being willing to turn that same critical lens back on one's own culture, including examining how one's cultural practices contribute to the oppression of other cultures.

Authors from this perspective emphasize the experiences and voices of multiple gendered/sexed experiences, particularly for racial minorities living in the West and those living in non-Western, nonindustrialized, noncapitalist countries. They argue that White, Western, educated feminists have had the most to say in defining women's experiences and have falsely assumed that their worldview represents all women, consequently portraying other women as passive, backward, unenlightened, oppressed, undereducated, and needing help.

Chandra Talpade Mohanty (2003) makes clear the failures of White Western feminists' studies of third-world women and women of color:

> To define feminism purely in gendered terms assumes that our consciousness of being "women" has nothing to do with race, class, nation, or sexuality, just with gender. But no one "becomes a woman" (in Simone de Beauvoir's sense) purely because she is female. Ideologies of womanhood have as much to do with class and race as they have to do with sex. Thus, during the period of American slavery, constructions of white womanhood as chaste, domesticated, and morally pure had everything to do with corresponding constructions of black slave women as promiscuous, available plantation workers. It is the intersections of the various systemic networks of class, race, (hetero)sexuality, and nation, then, that positions us as "women." (p. 55)

Mohanty (2003) urges everyone to recognize "the application of the notion of women as a homogeneous category to women in the Third World colonizes and appropriates the pluralities of the simultaneous location of different groups of women in social class and ethnic frameworks; in doing so it ultimately robs them of their historical and political agency" (p. 39).

Global feminists urge a consideration of all hierarchies and how they interact. A sex-only approach misidentifies third-world men as the root cause of third-world women's oppression, not capitalist colonial systems. This creates a dynamic that English professor Gayatri Chakravorty Spivak (1988) described as "White men saving brown women from brown men" (p. 297). This is not a dynamic confined only to colonial times. Dana Cloud (2004) provides a trenchant analysis of images circulated by Time.com of Afghan people while the U.S. administration was building public support for the 2001 invasion of and war in Afghanistan. Focusing on the women as veiled and oppressed, the images appealed to White men to save Brown women from Brown men and evoked a paternalistic stance toward the women of Afghanistan.

So-called third-world people and the colonization of them can exist in any country, including the United States. Chicana author and activist Gloria Anzaldúa explores the ways in which living on the U.S.-Mexican border shapes mestiza (mixed-race) women. Throughout her work, she moves between English and Spanish, detailing the process and purpose of communication, constantly reminding the reader of her role as a person positioned on the border between two cultures. As part of her exploration of political and personal borderlands, Anzaldúa, like other Chicana feminists, creates a space in which to perform multiple identities (Flores, 1996; Palczewski, 1996).

Rhetorician Raka Shome (1996) explains why the study of communication and imperialism is important and how it can be done. **Postcolonialism**, "a critical perspective that primarily seeks to expose the Eurocentrism and imperialism of Western discourses," asks two related questions:

> How do Western discursive practices, in their representations of the world and of themselves, legitimize the contemporary global power structures? To what extent do the cultural texts of nations such as the United States and England reinforce the neo-imperial political practices of these nations? (p. 41)

Shome explains that a focus on communication is necessary because "discourses have become one of the primary means of imperialism" (p. 42). Although "in the past, imperialism was about controlling the 'native' by colonizing her or him territorially, now imperialism is more about subjugating the 'native' by colonizing her or him discursively" (p. 42) by forcibly changing gender and national identities and values. The tremendous reach of Western media, the universality of English (a legacy of earlier territorial imperialism), the way in which academics have named and defined the "native" as "other," and the creation of economic dependency all mean that attention to communication patterns are central to understanding how colonialism persists (see also Shome & Hegde, 2002).

Queer Theory

Queer theorists challenge the very categories and binaries used in noncritical approaches: gender (feminine/masculine), sex (female/male, woman/man), and sexuality (homosexual/heterosexual). As a form of study, **queer theory** is the "process by which people have made dissident sexuality articulate," meaning "available to memory, and sustained through collective activity" (Warner, 2002, pp. 17, 203). In the process of studying those who do not fit into neat binaries, queer theory creates a language that names and makes present those who live outside the binaries. Queer theory critiques the categories used to understand gender, sex, and sexuality as part of the very hierarchies that maintain privilege for some groups over others.

This approach is overtly political in its aim, but *queer theory* is not meant to be an umbrella term for work on gays, lesbians, bisexuals, and transgender people. Instead, it is meant to question all forms of sex and sexuality categorization as it addresses "the full range of power-ridden normativities of sex" (Berlant & Warner, 1995, p. 345), particularly heteronormativity. Queer theory makes clear the variety of ways in which heterosexuality is composed of practices that have very little to do with sex (Warner, 2002, p. 198). When it comes to thinking about sex, sexuality, and gender, queer theory calls for a "rethinking of both the perverse and the normal" (p. 345). For queer theorists, desire is a focus of study, including the "categorization of desiring subjects" and what allows some desires to "pass as normal, while others are rendered wrong or evil" (Giffney, 2004, p. 74).

By recognizing and examining connections among sexual desire, gender, sex, and sexual orientation, this approach broadens the study of gender/sex in communication in important ways. For example, English professor Judith Halberstam (1998) writes about transgender persons' experiences. She shows that studying women performing masculinity may reveal more about cultural assumptions of masculinity than studying men, for whom society assumes the relationship is normal. Halberstam's (2005) study of drag kings (women and men who expressly perform masculinity, like Mike Myers in *Austin Powers*) exposes some of the absurdity of gender norms and how gender functions as a "*a kind of imitation* [or copy] *for which there is no original*" (Butler, 1991, p. 21, italics in original).

Critical/Cultural Approaches Conclusion

We have reviewed only a few of the critical/cultural approaches to gender in communication. Despite the range of approaches, critical/cultural approaches theorize that one can never understand gender and sex unless one studies broad cultural systems that sustain power differences. Critical/cultural approaches emphasize that reality is constructed through communication and that human reality contains systems of hierarchy and power differentials. Thus, gender differences are never seen just as differences but always as possible patterns that expose relations of power.

Conclusion

In this chapter, we outline the primary approaches used by researchers, popular media, and laypeople to explain gender in communication. Although these are not exclusively communication theories, they all reflect underlying assumptions about how people conceptualize and talk about gender/sex. Our goal has been to help readers better identify and examine their own assumptions as well as others'.

In this review of the biological, psychological, and cultural approaches to studying gender/sex in communication, we reach two conclusions: knowledge is culturally influenced, and a gender diversity, rather than a binary, perspective is best. Researchers bring their social and disciplinary assumptions and biases to the topic of study as well as to their choices of theories and research methods. More than one way exists to conduct research and build knowledge about gender in communication. How researchers define concepts such as gender, sex, difference, sexual orientation, ethnicity, and race, and the methods they choose to study these concepts, affects the conclusions formed about gender/sex in communication. Thus, one's perspective should recognize the existence of gender/sex diversity and not be limited by a gender/sex binary.

Throughout our discussion of biological, psychological, and critical/cultural theories, we have not been theoretically agnostic. We find the theories that account for power to be more persuasive than those that ignore power. However, we have been theoretically promiscuous; we find multiple theories and research practices useful, depending on the precise question studied.

Given that gender is complex and diverse, it makes sense that complex and diverse theories are necessary. For this reason, we embrace Nancy Henley and Cheris Kramarae's (1991) advice to quit arguing about whether gender is a product of nature *versus* nurture or cultural style *versus* domination. Rather, it is more useful to recognize the influences of intersecting identities (such as sex, gender, race, social class, and sexual orientation) *and* biology, psychology, culture, and social hierarchies.

Gender/sex is formed as a result of multiple influences, from biology, to internal psychological processes, to broader social norms and institutions. The challenge is to recognize that cultural influences are always at play, affecting the biological elements researched and the cultural value attached to them. To make clear the way the theories interact, we offer the following diagram (see Figure 2.3). Its goal is to both make clear how theories differ in the expansiveness of their cause of sex/gender and to make clear that even the most scientific of theories are embedded within larger cultural structures.

Given the multitude of variables that influence who persons are, it makes sense that there would never be just two gendered types of communication. Communication studies professor Celeste M. Condit (1998) outlines the four benefits of a **gender diversity perspective**. First, "The gender diversity perspective advocates respect and care for persons of all genders and gender types (as long as those types do not directly harm others or infringe on the human rights of others)" (p. 177). As Henley and Kramarae (1991) advise, gender diversity "assumes that

Figure 2.3   Theory Chart

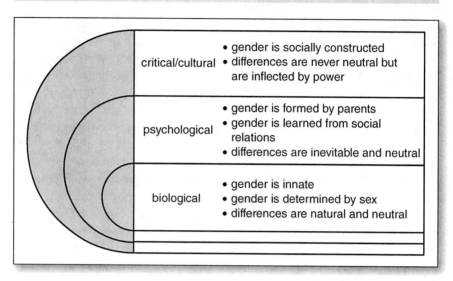

critical/cultural	• gender is socially constructed • differences are never neutral but are inflected by power
psychological	• gender is formed by parents • gender is learned from social relations • differences are inevitable and neutral
biological	• gender is innate • gender is determined by sex • differences are natural and neutral

gender is a combination of temporally and locationally specific interactions among biological, social, and individual components" (p. 177).

Second, it allows people to stop feeling like failures in the "ideal woman" and "ideal man" game (Condit, 1998, p. 179). For example, the theorists discussed earlier who celebrate the traditionally feminine attributes of nurturance, cooperation, and gentleness have much to recommend, yet "they ignore not only racial diversity, but class and regional diversity, as well as personal idiosyncrasy" (p. 180). They are prescriptive for how women should act, not descriptive.

Third, it makes clear that systems of patriarchy have costs for men, not just women, even though the form and size of those costs might differ. Some groups of men benefit from patriarchy more than other groups of men, yet all men share the burden of upholding the myth of men's superiority.

Fourth, it reorients research in an invigorating way: "Instead of trying to describe how men and women speak differently, we can begin to explore the range of gendered options available to people" (p. 183). It diverts attention from the study of how women's gender limits communication and directs it to the study of how a range of people have used diverse gender styles to speak passionately, ethically, and effectively to their audiences. A gender diversity approach provides a more realistic, more interesting, and wider scope for analyzing gender/sex in communication.

A more productive way to study the topic of gender in communication is to use a broader lens of analysis that recognizes that theory and knowledge construction are rhetorical and political acts, as are people's efforts to interpret, embrace, and reject them. This does not mean that there is no objective reality but rather that reality means nothing until people give that reality meaning as they play active roles in its construction and deconstruction. People's perceptions are their reality. This is no less true for researchers. Understanding the link between expectations and reality brings with it an awesome ethical responsibility to attend to how one communicates and how one studies this topic. It also represents an exciting adventure through which we travel in the remainder of this book.

KEY CONCEPTS

biological determinism 36	gender diversity perspective 51	psychoanalytic theories 36
biological theories 28		psychological theories 28
cognitive development 40	interpretive 29	queer theory 50
critical/cultural theories 29	objective 29	social learning 38
culture 43	patriarchy 46	social reality 43
ethnocentric 48	postcolonialism 49	stereotype threat 33

DISCUSSION QUESTIONS

1. What expectations do you have for appropriate gender-related behaviors? Where do you think these expectations come from? What are your underlying theories about gender given what you have identified as the sources of gender?

2. How do biological theories explain the formation of gender and its role in communication? Identify examples from popular culture that embrace this theory.

3. How do psychological theories (psychoanalytic theory, social learning theory, cognitive development theory) explain the formation of gender and its role in communication? Identify examples from popular culture that embrace this theory.

4. How do critical/cultural theories explain the formation of gender and its role in communication? Identify examples from popular culture that embrace this theory.

CHAPTER 3

Gendered/Sexed Voices

"Do women talk more than men?"

"Do men talk about their feelings?"

"Do women gossip more than men?"

"Do gays talk like girls?"

"Do men interrupt more than women?"

"Do women ask more questions?"

"Do men use more profanity than women?"

"Do women use better grammar?"

"Do women use more active-listening cues?"

O ver the last 50 years, the questions researchers have asked about sex differences in conversation cover topics such as politeness, pronunciation, word choice, topic initiation, types of question asking, hesitancy, overlapping speech, talk time, self-disclosure, assertiveness, silence, and social support. Despite all their research seeking to prove sex-based differences in communication styles, the results have been inconclusive (Canary & Hause, 1993; Dindia & Canary, 2006). Accordingly, we do not provide a simple list of gender/sex differences in communication to answer questions like those that open this chapter. We are not denying communication differences exist in gendered performances; we simply suggest the performance cannot be reduced to false binary differences. Our intent is to help you listen for the nuanced ways gender diversity is performed through conversation.

First, we explain that it is important to study gender in conversation because gender is created (and not just expressed) through communication. Second, using our critical vocabulary and review of research, we propose a set of criteria you can use to assess conclusions you hear about gender in communication, whether they are conclusions from research, popular culture, or even conclusions you find yourself reaching. Third, we use our criteria to examine what has been the most prominent approach to studying gender in conversation, the **two-culture approach** that assumes men and women speak as though they come from two distinct cultures. Given this approach is based on a binary view of gender, it reveals cultural expectations for how people are to perform gender and how people interpret others' behaviors. Fourth, we offer a critical ethnographic approach as an alternative. Using an example of actual conversation from a recent research project, we demonstrate how the criteria we propose can be used to test whether a study offers a realistic view of how diverse gender/sex identities and relationships are being constructed through discourse. Our intent is to enable you to critically analyze the diverse ways gender is performed in conversation. Research that reveals the realistic, context-specific ways in which intersectional gender identities are constructed through interaction is the ideal.

Conversation as Identity and Relationship Work

The most pervasive microprocess that creates gender is mundane day-to-day interactions: conversation. **Conversation** is the process of two or more parties working interactively to create meanings through the exchange of verbal and nonverbal cues within a given context. It includes content (i.e., verbal and nonverbal vocalizations) and structure (e.g., social expectations for turns at talk that build and end conversations). People create conversation when they follow socially recognized patterns in content and structure, such as politeness norms for greeting others (Baxter, 2011; Brown & Levinson, 1978). People negotiate their identities, status, and relationships through basic exchanges: greeting each other, negotiating dinner plans, or giving orders at work.

Speakers follow (or violate) the rules not just because they exist but also because they enable speakers to accomplish their goals. As goals are accomplished, so too are identities. Conversation is used to continually create individual, relational (interpersonal), and group identities. How speakers use the rules and norms can reveal much about the individual identities they are constructing, their group identities (e.g., gender, sexual orientation, ethnic identities), and the types of relationships they are attempting to negotiate (e.g., cooperative/combative, subordinate/superior, romantic/platonic). In conversation, people work at identity and relationships.

Conversation work, identity work, and relationship work intertwine:

- The concept of **conversation work** makes clear that intent, effort, and some degree of cooperation are required in the seemingly easy process of talking to others (Brown & Levinson, 1978). For example, when initially forming a romantic relationship with another, you might actually exert effort to think about topics to discuss or plan compliments to offer.

- Individuals do **identity work** through conversation by presenting to themselves and to others who they are at a given time and negotiating that identity with their conversational partner (Brown & Levinson, 1987; De Fina, Schiffrin, & Bamberg, 2006; Tracy, 2002). For example, when a student asks a professor for an extension on an assignment, the student might do some work that constructs an identity as an earnest and hardworking student, making clear the extension is an exception.

- Conversations are central to **relationship work**. Relationships take continuous effort by both parties. Conversations enable people to create, negotiate, maintain, and/or change their interpersonal connections with others (Baxter, 2011). It is difficult to sustain a relationship if only one person's topics are the focus of every conversation.

We focus on conversation as a building block to studying gender identity and gendered relationships with others. For example, a person engages in gender identity work when she chooses to introduce herself as Ms. instead of Miss, Mrs., Professor, or Doctor. Similarly, in a formal context where unspoken conversation rules discourage interruptions, the interrupter may be making a power move to dominate the conversation. In return, others' acceptance of the interruption contributes to the maintenance of the interrupter's power.

Another way people construct their identity through conversation is their choice of conversational style. **Conversational style** is one's tendency to communicate verbally and nonverbally in a particular way, such as being assertive, argumentative, or animated (Norton, 1983). It is created through the habitual use of particular verbal and nonverbal behaviors, such as rate of speech, vocal inflection, vocal pitch, pronunciation of words, volume, amount of talk and silence, how one tends to take turns in conversation, and even topic preferences. A style becomes unique to a person or group when distinct versions of these qualities are combined.

Conversational styles carry with them implicit values with which people judge others. People tend to prefer and value the styles they use, thus creating a less-than-objective means of assessing others' communication. Communication studies scholar Marsha Houston (2004) interviewed middle-class White women and African American women and found the White women described their style as using "proper" English and distinct pronunciation. They viewed African American women as speaking with a "Black accent," being less "proper," and being "pushy". The African American women viewed their own style as celebrating their "sense of self" and "speaking with authority" (p. 121–122). They viewed White women's style as passive, friendly but phony, and weak (Houston, 2000). In other examples, vocal profiling in telephone conversations has been used by mostly Whites to discriminate against African American and Latino-sounding people seeking jobs, education, housing, and other services (Baugh, 2003, 2007; Wiehl, 2002). These examples demonstrate that styles are not simply different and equal. Perceptions of conversational style have real consequences for individuals and groups.

Gender identity also is constructed when people respond to others in conversation. Social psychologists call this **altercasting**, a concept that "highlights how the way we talk to and act toward others (alters) puts them in roles (casts them)"

(Tracy, 2002, p. 23). Conversational partners may reinforce one's identity, restrict it, contest it, and/or add to it. Altercasting plays a central role in maintaining stereotypical gender role expectations. For example, after a 2012 Missouri senatorial campaign debate, Representative Todd Akin accused incumbent Senator Claire McCaskill of not being "ladylike" and said she acted like "somebody let a wildcat out of the cage" because she was "attacking in every different direction" (Mascaro, 2012, par. 3, 6). One might assume that in the context of a political debate, robust disagreement and argument would be expected. Representative Akin was engaging in altercasting, as he thought McCaskill was not acting ladylike because she was acting like a debater. Altercasting does not mean people have to accept the roles in which they are cast, but the potential for negative judgments should they violate expected roles exists.

Identity is not under the full control of an individual. Identity construction is produced and interpreted in conversation with other people or groups. Each person produces identity, and interprets others' identities, in each conversation. When people internalize predominant social expectations and perceptions of gender they, in turn, influence how people converse and thus how their gendered identities are defined. Sociologist Barbara Risman (1998) explains, "Gender structure exists not only on the institutional, individual, and interactional levels, but on all levels at the same time" (p. 157). Through conversations, people create patterns of interaction that can be identified and analyzed to gain insights into how the participants' intersectional gender identities are being constructed within relational dynamics.

Studying gender in conversation is important. The challenge is how to study it in ways that reduce the likelihood of further imposing problematic gendered/sexed expectations.

A Critical Gender Diversity Framework

Our approach to conversation and nonverbal communication moves away from the culturally dominant view of binary gender (masculine *or* feminine) and sex (male *or* female) differences and moves toward understanding how identities and relations are created strategically according to the demands of the specific context as constrained by social expectations. The strategic choices that individuals and groups make may reinforce stereotypical binary gender/sex expectations or they may resist the binary view, making more realistic intersectional gender diversity evident.

We base our criteria for researching gendered voices on the theoretical framework advanced by sociologists Candice West and Don Zimmerman called "**doing gender**" (1987). After reviewing research on gender across cultures and gender identities, they concluded that gendered behaviors in everyday life are not natural, universal, or essential. People "do gender" as a "routine accomplishment embedded in everyday interaction" (p. 125). Instead of describing a person as having a gender, or gender being something internal that a person expresses externally, they described gender as emerging in social interactions; gender is "an outcome of and a rationale for various social arrangements" (p. 126). In other words, gender comes into being as part of people's interactions with others.

By noting that people *do* gender, we do not mean to suggest people have limitless and consequence-free choice about how to do gender. On the contrary, social norms limit the range of ways gender can be done and which bodies can do what types of gendered activities. Judith Butler (2004) explains that even though "gender is a kind of doing, an incessant activity performed, in part, without one's knowing and without one's willing," that does not mean it is "automatic or mechanical" (p. 1). Instead, she describes gender as "a practice of improvisation within a scene of constraint" (p. 1). In Butler's view, people constrain their own doings of gender as a result of the social norms they have internalized and are constrained by others' social expectations of how gender should be done. Even when individuals feel they are not performing gender, their behaviors are likely to be read by others as if they are, and a person's performance of gender may be read by others through a binary gender lens.

By noting that people do gender, it is important to remember it is interdependently done with other identity ingredients of race, ethnicity, class, sexual orientation, and other socially recognized group identities (West & Fenstermaker, 1995). These other ingredients may actually play a more prominent role in a given interaction. If one studies only how people do gender, one ignores the ways in which doing gender is informed by the simultaneous and uniquely historical prescriptions to "do" race, class, and so on.

To equip you with the tools to interpret research on gender in communication from a "doing gender" perspective, we combine the critical gender vocabulary with our review of recent scholarship on gender in communication to provide some **critical research criteria**.

Criterion 1: Use an intersectional gender analysis to explore gender diversity, not sex difference only. To examine if this criterion is being addressed, ask, Is the observer/researcher looking for gender/sex differences only? If so, proceed with caution. Why?

First, the observer/researcher is likely asking the wrong question and will only reinforce essentialist views of gender/sex in communication. For example, the most studied individual conversational behavior is interruptions (Kitzinger, 2008). West and Zimmerman (1983) claimed men interrupt more than women in heterosexual relations as a way of controlling interactions. Their research propelled a wide variety of studies testing this conclusion (e.g., Cameron, 1995; DeFrancisco, 1991; Fishman, 1978). What some of this research revealed is that men do not always interrupt more than women, and researchers had largely failed to consider the dynamics in same-sex platonic or romantic relationships or in varying ethnic groups' use of interruptions. Interruptions are not always power moves to take over the conversation. Not all simultaneous talk is seen as an interruption. Interruptions can be used to create high involvement, enthusiasm, and collegiality in an interaction (Schegloff, 1997; Tannen, 1994a), and overlapping speech can show supportiveness (Coates, 1996). The relationship between conversational behaviors and relational dynamics is not straightforward or simple to identify (Mills, 2003). A conversational behavior can have multiple meanings and should not be studied in isolation.

Second, research that identifies only the sex of each person in the sample, and then draws conclusions about gender, is conflating distinct variables. It may not be that men interrupt more than women but that people with some conversational styles interrupt more than others.

Third, if the research results focus on differences, ask, How *much* difference was found? Just because something is statistically significant does not mean it is socially significant. For example, in a study on sex and self-disclosure (Dindia & Allen, 1992), the report focused on differences found, but as the authors themselves later point out, the degree of difference was small. About 85% of the time the behaviors of the sexes were similar. In fact, only about 1% of the variance in the participants' use of self-disclosure could be attributed to sex differences; the women and men in the study were far more similar in their use of self-disclosure than different (Dindia, 2006).

Finally, ask, Does the observer/researcher use an intersectional gender analysis and explore whether interdependent ingredients serve to influence the gender performance in unique ways yielding unique privileges or inequalities? No observer can identify all possible intersections in speakers' identities in a given interaction, but when observers/researchers move away from a simplistic focus on gender/sex differences toward studying people's conversations in the rich complexity of performing intersectional identities, some very enlightening patterns can emerge. One can begin to see outcomes of the interactions in terms of identity, social status, power struggles, and interlocking oppressions.

Keep in mind that identifying a difference tells one nothing about similarities, the degree of difference, why the difference exists, or what the social consequences might be for the participants. To examine how people communicate their way into particular intersectional identities with unique contextual opportunities and pressures, one needs to look beyond gender/sex. The main lesson here is that communication differences between people are rarely, if ever, determined solely by the sex of the speaker.

Criterion 2: Enough evidence should be provided to show gender emerged from the conversation, rather than being imposed by the observer/researcher. To examine if this criterion is being addressed, ask, Is the observer/researcher truly studying how communication is creating identity, rather than prematurely imposing gendered labels? U.S. society foregrounds the gender binary and privileges those who are **cisgender**—meaning one's sex and gender identity match predominant cultural expectations (female = high feminine, male = high masculine; Schilt, 2011; "Trans 101," 2011). This can lead people to attribute a gendered communication style to a person incorrectly; for example, hearing a feminine style whenever a woman speaks or not hearing it when men use it. Conversational style differences are not always an expression or performance of gender (McElhinny, 2003), and gender performances are not limited to only a masculine or a feminine conversational style. This is the most difficult criteria to assess because one reads the results of a study, rather than watches the observer/researcher in the process. The author needs to describe how any presumed gender links to verbal and non-verbal cues emerged from the conversation, rather than simply being the result of the researcher grouping participants into two preexisting categories of male/female and then making stereotypical attributions about masculine/feminine.

Unless researchers ask participants about their interpretations, they risk assigning binary masculine or feminine attributions to the behaviors observed. Researchers also likely assume all the speakers are cisgender. Psychologists have documented the tendency for researchers to impose gendered labels on behavior that the participants would not accept (Stokoe & Smithson, 2001). Researchers themselves altercast. This does not mean the speakers' reported performance intentions in a conversation are the absolute truth either. They may not be fully aware of their identity performance, but what they report is their reality. Thus, self-reflection about the observer/researcher's undue influence is essential (DeFrancisco, 1991, 1997; Kroløkke & Sørensen, 2006; Wodak, 2008). To resist altercasting, Baxter (2007), an applied linguist, recommends using a feminist method called **self-reflexivity**, which requires actively questioning your values, biases, and assumptions.

Some indicators of the observer/researcher resisting altercasting include the following:

- Did the researcher gather detailed, systematic observations (rather than anecdotal ones) of interaction over time, rather than using isolated one-time events that might lead to stereotypical illustrations?
- Does the researcher show how the participants negotiate their identity and relative status through "moment-to-moment negotiations" in conversation (Goodwin, 2006)?
- Does the researcher identify and explain patterns in the speakers' conversation that lead to designating behaviors as gendered/sexed or other identity intersections (Kroløkke & Sørensen, 2006)?
- Did the researcher consult with the participants to more fully interpret the interaction?
- Does the researcher's report document efforts to be self-reflexive?

By providing evidence to show gender emerged from the conversation, one ensures that the analysis is not forced by the observer/researcher. As the reader, you should be able to trace the author's analysis and see how interpretations were substantiated by the conversations analyzed. The researcher should adequately explain *how* gender/sex performances were identified in the conversation. The gender analysis should emerge from the bottom up, not imposed from the top down. The main lesson here is that you need to work to avoid imposing gendered expectations on others.

Criterion 3: The observer/researcher must demonstrate a context-dependent analysis. To examine if this criterion is being addressed, ask, Is the observer/researcher taking into account the context's influence on participants' behaviors? The concept of **communication context** refers to how physical, social, cultural, and psychological elements of a given interaction influence it. Physical context is the immediate setting in which an interaction occurs, including time, place, sights, smells, and surrounding sounds. Social context describes whether the interaction was intrapersonal, interpersonal, small group, organizational, public speaking, or mass media (West & Turner, 2010). Cultural context refers to norms, values, communication styles, languages, social relations and inequalities, popular icons, and much more (Campbell, Martin, & Fabos, 2013). Psychological context encompasses much of what is happening intrapersonally for the speaker in terms of emotions, moods, and health, as well as what is happening among the interactants, such as feelings of resentment, companionship, love, and hostility. For example, professors interact differently with you in class than during an office visit. Context matters, and if you generalize about your professor's conversational style based only on lectures, you would provide a woefully incomplete description of that person's style.

In most of the research on gender in communication, researchers do not take into account unique context influences (Dindia & Canary, 2006; Eckert & McConnell-Ginett, 1992/2011). This allows researchers to default to assigning binary gender attributions to behaviors. When researchers take into account the unique intersectional identities of the speakers, the type of relationship participants create (such as superior/subordinate or friends), and the type of contexts that call for unique norms of politeness (such as legal court hearings or classrooms), what were presumed to be gender/sex differences in behavior are better explained by other influences (Dindia & Canary, 2006; Hinde, 2005; Schleff, 2008). Feminist linguists Eckert and McConnell-Ginet (1992/2011) describe the research problem succinctly:

> Abstracting gender and language from the social practices that produce their particular forms in given communities often obscures and sometimes distorts the ways they connect and how those connections are implicated in power relations, in social conflict, in the production and reproduction of values and plans. (p. 573)

Contextual information helps researchers interpret the meaning of a specific interaction because most communication interactions can have multiple meanings and serve a variety of functions (Crawford, 1995; Tannen, 1994a). For example, when professors ask questions of you in a class, the function is very different from when a question is asked as part of a personal conversation.

How can researchers better account for context? First, instead of assuming a communication behavior always functions the same way, observers/researchers should look for *patterns*, such as how the forms of questions asked interact with who talks longer, who makes more eye contact, who interrupts and controls the conversational floor, and which people successfully develop their topic of interest most often (DeFrancisco, 1991; Eckert & McConnell-Ginet, 1999). If one participant uses more sarcastic questions, interrupts in an assertive fashion, and is more successful developing the topics that person raises, dominance may be at play. Each behavior becomes an interdependent context for interpreting the other behaviors. Second, observer/researchers should take into consideration the multiple layers and types of context that may be influencing the interaction. Third, when in doubt, researchers should ask the participants about their perceptions of the interaction.

The lesson here is that you should not assume a person always talks the same way, regardless of context. Someone you think of as aloof in one context might be quite open and warm in another.

Criterion 4: The observer/researcher's analysis should include an examination of communication as strategic. To examine if this criterion is being addressed, ask, Is the observer/researcher considering the strategic nature of gendered discourse? Communication is goal oriented, and thus, even if one's behaviors are the result of gendered norms internalized over time, the behaviors are still strategic. Speakers are rational beings who behave in meaning-making ways. To do so, they may apply a number of strategies in their conversations (Crawford, 1995). Thus researchers need to examine the multiple ways in which people use conversational behaviors to accomplish their goals (Tracy, 2002).

Furthermore, people can choose to strategically play with gender expectations in discourse to accomplish goals. Feminist linguist Mary Crawford (1995) suggests speakers "attempt to choose language that will 'work' interactionally. Their use of language is situated [context dependent] and strategic. And, what 'works' depends on the social status of the speaker and the power relations between speaker and listener" (p. 44). Communication choices are rarely innocent of persuasive intent. Examining the strategic aspects of conversation clarifies the active role individuals play in communicating gender.

For example, in her work on first-wave women's rhetoric, Karlyn Kohrs Campbell (1989, Vol. 2) analyzes women rhetors who strategically used cultural expectations of feminine speech style. Campbell argues female antislavery and woman suffrage speakers such as Maria Miller Stewart, Sarah and Angelina Grimké, Susan B. Anthony, and Elizabeth Cady Stanton lessened audience resistance because they "strategically adopted what might be called a feminine style to cope with the conflicting demands of the podium. That style emerged out of their experiences as women and was adapted to the attitudes and experiences of female audiences" (p. 12). Campbell argues their use of a feminine style consistent with the expectations of White middle-class femininity, even though they were not all White and middle or upper class, enabled them to push at sexist prohibitions against women speaking in public. In contrast, British suffragette and labor activist speakers used a more militant style, invoking their working-class backgrounds and their affiliation with workers' movements (Kowal, 2000). Instead of styles merely being some outward expression of inward identity, styles were used strategically, adapted to the context.

Most researchers fail to examine the strategic use of gender in communication. Recognizing strategic gendered communication is important because it offers a way to explain gendered communication not as a deficit or as a passive socialization processes but as an active choice. Speakers are rational and capable of using cultural norms (or violating them) to attain their strategic goals. The lesson here is to remember to look for expressions of speakers' improvisational agency, even as they perform within a scene of constraint.

As you read original research or popular writing on gender in communication, you should find these four criteria useful. Together they suggest one overall question: Is the observer/researcher challenging common assumptions about gendered interactions and trying to understand the participants' lived experiences? Questioning assumed binary differences in gender tied to sex reveals more diversity in interaction and more similarities.

While researchers use multiple approaches to study gendered voices, we have selected two to highlight. The predominant one, the two-culture approach, does not meet the criteria we outline. The second one, a critical ethnographic approach, does. However, we review the two-culture theory because it informs so much research and popular writing. If you are to become a critical reader of research on gender in communication, it is important for you to be able to see the problems with existing research.

The Two-Culture Approach

The **two-culture approach** is based on sociolinguists Daniel Maltz and Ruth Borker's (1982) paper "A Cultural Approach to Male-Female Miscommunication," in which they posit that communication problems between women and men are similar to problems that arise when persons from different language groups attempt to communicate. The two groups (men and women) have different cultural goals and rules for conversation (masculine and feminine style), which lead to communication problems or "miscommunication" (p. 196). The original scholars proposed this approach in earnest as a way to identify gender construction in talk, but it actually reveals more about society's gendered binary expectations regarding how to talk like a girl or boy, how to sound feminine or masculine, than about the diverse ways in which people actually do gender.

The two-culture approach, also called the *cross-cultural* view of gender, has been the pervasive approach in much social science research investigating gender and conversation for at least the last 30 years. Although this binary view of gender is increasingly inconsistent with the growing body of gender/sex research, it reflects social expectations about how people should perform gender. Masculine and feminine styles are predominant cultural expectations for gendered/sexed behavior from which people interpret and judge their own and others' behaviors. The styles then become cultural and individual communication preferences for how women and men should talk. These preferences should be familiar to you as they resemble society's predominant binary gender differences view.

According to Maltz and Borker (and later Tannen, 1990; Wood, 2013), feminine and masculine language groups come from sex-segregated child's play, where the rules of interaction differ. While some boys engage in girls' realm of make-believe, more girls tend to know the rules of feminine play:

- Talk *is* the game or goal, and the context is playing school or house (nonrule bound and noncompetitive games)
- Players learn a communication style for creating and maintaining close equal relationships:
  - o Be tactful when criticizing others
  - o Pay close attention to correctly interpreting others' behavior (Wood, 2013)

In contrast, the researchers argue, boys tend to play in larger, hierarchal groups in which the rules are predetermined, relying less on talk and more on action. More girls today are participating in so-called boys' games, but the suggestion is they are expected to follow boy-style rules:

- Competition and asserting oneself *is* the game or goal
- Players learn a communication style of dominance:
  - o Use communication to proclaim opinions and identity
  - o Use talk to achieve something, such as to solve problems or develop strategies
  - o Use communication to attract and maintain others' attention (Wood, 2013)

If the goals, functions, and styles of talk differ between the two groups, miscommunication is likely between members of the two groups.

Some of these rules may ring true to you, in that children, parents, and teachers often prefer and impose sex-segregated play that has rules tied directly to gender stereotypes of masculine and feminine styles of interaction (Eliot, 2009a; Kimmel, 2012a). However, for students who grew up in situations where same-sex playmates were not an option, or where neighborhood children played sports together, or where transgendered, androgynous, or gender nonnormative children felt more comfortable playing games with another sex, this explanation seems extremely unrealistic. It does not match the reality of many children's lived experiences. In particular, girls do learn the rules of and play so-called boys games, such as soccer and wrestling, even as many boys consider playing so-called girls' games taboo— not because they do not know the rules but because they are attempting to distance themselves from anything considered girly (Eliot, 2009a).

From sex-segregated play rules, two-culture theorists argue that adults develop different gendered conversational styles. The assumption in two-culture theory is that women tend to have one feminine style and men tend to have one masculine style, so that when women and men interact they often "talk at cross purposes" (Tannen, 1990, p. 120). Thus, gender in communication is portrayed as unrecognized cross-cultural conflict.

Feminine Style

The first and primary characteristic used to describe feminine style is **rapport talk**: talk that focuses on building relationship, connecting collaboratively with the other person, and showing empathy. Communication researcher Julia Wood (2013) explains, "For feminine people, talk *is* the essence of relationships" (p. 129). Talk is seen as a primary means of negotiating and maintaining relationships. To build rapport, speakers use verbal and nonverbal cues that convey support to the other person, offering affirmations or questions that convey interest, and seek cooperation rather than competition (Coates, 1997; Johnson, 1996; Tannen, 1990).

A second characteristic is the use of **indirect communication**, which includes hedges ("I am sort of thinking . . .," rather than, "I think what we should do is . . ."); qualifiers ("Well I may be wrong, but . . ."); tag questions ("I think we should do this, don't you?"); and indirect requests ("There is a hole in my glove," rather than asking, "Could you buy me some new gloves?"). Indirectness softens the claims or requests being made and is perceived as more polite (Mills, 2003). In what is considered a groundbreaking article, feminist linguist Robin Lakoff (1975) argued women strategically learn to use indirectness to better accomplish their goals as relatively powerless speakers in a patriarchal culture, similar to how a child might make a request of a parent or a slave of an owner.

Third, feminine storytelling is said to be more collaborative (Aries, 2006; Coates, 1996; Holmes, 1997). One person's story becomes the group's story or an invitation for others in the group to share their stories (Coates, 1997). The goal is to catch up on each other's lives by sharing intimate details (Holmes, 1997). As such, simultaneous talk is seen more as collaboration and enthusiasm, not as interruption, making the organization of the story less linear.

Masculine Style

The first and primary characteristic used to describe masculine style is **report talk**: talk that focuses on instrumentality or task orientation, asserting oneself, and competitiveness. Those who use a masculine style are said to use talk as a tool to accomplish a goal. The goal can be to complete a task, solve a problem, exert control, assert oneself, or gain independence and status (Cameron, 1997; Coates, 1997; Wood, 2013). Masculine style avoids personal disclosure and vulnerability, which is typically seen as the opposite of a feminine style. The focus on using talk to accomplish tasks also infers masculine speakers will talk less than feminine speakers; talk is a means to an end, not an end in itself as when using talk to do relational work.

Second, masculine talk is direct and assertive (Mulac, 2006; Wood, 2013). Being direct and assertive fits well with a speaker who is expected to be task oriented rather than relationally oriented and with one who uses communication to establish and maintain control or status.

Third, masculine storytelling is about status. Men studied tend to prefer to tell stories in ways that helped enhance their status and masculinity (Coates, 1997; Holmes, 1997). In an extensive study where the author looked at how gender emerged, linguist Jennifer Coates (2003) examined 32 transcribed conversations among primarily White, middle-class, adult male friends in the United Kingdom, identifying more than 203 stories with five prominent masculine features. First, the stories were about stereotypical masculine topics such as cars, sports, drinking, and technology; these topics helped detour the conversation away from personal self-disclosure and vulnerability. Second, the stories were told as a series of monologues, not interactively. Third, the organization of stories was chronological. Fourth, the men used profanity heavily. This was the most marked difference Coates found in comparison to her studies of women's conversations: "Swearing has historically been used by men in the company of other men as a sign of their toughness and manhood" (p. 46). Fifth, the men's stories stressed achievement or bragging rights. The men engaged in competitive storytelling, seeing who could tell the bigger "fish story"; storytelling became a competitive sport in a way Coates did not observe in women's conversations.

Two-Culture Gender Miscommunication

The feminine and masculine style features just described are a sample of the claims of the two-culture approach, but they clearly reduce the study of gender in communication to masculine and feminine speakers following narrowly defined styles that are described as the opposite of the other's. So what happens when people with masculine and feminine styles come together to converse? Based on the two-culture view, the result is inevitable miscommunication. The different styles lead to miscommunication or incorrectly interpreting another's behavior through one's own gendered frame of reference or communication preferences (Tannen, 1990; Wood, 2013).

Even though one may understand the other's language, speakers tend to prefer the conversational style they use and judge other styles more negatively (Norton, 1983). Feminine conversational style compels its speakers to focus on rapport-building interactions, using active-listening behaviors when needed and perhaps avoiding conflict through the use of indirect speech strategies. Masculine conversational style compels its speakers to focus on report interactions, such as a task that must be accomplished, using an assertive, independent means to do so. The likely result is that neither party accomplishes the desired goals to their mutual satisfaction in the interaction or the relationship. Popular writers claim this could be particularly problematic in intimate long-term heterosexual relations (Gray, 1992; Tannen, 1990) as well as in organizational work situations (Tannen, 1994b).

Most troubling about the two-culture approach is that communication problems are defined as conversational style differences, and the solution is simply for partners to try to understand that. Two-culture theory offers no critical cultural analysis about how the differences were created, if one group benefits more from them, or how these socialized differences contribute to a continuum of violence where seemingly innocent conversational styles contribute to a context in which some members of a culture are praised for being aggressive and others for being submissive.

In addition, researchers have shown conversational styles are simultaneously influenced by race, ethnicity, social class, national origin, region of the country, and language (Carbaugh, 2002; Hall, 2009; Kikoski & Kikoski, 1999; Kochman, 1990). The belief in only two gendered styles helps to maintain a White heterosexual normative style of speaking: "To treat asymmetries of interaction as style differences ignores social realities. Speakers do not speak in a vacuum" (Crawford, 1995, p. 44). Conversations occur in a political cultural context, one that unnecessarily pits women against men.

We ask one final question about two-culture theory: Where is the evidence? In detailed analyses of Tannen's (1990) claims about women's rapport and men's report talk, researchers found virtually none of her claims were adequately supported (Goldsmith & Fulfs, 1999), yet the myth lives on. Actual research conducted to test the two-culture theory shows gender differences of small degrees rather than of kind (Edwards & Hamilton, 2004; Michaud & Warner, 1997). Meta-analyses, a statistical method that allows a reviewer to accurately compare research results from massive numbers of studies regardless of the magnitude of differences among the studies, have consistently shown negligible gender/sex differences (Canary & Hause, 1993; Dindia & Canary, 2006; Hyde, 2005).

To help clarify research inconsistencies on direct and indirect speech styles, Leaper and Robnett (2011) conducted a meta-analysis of 29 studies. They found there was a statistically significant, but small, sex difference in the use of indirect behaviors. About 85% of the time the behaviors of the sexes were similar. When the researchers controlled for contextual influences, the sex differences fell even further into the negligible range, meaning about 92% of the time the behaviors of the sexes were similar, indicating context may determine indirectness more than a gendered style.

Although researchers find no support for the two-culture approach, cultural expectations continue to influence how speakers are judged. Perceived differences in gender/sex communication style far exceed any actual ones (Kirtley & Weaver, 1999). Even if persons do not communicate in ways that fit binary gendered norms, people expect them to. These expectations are real, and they have real consequences for people's identities and abilities to accomplish their conversational and relational goals.

We find the two-culture approach inadequate for revealing the actual ways people construct intersectional gender identities. However, the prominence of this approach does open one's eyes to the extent of predominant cultural expectations and preferences for how people communicate gender.

A Critical Ethnographic Approach

Many alternatives to two-culture theory exist; we focus on an ethnographic approach because it provides a promising set of methods that resist deductive, essentialist interpretations (Baxter & Wallace, 2009; Goodwin, 2006). A **critical ethnographic approach** includes observation over time, getting to know the speakers, interpreting conversations informed by their insider perspectives, and studying conversation in rich context—all of which better assure researchers are studying the dynamic ways intersectional gender identities are created in conversation.

Sample Conversation for Analysis

Sociolinguist Kira Hall (2009) conducted an extensive ethnographic study over several months, including participant interviews and 50 hours of ongoing conversations, among females participating in a support group for "women who are attracted to women" sponsored by a nongovernmental organization (NGO) focusing on HIV/ AIDS education in New Delhi, India. The participants were all born female and were East Indian bilingual Hindi and English speakers. Some identified as lesbian (e.g., Barbara) and some called themselves "boys" (e.g., Jess, Sarvesh, Priti, Bijay), meaning they did not see themselves as women.

The conversation that follows is a group discussion, one of many held by the NGO facilitator, Liz. She chose to discuss masculinity as a social construct versus a physical one as part of her project to build alliances among the group members. However, when she introduced the topic, one of the transboys, Jess, immediately shouted across the room to her, "What do *you* know about masculinity?" The group proceeded to have a 55-minute conversation, including this excerpt.

(English is in standard font, Hindi in italics)

1	Liz:	You- is there no room to be (.) f<u>e</u>mini-
2		to be a f<u>e</u>male (.) but masculine?
3		to be a f<u>e</u>male [but (.) to be masculine?]
4	Barbara:	[That's really-] that's
5		just the opposite of the masculine?
6		I suppose?
7	Liz:	No to be f<u>e</u>male and to be m<u>a</u>sculine.
8		Is there no [room for it?]"
9	Barbara:	[That's not] a way,
10		You make that all up (.) opposite things,
11		then (you're still a woman),
12	Liz:	No I'm not saying whether it becomes
13		permanent,
14		I'm saying for the individuals in this group.
15		tod<u>a</u>y.
16		who we are (.) sitting with?
17		Is there no room to b*e* a f<u>e</u>:male
18		and yet to be: (.) masculine.
19		<u>i</u>n that role?
20		to ↑ b<u>e</u>: like that?
21	Jess:	I th [ink]-
22	Liz:	[Why] doesn't society
23		allow for that?

24		Why can't we b<u>e</u> like that [t?]?
25	JESS:	[Well] because
26		that's -ss uh one of those things,
27		You have to follow a p<u>a</u>ttern.
28		You're a woman so you have to
29		↑[BE::: this this this] this.
30	LIZ:	[Yeah but ↑ WHY::.] Why?
31		You're- you're also- you're a woman,
32		but you are attracted to other w<u>o</u>men.
33		That's not acceptable to society,
34		but you <u>a</u>re b<u>e</u>ing like that,
35	JESS:	<quietly, rapidly> <*gālī detī hai.*
36		*mujhe* wom<u>a</u>n [*boltī hai.*]>
37	LIZ:	<falsetto> <[↑Well just]> [[feh-]]
38	JESS:	<loudly, rapidly> <[[*gālī*]] *detī hai.*
39		wom<u>a</u>n *boltī hai mujhe.*
40		*tereko abhī āg lagtī hu maĩ.*>
41	SARVESH:	[<laughs>]
42	PRITI:	[<laughs>]
43	BIJAY:	[<laughs>]
44	LIZ:	<rapidly> <NO. GUYS.>
45		I'm just asking the question, (.) basically.

Hindi Translation (for lines 35–40)

35	JESS:	<quietly, rapidly> <*She insults me.*
36		*She calls me* woman!>
37	LIZ:	<falsetto> <↑Well just> feh-
38	JESS:	<loudly, rapidly> <*She insults me.*
39		Woman *she calls me!*
40		*Now you think I'm fire (to burn you alive)?*> [refers to Hindu tradition of cremation]

from Kira Hall, "Boys' Talk: Hindi, Moustaches and Masculinity in New Delhi," 2009, 146–147. Reproduced with permission of Palgrave Macmillan.

Transcription Symbols

[ ]	Brackets indicate portions of overlap in speakers' talk
?,!.	Punctuation symbols mark intonation, not grammar
↑↓	Up/down arrows indicate upturn or downturn in vocal pitch
(.) or (.05)	A period in parentheses indicates a micropause in talk,
	(.05) mark silences in tenths of a second.
{ }	Uncertain transcription contained within

(Transcription key: Sacks, Schegloff, & Jefferson, 1974)

We use this example because the performance of gender is both an overt, and implicit, part of the conversation and because this example vividly illustrates the benefits of a critical ethnographic approach. The example illustrates the limitations of having only two gendered styles to draw from when interpreting this discourse. A discussion of each of our research criteria makes this clear.

Criterion 1: Use an intersectional gender analysis. When analyzing the conversation, Hall saw a resistance to Liz's idea that the participants in the support group share a commonality in their relationship to masculine identity. Jess, in particular, rejected this idea, perhaps because such a view denies Jess's physical experience—being born female but being male psychologically and wanting to be male physically. For Jess, masculinity is not a socially constructed choice. Jess identifies more with men than with lesbians. In asserting this, Jess is asserting a particular individual and group identity that is not accounted for in two-culture theory or commonly recognized in U.S. culture.

From the beginning, the composition of the group helped to prevent a binary analysis of gender. The participants were the same sex, so the analysis could not be split into female versus male. But Hall could have still fallen into the trap of labeling speakers as stereotypically masculine and feminine, according to whether they self-identified as boys or lesbians. She did not. She focused on what each person seemed to be strategically attempting to do (Criterion 4). She focused on how Liz was assertive in trying to get her conversational topic developed, perhaps by talking more (lines 12–20), increasing volume (line 20), and asking more questions (lines 3, 5, 8, 16, 19, 20, 23, 24, 30). Hall also noted how Jess used multiple strategies to resist this idea, such as volume prior to the conversation, interruptions by both speakers (lines 22, 25, 30, 35–38), and verbal arguments. Most tellingly, Hall focused on explanations for the language shifts by Jess (and other boys) that those who identified as lesbians did not use (lines 35–36 and 38–40).

Hall argues the language shift from English to Hindi better enabled the boys to create a distinct subgroup identity. The choices were not tied to their sex, as everyone there was female, but to their gender. The boys spoke Hindi seemingly strategically, to mark themselves as more masculine. Hall explains that Hindi is culturally associated with the ideals of masculine vulgarity and lower social class, as compared to the colonized language of English that still carries elitism. In contrast, the lesbians chose English in strategic places of conversation to connote an upper-class identity (e.g., in line 37, Liz does not respond in Hindi to Jess). In the conversation, the reader can see Jess's resistance to Liz's ideas build until Jess actually switches to speaking in Hindi. Imagine if the researcher had limited the study to a two-culture explanation, rather than one that included national identity, language, gender, sex, and sexual orientation. The richness of gender construction would be lost.

Criterion 2: Do not impose gender on people. Hall's interpretations are not based solely on this excerpt of conversation but on months of interactions. Hers are not isolated observations. She conducted a systematic analysis, looking for patterns in the interactions across time. The pattern that emerged most visibly was the boys' language switching at critical points where their assertion of masculine identity was needed.

Whether Hall, as an observer/researcher, exercised sufficient self-reflexivity in terms of how much her own view influenced the presentation of results is a personal judgment. Suffice it to say that after reading the larger body of work from which this excerpt comes, we felt Hall did meet this requirement. An endnote in her study demonstrates her self-reflexivity: "I am also indebted to a number of friends, students and colleagues who have helped me think through various ideas expressed in this chapter. . . . Above all, I would like to offer my heartfelt thanks to the lesbians and boys who agreed to participate in this study and who gave me many months of unforgettable Delhi-style fun" (Hall, 2009, p. 160).

Criterion 3: Conduct research in context. Hall's findings that the boys and lesbians in this study use language switching to construct unique intersectional identities demonstrate the power of context in influencing how people perform their identities in a given situation. Her study is rich with social-historical context information to help the reader understand how she came to the interpretations regarding social class and gender associations for speaking Hindi instead of colonized English. She traces for the reader how the NGO center socializes new members into using English words for discussions of sexuality and how Hindi words are perceived as too vulgar:

> The male-identified women who came to the Center in response to a local advertisement campaign were quickly socialized into new patterns of expression that relied on the ideological understanding of English as the appropriate language for discussion of sexuality, whether these discussions involved sexual practice, sexual desire, or sexual identity. Veteran group members, most of whom had come to identify as lesbian within the context of this transnationally funded NGO, viewed Hindi as unsuitable for the expression of a progressive sexuality. For them, the use of Indian languages in sexual discursive domains was backwards, rude and just plain vulgar, an interpretation that appears to be shared by many multilingual speakers of the educated Indian middle class. (Hall, 2009, p. 142)

The fact that the self-identified boys resisted this social conformity highlights how negotiating a specific gender identity happens in conversation and is responsive to unique contextual influences. The elitism of the English language versus Hindi becomes conflated with gender identity.

Criterion 4: Recognize the complex strategic nature of conversation. The actual shifts in languages from Hindi to English in this excerpt make the work of identity negotiation and power assertions particularly apparent. Given that English was the language of the NGO organization, and English is still seen as a more prestigious language in India, the boys' insistence on using Hindi to discuss sexual matters was strategic. Jess, in particular, asserted a masculine boy identity by shifting to Hindi and by further separating from Liz, referring to her in the third person, "Woman she calls me!"

Thus you can see how the speakers use language choice and conversation to negotiate identity and that this negotiation is a power struggle. Liz as the NGO worker was trying to maintain control and get her point across. One way she seemed to do this was through the use of questions rather than making statements. Liz asks nine questions in a short time frame. Given Liz is facilitating the discussion, Hall suggests her questions resemble a traditional Indian style of classroom interaction where teachers drill students for memorized answers in a quick pace that creates a power asymmetry and allows no room for students to do more thinking or talking than they are told to do. Questions function in a distinctive way in the Indian cultural context. Liz may be using the questions in an attempt to guide and control the direction of the conversation. The strategies she uses, however, also serve to contest the identities the boys are seeking to claim. Conversation work, identity work, and relationship work occur simultaneously and often conflict. Conversation is dynamic.

Hall argues that the boys' diverging choices in the conversation not only align them with particular sexual identities, but through this specific interaction, they are also performing their masculinity as required by their specific boys' sexual identity:

> [T]hroughout the discussion, Jess and the other boys use Hindi as a resource for the expression of an authentic masculinity that opposes the fictitious characterization of masculinity suggested by Liz's appeal to social constructionism. For the boys, maleness is an essential aspect of their understanding of self, not a constructed one, a point underscored by Jess in her [*sic*] decisive rejection of the membership category *woman*. And yet, Jess's contribution, in part because of the extremeness of its articulation, is very much recognized as a performance of masculinity by her fellow boys, who responded with uproarious laughter. (Hall, 2009, p. 148)

The boys' identity of masculinity "emerges from localized negotiations of the relationship between form and meaning" (Hall, 2009, p. 141). It is done in relationship with the lesbians with whom they interact.

Research on the speech patterns of gay, lesbian, bisexual, and transgender persons makes visible the notion that communication is strategic. When people do not fit into the normative heterosexual culture, they must overtly play with cultural norms of feminine and masculine conversational style if they want to construct an identity that is not heterosexual (Livia & Hall, 1997).

One additional note about what this example reveals. The criteria we propose are interdependent: When one studies conversation from an *intersectional* gender identity perspective, it necessitates the inclusion of contextual information in the analysis. When the analysis is studied with rich contextual information, the conclusions drawn will more likely emerge from the analysis, rather than solely from preexisting gender assumptions. The realities of the strategic work and power struggles involved in constructing identities and negotiating identities will be more visible as well. The criteria work together to reveal the ongoing construction of intersectional gender identities and relational identities and inequalities.

At this point, you might be thinking, given this, can researchers ever say anything about how men communicate and how women communicate? They cannot, and that is our point. People need to get beyond describing communication in ways that reinforce the binary of men communicating in a masculine way and women communicating in a feminine way. People need to quit talking about gender as if it is the only variable in communication styles.

Comparing Research Approaches

The following table makes visible key distinctions in the two approaches' underlying assumptions about gender. These assumptions influence the conclusions researchers reach about gender in communication.

Table 3.1 Key Distinctions

Key Distinctions	Two-Culture/Differences Approach	Gender Diversity Approach
Source of gender	Pre- or early determined and relatively fixed difference	Socially constructed, emerge in the conversation
Number of genders	Binary	Range to include transgender
Relationship among sex, gender, sexuality	Cisgender: presumes speakers are heterosexual females or males with consistent feminine/masculine gender identities	Multiple combinations of gender, sex, and sexual orientations
Presumed sexuality	Heteronormative	LGB and heterosexual
Communication styles	Two sociolinguistic styles	Socialized preferences and expectations as well as influence from other cultural identities and the immediate context
Gender identity performance	Unconscious	Can be unconscious and strategic
Gender as power	Apolitical, no one's fault/benefit	Social behavior always has the potential to be political; difference are rarely socially equal

Conclusion

Conversation is a primary means by which people and groups continually negotiate gender/sex intersectional identities. But contrary to popular assumptions, any presumed gender differences in conversation cannot be simply aligned with one's sex. Stereotypic cultural expectations and perceptions of gender/sex behavior do have the potential to strongly influence how people do gender and construct group identities and inequalities through talk. But people also make choices of behaviors according to their goals in unique situations. It is impossible and irresponsible to establish simple universal causal links between sex and gender and between gender and particular discourse strategies.

Because the construction and perceiving of gender are cultural, they are also potentially political. Understanding the power embedded in discourse helps answer the question of why differences rather than similarities are culturally emphasized. After reviewing a large volume of research on gender in communication, researcher Kathryn Dindia (2006) notes that with all the pressure for people to conform to different gender/sex expectations in communication styles, it is amazing how similar the sexes are in their communication. The similarities between women and men, and the variances among women and among men, offer evidence that differences are not innate or universal. Yet people still impose expectations on others based on perceived universal differences, so communication problems may emerge not from actual style differences in how people *do* talk but in different expectations of how people *supposedly* talk.

The methods observers/researchers select to guide their work will influence the results. If one looks only for sex differences, sex differences are what one will find. But if one realizes the researcher, too, is likely a product of the two-culture, gender binary worldview, and demands evidence in the interaction to support conclusions drawn, such binary views become less persuasive.

Individuals and groups must continually negotiate gender/sex tensions to assert their identities and specific communication goals in diverse cultural contexts. The selective use of feminine and masculine styles in politics, management, and cultures should help make clear that patterns of communication often emerge as a particular way to respond to a particular situation. However, as situations, people, and cultures change, so, too, does the utility of the styles and their labels.

Thus, rather than asking whether a person's speech is feminine or masculine, we advise people to ask, What wide variety of ways of speaking allows each person to communicate more clearly, effectively, ethically, and humanely? Rather than asking how women and men communicate differently, researchers should explore how the range of gender options might be a resource for everyone, whether in interpersonal, group, or public settings.

KEY CONCEPTS

altercasting   57

cisgender   60

communication context   61

conversation   56

conversation work   56

conversational style   57

critical ethnographic approach   68

critical research criteria   59

"doing gender"   58

identity work   57

indirect communication   66

rapport talk   65

relationship work   57

report talk   66

self-reflexivity   61

two-culture approach   56

DISCUSSION QUESTIONS

1. Why is it useful to study gender and identity in discourse? How might this contribute to the development of your critical gendered lens?

2. Have you observed the construction of gender through conversations in classrooms? At work? In social groups? In church? In your family? Describe them.

3. Describe your own conversational style and ask a friend to describe it as well. Look for similarities and differences in your descriptions. Do either of you include assumptions about gender, race, or class? If so, which identity ingredients are noted and which are not? Why not? What can you learn from this activity about your gender identity and performance in conversation?

4. How might employing diverse gendered styles become a communication resource for individuals? What are examples of this?

CHAPTER 4

Gendered/Sexed Bodies

Nothing is as intimately linked to your gender/sex identity as how you feel and act in your *body*. Unless people are intentionally challenging gender/ sex expectations, they tend to be less conscious of how they use their bodies to perform gender and how their bodies use them to maintain cultural norms regarding gendered identities. This is perhaps why many assume that communication through the body is more biologically determined than verbal communication.

This chapter clarifies that although your body may feel like your most private, natural possession, that assumption is part of what makes the body ripe for social control. It is a site of individual and social contest where consumer markets, religions, predominant cultural norms, medical practices, and even academic researchers attempt to police the boundaries of appropriate behavior (Langman, 2008). In saying this, we are not claiming *all* gendered behavior is bad or purely socially controlled. However, when one assumes choice exists where there is little, that is a powerful form of social control, and when some groups benefit more from these controls, that is the internalization of sexism, racism, homophobia, classism, and ableism.

To illustrate the unconscious controls at work on your body, try this thought experiment.

- If you identify as a woman, examine the way you are sitting. Now spread your body out, with your arms and legs farther apart (especially if in a skirt). How do you feel?
- If you identify as a man, examine the way you are sitting. Now pull your body in closer, with your knees together or legs crossed at the knees and fold your hands in your lap. How do you feel?
- If the labels *woman* and *man* do not feel comfortable for you, examine the way you are sitting. Now sit in a way that resembles one of the gendered expectations just listed. How do you feel?

If these behaviors make you uncomfortable, it is because your behavior is breaking a cultural norm. Gendered cultural norms dictate something as mundane as how you sit.

Gendered bodily communication is a primary way in which cultural expectations for binary and inequitable gender/sex identities are maintained, challenged, and changed. We prefer the term **bodily communication**, instead of what social scientists refer to as *nonverbal communication*, because it calls attention to body politics, the disciplining of the body, and the body as a locus of agency.

To explore bodily communication, this chapter focuses on three points. First, the body is political; that is, the body is a powerful social tool in which intersectional gender identities and inequalities are created. To demonstrate this, we employ the theoretical concepts of performativity and objectification. Second, the body is disciplined through cultural norms. We offer the examples of gendered appearance, prescribed rules about the use of physical space, and gendered movement. Third, bodies can be a locus of agency. Bodies not only are acted upon but can act. We offer multiple examples of how people strategically use their bodies to resist the command performance of prescriptive gendered behaviors.

Body Politics

Although biology and ethnicity contribute to a wide variety of distinctive sizes and shapes of bodies, social norms constrain bodily forms and expressions, the meanings of these, and one's very relationship to her or his body. Women are encouraged to be continually aware of their bodies as they prune, pose, provide sexual gratification, menstruate, give birth, and nurse children. Men tend to experience their bodies as a double bind: They dare not pay too much attention to their bodies for fear of appearing effeminate (Gill, Henwood, & McLean, 2005), but they must control and present their bodies in a particular manly way and use their bodies to control and restrict others' bodies. Further, men's bodies remain the norm to which women's bodies are compared and devalued. Men are to be strong, women weak; men should be tall, women should be short; men should be substantial, women should be slender. The result is not just gendered/sexed bodies but a system that requires particular groups of bodies to dominate over other bodies (Lorber & Martin, 2011).

Gender Performativity

West and Zimmerman developed the notion of "doing gender," meaning that gender is a continuous process of identity negotiation through conversation (1987). In this chapter, we add to this idea of doing gender philosopher Judith Butler's (2004) concept of **gender performativity** as the stylized repetition of acts. Butler's work builds on "doing gender" to point out people not only *do* gender in interaction, but the repeated style of interaction genders people.

Each person learns a script about how to act, move, and communicate gender. If gender is "a practice of improvisation within a scene of constraint" (Butler, 2004, p. 1), then it is a command cultural performance in which actors have minimal awareness of the cultural constraints imposed on their actions. Although some variation occurs, it is always within set limits. Through the repetition of gendered behaviors over time, people continually construct and constrict their gender identities. Butler argues this is how binary genders and compulsory heterosexuality are formed. The repetition is largely guided by social expectations of dominant groups and habit, not free will.

We agree with Butler. People do not get up each morning and consciously decide how they will perform their gender identity that day. Instead, people internalize predominant cultural norms that gender their bodies. However, we also believe people are goal oriented, and they can play with gender performativity to challenge gender/sex norms.

Drag shows demonstrate that gender is a prescribed set of actions in the staged performance of drag queens and kings (see Figure 4.1). The performers act in often exaggerated ways to appear as another sex as they sing, dance, model, or act on stage. By doing so, they challenge normative gender performances. The exaggerated performance of femininity opens up the possibility of questioning gender/sex pre-scriptions. When drag "mimics dominant forms of femininity" it can, at the same time, "produce and ratify alternative drag femininities that revel irony, sarcasm, inversion, and insult" (Halberstam, 2005, p. 130). Just because femininity is being mimicked does not mean it is being praised. At its core, doing drag recognizes the *performance* of gender.

Overt gender performance is not reserved to those who practice drag. Sociologists Richard Majors and Janet Billson (1992) observe how some young African American men challenge racial stereotypes through the performance of a cool pose. The pose was originally created by street pimps and includes a specific stance, walk, posture, and speech pattern, all of which suggest a relaxed, confident, and cocky masculinity. The walk is similar to a slow stroll, with parts of the body moving together, as if to announce oneself in a unique way. By posing, the men present themselves as a spectacle of self-expression, detachment, and strength. Majors (2001) argues that many have learned to use posing as a strategic tool to

Figure 4.1   Drag Queen (left) and Drag Kings (right)

Sources: © iStockphoto.com/karens4 and ZUMA Wire Service / Alamy

convey control and toughness when other resources of power and autonomy are not available to them. That very pose, however, may further prevent them from full participation by no longer passing in a privileged White masculine culture (Johnson, 2010).

The concept of performativity points out that when people internalize social expectations about gender tied to their body's sex, it becomes difficult for them to realize gender/sex expectations construct their gendered/sexed identities. Objectification theory explains a more specific way society disciplines the performance of gendered bodies.

Objectification

You have probably heard the statement that mass media objectify girls and women, but what does that mean? **Objectification** occurs when people are viewed as objects existing solely for the pleasure of the viewer, rather than as agents capable of action. The person being objectified often is reduced to body parts: breasts, genitalia, muscles, curves, buttocks, and hair. The person is no longer human but commodified—turned into a market commodity like other inanimate products, free to be bought and fondled (even if only by others' eyes). **Self-objectification** occurs when people internalize the objectifier's view of their body and "participate in their own objectification" by seeking to exert a limited power linked to their ability to attract the gaze of others (Lynch, 2012, p. 3).

People who internalize objectification engage in heightened **body surveillance**; they critically look at and judge themselves. Objectified people's perceived physical and sexual attractiveness may become more important to them than their morality, honor, intellect, sense of humor, or kindness. Unrealistic, narrow standards of attractiveness can lead to perfectionism and body shame. Researchers have linked objectification to low self-esteem, depression, anxiety, disordered eating, muscle dysmorphia (obsession with building muscles), and suicide, particularly for women (Moradi & Huang, 2008; Travis, Meginnis, & Bardari, 2000) but also for puberty-aged children, including boys (Grabe, Hyde, & Lindberg, 2007).

Sexual objectification is not limited to mass media. Researchers continue to identify women and girls as particularly vulnerable in daily life (Moradi & Huang, 2008). Feminine gender socialization exposes women and girls to being viewed solely as a sexual entity (Bartky, 1990; Young 1990), and the process happens younger than one might think (Levin & Kilbourne, 2009). Beauty pageants, such as Dream Girls U.S.A. and Real Girls U.S.A., start at age 4; others start even younger.

Figure 4.2 Eden Wood, from *Toddlers and Tiaras,* promotes her new LOGO docu-series *Eden's World.*

Source: Anthony Behar/Sipa Press (Sipa via AP Images)

These messages are being internalized. In a study of 60 6- to 9-year-old girls in the Midwest, the girls chose a sexualized paper doll as their ideal self (68%) and the doll that would be popular (72%; Starr & Ferguson, 2012). Researcher Christy Starr said, "It's very possible the girls wanted to look like the sexy doll because they believe sexiness leads to popularity, which comes with many social advantages. Although the desire to be popular is not uniquely female, the pressure to be sexy in order to be popular is" (cited in Abbasi, 2012, pars. 6–7). Not all the girls chose the sexualized doll as their ideal self: Girls who took dance classes, had maternal influences that did not self-objectify, had been taught to view media critically, and/or were raised with strong religious beliefs were more likely to choose the doll with more clothing as their ideal self.

Figure 4.3   Paper dolls used in Starr and Ferguson study

Source: Dollz Mania's ChaZie Dollmaker, http://dollzmania.net/ChaZieMaker.htm. Retrieved from www.livescience.com/21609-self-sexualization-young-girls.html

Increasingly, men and boys are victims of sexual objectification (Moradi & Huang, 2008), but they are less likely to negatively internalize the messages (Grabe, Hyde, & Lindberg, 2007). Indicators of this trend are the growth in sales of cosmetics for men, greater stigma for men perceived as fat, and hair transplants for balding heads (Shapiro, 2010). Men and masculinities scholar David Buchbinder (2013) argues the difference in men's self-objectification is that it is not for women's pleasure as much as it is to compete with other men. Men who are members of oppressed groups due to race, ethnicity, and/or sexual orientation are most often the recipients of objectification (Teunis, 2007; Whitehead, 2002). The objectification marks them as not quite men, or certainly not as normative White men.

Black men's bodies are objectified when they are reduced to violent, sexual, aggressive, and athletic (Jackson & Dangerfield, 2003). African American gay men may become sexual objects of desire by some White gay men because of the stereotype that they are endowed with larger penises, and Asian and Hispanic American men may be labeled exotic objects of sexual pursuit. When "the sexual objectification of men of colour forces them to play specific roles in sexual encounters that are not necessarily of their choosing" (Teunis, 2007, p. 263), many gay communities uphold normative White masculine domination (McKeown, Nelson, Anderson, Low, & Elford, 2010).

The performance of gendered bodies is far from natural. The theoretical concepts of performativity and objectification explain why bodies are a site of political struggle. For more than 40 years, researchers have documented the negative effects of bodily cultural norms that objectify women and feminine men, creating prejudices against them, low self-esteem, the glorification of masculine violence, sexual violence, sexual harassment, domestic physical and emotional abuse, homicides of domestic partners, higher suicide rates for homosexual teens, and violence against people who are LGBTQ. These negative effects quite overtly discipline bodies to perform gender in particular ways.

Disciplining Gendered Bodies

Communication scholar John Sloop (2004) used the term **disciplining gender** to make visible the multiple ways in which people and cultures consciously and unconsciously maintain rigid norms of binary, heteronormative gender performance. Common body practices, or signifiers, are so intertwined with gender expectations that it is difficult to recognize these are socially constructed practices. Sloop explains,

> Just as with a child's clothing and hairstyle, a single set of signifiers (gait, gestures, body movements, rough-an-tumble play, and the stance for urination) are used to illustrate masculinity and femininity in binary fashion regardless of whether gender is posited as a product of socialization or the materiality of the body, that is, its sex. In terms of gender culture, we clearly see . . . the signifiers that are employed in the judgments people make about one another and themselves in their evaluations of gender performance. . . . Heterosexuality is signified, indeed emphasized, as a norm in the performance of gender. (pp. 36, 40)

What follows are three examples of how heteronormativity disciplines as it genders the body.

Attractiveness

People speak of natural beauty, but most human beauty is constructed, perceived, and regulated through a narrow cultural lens of what is defined as **gendered attractiveness**: heteronormative physical appearance that is seen as pleasing, beautiful, and having sexual appeal. The norm of attractiveness that merges beauty and sexuality "moves sexuality into the public realm . . . and thereby [makes it] amenable to inspection, definition, social monitoring, and control" (Travis et al., 2000, p. 239). People's sexualities are not private; through attractiveness norms, they become public, social property. Gendered attractiveness norms reinforce and privilege White heterosexual gender expectations and help maintain women as objects (Felski, 2006).

Attractiveness norms are maintained and changed through consumer markets. The dominance of Western capitalism and commercialization has imposed a narrow definition of attractiveness worldwide (Bordo, 2003). Consumers, particularly women, spend millions of dollars annually to buy cosmetics, diets, hair products, beauty advice, plastic surgeries, clothing, and accessories. Beauty *costs*, as Table 4.1 on personal care reveals, and standards of attractiveness are increasingly costing men, too (Buchbinder, 2013).

Table 4.1 Personal Care Market Value (2007, in millions of dollars)

	Male	*Female*	*Total*
France	4,163.4	10,268.6	14,432.1
Germany	3,879.6	9,285.1	13,164.8
Italy	2,897.0	7,036.9	9,933.9
Netherlands	816.6	1,889.2	2,705.9
Spain	2,877.7	4,529.9	7,407.5
Sweden	445.7	1,219.5	1,665.2
UK	3,633.4	8,261.5	11,895.0
US	11,059.8	27,638.8	38,698.6
Australia	840.8	2,001.0	2,841.8
Brazil	3,875.9	7,718.4	11,594.3
China	3,828.1	7,002.8	10,830.9
India	1,645.3	2,311.5	3,956.8
Japan	5,927.6	19,780.7	25,708.3
Korea	1,285.9	3,219.8	4,505.7
Russia	2,067.3	5,481.8	7,549.2

Source: as cited in Romanowski (2010).

Attractive Men

Feminist sociologists Judith Lorber and Patricia Yancey Moore (2007) describe a "hot" man's body:

> In Western contemporary cultures, a sampling of popular images would suggest that the ideal male body is over six feet tall, 180 to 200 pounds, muscular, agile, with straight white teeth, a washboard stomach, six-pack abs, long legs, a full head of hair, a large penis (discretely shown by a bulge), broad shoulders and chest, strong muscular back, clean-shaven, healthy, and slightly tanned if White, or a lightish brown if Back or Hispanic. Asians . . . are rarely seen. (p. 114)

Size matters. Social norms dictate that attractive men are big—but muscular, not flabby. They are tall. Lorber and Martin (2011) note, "We may say that intelligence and competence count for much more than physical appearance, but only a few presidents of the United States have been shorter than 6 feet tall, and research on corporations has shown that approximately 10% of a man's earnings can be accounted for by his height" (p. 282). Interpersonally, many women who marry men shorter than they consciously choose to wear flat shoes on their wedding day to deemphasize the man's height. Men's studies scholar R. W. Connell (1995) explains the social significance of expecting men to be bigger than women: "Visions of hegemonic masculinity help to legitimize a patriarchy that guarantees the dominant physical position of men and subordination of women" (p. 77).

Consider the well-known G. I. Joe action figure (see Figure 4.4). In its 40 years on toy shelves, the doll's size has ballooned, from its 1960's life-size equivalent of 5'10" tall (unchanged for 40 years) with biceps of 12" and a chest of 44" to 2011's biceps of 27" and chest of 55". Given these measurements, "GI Joe would sport larger biceps than any bodybuilder in history" (Pope, Olivardia, Gruber, & Borowiecki, 1999; see also Olivardia, Pope, Borowiecki, & Cohane, 2004). At the same time, on girls' toy shelves Barbie celebrated her 50th anniversary in 2009. Estimates are that a life-size Barbie would have a height of 6'9", with only a 20-inch waist but a 41-inch bust. The story commonly told is she would not be able to stand up. The odds of a woman having these proportions are 1 out of 100,000 ("As G.I.," 1999; BBC, 2009).

When one compares current cultural norms of men's attractiveness to current cultural norms of women's attractiveness, an interesting insight emerges: As women are encouraged to become smaller, men are encouraged to become larger. Even as children, size matters. Shorter boys are bullied more (Voss & Mulligan, 2000).

Body image is not just a women's problem. Negative body image is affecting men in increasing numbers, although doctors have been slow to diagnose it and researchers have been slow to document the effects (Kreimer, 2011; Phillips, Menard, & Fay, 2006). Researchers in one study found the percentage of men dissatisfied with their overall appearance almost tripled in 25 years (to 43%), and the men report being nearly as unhappy with how they look as women report (Pope, Phillips, & Olivardia, 2000).

Figure 4.4   (Left) G. I. Joe, 1964; (Right) G. I. Joe, 1992

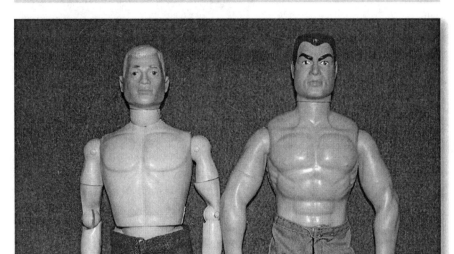

Source: From the collection of Tom Stewart.

Instead of women's concerns about thinness, men are concerned about being underweight and lacking body muscularity. Muscle dysmorphia is a preoccupation with muscularity and the misperception of one's physique as small, often despite distinct muscularity and size (Pope et al., 1997). This psychological disorder leads to compulsively working out, weight lifting, and rigid low-fat diets. The causes are attributed to increasing social pressures for boys and men to be large, muscular and athletic: "For many men today, muscles—literally—make the man. . . . Men in the new millennium are becoming obsessed with their body image in higher numbers than ever before" (Olivardia, 2001, p. 11).

In a study of 154 college men, predominantly White Catholics ages 18 to 30, the researcher not only found the men displayed substantial body dissatisfaction with their muscularity, but they explained why. Their concerns were tied to competing with other men and gaining their respect (Olivardia, 2000). The results showed a large—and likely unhealthy—gap between some men's ideal body images and their own body realities. This gap can lead to health problems related to excessive exercise, anabolic steroid use, and eating disorders. Problems such as these may go undiagnosed because heterosexual men tend to be more reluctant to seek help for fear of appearing weak, feminine, or gay.

Gay men have been identified as having the greatest tendencies toward eating disorders among men. Many gay cultures place a higher value on physical attractiveness than heterosexual men's cultures, and some gay men report stresses similar to those heterosexual women report who work to make themselves attractive to men (Olivardia & Pope, 1997). It seems that for women and men, the more one's value is reduced to one's sexual attractiveness, the more one is likely to engage in self-destructive practices.

Attractive Women

Cultural ideals of attractiveness are impossible to attain because they keep changing. For example, in the 1910s and 1920s, when women entered the U.S. workforce in larger numbers and gained the right to vote, women's fashion trends seemed to counter this political progress by becoming more restrictive of movement and more revealing of the body. Sexual appeal became about external appearance, with short flapper-style dresses. Pale white complexions, slender legs, narrow hips, and flat breasts were the ideal, causing many women to bind their breasts and shave their legs and armpits. In the 1950s Marilyn Monroe became a beauty icon. As the first woman to be featured naked in *Playboy*, Monroe exhibited the larger breasts and hips that became sexy. Her size 12 is considered large by today's beauty standards. U.S. women are now presumed to have the most gender/sex equality in history, yet the predominant notion of feminine beauty has become even more impossible to attain.

The ideal woman's body type has become increasingly thinner, both in reality and as a result of photo alteration. Current *Playboy* centerfold models are 10% to 20% thinner than most women. According to advertising analyst Jean Kilbourne (2010), only 5% of today's women fit the preferred body type, which leaves 95% of women wondering what is wrong with their bodies.

Now, the thin, White, blonde Barbie doll physique dressed in tight-fitting, revealing clothing captures predominant expectations of women's beauty. In a survey of 4,000 people across ages, results echoed this narrow definition (Brumbaugh & Wood, 2009). This beauty ideal is normative, even though it is not the norm. The White upper-class ideal of beauty is impossible for most women, but the ideal particularly disciplines women who have disabilities, darker skin, larger bodies, kinky hair, or limited money (Gerschick & Miller, 2004; Kramer, 2005; Lorber & Martin, 2011; Shapiro, 2010). Body size, especially for women, tends to affect popularity, dating and marriage opportunities, educational and economic accomplishments, susceptibility to job discrimination, and work environments (Fredrickson & Roberts, 1997). Women who do not comply with social demands regarding beauty regularly experience humiliation, harassment, and discrimination. They are called lazy, mentally ill, unfeminine, and asexual (Lorber & Martin, 2011; Travis et al., 2000).

A clear indication that women's attractiveness is a social construction is apparent when comparing Western ideals to other cultures' traditional notions of beauty. Azawagh Arabs of Niger defined ideal femininity as extreme fatness. Expansive thighs, belly rolls of fat, and stretch marks were seen as indicators of sexual desirability and upper-class status, for they rendered the woman unable to work (Popenoe, 2004). Latino American and African American cultures traditionally defined larger-sized women as voluptuous and physically and emotionally strong (Patton, 2006). Traditional Asian Hmong culture valued sturdy women who could work hard, making larger waists and hips attractive.

But Hmong immigrants in the United States are assimilating to Western notions of thinness (Lynch, 1999). Even more indicative of Western influence, White skin and round eyes are now markers of social status around the world. Skin-whitening products and plastic surgeries are believed to help women's earning potential and marital prospects in countries such as Hong Kong, India, Japan, and Korea (Glenn, 2008; Li, Min, Belk, Kimura, & Bahl, 2008). The message is clear: The natural body is sick or unacceptable, and altering one's body through products or surgery is the way to fix it. Western beauty ideals have become a tool to colonize women around the world (Hegde, 1995).

One of the ways body disciplining becomes visible is when individuals internalize the message so severely, they risk their physical and mental health. This is not to say eating disorders are simply about media messages to be thin. They do not have a single cause or a simple cure (Wilson, Grilo, & Vitousek, 2007): "Eating disorders are behavioral problems brought on by a complex interplay of factors, which may include emotional and personality disorders, family pressures, a possible genetic or biologic susceptibility, and a culture in which there is an overabundance of food and an obsession with thinness" (University of Maryland Medical Center, 2011, par. 1). Young women are the cohort most frequently diagnosed with eating disorders, and concerns about weight and body shape play a role in all eating disorders. The National Eating Disorder Association (n.d.) explains, "While eating disorders may first appear to be solely about food and weight preoccupations, those suffering from them often try to use food and the control of food to cope with feelings and emotions that may otherwise seem overwhelming" (par. 2). Starving and purging provide a temporary sense of control over one's body until the compulsion to starve and/or purge begin to control the person (American Psychiatric Association, 2012). In the United States, 10 million men and 20 million women will suffer from disordered eating at some point in their lives.

Turning an unrealistic mirror on oneself may induce body shame, anxiety, low self-esteem, depression, sexual dysfunction, and eating disorders (Moradi & Huang, 2008). The result is an efficient form of social control, a hegemonic notion of beauty and sexuality (Bordo, 1997a). The desire for perfection and control, as well as self-hatred, drive destructive cycles of eating disorders such as anorexia and bulimia nervosa (Kilbourne, 2010).

Although there are cultural differences in overall body satisfaction and what influences girls and women to develop eating disorders, surveys make clear that U.S. women across racial and ethnic groups, and inherent body types, have eating disorders (Grabe & Hyde, 2006; Vince & Walker, 2008). A meta-analysis comparing 98 studies of African, Asian, Hispanic, and White American women, shows that all the groups of women studied reported significant dissatisfaction with their body image, with White, college-age women slightly more dissatisfied (Grabe & Hyde, 2006). Native American women suffer from eating disorders at nearly the same rate as White American women (Striegel-Moore et al., 2011).

In a national survey of 7,272 adolescent girls, participants saw themselves as overweight, regardless of their actual weight. Half of the girls acknowledged trying to lose weight by dieting, exercising, taking pills, and vomiting. Interestingly, this pattern was most pronounced among White and Hispanic girls who had good grades in school, were involved in school activities, and had more friends, suggesting a strong perfectionist pressure, including appearance pressure, at an early age. African American girls seem less susceptible to the predominant thinness ideal (Botta, 2006; Boyd, Reynolds, Tillman, & Martin, 2010), although they tend to be negatively influenced by media images of thinness just as White girls, and they are just as likely to engage in eating disorders (Botta, 2006). Hispanic American teenage girls seem to be less affected by media images of thinness; competition with other females is often what propels their eating disorders (Ferguson, Munoz, Contreras, & Velasquez, 2011).

Although women's experience with eating disorders was once thought to be limited to the United States, there is growing evidence that women across a wide range of ethnicities and nationalities are suffering from these illnesses (Pike & Mizumshima, 2005). The findings from a study of a subculture of women in Curacao, a Caribbean island, suggest why the disorders are spreading. The women who experienced eating disorders were from a privileged socioeconomic class, had traveled to the United States, and desired to assimilate with the White elite, including its beauty standards (Katzman, Hermans, Van Hoeken, & Hoek, 2004). Similarly, after television was introduced to the island nation of Fiji in 1995, eating disorders increased fivefold in just 5 years (Becker, Burwell, Herzog, Hamburg, & Gilman, 2002). Western influence through commercialism, particularly popular culture, fashion, and higher U.S. status, seems to be spreading eating disorders around the world.

Clothing Trends

It is not coincidental that the beauty and fitness industries benefit economically from shifts in beauty ideals. Capitalism shifts consumer desires to keep demand alive. Clothing and accessories play a part of shifting trends. Clothing designated for girls and women tends to be restrictive, following the contours of the body. Men's clothing, in contrast, tends to be loose fitting, has pockets, and allows movement. Sociologist Ruth Rubinstein (2001) argues that gendered clothing is a social tool to reinforce heteronormative gender/sex differences in society and to "alert an approaching individual about suitability for sexual intercourse" (p. 103).

As some gendered distinctions in dress disappear, others appear. In the United States, women's professional clothing restrictions have lessened. Politicians such as Hillary Rodham Clinton wear pants instead of dresses, and men like David Beckham, famous British soccer player turned sex symbol, wear earrings. However, women's stiletto high-heel shoes, a marker of sexiness, are as popular as ever, even though they are more restrictive and harmful than men's flat shoes (Harris, 2003).

The continued disciplining of gender attractiveness through dress is apparent in responses to cross-dressing. People in the United States tend to be uncomfortable with and ridicule cross-dressers because they do not conform to the norm. In reality, everyone engages in some degree of cross-dressing as they adapt their dress to specific situations. During cold weather, women tend to wear pants, as do men. During hot weather, men tend to wear shorts, as do women.

Why is the vision of men in skirts laughable? There is no biological reason, and in many places men do wear skirts in the form of kilts, sarongs, caftans, or djellabas. Ridicule is an indication of the disciplining power of clothing to dictate social norms for gender/sex and sexual orientation. But people who break gender norms, by wearing androgynous clothing or clothing ascribed to another sex, broaden dress options for everyone.

One father, from Berlin, Germany, donned a skirt to support his son's wish to wear dresses in public. As for the son, "he smiles when other boys (it's almost always boys) want to make a fool out of him and says: 'You just don't dare to wear dresses and skirts because fathers don't dare to'" (Pickert, 2012). (For an image of the two together, see www.dailymail.co.uk/news/article-2195876/Nils-Pickert-German-father-wears-womens-clothing-solidarity-cross-dressing-year-old-son.html.)

Embodied Space

Embodied space refers to the holistic way in which people experience their bodies in physical spaces, often in relation to others (Low, 2003). In the field of communication studies, the study of embodied space is referred to as **proxemics**, the analysis of the invisible area around a person that is considered her or his private territory (Hall, 1966). Generally, advancing toward another person signals the wish to establish closer intimacy; moving away indicates a desire to protect one's privacy or that one feels spatially threatened. The size of personal space with which a person feels comfortable varies greatly by culture, situation, status, and type of relationship (Hall, 1966). In many so-called contact cultures (e.g., Arab, Latin American, some Asian, southern European), sitting close, holding hands with friends, and touching is normal (Low, 2003).

In the United States, taking up personal space with one's body, gestures, or property is commonly associated with power and status. Consider who tends to have her or his own chair designated at the family dinner table or in front of the television and where the remote control for the television sits in proximity to that chair. These are often unspoken claims of status. Who is permitted to invade another's space also can reveal intimate relations and/or power differentials (Khan & Kamal, 2010).

The size of one's interpersonal space also tends to be gendered/sexed, as the activity at the beginning of this chapter illustrates, with men permitted to sprawl out and women taking up less space (Gillespie & Leffler, 1983; Henley, 1995). Heightened awareness of one's body as an object for others' observations has been found to help explain some women's discomfort in taking up space around others (Kwan, 2010). Our goal in exploring gender in interpersonal space is to examine this invisible gendered boundary and how it is used to discipline the self and others according to predominant gendered expectations.

Obviously, the relative size of one's body influences the amount of personal space one takes. Thus, the cultural norm that masculinity be signaled by more muscular and taller bodies makes the larger use of space more legitimate for men, even if many men are not larger than many women. Great variances in size among women and among men exist, but social expectations persist. For example, from the 1950s to 1990s, U.S. doctors prescribed the sex hormone synthetic oestrogen to treat what was called an "abnormality of tall stature in females" (Rayner, Pyett, & Astbury, 2010, p. 1076). Although there is no evidence to suggest tallness hurts women's health or reproductive ability, tallness was diagnosed as a psychological threat.

Size has its limits for all people. Women and men with large, less muscular bodies experience discrimination from what sociologist Samantha Kwan (2010) calls **body privilege**: "an invisible package of unearned assets that thin . . . individuals can take for granted on a daily basis" as they navigate public space in their daily life (p. 147). Critical studies scholar Samantha Murray (2008) argues that fatness has become gendered; men who are seen as fat are feminized. Their masculinity is stripped away from them, meaning they cannot be fat and manly, too.

In her interviews with 42 overweight women and men, they noted discrimination and humiliation when doing such basic things as trying to sit in classroom chairs, buying clothing, ordering food, and trying to enjoy food in public. White and Hispanic women seemed to especially internalize these negative experiences. While large, muscular men are rarely judged as taking up space illegitimately, women and men considered obese are (Buchbinder, 2013).

Given that women tend to be disciplined more severely by how they look, it is no surprise obese women report being the target of frequent ridicule from strangers and acquaintances alike. In a critical review of research, Janna Fikkan and Ester Rothblum (2012) found discrimination against obese women, and particularly obese poor women and women of color, exists in workplaces, education, health care, media representations, and opportunities for romantic relationships.

Body Movement

We use the term **body movement** to refer to how people ambulate, flow, travel, move in their bodies in daily life, and how it feels to move. It includes one's demeanor, which sociologist Nancy Henley defines as how one physically carries oneself (1977). Although gender is one of many influences (e.g., physical ability, age, ethnicity, race, class, perhaps sexual orientation) on how you move, strong cultural expectations discipline gendered movement.

People tend to think of demeanor as something unique to an individual, but Henley (1977) points out that demeanor can have gender/sex and power/status attributions. Sociologist Erving Goffman (1963) found that demeanor can be used to mark upper and lower status and that higher-status persons may tend to have more latitude in their behavior. They may carry their bodies more loosely. Persons of lower status may be tighter, more attentive to their physical demeanor. Philosopher Iris Marion Young (1990) observes how this might affect some girls' movements:

> walking like a girl, tilting her head like a girl, standing and sitting like a girl, gesturing like a girl, and so on. The girl learns actively to hamper her movements. She is told that she must be careful not to get hurt, not to get dirty, not to tear her clothes, that the things she desires are dangerous for her. Thus she develops a bodily timidity that increases with age. (p. 154)

How people move and use their bodies can influence long-term health, social group affiliations, and identity.

Criticism of women athletes reinforces the presumption that a woman should be slight yet large breasted and not commanding on the sports field. Female athletes are seen as exceptional women, as in the case of African American tennis stars Venus and Serena Williams, who are dismissed as merely natural athletes because of their race (Douglas, 2002), or not women at all, as in the case of South African world track champion Caster Semenya who was challenged for her masculine build, deep voice, and tendency to wear pants (Sloop, 2012).

The status of girls and women in sports has improved markedly since the historic passage of the 1972 civil rights law, Title IX, which made it illegal to discriminate on the basis of sex when participating in federally funded educational programs. Girls increasingly joined sports (formerly designated for boys) such as hockey, wrestling, and football. In hockey alone, the number of girls participating in high school teams went from 96 in the 1973–1974 school year to 8,254 in 2009–2010 (Anderson, 2012).

U.S. culture is obsessed with sports and disciplining those who cannot fit the elite group of gifted athletes. The disciplining often happens in seemingly innocent messages of encouragement. Boys are told to "man up," meaning, "don't be a pussy, brave it, be daring," put your body in harm's way (Urban Dictionary, n.d.). And boys and girls are told, "Don't throw like a girl," making the point that the worst athlete is one who acts feminine.

The social importance of this phrase is further demonstrated by academic research. As early as 1966, psychologist Erwin Straus examined a series of photographs of young girls and boys throwing baseballs and was struck by the differences he saw in how they used space and motion:

> The girl of five does not make any use of lateral space. She does not stretch her arm sideward; she does not twist her trunk; she does not move her legs, which remain side by side. All she does in preparation for throwing is to lift her right arm forward. ... The ball is released without force, speed, or accurate aim. ... A boy of the same age, when preparing to throw, stretches his right arm sideward and backward; supinates the forearm; twists, turns and bends his trunk; and moves his right foot backward. From this stance, he can support his throwing almost with the full strength of his total motorium. ... The ball leaves the hand with considerable acceleration; it moves toward its goal in a long flat curve. (pp. 157–160)

In other words, Straus observed that the girls did not tend to bring their whole bodies into motion, but the boys did. Years later, the relative power of men's throwing was supported in a statistical meta-analysis of a wide variety of gendered behaviors. Psychologist Janet Hyde (2005) found velocity and distance throwing was one of the few consistently large differences in women's and men's behaviors.

The question is how to explain these differences. Straus considered biological origins, but he observed that the children had not reached puberty so possible sex differences in muscle mass and bone size were not likely. Similarly, the girls did not have breasts that might inhibit their throwing. Straus had to dismiss the idea that the girls were simply weaker, because a weaker person would likely throw the whole body into the movement to compensate. Instead, he concluded that the difference in style came from what he vaguely referred to as a "feminine attitude." He did not consider the possibility that the boys had been taught to throw and the girls had not. Nor did he consider that girls who throw like a boy may be ridiculed as unfeminine tomboys, and boys who throw like girls often are ridiculed as feminine and gay.

Twenty-four years after Straus's work, Iris Young (1990) examined his observation in regard to what it means to "throw like a girl." Young compared the assumption of gender/sex differences in throwing to other presumed gender/sex differences in body movement to make clear girls are *taught* what to do and what not to do, just as many boys are *taught* how to throw with force.

Not only is there a typical style of throwing like a girl, but there is a more or less typical style of running like a girl, climbing like a girl, swinging like a girl, hitting like a girl. They have in common first that the whole body is not put into fluid and directed motion, but rather . . . the motion is concentrated in one body part; and . . . tend not to reach, extend, lean, stretch, and follow through in the direction of her intention. (p. 146)

While current generations of girls are challenging Young's description of gendered expectations, her key point is that people tend to experience their bodies in uniquely gendered/sexed ways that matter. Many girls and women experience their bodies in more guarded ways than boys and men because of how they are *taught* to use and relate to their bodies. So, what does it now mean to "throw like a girl"?

"You throw like a girl" has been a common taunt for decades. Traditionally it was a criticism, meaning the person threw with little force. Although the meaning is being partially resignified as girls and women come into their own successes in competitive sports, and display "throw like a girl" and "I am one" on T-shirts as a badge of honor (see Figures 4.5, 4.7, and 4.8), not even the president of the United States could escape this criticism (see Figure 4.6).

Masculinities scholars observe that most men do not experience their bodies in the guarded way girls and women tend to (Buchbinder, 2013; Forth, 2008; Whitehead, 2002). In fact, they are taught that their bodies are to be used and abused. Stephen Whitehead (2002) describes masculine bodily experiences: "The male/boy/man is expected to . . . place his body in aggressive motion . . . in so doing posturing to self and others the assuredness of his masculinity" (p. 189). Social norms of masculinity

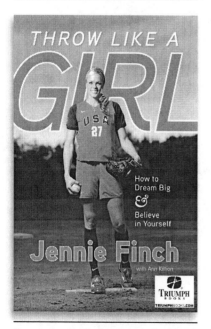

Figure 4.5 U.S. softball Olympian Jennie Finch's book *Throw Like a Girl* (Triumph Books)

Source: Jennie Finch's *Throw Like a Girl: How to Dream Big and Believe in Yourself* (9781600785603) was published by Triumph Books.

Figure 4.6 Barack Obama partakes in the U.S. presidential tradition of throwing out the first pitch for the Major League Baseball season in 2010. He is criticized on the web as "throwing like a girl" (e.g., YouTube; Sodahead.com; Sweetness and Light; http://lonelyconservative.com/wp-content/uploads/2012/07/Obama-Wimp-Throws-Like-a-Girl.jpg).

Source: AP Photo/Nam Y. Huh

encourage boys and men to physically exert their bodies to extremes. Consider that from 250,000 to 300,000 people a year, almost exclusively athletes, injure their ACLs (anterior cruciate ligament in the knee). Men's studies scholar David Buchbinder (2013) explains the demands placed on men's bodies:

> Traditionally women have been constructed as coextensive with their bodies (they are bodies), whereas men are deemed to *use* their bodies. The latter principle is observed, for example in the gymnasium, where the motto, "No gain without pain" makes explicit the secondary and subordinate nature of the body. Even where the aim is the enhancement, whether merely physical or also visual, of the body itself, the [man's] body must be subjected to a rigorous discipline in the cause of achieving an idealized goal outside and beyond it. (p. 123)

The social significance placed on men's bodies as large, strong, and agile heavily influences many men's gender identities (Connell, 1995). While there are increasing exceptions to these norms for women and men, Whitehead (2002) notes, "We should not allow the exceptions to deny the differing realities of the lived experiences of most women's and men's bodily existence" (p. 190).

Figure 4.7   Erin DiMeglio, the first girl to play high school quarterback in the state of Florida, warms up before a preseason game on August 24, 2012, and shows that throwing like a girl can be strong, accurate, and powerful. (Jim Rassol/Sun Sentinel/MCT via Getty Images)

Figure 4.8   Megan Schachterle is an 11-year-old softball pitcher from Iowa. She opens her body widely and grunts every time she pitches. She has been playing softball since she was 3, and her hero is Jennie Finch. Megan takes "you throw like a girl" as a compliment, especially given her mission in life is to be a pitcher for Team USA.

Source: MCT via Getty Images

Source: Victoria DeFrancisco

Researchers also have examined countless other ways bodily movement tends to gender/sex people through quantitative studies of differences in smiles, gaze, nods, gestures, self-touch, expressiveness, accuracy in interpreting others' emotion, loudness, and speech errors (Dindia & Canary, 2006; Mast & Sczesny, 2010). Much of this research is inconsistent, and where gender/sex differences have been found, perceived expectations explained the differences more than actual behaviors (Hall et al., 2005).

Refusing the Command Performance

Even though binary gendered/sexed bodies seem permanent, people push at the disciplinary norms. That pushing by individuals and groups helps propel social change. The very tools used to discipline people's bodies also can be used to challenge these restrictions. To explore the multiple ways people resist and change the command performance, we first introduce the concept of agency. We believe that even as bodily communication is used to differentiate and oppress, people also can be agents and use the body to bring about self-empowerment and social change. We then turn to specific strategies people use to challenge the constraints within which they improvise.

Agency

Even in the face of social constraints on gendered bodies, people exert agency in diverse ways. **Agency** is the ability to act or the degree to which people can control their experience or identities in a given situation through creative communication strategies and/or the manipulation of contextual circumstances (Campbell, 2005). Agency means people are not helpless victims; even people in oppressed groups find ways to survive, to make needed changes and gain some control over their own destiny (Scott, 1992). Resistance is not easy, and only a fine line separates actions that exert individual agency and those that comply with cultural pressures to conform. For example, do men who body build constitute agents in control of their own bodies? Do pro-Ana (pro-anorexia) websites' support of peers' eating disorders really represent positive control over one's body? Do breast cancer survivors who have had mastectomies and opt for breast implants show self-empowerment? As gender/sex is reiterated through performance, the reiteration also creates "gaps and fissures," instabilities and something "which escapes or exceeds the norm," that allow agency and resistance of the command performance (Butler, 1993, p. xix). No repetition is a perfect reproduction of gendered body expectations. These seeming imperfections provide avenues for oppositional performance.

Using Norms Against Each Other

One of the most traditional norms about women's bodies is that of being a mother. The role of mother creates social expectations about how women should act: listening, attending to others' needs, remaining in the private sphere. Over time and across cultures, women have used this role of mother as their foundation for public advocacy. They manipulate the expectations of being caretakers to seek social justice. The Mothers of Plaza de Mayo formed in 1977 to protest the "disappearance" of their children under the repressive military regime that ruled Argentina from 1976 to 1983. Communication scholar Valeria Fabj (1993) explains that a verbal response by men was not possible because the society was repressive, yet women as mothers were valued and could protest the state's murder of their grown children. Wearing their children's cloth diapers as headscarves (embroidered

Figure 4.9   Mothers of Plaza de Mayo plead their case with men politicians in 1977.

Source: Presidencia de la Nación Argentina

Figure 4.10   Mothers of Plaza de Mayo protesting in 2006.

Source: Wikipedia/Roblespepe

with the children's names and dates of disappearance) and carrying pictures of their disappeared children, the mothers marched around the plaza at a time when public protest was prohibited. Fabj argues it was the very "myth of motherhood," the social beliefs attached to the women's bodies, that allowed them "to draw from their private experiences in order to gain a political voice, discover eloquent symbols, and yet remain relatively safe at a time when all political dissent was prohibited" (p. 2).

Because they were fulfilling social expectations attached to devoted motherhood, they were able to violate social and legal norms that no one else could. In a situation where verbal argument was not an option, bodily communication linked to women's traditional role was necessary.

In Nigeria, women also used the threat of their public bodies as a form of silent protest. From July 2002 to February 2003, thousands of Nigerian women ranging in age from 30 to 80 peacefully seized Chevron-Texaco's terminals, airstrip, docks, and stores, disrupting oil production (Agbese, 2003; Turner & Brownhill, 2004). The women demanded jobs for their sons, schools, scholarships, hospitals, water, electricity, and environmental protection. They wanted some of the wealth being pumped out of the ground to be pumped back into their communities. As part of the protests, a group of women threatened public nudity if their demands were not met, an act that was culturally understood to shame men. The women explained, "Our nakedness is our weapon" (quoted in Wysham, 2002, n.p.).

The Nigerian and Argentinian women used social norms and prohibitions to pressure those in power to meet with them and to give in to their demands. The social norms demanding that women be good mothers can be used to violate other social norms. When social norms concerning how one should be in one's body contradict or conflict, as in the earlier examples, the gaps and fissures that emerge can be productive places to explore new ways to be in one's body.

Making Norms Visible

The Guerrilla Girls, a New York–based group formed to protest the exclusion of women from the art world, employ the tactic of "zap actions"—placing posters around New York City (Demo, 2000). Their first action was in 1985 and focused on the absence of women in the major museums and galleries in New York. "Using mass-media techniques and advertising world savvy" (Guerrilla Girls, 1995, p. 10), they quickly gained notoriety.

Their emblematic poster, which appeared in 1989 on buses in lower Manhattan, refigured Ingres's *Odalisque*,

> a reclining figure whose sinuous nude back and hips have long stood for idealized female beauty. Rather than meeting the classical profile of Ingres' original, however, our eyes confront a large shaggy gorilla head, mouth open, teeth glistening. Twisted to meet us eye to eye, it challenges instead of seducing. (Guerrilla Girls, 1995, p. 7)

Challenging the objectification of women's bodies and positioning women as artists, the poster makes visible the naked body of a real woman, challenging the fetishized, artistically rendered bodies in museums. It refigures what it means for women to be present, and it blocks the ability of museum defenders to claim that women are present as more than bodies on canvases (Demo, 2000). The poster makes visible the norm of women as objectified bodies even as the alternative of women's bodies as artists is offered (see Figure 4.11).

Figure 4.11   Guerrilla Girls 1989 poster

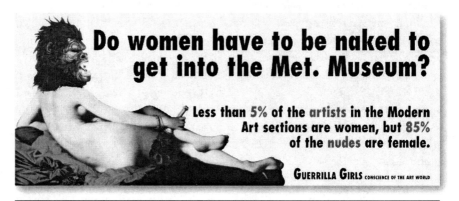

Source: Copyright © 1989 by the Guerrilla Girls. Courtesy of www.guerrillagirls.com

Communication scholar Bonnie Dow (2003) analyzes feminists' protest against the 1968 Miss America Pageant. In the second-wave feminists' first major public event, women made the extreme social expectations of women's attractiveness visible. Women threw into trash cans bras as well as "girdles, high heels, cosmetics, eyelash curlers, wigs, issues of *Cosmopolitan*, *Playboy*, and *Ladies Home Journal*— what feminists termed 'instruments of torture' to women" (pp. 130–131). Although media coverage of the event referred to bra burning, *no bras were burned*. This event provides an interesting example of how those who attempt to make oppressions visible often are disciplined. Dow explains how the false claim of bra burning was used against the protestors. In a society obsessed with breasts, accusations of bra burning were a way of sexualizing and trivializing women's demands. For example, two years after the protests, Senator Jennings Randolph described feminists as "braless bubbleheads" in his response to the Women's Strike for Equality in 1970 (as cited in Dow, 2003, p. 130). But, more than 35 years after this initial protest, it is clear that many of the women's movements' challenges to attractiveness have taken hold (girdles, anyone?) even as new norms have replaced them (breast implants, anyone?).

Overtly Challenging Norms

In the last 40 years, tattoos and body piercing have become increasingly popular across gender, sex, age, social class, nonathlete, athlete, African American, Latino, and White identities (Kosut, 2006; Mayers & Chiffriller, 2008). Women and men are now getting tattoos at comparable frequencies (Adams, 2009).

Women still outnumber men in body piercing, but men are getting piercings more than ever before, and there is a trend for women and men to have multiple piercings on tongues, nipples, navels, eyebrows, noses, lips, and genitals (Mayers & Chiffriller, 2008).

Historically in the United States, inscribing one's body with tattoos was reserved for particular subcultures of men: Civil War soldiers, sailors, incarcerated men, bikers, gangs, and working-class men (Fisher, 2002; Kosut, 2006). Tattoos inscribed masculinity on men's bodies—strong, brave, heroic, macho, and perhaps threatening (Atkinson, 2002; Braunberger, 2000; Gill, Henwood, & McLean, 2005).

Body piercing was limited to girls and women, particularly in Hispanic and Latina cultures. Earlobe piercing for U.S. men became popular in the 1980s, with young gay men piercing their right lobe as an identifier to other gay men. Young heterosexual men quickly took on the style and wear earrings in one or both ears. Popular icons, such as professional athletes and actors, wear earring studs and multiple visible tattoos. While tattoos have long been a statement of masculinity, when women *and* men use multiple tattoos and move beyond earlobe piercing, gender distinctions begin to blur. The result is often a more androgynous look (Shapiro, 2010).

Figure 4.12 Tattoos and piercing

Source: Ryan McVay/Digital Vision/Thinkstock

Part of the popularity of tattoos seems to be the appeal to inscribe one's body in a way the predominant culture views as taboo (Adams, 2009). The symbols are self-expression and cultural resistance at the same time (Braunberger, 2000; Santos, 2009). Sociologist Mary Kosut (2006) argues that tattooing "suggests a degree of agency that is unlike the consumption of other bodily goods. . . . The painful and ritualistic tattoo process involving the penetration of the body, coupled with the ongoing live-ness of the tattoo, creates a unique and potentially agentic consumer experience" (p. 1042). Sociologist Michael Atkinson (2002) adds that women who "radically mark [their] bodies tend to subvert hegemonic ideologies about femininity—especially images of the weak, sexually objectified, or otherwise submissive woman" (p. 220). One of the participants in his study of women with tattoos said,

> I made the conscious choice to tattoo my body, and I'll never regret it. It was probably the defining moment in my life so far . . . it was the only time I did anything solely for myself, to display who I am as an individual. Still, I'm not indifferent to ridicule from other people about my tattoos so I keep them under wraps most of the time. (Adele, age 23, p. 231)

Thus, Atkinson found the choice to tattoo can be simultaneously one of personal expression and gender resistance but still have some semblance of compliance to gendered norms, as in the relative size and nature of the tattoo and where it is placed (Atkinson, 2002).

Revaluing the Body

Bodies that have been denigrated can be respected and acknowledged. Fat activists reject pressures to pathologize large bodies as abnormal. Feminist scholar Cecilia Hartley (2001) argues that the lack of social acceptance for fat bodies helps to create and maintain not only the cultural criticism of fatness but also the unrealistic ideal of thin bodies. In both cases, bodies are controlled, regulated, disciplined, and live in fear.

In 2012, Jennifer Livingston, a weather reporter on a local television station in Milwaukee, Wisconsin, fought back against such discipline. She publicized a scathing e-mail ridiculing her for being fat:

Hi Jennifer,

It's unusual that I see your morning show, . . . I was surprised indeed to witness that your physical condition hasn't improved for many years. Surely you don't consider yourself a suitable example for this community's young people, girls in particular. Obesity is one of the worst choices a person can make. . . . I leave you this note hoping that you'll reconsider your responsibility as a local public personality to present and promote a healthy lifestyle.

Ms. Livingston responded on air:

The truth is: I am overweight. You could call me fat. And yes, even obese, on a doctor's chart. But to the person who wrote me that letter: Do you think I don't know that? That your cruel words are pointing out something that I don't see? You don't know me. You are not a friend of mine. You are not a part of my family and you have admitted that you don't watch the show. So you know nothing about me but what you see on the outside. . . . And I am much more than a number on a scale. And here is where I want all of us to learn something from this . . . bullying . . . is a problem that is growing every day in our schools and on the Internet. It is a major issue in the lives of young people today. . . . But what really angers me about this is there are children who don't know better; who get e-mails as critical as the one I received, or in many cases even worse, each and every day. . . . This behavior is learned. It is passed down from people like the man who wrote me that e-mail. If you are at home, and you are talking about the fat news lady, guess what? Your children are probably going to go to school and call someone fat. . . . To all of the children out there who feel lost, who are struggling with your weight, with the color of your skin, your sexual preference, your disability, even the acne on your face, listen to me right now. Do not let your self-worth be defined by bullies. Learn from my experience; that the cruel words of one are nothing compared to the shouts of many.

By using the media, one courageous journalist was able to take what was a personal attack and make it a public issue to be addressed. She moved the attack from being about her body to being about the bullying of the writer and others like him. She rejected the heightened sexual objectification of appearing on television and reclaimed the value of her body.

Conclusion

For every norming of people's bodies through expectations concerning bodily communication, locations of resistance arise. Yet that resistance will face a response. Although the Mothers of Plaza de Mayo faced fewer reprisals than other activists, the government punished many of them. Although the Guerrilla Girls have been active for nearly 30 years, women continue to be underrepresented in major galleries and museums. Although dress standards have changed remarkably in the last 100 years, the range of individual expression in terms of dress really is quite limited (look around your classroom if you are unconvinced). Even as the most marginal of bodies are made visible, that does not mean they are accepted. Even if one recognizes that bodies' performances of gender are not natural, that does not mean it is easy to change the performance.

"Throwing like a girl" and "throwing like a boy" are far from natural behaviors. Social norms train people to throw, sit, walk, move, dress, and be in ways appropriate to what a person's gender/sex is perceived to be. Cultures label particular movements of the body as gender/sex specific, and members of the culture then ridicule those who do not follow the prescribed behaviors. Over time, routinized movements of the body in gendered/sexed ways appear natural. The body is an important location on which gender/sex identities are communicated, constructed, maintained, and challenged.

KEY CONCEPTS

agency 95

bodily communication 78

body movement 90

body privilege 90

body surveillance 80

disciplining gender 82

embodied space 89

gender performativity 78

gendered
   attractiveness 82

objectification 80

proxemics 89

refusing the command
   performance 95

self-objectification 89

DISCUSSION QUESTIONS

1. Do you agree with Whitehead that men do not tend to experience their bodies in the guarded way women do? Why or why not?

2. Why is Butler's notion of gender as performance particularly relevant here?

3. Identify examples of how objectification is present in your everyday life.

4. What are the primary ways in which persons have refused the command performance? Are there any ways you have refused a command performance?

CHAPTER 5

Gendered/Sexed Language

U nderstanding gender/sex in communication requires an understanding of language's power to subordinate *and* liberate. In interpersonal communication, language can be used to injure. In organizational communication, language can be used to exert power. In public communication, language to name a problem is necessary before one can solve it. In many ways, struggles over gender/ sex are struggles over language. An example illustrates why understanding language is central to understanding gender/sex in communication.

Prior to the 1970s, *sexual harassment* as a term did not exist, even though the activity did. During slavery, African American women were sexually used and raped by their White masters. During industrialization, immigrant women were forced by economic necessity to acquiesce to the demands of their employers. Even during contemporary times, women (primarily) are subjected to work environments where their sex is used as a basis of ridicule, often in the hopes of driving them from the workplace. When women experienced hostile, abusive, and violent workplaces, it was explained as having a "bad boss" or as further proof that women did not belong in the rough world of paid employment. With the burgeoning of the second wave of women's movements, women developed a language that made their interests articulable. The Women's Center at Cornell University held the first speak-out in 1975, where women around the country came together to name these experiences "sexual harassment" and articulate the harm as discrimination. In 1980, the Equal Employment Opportunity Commission (EEOC) issued guidelines recognizing **sexual harassment** to be a violation of Title VII of the Civil Rights Act of 1964.

According to the U.S. Code of Federal Regulations, which the EEOC enforces,

(a) Harassment on the basis of sex is a violation of section 703 of title VII. Unwelcome sexual advances, requests for sexual favors, and other verbal or physical conduct of a sexual nature constitute sexual harassment when (1) submission to such conduct is made either explicitly or implicitly a term or condition of an individual's employment, (2) submission to or rejection of such conduct by an individual is used as the basis for employment decisions affecting such individual, or (3) such conduct has the purpose or effect of unreasonably interfering with an individual's work performance or creating an intimidating, hostile, or offensive working environment. (29 C.F.R. § 1604.11)

In 1986, in *Meritor Savings Bank v. Vinson* (477 U.S. 57), the Supreme Court held that creating a hostile work environment is actionable under Title VII, explaining that the prohibition against employment discrimination "is not limited to 'economic' or 'tangible' discrimination" like losing a job (p. 64). The courts also recognized that acquiescing to sexual demands was not necessary to prove an injury. One person did not need to touch another to harm another. Instead, the courts recognized that what people said, only words, could create an environment in which it was impossible to work. Language could be used to subordinate another on the basis of sex. The Eleventh Circuit Court offered a compelling explanation:

> Sexual harassment which creates a hostile or offensive environment for members of one sex is every bit the arbitrary barrier to sexual equality at the workplace that racial harassment is to racial equality. Surely, a requirement that a man or woman run a gauntlet of sexual abuse in return for the privilege of being allowed to work and make a living can be as demeaning and disconcerting as the harshest of racial epithets. A pattern of sexual harassment inflicted upon an employee because of her sex is a pattern of behavior that inflicts disparate treatment upon a member of one sex with respect to terms, conditions, or privileges of employment. There is no requirement that an employee subjected to such disparate treatment prove in addition that she has suffered tangible job detriment. (*Henson v. City of Dundee*, 682 F.2d at 902 [1982; footnote omitted])

Although the child's rhyme proclaims, "Sticks and stones may break my bones, but words will never hurt me," the law recognizes that words, indeed, can injure.

This example demonstrates the complex ways language is part of gender in communication. Women experienced violence via a form of interpersonal communication. Until they could name that violence, nothing could be done about it. By coming together in small groups and developing a vocabulary that could articulate their interests, women were able to take their demands to the public, eventually effecting legal change, giving them grounds on which to contest illegal, not just inappropriate, forms of interpersonal communication and to demand changes in social norms. These efforts continue today.

Lani Shotlow-Rincon created the "Don't Call Me Baby" project for a class on designing public campaigns. She explains, "My project outlined how an effective campaign could be created for the USC Campus area" (Stop Street Harassment, 2011). As part of the campaign, she created a website, an art exhibit, a flash mob, and public service announcements. The graphic below was created as the centerpiece visual of the campaign, illustrating the fundamental message that words can negatively impact others. For more on the campaign, see www.stopstreetharassment. org/2011/03/the-dont-call-me-baby-project

Language is more than a tool used to transmit information or a mirror to reflect reality. Words *do* things. Saying something is as much an action as moving something. However, people do not always recognize that every time they communicate, they engage in symbolic action, action that constructs social reality.

Language structures people's understanding of social reality, and insofar as gender/sex is part of social reality, language about gender/sex structures understandings of gender/sex and hence structures gender/sex. People literally speak and perform their bodies and identities into being. Australian scholar Dale Spender (1985) described language as "our means of ordering, classifying and manipulating the world. It is through language that we become members of a human community, that the world becomes comprehensible and meaningful, that we bring into existence the world in which we live" (p. 3).

How language names a person as a sex and a gender determines how that person is perceived as a sex and a gender. For example, because the English language tends to recognize only two "opposite sexes"—female and male—it does not recognize the existence of intersex people. The result of that linguistically constructed sex binary, which does not accurately represent the range of biologically possible sexes, is a demand to make the world fit people's understanding of it. Thus, intersex babies were surgically altered to fit the binary. People's language induced them to intervene in the biological world to make it match the social world that created a sex binary. Quite simply, language has power—to oppress, deny, and subordinate. But language can also liberate, witness, and empower.

Understanding how cultures teach gender and enforce sex, and how to challenge existing constructions of gender and sex, are communication issues. Thus, this chapter focuses on patterns of communication embedded in language that speak to how sex and gender have been structured and, in turn, have structured the world. Sex is not a thing (even though the word is used to describe the human body), and gender cannot be held in your hands. Instead, when you study sex and gender, you study the trace evidence of them in language. To understand this, we first explore theories explaining the power of language. We then identify ways in which language is used to subordinate and to liberate.

The Power of Language

Rhetorical scholar Kenneth Burke (1966) argued that human beings are "symbol-using (symbol-making, symbol-misusing)" creatures (p. 16). He did not stop at this description. Instead, he asked, "Do we simply use words, or do they not also use us?" (p. 6). Linguist Robin Lakoff (1975) answered this question: "Language uses us as much as we use language" (p. 3). Burke's question and Lakoff's answer direct students of language to consider how words circumscribe people's interactions with each other and the world.

Words do not exist in isolation but combine to form **terministic screens** that direct people's attention away from some things and toward others. Burke's (1966) view of language highlighted the "necessarily *suasive* nature of even the most unemotional scientific nomenclatures" (p. 45). All communication is persuasive because "even if any given terminology is a *reflection* of reality, by its very nature as a terminology it must be a *selection* of reality; and to this extent it must function also as a *deflection* of reality" (p. 45). The point is not just that a word constructs the way you see the world. Instead, Burke's point with terministic screens is that words interact with one another to form a screen through which you view the world. Thus, people in the United States tend to operate with a sexed and gendered screen, one that directs their attention to see some things about gender/sex and not others.

An example clarifies Burke's point about how language directs attention. Reproductive freedom and abortion are rhetorically charged issues in the United States. Two main sides have long dominated the controversy: pro-life and pro-choice. People who are pro-life tend to refer to the "reality" as a *baby*, whereas those who are pro-choice tend to refer to the "reality" as a *fetus*. Each term selects, deflects, and reflects reality in a particular way and calls forth different clusters of terms that accompany it.

Baby accurately reflects reality insofar as some people often ask, "When is the baby due?" and some people perceive miscarriage as the loss of a baby. *Baby* also selects a particular aspect of reality to highlight; it focuses attention on how the reality is a fully formed human being separable from its gestational location. A person could leave a baby in a room unattended (but of course safely ensconced in a crib). However, when in the womb, it cannot be separated from its location. *Baby* also selects a particular type of relationship to other human beings; *babies* have mothers and fathers, not women and men. *Baby* also calls forth positive associations because U.S. culture is pronatal; it celebrates the arrival of babies. People think of babies as innocent and pure. Once people think of the "reality" as a separate and distinct human being, to terminate its existence means that someone has committed murder.

In the process of selecting some parts of reality to highlight, *baby* also deflects part of reality. It deflects that the "reality" is located within a woman's body, and it deflects the possibility that women can be something other than mothers; if there is a baby, there is a mother. It also deflects the fact that people recognize stages in development in the human as it undergoes gestation, from zygote to embryo to fetus.

In the same way that *baby* reflects, deflects, and selects parts of reality, so does the term *fetus*. *Fetus* selects those very parts of reality that *baby* deflects. It selects the reality that is described in medical and scientific terms, that gestational stages exist, and that a fetus cannot exist without a woman to carry it. In fact, *fetus* reverses the relationship: Babies *have* mothers, whereas women *carry* fetuses. In selecting the medical reality, *fetus* highlights a not yet complete human being. Although people may fondly imagine cuddling a baby while sitting in a rocking chair, imagining cuddling a fetus is not quite the same. *Fetus* highlights the incompleteness of the human.

In the process of selecting, *fetus* also deflects attention away from the very things *baby* selects. *Fetus* deflects the emotional attachments people tend to have to small human forms, and it deflects the possibility that the fetus can be murdered. Fetuses are not murdered; instead, pregnancies are terminated.

Ultimately, words contain within them implicit exhortations to see the world in one way rather than another. Words "affect the nature of our observations" (Burke, 1966, p. 46). However, Burke (1966) went even further, positing that "many of the 'observations' are but implications of the particular terminology in terms of which the observations are made" (p. 46). People see only that for which they have words.

Lexicographer Julia Penelope (1990) extended this analysis from a gender/sex perspective to highlight how systems of sexism have influenced the words available:

> Language draws our attention to only some experiences in some ways, making it difficult to grasp and articulate those it doesn't provide labels or descriptions for. We can describe feelings and perceptions English doesn't provide words for, but finding an accurate description takes time and patience and some fluency with the language. Because English foregrounds only some aspects of experience as possibilities, we have a repertoire of specific gestures, sounds, words, sentence structures, metaphors, that focus our attention on just those activities named by patriarchy. (p. 204)

Given this, it is important to understand the patterns present in language that privilege some views of the world, while displacing others. One way to track power's presence in language is to identify when some groups' perspective can be found in language, and other groups' is not.

Muted Group Theory

In 1963, when Betty Friedan identified women's discontent caused by sexism as "the problem that has no name" (p. 11), she recognized that the English language does not serve all its users equally. Language is a social product. It is created, maintained, and changed by its users, but not all users have equal access to influencing the language. Those who belong to dominant groups within a culture have more influence over the language and, hence, over the terms that form a culture's terministic screen.

Social anthropologists Edwin Ardener and Shirley Ardener originally proposed **muted group theory** to explain why some people are unable to express themselves even when they have the physical ability to speak. The theory highlights how dominant and nondominant groups within a given culture have different cultural boundaries in their perceptions, as well as related language (E. Ardener, 1973; S. Ardener, 2005).

Because of their muted positions in culture, persons in nondominant groups constantly must translate their ideas into forms that will be accepted by the dominant groups. They do not have the natural or easy access to communication possessed by those in the dominant groups. This affects not only their quantity of talk but also the content, timing, and mode of communication (S. Ardener, 2005). African Americans who speak Ebonics, or Black English, understand this. The pressure to speak dominant English is a pressure to "pass," to learn to speak White to be accepted or just to get by in dominant White culture. Even though in 1996 the Oakland, California, school board recognized Ebonics as a second language ("Oakland School Board," 1997, p. 12) and in 1997 the Linguistic Society of America recognized Black English as a legitimate language with its own grammar structures, semantics, and style ("LSA Resolution," 1997), it still is not accepted in dominant U.S. culture. Resistance to the creative expansion of language makes evident the politics of language.

Communication studies professor Cheris Kramarae (1981) extended the Ardeners' theory to explore the role of communication in processes of domination by focusing on how men as the dominant group block the ability of women to fully express their experiences. She described how muting occurs on two levels:

1. "Women (and members of other subordinate groups) are not as free or as able as men are to say what they wish, when and where they wish, because the words and the norms for their use have been formulated by the dominant group, men."

2. "Women's perceptions differ from those of men because women's subordination means they experience life differently. However, the words and norms for speaking are not generated from or fitted to women's experiences." (p. 1)

Intercultural communication scholar Mark P. Orbe (1998) further extended muted group theory with research on people of color, women, LGBTQ people, and those from lower socioeconomic classes to develop a theory of cocultural communication. He identified the factors that influence communication from nondominant group members to dominant group members:

Situated within a particular field of experience that governs their perceptions of the costs and rewards associated with, as well as their ability to perform, various communicative practices, co-cultural group members will strategically adopt a communication orientation—based on their preferred outcomes and communication approaches [e.g., assertive, nonassertive, aggressive]—to fit the circumstances of a specific situation. (p. 19)

These elements influence communication practices, such as emphasizing commonalities, self-censorship, avoiding controversy, bargaining, ridiculing self, confronting, and avoiding.

Muted group theory provides a way to understand that simply adding women's and other oppressed groups' voices will not create equality. Dominant groups mute through control of language (S. Ardener, 2005). Those who resist must adapt or change the language.

Although nondominant groups may be at a disadvantage in language access, speakers are resilient. Orbe (1998) made clear that "muted group status is not fixed; it is constantly reinforced, augmented, or challenged" through communication practices (p. 10). Oppressed and subordinated groups can speak to the challenge presented by problems without names. Some women keep diaries or journals (Kramarae, 1981). In the United States in the 1960s, consciousness-raising groups were used by many White, middle-class women to talk about subjects considered taboo, such as their sexuality (Campbell, 1973). Writers such as Gloria Anzaldúa used poetry, slang, multiple languages, unique forms, and profanity in academic writing (Palczewski, 1996). Sociolinguist Braj Kachru (1982) documented ways in which second-language speakers of English adapt the language to better reflect their worldviews, resulting in multiple world Englishes.

The Patriarchal Universe of Discourse (PUD)

Not only language but the rules of language usage mute people. Penelope (1990) focused on the grammatical rules that govern language use, as well as the words. She argued that the English language is not neutral but supports patriarchy insofar as English creates a **patriarchal universe of discourse (PUD)**:

A "universe of discourse" is a cultural model of reality that people use daily to decide how to act and what to say in specific contexts. . . . It is the same thing as "consensus reality," and those who accept its terms assume that it is an accurate description of reality. . . . In fact, people can be so attached to "consensus reality" that its assumptions and predictions override contradictory evidence. (pp. 36–37)

When the model of reality is one in which a patriarchal system dominates, then that model tends to hide the exercise of male privilege.

The existence of a consensus reality explains why thinking critically about gender/sex can be so difficult. The language system pushes people to see things in a particular way. For example, according to the existing consensus reality, there are only two sexes, the sexes are opposite, and the words used to describe those sexes are not semantic equivalents. Penelope argued, "PUD divides the world into two, unequal, stereotypical spheres in . . . well-defined, discrete areas of the English vocabulary that name people, their behaviors, attitudes, and activities in the world" (p. 38).

The interesting move in Penelope's analysis is that she made clear that once people accept that language has power, then they need to start thinking about how those with power deploy language to maintain and extend power: by denying access to it (e.g., refusing education or public speaking forums), by stripping others of their languages (e.g., the forced suppression of Native American languages in Bureau of Indian Affairs schools beginning in the 1880s and continuing until passage of the Native American Languages Act of 1990), by generating rules of proper usage (e.g., proper English as a class and race marker), and by structuring the language in such a way that it masks power.

Language Can Be Used to Oppress and Subordinate

Thus far, we have described how dominant groups structure reality through language. We now identify some specific examples of language-based gender/sex privilege. Of course, some of the examples may seem natural, unremarkable, or insignificant. This is part of the power of language. Linguist Deborah Cameron (1998) noted, "Language is ideological. The same reality can be represented in any number of ways, and the power of linguistic conventions lies precisely in the selectiveness with which they represent the world, making one way of perceiving reality seem like the only natural way" (p. 161).

As we trace the locations of sexism in language, keep in mind that the examples are mostly derived from the United States. Our hope is that by learning to recognize the language patterns that reinforce sex and gender inequality, you will develop the critical faculties to think more politically about all language use, your own included. We happily admit that our discussion of language is prescriptive; part of our job as communication scholars is to identify problems and offer solutions.

He/Man Language

The element of sexist language that has received the most attention is the use of sex-exclusive language such as the generic *he* or *man* used to refer to any person (female or male) or to all people (women and men). Research conclusively demonstrates that sex-exclusive language does influence the perception of those who read and hear it. Here is only a partial list of the studies that prove influence: Martyna, 1980a, 1980b, 1983; McConnell & Fazio, 1996; McConnell & Gavanski, 1994; Newman, 1992; Ng, 1990; Wilson & Ng, 1988. People do not read and hear *man* as a referent to all human beings, female and male, and people do not read and hear *he* as a referent for a woman. Every major style manual (APA, MLA, Chicago, Turabian, *New York Times*) requires sex-inclusive language that does not exclude half the population.

Most people forego sex-exclusive language in regular conversation. In a study of the actual use of the generic *he*, researchers Jeffrey L. Stringer and Robert Hopper (1998) found that the "generic he occurs rarely, if at all, in spoken interaction" (p. 211). In an analysis of scholarly writings and the *New York Times* from 1970 to 2000 and a comparison of personal writing from 1990 to 2008, cognitive scientist Brian D. Earp (2012) found "he/man language is increasingly less used, and nonsexist alternatives are on the rise" (p. 15). His conclusion? "We may be well on our way to seeing the ultimate extinction of masculine generics in the English language. It would be about time" (p. 16).

People no longer use the generic *he* in conversation, and style manuals discourage it in written communication. Thus, the debate over sex-inclusive language is resolved. Sex-exclusive language should not be used. Sex-inclusive language should be used.

Semantic Derogation

Semantic derogation occurs when two terms ought to represent parallel concepts, but one term is derogatory while the other is not (Schulz, 1975). Penelope (1990) describes these terms as "semantically symmetrical (paired), but conceptually asymmetrical" (p. 48). Some scholars argue that derogation is sex based: "Because naming and defining is a prerogative of power, semantic shifts in vocabulary have been determined largely by the experience of men, not women" (Miller & Swift, 1993, p. ix).

Is this true? Consider the degree college students earn: the bachelor's degree. The parallel term for bachelor is *spinster*, yet spinsters are thought of as dried-up old women who never married. The etymology of *spinster* indicates that positive meanings were once attached to it but have atrophied over time. Originally, *spinster* referred to women who spun fibers into thread and yarn. When men began to spin, the term referred to men, too. In the 17th century, the term began to refer to unmarried women (although some resisted this usage because *spinster* also was a colloquial term for "harlot"); the term became sexualized and derogated. Whereas *bachelor* referred to any unmarried man, a *spinster* was an unmarried woman beyond the marriageable age, making clear that men are never too old to marry but women can be. Other examples include *mistress/master; lady/lord; womanly/manly; tramp* (sexually active woman)/*tramp* (homeless man); *to mother children/to father children; governess/governor;* and *madam/sir.*

An interesting pattern emerges in the derogation of nouns: Sexuality is used to derogate women. *Bachelor* and *spinster* ought to be equal, but *spinster* connotes someone who cannot get any sex. *Lord* and *lady* ought to be equal, but *lord* designates a ruler, whereas *lady* contains a prescription for how women should act. *Master* and *mistress* ought to be equal, but a *mistress* is a kept woman who gets sex by "stealing" it from another woman. *Governor* and *governess* ought to be equal, but again the masculine term connotes political power, whereas a *governess* is a person who takes care of others' children.

Semantic Imbalance

Semantic imbalance refers to an overabundance of terms to describe something related to one group but few terms existing to describe the other. Answer this:

How many terms can you think of that describe a sexually active woman? A sexually active man?

The number of terms available that negatively describe women swamps the list of terms that describe men. Only recently have terms like *player* come to carry negative connotations typically associated with *slut*, but even now *player* is not nearly as bad a name as *slut*.

Semantic imbalance is created not only when there are too many words but also when there are too few. Women often are referred to as *hysterical* (*hysteria*, derived from the Greek word for women's reproductive organs), yet men are not referred to as *testerical*. Similarly, men may be referred to as *womanizers*, but women are not *mannizers* (Penelope, 1990, p. 187).

Semantic Polarization

Semantic polarization occurs when two parallel concepts are treated as though they were opposed, like "opposite sexes." In case you had not noticed, we avoid that phrase because it structures a perception of the world that we find problematic. The sexes are not opposite; all are human and may have more in common with those who are a different sex than with some who are the same sex. However, by framing the sexes as opposite, language reentrenches the notion that there are two and only two sexes and that the characteristics of one cannot be possessed by the other. Communication scholar Barbara Bate (1988) explains, "If you see women and men as polar opposites, you are likely to believe that any features or quality of men should be absent from women, and vice versa" (p. 16).

Marked and Unmarked Terms

When one sex or race tends to dominate a category, people may sex or race mark the category only when a nondominant person fills it. This creates the impression that a person is violating a norm. Because the nursing profession is dominated by women, people tend to refer to "the nurse" when the nurse is a woman but refer to "the male nurse" when the nurse is a man. Similarly, you often see references to "female police officer" but not "male police officer," "male slut" but not "female slut," and "Black professor" but not "White professor." In all of these examples, the race and sex of the person is incidental or irrelevant to the job being performed. This construction is not as common as it once was, but it still is an interesting tendency to track. It reveals a great deal about cultural expectations and designated roles, which may explain why it is most persistent in university sports teams: The men's team is the "Bears," and the women's team is the "Lady Bears."

Trivialization

Trivialization refers to the use of diminutives to refer to a disempowered group member. Historically, Black men's masculinity was demeaned by the use of the term *boy*. Although *boy* does not initially seem like a derogatory term, when used by a White person (often younger) to refer to a Black man (often older), it exposes the power dynamic at play. No matter how old, wise, or respected, a Black man was forever diminished as an immature person—a boy. Women also often are referred to in ways that strip them of stature. Women are referred to as desserts: *honeybun, cupcake, sweetheart, tart.* Linguist Caitlin Hines (1999) argues that this is no accident, insofar as dessert metaphors refer to women not just as "objects, but sweet (that is compliant, smiling), and not just desserts, but *pieces* or *slices*" (p. 148).

To correct semantic imbalance and derogation, trivialization, and marked terms, it is not enough simply to erase them from our vocabularies. Cameron (1998) points out, "The crucial aspect of language is meaning: the point of non-sexist language is not to change the forms of words just for the sake of changing, but to change the repertoire of meanings a language conveys. It's about redefining rather than merely renaming the world" (p. 161). Therefore, attention to the vocabulary people have—or lack—becomes important.

Naming

Another place where trace evidence in language points to a power imbalance between the sexes is in relation to naming practices upon heterosexual marriage. Historically in the United States, women lost their names upon marriage, becoming "Mrs. John Smith." Women's marriage status was embedded in their names; married women were addressed differently than unmarried: *Mrs.* versus *Miss.* As early as the 1600s, the alternative of *Ms.* was proposed as a way to make designations parallel: Men were *Mr.* whether married or unmarried and so women, too, could be *Ms.* whether married or unmarried. In addition, the option of keeping one's name upon marriage was introduced. In the 1970s only 1% of women kept their name, in the 1980s it was 9%, and in the 1990s a high of 23% kept their name. Then, in the 2000s, the percentage leveled off at 18% (Kopelman, Shea-Van Fossen, Paraskevas, Lawter, & Prottas, 2009). Even when women do keep their birth names or hyphenate, an overwhelming majority still give their children their husband's name (Emens, 2007).

Scholars who study naming practices see it as a "window into gender attitudes" (Hamilton, Geist, & Powell, 2011, p. 145). Of respondents in one study, 72.3% agree that "it is generally better if a woman changes her last name to her husband's name when she marries" (p. 156), so much so that 49.9% thought states should "legally require a woman to change her name" (p. 157). Despite this, some women do keep their names upon marriage. As an intersectional approach might predict, other factors than sex predict one's naming practice. Kopelman et al. (2009) found that women with high-level jobs like CEO, professional occupations like doctor, and those in the arts or entertainment fields tended to keep their name more often.

Lack of Vocabulary

The foregoing examples are ways language subordinates. However, as muted group theory clarifies, an equally challenging problem is a lack of language. Friedan's writing about problems without names highlights second-wave feminism's struggle to talk about sexism, sexual harassment, date rape, and marital rape. It is impossible to develop solutions to a problem when it has no name and, hence, is neither identifiable nor observable.

Spender (1985) argues, "Historically, women have been excluded from the production of cultural forms, and language is, after all, a cultural form—and a most important one" (p. 52). Its import stems from language's ability to "form the limits of our reality" (p. 3). Because of women's exclusion from the "production of the legitimated language, they have been unable to give weight to their own symbolic meanings, they have been unable to pass on a tradition of women's meanings to the world" (p. 52). The fact that women have not had the same opportunity does not mean they have had no opportunity. One example of language development occurred during the debates over pornography that dominated women's movements in the 1980s.

Although men (as religious figures and political leaders) historically controlled the definition of *pornography*, they no longer monopolize its meaning. Historically, *pornography* possessed two meanings: speech and in the 1500s, images used as an insult to the church and state (Hunt, 1993). These interpretations dominated *pornography*'s meaning until the second wave of feminism began to challenge the way women's sexuality was defined. Andrea Dworkin and Catharine A. MacKinnon (1988; among many others) focused on pornography's effect on women and redefined *pornography* as an act of sex discrimination, in the process rejecting a focus on pornography's effect on society's moral fiber (Palczewski, 2001). Although the municipal ordinance they wrote did not survive judicial scrutiny, they influenced Canadian law regarding sexually explicit, violent, and sexist materials.

Developing a vocabulary enables you not only to name your experience but also to critically reflect upon it—an important component of coming to political agency. African American feminist theorist bell hooks (1989) explains how "simply describing one's experience of exploitation or oppression is not to become politicized. It is not sufficient to know the personal but to know—to speak it in a different way. Knowing the personal might mean naming spaces of ignorance, gaps in knowledge, ones that render us unable to link the personal with the political" (p. 107). For hooks,

> Politicization necessarily combines this process (the naming of one's experience) with critical understanding of the concrete material reality that lays the groundwork for that personal experience. The work of understanding that groundwork and what must be done to transform it is quite different from the effort to raise one's consciousness about personal experience even as they are linked. (p. 108)

In other words, the development of a vocabulary with which to accurately describe one's experiences is an important process during which one needs to reflect on the political implications of that experience.

The Truncated Passive

Grammatical patterns as well as words provide evidence of sexism in language. Penelope (1990) argued that grammatical structures enable speakers to deny agency and perpetuate oppression. The prime culprit is the **truncated passive**, in which the use of a passive verb allows the agent of action to be deleted (or truncated) from the sentence. This example demonstrates the difference between when passives are and are not used:

Active voice: That man raped that woman.

Passive without truncation: That woman was raped by that man.

Truncated passive: That woman was raped.

Each sentence is grammatically correct but operates very differently in its depiction of the event. Sentence constructions using the truncated passive enable blaming the victim because the victim is the only one present in the sentence.

Individuals who attempt to avoid explicit responsibility for the consequences of the power they exercise often use truncated passives. The result of "agent-deletion leaves us with only the objects of the acts described by the verbs. Passives without agents foreground the objects (victims) in our minds so that we tend to forget that some human agent is responsible for performing the action" (Penelope, 1990, p. 146), as in the phrases "mistakes were made," "Hanoi was bombed," or "the toy got broken." Penelope explains, "Agentless passives conceal and deceive when it doesn't suit speakers' or writers' purposes to make agency explicit" (p. 149). As a result, "This makes it easy to suppress responsibility" and enables "protection of the guilty and denial of responsibility, . . . the pretense of objectivity, . . . and trivialization" (p. 149).

The Falsely Universal *We*

Political scientist Jane Mansbridge (1998) analyzes how the use of the collective *we* in political discourse can be used to represent a particular few by making invisible a distinct other. She explains, "'We' can easily represent a false universality, as 'mankind' used to" (p. 152). Thus, "the very capacity to identify with others can easily be manipulated to the disadvantage of" a subordinated group because "the transformation of 'I' into 'we' brought about through political deliberation can easily mask subtle forms of control" (p. 143).

One often hears politicians talk about how *we* need to do something or that *we* as a nation believe in particular values, when in reality they are referencing a particular segment of the population who they hope will vote for them. It is extremely easy to fall into using *we*, especially when you want to create a sense of identification and community. However, as Burke (1969) pointed out, any time identification is used, one must "confront the implications of *division*. . . . Identification is compensatory to division" (p. 22). When a group says, "We are alike," it also necessarily implies that others are *not* like them.

The Deverbing of Woman

Semantic imbalance and derogation also occur in verbs. The distinctions between the meanings of the verbs *to man* and *to woman*, which ought to be parallel, are intriguing. The *Compact Edition of the Oxford English Dictionary* (1971) listed the primary definition of the verb *man* as "to furnish (a fort, ship, etc.) with a force or company of men to serve or defend it" (p. 1711). Its definitions of the verb *woman* included "to become woman-like; with *it* to behave as a woman, to be womanly. . . . To make like a woman in weakness or subservience. . . . To make 'a woman' of, deprive of virginity. . . . To furnish or provide with women; to equip with a staff of women" (p. 3808). *Man* carries implications of acting, typically in battle and on ships. *Woman* carries implications of being acted upon. To *woman* is to become womanlike, to be made a woman, or to be deprived of virginity. Today, in contrast to the verb *man*, the word *woman* is seldom thought of as a verb at all.

The pattern described between *woman* and *man* also is present in other verb forms, such as *lord* and *lady* and *master* and *mistress*. *Lord*'s primary definition is "to exercise lordship, have dominion" (p. 1664). In contrast, the definition of the verb *lady* is "to make a lady of; to raise to the rank of lady . . . to play the lady or mistress" (p. 1559). Female verbs deny agency. Male verbs highlight it.

Master's primary verb form means "to get the better of, in any contest or struggle; to overcome defeat . . . to reduce to subjection, compel to obey; to break, tame (an animal)" (p. 1739). *Mistress* means "to provide with a mistress . . . to make a mistress or paramour of . . . to play the mistress, to have the upper hand . . . to dominate as a mistress" (p. 1820). Again, mastery involves agency, getting the better of, subjecting, compelling others to obey. *Mistress*, in contrast, is passive. A woman is provided for as a mistress; she does not mistress. Or she is made a paramour. Or she merely plays at being mistress. Or, if one focuses on the latter definitions in which agency is expressed, one realizes that it is often a false agency, for when a woman dominates as a mistress, she dominates (typically) "servants or attendants . . . household or family" (p. 1820). Agency is rarely involved; rarely is control possible and never over masters.

Language as Violence

The previous sections focused on how specific parts of language (pronouns, nouns, and verbs) construct sex privilege. However, particular forms of language are not the only way in which subordination is manifested. People use language itself as a form of violence. Critical race theorists examine the function of hate speech, recognizing the "relationships between naming and reality, knowledge and power" (Matsuda, Lawrence, Delgado, & Crenshaw, 1993, p. 5). They argue that hate speech (racist, homophobic, sexist, anti-Semitic) causes harm. Although the First Amendment has protected such speech, legal scholar Mari Matsuda (1993) argues that "an absolutist first amendment response to hate speech has the effect of perpetuating racism: Tolerance of hate speech is not tolerance borne by the community at large. Rather it is a psychic tax imposed on those least able to pay" (p. 18).

The distinction between words and actions may not be as clear as once thought. Matsuda (1993) explains, "The deadly violence that accompanies the persistent verbal degradation of those subordinated because of gender or sexuality explodes the notion that there are clear lines between words and deeds" (p. 23). Although First Amendment absolutists argue that the appropriate response to "bad" speech is more speech, such an alternative is not always viable for those targeted by hate speech. Legal scholar Charles R. Lawrence III (1993) demonstrates how words are more than what they denote.

> Like the word "nigger" and unlike the word "liar," it is not sufficient to deny the truth of the word's application, to say "I am not a faggot." One must deny the truth of the word's meaning, a meaning shouted from the rooftops by the rest of the world a million times a day. The complex response "Yes, I am a member of the group you despise and the degraded meaning of the word you use is one that I reject" is not effective in a subway encounter. (p. 70)

Of course, just because one recognizes that language acts does not mean that one automatically accepts the need for legal redress. Debate over hate speech dominated the 1990s. Those working against sexism, racism, religious intolerance, and homophobia disagree on the appropriateness of legal prohibitions against words that wound, noting the danger of collapsing a word into an action (Butler, 1997). However, all agree that we must respond to, answer, deny, reject, and condemn the use of language as a mechanism of violence.

Language as Resistance

If language has the power to create inequality and injustice, it also has the power to resist them. Although as communication studies scholars we *focus* on language, we do not dismiss the importance of economics, politics, and law to social change. Language is a precursor to recognizing the need for and the possibility of change in these other areas. Penelope (1990) argues, "Changing our descriptions won't immediately change reality or eliminate white supremacy or male dominance, but it will change the way we perceive power imbalances and the conceptual structures that make them appear to make sense to us" (p. 214).

Through language, people can rename, reenvision, and reimagine the world. Penelope (1990) explains, "Language is power, in ways more literal than most people think. When we speak, we exercise the power of language to transform reality" (p. 213). This section highlights the theories that explain the emancipatory potential of language.

Talking Back

In *Talking Back* (1989), bell hooks outlines how simply speaking can function as an act of resistance. For those who have been named subordinate, speaking rejects that naming. For any subordinated group, hooks explains,

> True speaking is not solely an expression of creative power; it is an act of resistance, a political gesture that challenges politics of domination that would render us nameless and voiceless. . . . Moving from silence into speech is . . . a gesture of defiance that heals, that makes new life and new growth possible. (p. 8)

"Talking back" is not talking for talk's sake but "is the expression of our movement from object to subject—the liberated voice" (p. 9). As we talk about language in this chapter, we talk about not only the words themselves but also who is authorized to use them, on which subjects, from which social locations, and with what critical perspectives.

For hooks, talking back is not simply the screaming of frustration, nor do all people speak as subjects and with a liberated voice every time they speak. She clarifies that "to speak as an act of resistance is quite different than ordinary talk, or the personal confession that has no relation to coming into political awareness, to developing critical consciousness" (p. 14). The distinction between ordinary talk and talking back is necessary for three reasons. First, it avoids trivializing or romanticizing the process of finding a voice; coming to voice is difficult political work. Second, it avoids privileging "acts of speaking over the content of the speech" (p. 14); when talking back, what is said matters. Third, it prevents the commodification of oppositional voices; when one recognizes the oppositional element of talking back, one can no longer treat it as mere spectacle. Talking back is not mere talk but talk with a political consciousness.

Developing a New Language

If existing language does not provide names for a person's experiences, as in the example of sexual harassment that opened this chapter, then one of the most profound acts of resistance is to develop new language. Philosopher Mary Daly (1987) explains, "New Words themselves are Mediums, carriers of messages" (p. 10). New words enable people to see new social realities.

Philosopher Sandra Harding (1995) outlines the power of naming for a marginalized group—in this case, women:

> For women to name and describe their experiences in "their own terms" is a crucial scientific and epistemological act. Members of marginalized groups must *struggle* to name their own experiences *for* themselves in order to claim the subjectivity, the possibility of historical agency, that is given to members of dominant groups at birth. (p. 128)

In order to become agents, or people who act rather than people who are acted upon, a language on and of one's own terms is essential: "For marginalized people, naming their experience publicly is a cry for survival" (p. 129).

Examples of developing language abound. Feminist lexicographers have made efforts to create alternative dictionaries to reclaim the English language, using concepts and definitions that reveal and reflect the diverse experiences and oppressions of women, persons of color, working-class people, gays, lesbians, bisexuals, transgender people, and people with disabilities (e.g., Daly, 1987; Kramarae & Treichler, 1992; Mills, 1993). Going beyond the creation of new words, Suzette Haden Elgin (1984/2000, 1987/2002a, 1993/2002b) developed an entire language, Láadan, for her fictional *Native Tongue* trilogy ("Suzette Haden Elgin," 2004).

Women in other nations and in other times also have developed languages in which to come to voice. Communication scholar Lin-Lee Lee (2004) studied how, more than 1,000 years ago in China, women developed *Nüshu*, a female discourse used in "texts sung and chanted by rural woman over their needlework on pieces of red fabric, handkerchiefs, and fans" (p. 407). Chinese women were excluded from formal education in *Hanzi*, the official Chinese script that "was created by men for the use of men." Nüshu offered an alternative as "an oral phonetic transcription passed from generation to generation by women" (pp. 408–409). It developed in an area governed by patriarchal Confucian systems, in which men dominated women and subservience to superiors was morally required. Nüshu texts describe the details of a woman's life and express feelings about "sexual inequality, low social status, and bad treatment" (p. 411). No one trained in ordinary Chinese can read Nüshu. Men who heard it could "understand it when performed, but they could not perform it, read it, or speak it themselves" (p. 409). This distinctive language "allowed women to have a voice, to create an individual and collective subjectivity that enabled them to confer value on and give importance to their lives" as it "transformed the hardships of women into tales that validated their lives and experiences" (p. 410).

Resignification

The recent debate over the naming of SlutWalks is an example of **resignification**, the linguistic practice in which one rejects a term's existing meaning's normative power, exposes how the term's meaning is constructed, and attempts to change its connotation. Historically, the word *slut* referred to a slovenly girl; in contemporary usage, it refers to a sexually promiscuous woman and has risen to the status of being a "four-letter word" (Nunberg, 2012). However, the meaning of the term was contested in the spring of 2011. After a police officer at a York University panel on campus safety said women, to avoid sexual assault, should not "dress like sluts" (implying that women who do are "asking"—or deserve—to be raped), campus activists responded by embracing the term and planning a SlutWalk. Since that first protest, an estimated 32,827 people have marched in 45 cities and 31 countries, including Argentina, Australia, Belgium, Brazil, Canada, China, Costa Rica, England, Finland, France, Germany, Honduras, Hungary, India, Ireland, Mexico, Netherlands, New Zealand, Nicaragua, Norway, Panama, Peru, Poland, Portugal, Romania, Scotland, Singapore, South Africa, South Korea, Tunisia, and the United States of America. Organizers of SlutWalk Seattle made clear the importance of the term: "One of the most effective ways to fight hate is to disarm the derogatory terms employed by the haters, embracing them and giving them positive connotations" (as cited in Thompson, 2011, p. 14). SlutWalks, and the activism around them, have embraced the term *slut* and sought to change its meaning (Kapur, 2012).

However, not all agree that *slut*, as a term, is something to be embraced. Professors Gail Dines and Wendy J. Murphy (2011) described the attempt to change *slut*'s meaning as a "waste of precious feminist resources" given how the term is "so saturated with the ideology that female sexual energy deserves punishment" (p. 25).

A group of Black women also challenged the SlutWalk movement to rename and rebrand itself. Calling for an intersectional approach, they argue, "As Black women, we do not have the privilege or the space to call ourselves 'slut' without validating the already historically entrenched ideology and recurring messages about what and who the Black woman is. We don't have the privilege to play on destructive representations burned in our collective minds, on our bodies and souls for generations" ("An Open Letter," 2011, par. 1).

Blogging About Language

For an extended consideration of the possibility of resignifying *slut*, see Meghan Murphy's May 7, 2011, "We're Sluts, Not Feminists. Wherein my Relationship with Slutwalk Gets Rocky" posted on The F Word: Feminist Media Collective, available at http://feministcurrent.com/2585/were-sluts-not-feminists-wherein-my-relationship-with-slutwalk-gets-rocky.

Well, Slutwalk, I also "grapple with the word slut." This word, as I have mentioned, has been used in a myriad of ways to hurt me. I have been called a slut for having sex, for not having sex, and for being coerced into sex. I have been called a slut by partners, by friends, and by acquaintances. I wish that this word did not hold the power it does. I wish that it had not been used to hurt and abuse me. But it has. There is no erasing that. Regardless of whether or not I decide to redefine the word. It continues to be used in this way. And so I still "grapple" with the word, "slut." While some may have decided to reclaim it or redefine it for their own personal empowerment, I'm afraid that this does not change my experiences.

This is not to say that attempting to change language is not a purposeful endeavour. Or that to take away the power a word has to hurt and abuse people is impossible. But rather that this is something that we must not only agree upon, as the oppressed group who has decided to reclaim the oppressive word, and that this takes time. While the argument has been made that the intent is not to force this supposed "reclaimation" on others, that, rather, anyone can volunteer to be a "slut or an ally," the very uncomfortable fact that Slutwalk pressures women (and men!) into accepting this word, a violent word, as part of their empowerment discourse, it [*sic*] not addressed. In fact it seems to go unnoticed. I may well be, in theory and in life, the "ally" of a self-described "slut." But I am not about to call her one.

Source: Rabble.ca, News for the Rest of Us. http://rabble.ca/news/2011/05/we%E2%80%99re-sluts-not-feminists-wherein-my-relationship-with-slutwalk-gets-rocky

---

Scholars have written about the need to resignify or reclaim words. Randall Kennedy's *Nigger* (2002) explores the history of that term and its recent resurgence as an in-group way to name African Americans. Inga Muscio's *Cunt* (2002), as well as Eve Ensler's *The Vagina Monologues* (2000), reclaim *cunt*. Politicized sex workers resignified *whore*, as in Gail Pheterson's *A Vindication of the Rights of Whores* (1989). Elizabeth Wurtzel's *Bitch* (1998) praises difficult women, *Bitch* magazine offers a feminist response to pop culture, and Meredith Brooks's song "Bitch" proclaims "I'm a bitch / I'm a lover / I'm a child / I'm a mother / I'm a sinner / I'm a saint / I do not feel ashamed. . . . So take me as I am / This may mean / You'll have to be a stronger man."

Interestingly, when a word's history is researched, it almost always turns out that the word originally had a positive meaning and only recently came to carry negative connotations. When Muscio researched *cunt*, she found that its precursors originally were related to titles of respect for women or names of goddesses and that "the words 'bitch' and 'whore' have also shared a similar fate [to *cunt*] in our language. This seemed rather fishy to me. Three words which convey negative meanings about women, specifically, all happen to have once had totally positive associations about women" (p. 6). Urvashi Vaid (1995), in her analysis of LGBTQ rights, found that *queer* originally was used as a form of self-naming by homosexuals. By the 1910s and 1920s, men who thought of themselves as different because of their homosexual attraction to other men rather than because of their feminine gender appearance called themselves *queer* (p. 42). *Queer* later developed the negative connotation still heard as an epithet in playgrounds and streets. This meaning did not develop overnight, but, as Butler (1993a) explained, "'Queer' derives its force precisely through the repeated invocation by which it has become linked to accusation, pathologization, insult" (p. 226).

This hints at the difficulty involved in resignifying a term. People cannot simply wish a term's connotation to change. Butler's theory on the performativity of gender explains why this is the case: People tend to be "ventriloquists, iterating the gendered acts that have come before them" (Hall, 2000, p. 186). How does one get out of this repetitive loop? By resignification—the repeated invocation of a term that links it to praise, normalization, and celebration. Unfortunately, even when a term may be resignified within a group of people, that does not mean the new meaning carries beyond that group. Butler (1993a) noted, "As much as it is necessary to . . . lay claim to the power to name oneself and determine the conditions under which the name is used, it is also impossible to sustain that kind of mastery over the trajectory of those categories within discourse" (p. 227). However, that may be one's only option.

Butler (1997) writes that people sometimes "cling to the terms that pain" them because they provide "some form of social and discursive existence" (p. 26). Guided by Althusser's theory of interpellation (whereby one becomes a subject because one is recognized by another), Butler posits, "The act of recognition becomes an act of constitution: the address animates the subject into existence" (p. 25). Thus, she posits it is understandable that one might prefer being known as a *queer* or a *nigger* or a *bitch* to not being known at all. Additionally, even as dominant naming may disempower, it also creates locations for resistance, for "opening up of the foreclosed and the saying of the unspeakable." For Butler, "The resignification of speech requires opening new contexts, speaking in ways that have never been legitimated, and hence producing legitimation in new and future forms" (p. 41).

Even though resignification is difficult, it is not impossible. *Queer's* meaning has been altered (although not completely) with the emergence of queer theory and queer studies in the academy, as well as Queer Nation's chant, "We're queer, we're here, deal with it." During the 18th century, *woman* was used in contrast to *lady*, the latter indicating refinement and the former connoting sexuality (Mills, 1993, p. 267). However, *woman* is now the preferred term because it connotes power and agency, whereas *lady* tends to connote prissiness. *Lady* prescribes that one should act in a restrained manner ("like a lady"), and it implies a class distinction (ladies are of a higher class). In an interesting twist, though, many women's sports teams still are called the Lady Cats, Lady Cavaliers, Lady Mocs, or Lady Tigers, perhaps implying they are not true athletes by linguistically marking them as female.

Strategic Essentialism and Rhetorics of Difference

Communication involves not only what people speak but who people speak as. People perform identities. Often, those who are most marginalized are those most strongly denied a language with which to speak. Yet when challenging oppressions, many people choose to speak from the very identity ingredient that has been the basis of their oppression. When people speak as women, as people of color, as queer, as third-world women, as indigenous people, they thematize their named identities as a legitimizing force of their rhetoric.

The relationship between identity categories and political action is complex. Although we are wary about claims of some innate or biological sense of identity, we also recognize that each person is categorized and that those categories have real effects. Even if there is no biological foundation to race, people categorized as Black, Hispanic, Arab, Asian, and Native American are subjected to stereotypes on the basis of that categorization. In terms of sex, even if the differences between women and men are infinitesimal, people treat men and women as different. Identity categories might be artificial, but they have real, material effects. Given that linguistic categories of identity difference do exist, how might they be challenged? One way is to be constantly vigilant about whether the perception of differences is warranted. Another way is to engage in what Gayatri Spivak (1996) has called *strategic essentialism* (pp. 159, 214).

Strategic essentialism has two important characteristics. First, the so-called essential attributes of the group are defined by the group members themselves. Second, even as group members engage in essentialism, they recognize that it is always an artificial construct. They do not deny they are a group but, instead, seek to control what it means to be part of that group. This reclaims agency. Jaqui Alexander and Chandra Talpade Mohanty (1997) explain: "Agency is . . . the conscious and ongoing reproduction of the terms of one's existence while taking responsibility for this process" (p. xxviii). The marginalized become actors instead of the acted upon.

For example, consider how Black women's identities are constituted by the dominant public sphere. Alexander and Mohanty posit that the taxpaying consumer is the model of citizenship in the United States. If you doubt this, think back to what U.S. citizens were asked to do in the wake of the 9/11 attacks. President George W. Bush, New York Mayor Giuliani, and Senators Daschle and Kerry all urged U.S. citizens to go shopping (Apple, 2001; Crenson & Ginsberg, 2002; Kowalczyk, 2001). In contrast to the consuming and taxpaying (White) citizens, much public discourse defines poor women of color as the "paradigmatic welfare recipients (when in fact, White women constitute the largest group on welfare) and the discourses of dependency, cultural deprivation, and psychological personality characteristics . . . used to discipline these women indicate that (Black) women on welfare are, by definition, neither consumers or taxpayers and, thus, are noncitizens" (Alexander & Mohanty, 1997, p. xxxii). In response, Black women such as bell hooks, Ruby Duncan, Angela Davis, Patricia Hill Collins, and Lani Guinier and the Black women's welfare rights movement (Nadasen, 2005) have sought to redefine Black women's identities, interests, and needs.

Even as scholars recognize that identities are fluid and contingent, and that clinging to them carries danger, scholars also understand "'identities' as relational and grounded in the historically produced social facts which constitute social locations" (Moya, 1997, p. 127). Identities matter insofar as they determine where a person fits within the social order as it presently exists. When one is positioned at the margin, this does not mean that one automatically articulates counterdiscourses but that such a person can provide a location from which a group oppositionally can "provide us with a critical perspective from which we can disclose the complicated workings of ideology and oppression" (p. 128). English professor Paula M. L. Moya (1997) argues that the external construction of identities influences experiences, and those experiences then inform what people know and how they know it. Moya urges everyone to remember that although "people are not *uniformly* determined by any *one* social fact, . . . social facts (such as gender and race)" *do* influence who we are (p. 132).

An excellent example of strategic essentialism is communication scholar Lisa Flores's (1996) study of Chicanas' development of a rhetorical homeland. Flores examined how Chicana feminists' creative works create a discursive space, distinct from the liminal borderlands in which they live—the space between the United States and Mexico that Chicana lesbian feminist Gloria Anzaldúa (1987) described as where the "Third World grates against the first and bleeds" (p. 3). Flores explained that because Chicana feminists live between worlds—physically unwanted in the United States and not wanting to return to Mexico, emotionally seeking the safety of family while seeking respect as women—they must create their own homeland.

The development of a space of belonging, where they can assert agency in relation to their identity, cannot occur in the public sphere given their limited access to it, so Chicana feminists turn to what Flores called private discourse: "Through the rejection of the external and creation of the internal, marginalized groups establish themselves as different from stereotyped perceptions and different from dominant culture" (p. 145). Importantly, Chicana feminists do not remain an insular group. After they "carv[e] out a space within which they can find their own voice . . . they begin to turn it into a home where connections to those within their families are made strong" (p. 146). Once the homeland is firmly established, "recognizing their still existing connections to various other groups, Chicana feminists construct bridges or pathways connecting them with others" (p. 146). Constructing a Chicano homeland is not limited to women. In a fascinating study of the effects of diaspora on Mario, a Chicano, B. Marie Calafell (2004) describes the way she is his "Chicano space" because she is the only other Chicana/o Mario knows (p. 188).

Across this discussion, we have tried to make clear that even as people strategically appeal to essential identities as locations from which to develop knowledge, create solidarity, and resist dominant definitions, the identities also are always critically examined. Sometimes the identities are strongly embraced in order to create a sense of belonging. Other times, some identity ingredients are deemphasized so that alliances can be built on the basis of other ingredients. Gloria Anzaldúa elegantly described this multilayered process as creating bridges, drawbridges, sandbars, or islands (1990). Even as groups build bridges to others, sometimes moments of separation are needed, and the drawbridge is raised.

Although many attempt to use strategic essentialism, its political success is not guaranteed. Spivak (1993) herself claimed the strategy "has served it purpose" (p. 17), but others still advocate it. One of the concerns is that even if people are conscious of their participation in essentialism, "strategic essentialism keeps alive the image of a homogeneous, static, and essential third-world culture" and can also limit people to only claiming knowledge about the identity they embrace (Lee, 2011, p. 265). The question remains: Do the short-term political benefits outweigh the long-term costs of accepting reductive definitions of self (Eide, 2010, p. 76; Lee, 2011, p. 265)?

Moving Over

Building alliances and creating solidarity across identity categories is a good thing. People ought to think about ways to build coalitions. However, whenever one seeks to represent others, one must be attentive to how one speaks for, about, or in solidarity with that other. The issue of who can speak for whom is complex. Those working in solidarity with marginalized groups have long grappled with it. English professors Judith Roof and Robyn Weigman edited a collection of essays that address this very issue, *Who Can Speak? Authority and Critical Identity* (1995). In it, scholars explored the problems presented by the act of speaking for others. When a White, college-educated, middle-class, Christian woman who is a U.S. citizen claims to speak for all women, she potentially erases most other women. This woman's concerns are probably not identical to those of a third-world, poor, Muslim woman of color. Members of a privileged group also may erase others when they seek economic advantage by passing themselves off as members of a marginal group. People need to be wary of instances of speaking for others, because it "is often born of a desire for mastery, to privilege oneself as the one who more correctly understands the truth about another's situation or as the one who can champion a just cause and thus achieve glory and praise. The effect of the practice of speaking for others is often, though not always, erasure and a reinscription of sexual, national, and other kinds of hierarchies" (Alcoff, 1995, p. 116).

However, this should not be taken as an excuse to not speak: "Even a complete retreat from speech is of course not neutral since it allows the continued dominance of current discourses and acts by omission to reinforce their dominance" (Alcoff, 1995, p. 108). Sometimes, when a group cannot speak for itself (e.g., due to political repression, lack of time or resources), then those with power have a responsibility to speak. Philosopher Linda Alcoff explains, "A retreat from speaking for will not result in an increase in receptive listening in all cases; it may result merely in a retreat into a narcissistic yuppie lifestyle in which a privileged person takes no responsibility whatsoever for her [or his] society" (p. 107).

One interesting case exists in which a race-privileged person stepped aside when asked by those for/as whom she was speaking. Anne Cameron, a well-known White Canadian author, wrote first-person accounts of the lives of Native Canadian women. Lee Maracle, a Native Canadian author of Salish and Cree ancestry and a member of the Sto:loh Nation, was sent as a spokesperson for a group of Native writers who met and decided to ask Cameron to "move over" at the 1988 International Feminist Book Fair in Montreal. When asked, Cameron did, indeed, move over (Maracle, 1989, p. 10).

The Native women's concern was that as long as Whites writing as Native women filled stores' bookshelves, no room was left for Native women. Maracle explained, "Anne is occupying the space that has no room for me. So few Canadians want to read about us that there is little room for Native books. There is little space for Native writers to trot their stuff. If Anne takes up that space there is no room for us at all" (p. 10). This example is fascinating because of the deep level of respect all the people involved had for each other. Maracle and the other Native Canadian women did not see Cameron as their enemy, and Cameron understood the basis of the request and honored it. The point is that sometimes material realities (monies for publishing, contracts, space on bookstore shelves) can inhibit the possibilities of the marginalized to be heard. People with privilege, whether race, class, sex, nationality, or religion, may need to step aside, move over, and make space when others wish to speak.

Verbal Play

Even though language matters and is a place of subordination as well as liberation, it also is a place of play, as demonstrated by Celeste Condit's (1992) playful reformulation of Burke's "Definition of Man." Condit believes people should think of themselves as

> People [who] are players with symbols inventors of the negative and the possibility of morality grown from their natural condition by tools of their collective making trapped between hierarchy and equality (moved constantly to reorder) neither rotten nor perfect, but now and again lunging down both paths. (p. 352)

So, how do people play with examples of language as subordination? Taking the example of the deverbing of *woman*, we now play with *woman*, *mistress*, and *lady* as verbs (see Palczewski, 1998).

We could integrate new vocabulary into our repertoire that recognizes *woman*, *lady*, and *mistress* as active. If a woman is "an individual human being whose life is her own concern" (Cicily Hamilton, quoted in Kramarae & Treichler, 1992, p. 490), then *woman* as a verb can mean "to populate a place with courageous, self-identified people." *To woman* is not to populate a place for military battle, nor is it to prepare for a show of deference to hierarchy, but instead it is the creation of a critical mass of souls who are willing to do what needs to be done to maintain and create life-giving forces. For example, "We need to woman the world with crones, hags, spinsters, harpies, and viragos."

An additional, special use of *to woman* exists with language as its object. For example, if one *womans* the language, then one raises gender/sex questions about language, not so much to occupy it as to open it to inspection. For example, when *history* is womanned to *herstory* (even though *history* is not etymologically sexed), gender/sex questions are raised that heretofore have been unasked, in part because history was not open to inspection.

Accepting conventional meanings of *mistress* as someone who controls, someone who teaches, and someone who is sexual, we can brew up an interesting verb form. *To mistress*, then, means to determine one's own sexuality or to teach your body to be sexual in the way you want it to be and not the way society demands. Here, control is not an issue of restraint but one of self-determination. For example, "I have mistressed the lusty powers of my body; they are mine and no one else's."

Lady derives from an Old English term meaning both *loaf* and *knead* (Mills, 1993, p. 133). Accepting those roots, *to lady* means to knead an idea and then to let it set and rise; *to lady* an idea allows it time to grow. Unlike *lord*, *lady* is not an indication of control but denotes active involvement (kneading) and recognition of another's need for space and time in which to develop. For example, we ladied this chapter through its many stages, occasionally kneading ideas and at other times letting them alone to mature.

In addition to offering *woman/mistress/lady* as counters to *man/master/lord*, we also can explore language for sexings of its verbs by playing with inclusive or generic verb forms. Although *people* already is a verb form, meaning "to furnish or fill with people or inhabitants; to populate" (*Compact Edition of the Oxford English Dictionary*, 1971, p. 662), perhaps we also need to expand our language so that we are able to *human* and *person* things as well. Gender- and sex-inclusive terms must develop, as well as womanned terms, to counter the phallocentrism inherent in male action verbs.

Conclusion

Language orders the world, directing a person's attention in one way rather than another. Thus, this chapter is not about being politically correct but about being an ethical, conscious, and critical communicator. The theories reviewed explain the significance of individual words, the power of symbol systems, and how particular symbols systems can dominate others. Words are never "only words."

Language is fun, fascinating, and of real consequence. Learning to speak clearly, vividly, passionately, and with joy is not drudgery. Work is work, but work also can be play. However, even as we play, we still must recognize that rules exist. Almost everyone is familiar with Robert Fulghum's book *All I Really Need to Know I Learned in Kindergarten* (2004) and its list of rules. The first few are "Share everything. Play fair. Don't hit people. Put things back where you found them. Clean up your own mess. Don't take things that aren't yours. Say you're sorry when you hurt somebody" (p. 2). Although most people may have learned these rules in kindergarten, translating them into language rules may not happen until later (college, maybe?).

Here is our playful reinterpretation of the rules. Like Anne Cameron, share, even if it means moving over. Be fair in the way you describe the world, giving all people recognition of their existence by avoiding the falsely universal *we* and sexist language. Do not use violent language. When you use words borrowed from another, make sure you make clear where you found them. If your language is messy, imprecise, or causes messes because it is violent or uses truncated passives, clean up your language. If a term has a specific meaning as part of a coculture, do not use it unless granted permission. And should you ever hurt someone with your language, apologize. Sticks and stones may break bones, and words may break spirits.

Understanding the power of language requires all language users to be more conscious of the words they use and the worlds they construct. Native Canadian author Jeanette Armstrong (1990) outlines a powerful language ethic held by her people:

> When you speak, . . . you not only have to assume responsibility for speaking those words, but you are responsible for the effect of those words on the person you are addressing *and* the thousands of years of tribal memory packed into your understanding of those words. So, when you speak, you need to know what you are speaking about. You need to perceive or imagine the impact of your words on the listener and understand the responsibility that goes with *being* a speaker. (pp. 27–28)

Even though she describes her nation's ethic, Armstrong believes responsibility is shared by all who use language:

> We are all responsible in that way. We are all thinking people. We all have that ability and we all have that responsibility. We may not want to have that responsibility or we may feel unworthy of that responsibility, but every time we speak we have that responsibility. Everything we say affects someone, someone is hearing it, someone is understanding it, someone is going to take it and it becomes memory. We are all powerful, each one of us individually. We are able to make things change, to make things happen differently. We are all able to heal. (p. 29)

This call to a language ethic may seem strange, given that we have noted the permeability of language. Sometimes, a person may use a term and not recognize that its meaning may have moved on. Mistakes do happen, but as Alcoff (1995) is quick to remind, "a *partial* loss of control does not entail a *complete* loss of accountability" (p. 105).

So, speak, speak out, speak loudly, speak softly, speak kindly, speak kindness, play with what you speak, speak playfully, speak in solidarity with others, speak with power, speak truth to power, speak back to power, talk back, talk.

KEY CONCEPTS

developing a new language   118

deverbing of woman   115

falsely universal *we*   115

he/man language   110

lack of vocabulary   113

language as violence   116

marked terms   112

moving over   124

muted group theory   108

patriarchal universe of discourse (PUD)   109

resignification   119

rhetorics of difference   122

semantic derogation   111

semantic imbalance   111

semantic polarization   112

sexual harassment   103

strategic essentialism   122

talking back   117

terministic screens   106

trivialization   112

truncated passives   114

DISCUSSION QUESTIONS

1. The authors argue language can oppress and liberate. Why is recognizing both the liberatory and oppressive potential of language important?

2. What is the ethical debate regarding "speaking for others"? How do the authors suggest we address the debate? Do you agree or disagree and why?

3. For each language form that constrains outlined in the chapter, find one example in contemporary discourse.

4. Do you think resignification is possible? Why or why not? Why would some groups or people choose such a strategy?

PART II

Institutions

CHAPTER 6

An Introduction to Gender in Social Institutions

Thus far, we have focused on a person's performance of gender though speech style, body, and language. We hope we have made clear that a person's sex does not biologically determine the performance of a person's gender. However, as a result of social practices, sex and gender are intertwined. Even though differences are not biologically caused, perceptions of gender/sex differences persist. They have real-life consequences, both positive and negative, for individuals and for groups. Which raises this question: What are the sources of these differences?

Gender/sex differences exist because of social forces, particularly institutions. They push particular sexes to perform gender in a particular way. There are multiple social institutions in a given culture. Each exists to serve a specific function. For example, educational institutions create and enforce rules, and religions teach beliefs by which members should live. Through the establishment of rules, norms, and roles, social institutions create predominant cultural expectations for patterns of behavior "with rights and duties attached to them" (Andersen, 2011, p. 31).

Thus, in order to understand gender in communication, one needs to study not only the micropolitics of personal gender performances and interpersonal interactions but also the related macropolitics of institutions—how they communicate and normalize particular understandings of gender through cultural expectations of patterned behaviors.

Sociologist Patricia Yancey Martin (2004) outlines 12 characteristics of **social institutions**. Institutions:

(1) are social,

(2) persist across time and space,

(3) have distinct social practices that are repeated,

(4) constrain and facilitate behavior,

(5) designate social positions characterized by expectations and norms,

(6) are constituted by people,

(7) are internalized as part of people's identities,

(8) have a legitimating ideology,

(9) are contradictory,

(10) continually change,

(11) are organized and permeated by power, and

(12) are not separable into micro and macro phenomena. (pp. 1256–1258)

These characteristics foreground how people compose institutions and, vice versa, how "institutions define reality for us" (Andersen, 2011, p. 31). They also help explain why studying the role of institutions in gender communication is challenging. First, institutions are amorphous. They are not reducible to specific organizations or groups but are composed of the practices and beliefs that link groups and organizations together. Second, they are large and pervasive in society. Third, they are interdependent. They support each other. Fourth, they normalize rules and values—make them seem natural and universal. Fifth, institutions change constantly and embrace contradictory values and norms. This makes them difficult to grasp. But these characteristics are also what make them powerful.

Institutions' power to normalize is why analysis of their communicative practices is essential to developing one's critical gendered lens. Sociology professor Kathleen Gerson (2004) explains that "private choices are rooted in social arrangements over which individual women and men have only limited control" (p. 164). To assume individuals act completely independent of external influence is to ignore the larger elephant in the room—the institutional forces that influence how people perform their gender identities. Sociologist Margaret Andersen (2011) explains,

> gender is not just an attribute of individuals; instead, gender is systematically *structured in social institutions*. . . . Gender is created, not just within families or interpersonal relationships . . . but also within the structure of all major social institutions, including schools, religion, the economy, and the state. . . . These institutions shape and mold the experiences of us all. (p. 31–32; italics in orginal)

Institutions, like individuals, communicate gender and are gendered through communication. Thus, to more fully understand gender in communication, one must study how predominant social institutions' communication influences an individual's life choices and conversely, how individuals can affect the policies, procedures, and practices of social institutions.

Studying gender/sex in communication is complex because gender/sex is constructed and communicated on the personal and interpersonal microlevels and the public and social macrolevels simultaneously. One can talk about the macro- and microlevels as theoretically distinct, but they overlap in practice. This means the relationships between the levels and influences are difficult to outline in a clear, cause-and-effect fashion. Thus, we devote the remainder of the textbook to some key institutions that normalize particular understandings of gender: family, education, work, religion, and media. Before we explore each of those, however, we want to first make clear the relationship between communication and institutions.

Prejudice Versus Institutionalized Discrimination

We embrace an analytical approach that interrogates the interrelations between micro (interpersonal) and macro (institutional) practices of gender. We seek to make clear that personal prejudice is distinct from institutionalized discrimination. Prejudice in the form of individuals' false or bad beliefs does not *cause* sexual and racial inequalities. Instead, **institutionalized discrimination** is maintained through complex sets of social institutions that interact with, structure, and influence individual beliefs and prejudices. Although persons may possess prejudices, to think of sexism or racism as exclusively lodged within individuals is to misdirect attention.

Obviously, individual prejudice contributes to the maintenance of systems of discrimination. Still, the most powerful engines that drive and sustain racism, sexism, and heterosexism (and hence construct race, gender, and sexuality) are embedded in a society's institutions. Philosopher Sandra Harding (1995) argues that one should view inequality as "fundamentally a political relationship," as a strategy that "privileges some groups over others" (p. 122). Because discrimination is made normal and unconscious through institutionalization, to end discrimination people must identify how it operates on an institutional level via its communicative practices. Attention must turn to the institutions that structure people's relationships to themselves, to each other, and to society.

You probably have heard the phrases *institutionalized racism* and *institutionalized sexism*, but what do they mean? Sexism, racism, homophobia, classism, and other inequalities are not institutions in and of themselves, but they become so embedded in institutional communicative practices and norms that it becomes almost impossible to identify them as forms of discrimination. Unlike intentional expressions of prejudice, institutional sexism and racism often are unconscious. When someone hurls a sexist or racist epithet at another human being, it is easy to identify the presence of prejudiced attitudes. However, when one looks at systemic inequalities, it is difficult to identify who is responsible (because no one single person is), and it is impossible to locate the intent to discriminate (because no single person is behind the discrimination).

Subtle forms of discrimination occur when a person's gender performance conflicts with institutional expectations. For example, why do males continue to be statistically underrepresented in the professions of nursing (from 6% to 8%) and elementary school teaching (18%; U.S. Census Bureau, 2012c)? No one is barring men from nursing or elementary education classes. Because these professions are considered caring professions, the gendered expectations attached to the male sex may make it seem as though men are unfit to perform these roles. And the few men who enter caring professions often experience discrimination.

The practices of institutions can result in inequality. Just because one cannot directly identify and locate intent does not mean that no discrimination occurs. Communication analyses of institutional practices and norms can reveal possible contributors to inequality. For example, political communication scholars study whether U.S. citizens define citizenship and leadership in ways that are sexed and gendered in order to explain why so few women are in the U.S. Congress (Panagopoulos, 2004). Communication education scholars study whether the sex of a speaker affects peer assessments (Sellnow & Treinen, 2004). Media scholars study how television news and crime dramas contribute to the overrepresentation of African American men as criminals (Entman & Rojecki, 2001). Rhetoric scholars study how representations of women's bodies as objects undermine women's credibility as public speakers (Bizzell, 2010). Organizational communication scholars study whether corporate culture contributes to the lower presence of women of color, particularly African American women (Richardson & Taylor, 2009). To identify the communicative practices that maintain gender and sex norms, norms that often dictate different and unequal treatment, one must examine how institutions maintain and perpetuate gender.

Institutional Control

Institutions wield a great deal of power via social control. Social institutions distribute cultural resources, constrain and facilitate actions, allocate power, and assign rights and responsibilities (Lorber, 1994; Vannoy, 2001). Institutions' maintenance of gender/sex differences is why they are widely believed and accepted as truisms. For example, how many times have you heard or said, "Men and women are just different." Why does society focus on gender/sex differences rather than similarities, which research shows are far more prevalent (e.g., Dindia & Canary, 2006)? Our central point is that the differences that are noted, viewed as significant, and praised are those that are normalized by institutions. The functions institutions serve are not value free, apolitical, or universally positive.

Not surprisingly, social institutions are largely created and maintained by the predominant groups within particular historical, cultural, and political environments. As such, the institutions help to maintain the values, ideology, and worldview of the predominant groups. The discussion of sexism and racism in language demonstrates this. Social institutions, communicating through the dominant language, sustain and create cultural hegemony, whereby the beliefs and interests of dominant groups dictate what is considered common sense. Institutions' power comes not from a single act of enforcement but through subtle forms of social control of which people may not be aware.

Social institutions use **cultural ideology**—the ideas, values, beliefs, perceptions, and understandings known to members of a society that guide their behaviors.

Italian political theorist Antonio Gramsci's concept of hegemonic or ruling ideology (Zompetti, 1997) is useful here. Gramsci argues that social control, **hegemony**, is accomplished primarily through the control of ideas. People are encouraged to see an idea as common sense, even if it conflicts with their own experiences. By following the cultural norms that guide behaviors, members uphold the ideology. By recognizing how gender is embedded within social institutions, one is better able to recognize the falsehood of such commonsense assumptions and instead realize the diversity of gender/sex experiences (Buzzanell, Sterk, & Turner, 2004).

Here are a few U.S. examples of compliance with hegemonic norms that people believe to be voluntary:

- In heterosexual marriages, women tend to adopt their husband's name.
- School holidays are structured around Christian holy days.
- Boys are not allowed to play with dolls (but action figures are okay).
- Shopping is considered an acceptable leisure activity, particularly for women.
- Men do not wear skirts.
- Women shave their legs.

Can you think of more?

The point is that in everyday life, social control happens without guns or overt threats. It happens seemingly innocently as people comply without much thought to social expectations.

Institutions enforce and sustain gender expectations. Enforcement mechanisms can appear less coercive for those who abide by socially sanctioned gender roles. But for those who violate role expectations, the coercive power of institutions becomes overt. When biological men exhibit femininity, they are disciplined, sometimes through overt violence, as was army private Barry Winchell who was murdered by two other soldiers because of his relationship with a preoperative male-to-female transsexual (Sloop, 2004). When biological women exhibit masculinity, they, too, face violence, as is made clear by the murder of Brandon Teena, a story cinematically told in *Boys Don't Cry* (Sloop, 2004). Challenges to gender norms usually do not pass unremarked and unnoticed by dominant institutions.

Institutionalized Gendered/Sexed Violence

Institutionalized violence occurs when overt and subtle forms of violence become normalized as a result of institutional rules and norms. In the United States, gendered/sexed violence and violent thinking are part of hegemonic masculinity, meaning that men are expected to be violent and women are not. Masculine violence has become so normalized as a form of communication that people often do not recognize the violence when they speak or hear it. Men's studies scholar Michael Kimmel (2012a) says violence is so ingrained in daily life that it is commonplace in the closest relationships, including families, friends, and lovers.

Does this mean that all men are violent? No. But, because masculine men need not devote time and energy to thinking about how to avoid violence, all masculine men benefit from the institution of gender that normalizes violence against women and feminine men. Does this mean that all women are victims? No. But, as long as masculinity is predominantly defined as being an aggressor and femininity is defined as being submissive, all women potentially can be victimized. Does this mean men cannot be victims, too? Men absolutely can be victims of other people's hypermasculinity. What does this mean for men who work to prevent violence? Their efforts are often not counted and they are emasculated. What does this mean for women who are violent? Women, too, are socialized in a world in which violence equals power and many enact it. In heterosexual relationships, women's violence is sometimes reciprocation of a male partner's abuse (Kelly & Johnson, 2008).

The institutionalization of violence has effects beyond the microlevel of interpersonal relations. The fear of sexual violence affects women's participation in civic institutions. Political scientist Amy Caiazza (2005) analyzed factors affecting men's and women's levels of civic participation. She asked, "Do perceived levels of safety from crime or violence influence men's and women's decisions to become involved in their communities?" (p. 1607). Because many activities involved with civic participation occur at night, when women feel most vulnerable to attack, it is important to start thinking about the way systemic, institutionalized forms of sexism might influence women's full civic participation.

Caiazza studied women's levels of participation and correlated them to women's fear of potential violence. She found that "for women as a group, a sense of perceived safety is strongly related to involvement in the community, while a lack of perceived safety is linked to disengagement. In contrast, among men as a group, safety plays a relatively insignificant role in encouraging or discouraging engagement" (p. 1608). Of course, this conclusion is moderated when one recognizes that safety is not experienced equally by all women; poor women tend to be less safe, and so their participation is not influenced by the perceived loss of safety (which they normally lack anyway) but by other factors. Caiazza's research makes clear that "gender-based violence is an issue relevant to political and civic participation" (p. 1627). Some women participate less than men in politics, city councils, and legislatures not because they are disinterested in politics but because their fear of violence functions as a deterrent to participation.

When sexual violence is examined in this way, antiviolence measures are no longer just a way to decrease crime or maintain law and order. They are a means to fortify democracy and everyone's access to it (Caiazza, 2005). This exposes how gender/sex affects something as taken for granted as citizenship. Although every person is equal under the law of the land, the reality is that gender, and the institutionalization of gender/sex violence, make women's ability to participate unequal to men's.

Understanding the complex ways in which violence is normalized by communication practices across social institutions reveals the sources of gender oppression and social control for all people and identifies paths toward cultural change (Kimmel, 2012a; Miedzian, 1993). Communication scholar Julia Wood (2013) writes, "Individual pathologies can't explain why violence is pervasive and why it is disproportionately inflicted on certain groups. Widespread violence reflects social definitions of femininity, masculinity, and relationships between women and men" (p. 291). By examining violence as gendered, one can begin to identify how it is socialized into such things as raising boys not to cry, sexual harassment in the workplace, bullying in schools, honoring martyrdom in religions, and the wide variety of extreme violence and pornography created in commercial media.

One can also begin to understand how institutions contribute to and are related to a continuum of violence around the world: from gender intimidation to verbal and psychological abuse, to sexual coercion, to physical abuse and murder (Kramarae, 1992). The subtler forms create a context in which even the more explicit forms of violence become normalized. As you are confronted with the multiple forms of violence in society on a daily basis, remember that most are not isolated cases. Rather, they are systemically related to the institutions and the communication acts that maintain those institutions. In the chapters to follow, we hope to help you identify the links among gender, violence, social institutions, and communication.

Preview

Every major social institution in a culture affects the construction of gender/sex, and gender/sex influences the functioning of every institution. Martin (2003) points out, "Gendered practices are learned and enacted in childhood and in every major site of social behavior over the life course, including in schools, intimate relationships, families, workplaces, houses of worship, and social movements" (p. 352).

We begin our discussion of specific social institutions by examining the one perhaps most immediately experienced by each person: family. Family communication is heavily influenced by gendered/sexed cultural expectations of family, and these, in turn, affect the gender identity development and communication of individuals. Understanding the family as an institution makes clear that the family you came from was determined not only by the individuals who populated it but also by the cultural institutional structure of family itself. In order to understand communication within the family, one must also investigate how society communicates about the family.

Education is an institution that affects persons from childhood on. Children who graduate from high school have a minimum of 12 years of formal educational influence during their most formative psychological, physical, moral, and intellectual developmental period. That influence stems from classroom and extracurricular interactions with teachers and peers, interactions that tend to covertly teach heteronormativity. It is not surprising that education's influence extends beyond the classroom and educational material taught.

Work includes the gendering of paid and unpaid labor, organizational cultures, and gendered/sexed barriers such as sexual harassment. In the United States, there is an expectation that all people ought to *want* to work hard, even if they do not like their jobs, because work itself is considered a good thing. The almost unquestioned belief that work is good and the demonization of those on welfare demonstrates the way rhetorical constructions of work maintain its function as a social institution (Schram, 1995). Work expectations are not consistent across sexes. Work is not a gender- or sex-neutral institution. In fact, most organizations are masculinized (Britton, 1999). Thus, as we describe how work is an institution, many of the characteristics also will make clear how it is a *masculine* institution that helps to uphold caretaking in the family as a feminine trait and responsibility.

We turn next to religion. While most gender research fails to address religion, few other social institutions can rival the power of religious doctrine, culture, and practice in establishing and controlling one's deep-seated identities and values. Religious institutions participate in the construction of sex, gender, and sexuality, and while much of this influence seems to impose rigid binary gender/sex behaviors and beliefs, many individuals find ways to create spaces of liberation. Regardless of whether one is examining the general functioning of religion or a specific religious tradition, using a critical gendered lens enables one to understand more about how gender influences religious identity and how religion influences the construction of gender. Especially given the energy religion expends on delimiting acceptable forms of sexuality (virtually every religion views human sexuality as a source of sin), the study of religion is central to understanding the construction of and intersections among sex, gender, and sexuality.

We end with a discussion of media, a communication institution in its own right that also functions as an amplifier for other institutions. We approach media as an institution to make clear that to focus on a particular broadcast or single medium is inadequate. Media share conventions regarding construction of content and construction of audience. Additionally, media are one of the primary mechanisms that reiterate gender while also providing locations in which resistance can occur, in both construction and reception. However, even as we discuss the possibility of oppositional readings of media messages, we emphasize that such readings are not equally available to all audiences and that when they are available, they are not readily transformed into counterhegemonic politics.

Given that the United States is a consumer culture, understanding media is one way to understand how power, an element of media as an institution, manifests itself. As Martin (2004) notes, "Institutions are organized in accord with and permeated by power," insofar as they both constrain and facilitate behavior by members of a society in which the institution exists (p. 1258). Media exert power over how people do gender. Although it is true that a movie is a movie and an advertisement is an advertisement, neither is ever *just* a movie or *just* an advertisement. These media forms also always influence social norms concerning gender, race, class, nationality, and all the other ingredients that constitute identity, for they provide models of what it is to be feminine or masculine and encourage people to buy products that will make them more so.

Together these chapters illustrate the power macrolevel social constructions communicated in, by, and about institutions can have on individuals' and groups' daily lives. Much of the power comes from the ways in which social institutions interlock to influence each other. We argue the key to bringing about social justice is through the critical analysis and change of these social institutions. This is not to dismiss the important roles such institutions play in reducing the uncertainty of social life, creating a sense of belonging, offering shelter, providing order, and organizing mass initiatives. Rather, the ultimate goal is to recognize these important needs and see how all people could be better served. As you delve into the specific dynamics of each social institution, we suggest you look for key institutional characteristics described in the present chapter to see them at work in constructing, maintaining, and changing gender identities and dynamics. In what ways do the unique institutional norms liberate and/or restrict gender identity constructions?

KEY CONCEPTS

cultural ideology   134

hegemony   135

institutionalized
discrimination   133

institutionalized violence   135

social institutions   131

DISCUSSION QUESTIONS

1. What is privilege? Can you identify ways in which your sex, gender, race, sexual orientation, and/or able body privilege you?

2. How do institutions wield power? What are cultural ideology and cultural hegemony?

3. What is institutionalized gendered/sexed violence? What evidence of it did you discover? Is it necessary to address violence in the study of gender in communication? Why?

4. Why is an institutional approach to gender in communication important?

CHAPTER 7

Families

Beck Laxton and Kieran Cooper, a heterosexual couple from England, wanted to raise their child free from the stereotypical demands of gender. They wanted Sasha to be free to play with toys commonly associated with girls or boys. They took this commitment so seriously they asked not to know the sex of their child until 30 minutes after the birth and gave Sasha a gender/sex–inclusive name. Sasha's sex was not revealed to others until kindergarten, when the parents felt they would no longer be able to control the knowledge of it. Their gender-neutral approach to parenting elicited a great deal of attention. In response to an article about the family appearing in *Mail Online* (Wilkes, 2012), readers posted the following comments (which the paper capped at 1,450).

A case of brain cell deficient parents. Poor child. Ed, UK, 21/1/2012 10:07

What a gorgeous little boy, but he does look very much like a boy so I wouldn't imagine many people were fooled. What silly people, with so much more serious stuff going on in the world. Caroline, England (Still?), 21/1/2012 10:07

My daughter plays with Lego and dolls, dresses up like a princess and a pirate, does ballet and plays football . . . isn't that just how children play? paul, east yorkshire, 21/1/2012 10:06

I feel sorry for any of the parents at the school this child goes to, nightmare. Andy, Bath, 21/1/2012 10:00

They obviously wanted a daughter. Suzee, Usa, 21/1/2012 9:58

Calling your son "the infant" is possibly the most cold term you could use to refer to your child. Idiots! Ben, Birmingham, 21/1/2012 9:57

Figure 7.1 Beck Laxton with her child Sasha

Source: Retrieved from www.dailymail .co.uk/news/article-2089474/Beck-Laxton-Kieran-Cooper-reveal-sex-gender-neutral-child-Sasha.html (photograph by Warren Gunn)

We fight for the right of parents to educate their kids how they wish, at home or in a private school, we are happy for parents to impose religious orientation on their children. So why is everyone so angry if the parents choose to bring their child up gender neutral. They are not denying or trying to change is [*sic*] sex nor his sexual orientation but have concerns, which we may not all share, about the stereotyping of dress and behaviours. It's only taking it a little bit further than the common practice amongst caring parents to ensure that their little girl not only gets to play with dolls and my little pony but also meccano, Lego, chemistry sets and telescopes. Richard, Cheltenham, 21/1/2012 6:33

The volume of responses to this article suggests people have strong opinions on how to raise children and a strong resistance to efforts to embrace more fluid gender learning in the home. What do the responses reveal about relationships between gender/sex and family communication? Why is gender-neutral parenting receiving so much feedback? How do you react to the photo of Sasha? Do you have an overwhelming need to know Sasha's sex? Why?

We open with this example because when people choose to resist cultural norms, they make cultural norms visible as institutional social constructions. Assumptions that boys will be boys, girls will be girls, and they should perform their genders accordingly, are deeply entrenched in family communication.

In this chapter, we explore how gendered expectations about parenting tend to constrain families. To understand how gender is constructed through families and how gender organizes families, we unpack the ideology and myths associated with families. The first myth is that there is only one normal form of family. The second myth is that because of variations from this norm, the well-being of the family and society generally are threatened.

To unpack the myths and show how they influence families' gendered communication, we provide historical information to challenge each myth. The first myth relies on the ideology of dating, romance, and the compulsion that everyone be coupled in a heterosexual family. In response to the second myth, we explain why some believe the family is in crisis: relaxed gender expectations, more women working outside the home, cohabitation, same-sex marriage, and divorce.

With the myths unpacked, we then explore how traditional gender norms play out *and* get challenged in parent-child communication, sibling communication, marital communication, and domestic violence. We end with a discussion of a more positive picture of the state of families. Researchers note that U.S. people tend to value family life as much as ever, the structure of families and roles of members are more diverse, and fluid gender identities are the solution for maintaining families as a vital aspect of culture (Gerson, 2010; Walsh, 2012).

Defining Family and Gender/Sex Roles

The concept of family is difficult to define, as there is no set structure, purpose, or communicative meaning-making process that defines family (Segrin & Flora, 2011). Instead, multiple family structures exist (e.g., single parent, extended, stepfamilies, child-free couples, LBGT couples, nonbiological families of choice). The structures shift across time and cultures, and the functions families provide as well as the meanings created are diverse (Karraker & Grochowski, 2012). Because family is not a fixed concept, it requires a fluid description (Hoover, Clark, & Alters, 2004). How researchers define family influences what types of families are studied and further legitimized. Thus, we adopt a definition of **family** that takes into account the structure, purpose, and communicative processes involved in families:

> Any group of people united by ties of marriage, blood, or adoption, or any sexually expressive relationship, in which (1) the adults cooperate financially for their mutual support, (2) the people are committed to one another in an intimate interpersonal relationship, (3) the members see their individual identities as importantly attached to the group, and (4) the group has an identity of its own. (DeGenova, Stinnett, & Stinnett, 2011, p. 5)

The institution of family governs norms of gender/sex, sexual orientation, race, ethnicity, and class. Quite simply, "Families and gender are so intertwined that it is impossible to understand one without reference to the other. Families are not merely influenced by gender; rather, families are *organized* by gender" (Haddock, Zimmerman, & Lyness, 2003, p. 304). This organization is apparent in the prescribed roles played in many families: mother, father, daughter, son, sister, brother, grandmother, grandfather, aunt, uncle, in-laws. These roles are sex marked and designate responsibilities, expectations, and power. The term **gender/sex roles** refers to binary gender social expectations based on a person's sex (Ryle, 2012).

You may think, "Strict gender/sex roles aren't true today . . . at least not in my family." Although stereotypes do not define families completely, the awareness of noncompliance means the stereotyped expectations still persist. Most people think of themselves as the exception to the norm. If you like to cook, being the primary food preparer does not seem like a gender/sex role demand (or burden). However, this leaves unanswered the question, why are more women than men socialized to like cooking and expected to be skilled at it? Why are more men than women socialized to like working on cars and expected to be skilled at it? Even when people do not want to or are unable to live up to gender/sex roles, they still are judged against the norms.

By focusing on family as an institution, we make clear how family practices contribute to the institutionalization of gender/sex discrimination. Micropractices (who cleans the toilet?) are maintained by individual socialization (who is typically assigned the chore of cleaning the toilet?) as well as macrostructures of discourse (how often is toilet bowl cleaner advertised during the Super Bowl versus weekday television soap operas?) and law (what is a fair wage for those who clean toilets versus those who mow lawns?).

Myth #1: The Nuclear Family as the Norm

Where did the stereotypes of gender/sex prescribed family roles come from? During the Industrial Revolution of the 1800s, current stereotypical notions of masculinity and femininity emerged along with the concept of the nuclear family.

The **nuclear family** presumes a self-supporting, independent unit (excluding extended family) composed of two heterosexual parents legally married performing separate masculine and feminine family roles. For nuclear families, the male is the primary wage earner and the female is the primary homemaker. The nuclear family is considered the embodiment of a healthy family and the foundation of society (Ruane & Cerulo, 2008; Walsh, 2012). In reality, though, the nuclear family has never been the most common family structure, and any family structure is susceptible to being unhealthy.

Sociologists describe the nuclear family as the elusive traditional family because historians cannot point to one specific time when this family structure actually prevailed (Coontz, 1992, 1997, 2006). Most scholars have concluded that "the form of the 'typical' American family has changed quite frequently throughout our nation's history. Indeed, historically speaking, the nuclear family is a fairly recent as well as a relatively rare phenomenon" (Ruane & Cerulo, 2008, p. 208). Even during the Industrial Revolution, it was an ideal, a status symbol, achieved for some on the backs of the working class—racial and ethnic minority families where the women were domestic help in other people's homes.

In preindustrial, pre-mass production times before the 1700s, families were work units, and all members (including children, boarders, and hired hands) worked to contribute to a family's economic livelihood. Work was shared across sexes and age groups, extended family lived under one roof, and single-parent households were common due to early mortality. As the Industrial Revolution progressed, manliness was demonstrated by a man's ability to support his family with his income alone. As such, the public sphere of business was thought to be exclusively for men, even though not all families could afford to live on the man's wages alone, nor did all families have men. Only middle- and upper-class White Western women were able to focus exclusively on the family's social activities and household needs. Although not all women could afford to stay at home, domesticity became the norm for judging women's worth. True womanhood was defined as pure, pious, domestic, and submissive (Welter, 1976).

In spite of the influence of the Industrial Revolution, the nuclear family and its rigid gender roles did not become more firmly planted into U.S. ideology until the 1950s. Rapid economic growth enabled and popular media representations normalized the male wage earner. Situation comedies such as *Father Knows Best* (1954–1960), *Ozzie & Harriet* (1952–1966), and *Leave It to Beaver* (1957–1963) modeled White, middle-class nuclear families. Interestingly, during this time there was also an increase in consumer demands, which resulted in an increase of 2 million White, middle-class women working outside the home. Most poor White, African American, Asian American, and Hispanic American women never left the workforce; they have always had to juggle work and family demands (Ruane & Cerulo, 2008).

The assumption that heterosexual romantic love should be the basis of marriage and family is a prominent U.S. value, but it is not universally shared and was never the basis of all marriages. Into the 1800s, marriage was based on financial need, control of reproduction, political concerns, and family arrangements, not love (Cancian, 1989). These factors still play a role in many marriages, particularly outside the United States. Passionate love is one form of love between sexual partners, and it does not tend to be the most enduring.

Why and how has the myth of the nuclear family and its accompanying gender roles persisted in the face of diverse and rapidly changing families? People have internalized this model as the ideal. Although many people assume their family structure will mirror the nuclear family ideal, in reality, what is most common is quite different and decidedly *not* the nuclear family.

A major contributor to maintaining this myth is heteronormativity. **Heteronormativity** encompasses legal, cultural, organizational, and interpersonal practices that reinforce unquestioned assumptions about gender/sex. These include

> the presumptions that there are only two sexes; that it is "normal" or "natural" for people of different sexes to be attracted to one another; that these attractions may be publicly displayed and celebrated; that social institutions such as marriage and the family are appropriately organized around different-sex pairings; that same-sex couples are (if not "deviant") a "variation on" or an "alternative to" the heterosexual couple. (Kitzinger, 2005, p. 478)

In addition, the "socially approved economic and sexual union" represented by heteronormative romance and heterosexual marriage is the cornerstone of the traditional nuclear family (Ruane & Cerulo, 2008, p. 215).

To be perfectly clear, we are not criticizing individual families who fit the nuclear family model nor are we suggesting this structure of family is innately harmful. We are criticizing prominent ideologies that insist there is only one type of normal family. We want to explore how this narrow, unrealistic concept of family became and remains pervasive. Whether in a nuclear family or not, the narrow definition of family directly or indirectly affects everyone. Even in non-U.S. cultures, the ideal of the nuclear family is increasingly becoming the standard from which one judges her or his own and others' families (Ingoldsby & Smith, 2006). The heteronormative nuclear conception of family affects how people approach friendships, dating, and the social ritual of weddings.

Friendship

An indication of the ideological power of heterosexual romance is how platonic friendships tend to be devalued in U.S. culture. Friendships receive no ceremonial celebration; no legal, political, religious, or other institutional support; and people are encouraged to have same-sex platonic friends rather than cross-sex friends. Over the course of one's life, friendships typically receive less time and attention than family relationships. Cross-sex friendships among heterosexuals and perhaps same-sex friendships among LGBTQ people are often seen as a threat to committed romantic relationships (Bleske-Rechek et al., 2012). Thus, the threat upholds marriage as the most important relationship. Take an inventory of your own friendships with the following questions.

> **Consider who you call a close friend. How many share your**
>
> gender/sex?
>
> sexual orientation?
>
> race/ethnicity?
>
> age range?
>
> nationality?
>
> religion?

Although choices in friendship may seem personal, cultural norms largely constrain one's choices. You may find yourself continually defending friendships you choose outside these categories (Ryle, 2012). Fortunately, many people now report enjoying cross-sex nonromantic friendships and the taboos regarding them seem to be lessening with each generation (Monsour, 2006).

Even in a heteronormative culture that encourages people to have same-sex friends, there is often competition among young adult same-sex friends, making genuine friendship a challenge. Consider the following college women's comments about same-sex friends:

> "Girls are just mean. Even when they don't know each other they are so negative and judgmental."

> "All of my friends are guys because girls are never nice to me."

> "I think all girls view each other as competition in some way or another."

> (Norwood, 2006, p. 2)

Research on women's friendships consistently demonstrates that ideals of feminine beauty and heternormativity encourage girls and young women to see each other as competition for male attention.

Heteronormative hegemonic masculinity sets limits on men's friendships, too. Often men are encouraged to compete and prove who is more masculine. However, unlike women who compete for the attention of men, men's studies scholar Michael Kimmel (2008) suggests men's performance of masculinity is done more to gain the approval of other men than to attract women.

Dating

Heterosexual dating is the most studied type of nonmarital relationship—a fact that indicates the social privilege attached to it. Relatively little research examines the role of gender in dating relations for same-sex partners, transgendered persons, non-White couples, or non-Western couples. What is known is that even though dating patterns have changed tremendously in the United States (more hooking up instead of dating, more couples cohabitating, and more persons delaying marriage or choosing not to marry), the ideological normativity of heterosexual intimacy persists.

This ideology of intimacy is manifested primarily through romance expectations. Images of heterosexual relationships in movies demonstrate this. The most desired romance is young, between an attractive masculine man and an attractive feminine woman, usually of the same race or ethnic group, and it hinges around passionate sexual attraction, an attraction that is usually initiated by men. Movies that consistently show up on lists of the top 100 romantic comedies posted on the Internet Movie Database (IMDb) make clear how, across time, this dynamic operates. As these movies demonstrate, the focus is on young, white, heterosexual couples shown in poses that indicate romantic, if not sexual, attraction (see Figure 7.2).

Figure 7.2

In a review of the literature, communication scholar Sandra Metts (2006) identifies general patterns in the **gender role scripts** of dating relationships, noting "both gender and dating are social constructions enacted through communication" (p. 25). A few of the dating gender role scripts Metts (2006) identifies include the following:

- Regardless of sexual orientation, men place priority on a date's physical attractiveness and women on personality.
- Women should make themselves attractive to men.

- Men should take the lead in initiating first activities, from dates, to saying "I love you," to sexual relations.
- Women should take the lead in relationship maintenance.
- Sexual relations are an expected part of relational progression, but they need not wait for a verbal expression of love.

In terms of heterosexual dating norms, the predominant expectation is still that men will initiate dates and physical intimacy and that women will take primary responsibility for relationship maintenance (Laner & Ventrone, 2000).

White Weddings

In U.S. culture, the purpose of heterosexual dating is to find a suitable partner for marriage. Many girls and some boys, including those who are LGBTQ, begin rehearsing wedding ceremonies as children. Marriage, and more immediately the wedding, has become a symbol of attaining adulthood in U.S. culture. Weddings are the ultimate heteronormative tradition with families spending well beyond their means to host them.

The Cost of White Weddings: A $9 Billion Industry

According to a survey of 18,000 couples married in 2011,
   The average wedding budget (excludes honeymoon) was $27,021.
   The average cost per guest was $196.
The survey was conducted via the Internet, by two websites (theknot.com and weddingchannel.com) targeted at helping couples plan the perfect wedding. Cited in Kim (2011).

From early on, girls and boys are pressured: to have boyfriends or girlfriends; to learn to flirt with the other sex; to devalue, distrust, and compete in nonromantic same-sex friendships; and to see marriage as a life accomplishment. In the best-known fairy tales such as *Cinderella* and *Snow White*, strong, young, White men save and then marry beautiful, young, White women, living happily ever after. Such fairy tales, popularized by Disney, contribute to unrealistic romantic expectations and enforce the notion that women are weak and need to be saved by men and that men are strong and never need to be saved (Bell, Haas, & Sells, 2008; Do Rozario, 2004; Hoerrner, 1996). The fantasies largely ignore people of color, as if to say they cannot have such dreams; even when other races are present, they are treated as an exotic other, not a character with which to identify (Lacroix, 2004).

Yet regardless of race, class, or sexual orientation, people are socialized to want marriage. Related rituals reinforce the desire. The debutante ball from African American culture and quinceañera from Latin American culture are coming-out parties families throw for their daughters when they turn 15 or 16. Girls wear fancy white gowns, and the family invites everyone they know to a dinner dance. The events mark a girl's transition into womanhood. Purity balls are a more recent trend (1998 was the first) among some conservative Christian groups where fathers are the daughters' date for a formal evening culminating in the girls promising their fathers chastity until marriage and their fathers promising to protect and guide their daughters' lifestyle ("Purity Ball," 2012). Held about the time of a girl's onset of menstruation, they mark her entry to womanhood, but it is a particular type of womanhood—a virginal, upper-class, largely White heterosexual one.

You might notice there seems to be no parallel public event for young men. A possible exception is the Jewish coming-of-age celebrations, Bar Mitzvah for 13-year-old boys and Bat Mitzvah for 12-year-old girls. While clearly gendered/ sexed events, these are not tied to marital availability.

Ingraham (2008) believes that the romanticized white wedding (and we would add the debutante ball, quinceañera, and purity ball) is a primary cultural tool for institutionalizing heterosexuality as the norm, the standard from which all relationships are judged. Marriage (especially if it results in children) remains a primary way people can raise their socioeconomic status.

Myth #2: The U.S. Family Is in Decline

A quick survey of the Internet would have you believe the U.S. family is in crisis, under attack, and in decline. This view has been around since the early 1990s when U.S. politicians and clergy repeatedly used the slogan "family values," in which *family* means nuclear family (Cloud, 1998). The slogan refers to a heterosexual married couple and multiple children living together in a home guided by conservative Christian principles and blames increasing diversity of family structures for the decline of the family. Presidential candidate Pat Buchanan used "family values" in the 1992 presidential election to advance a "cultural war . . . for the soul of America" (par. 37).

In contrast, we argue the institution of the family is in transition. Most U.S. people want to marry, including same-sex couples seeking legal marriages. But as of 2011 only 51% of people 18 or older are married, down from 72% in 1960 (Cohn, Passel, Wang, & Livingston, 2011). More people are cohabiting instead of marriage (10%, LGBTQ and heterosexual), cohabiting before marriage, marrying later in life (age 26 for women, 28 for men), not marrying because of pregnancy (Gibson-Davis, 2011), and staying single (LGBTQ and heterosexual; U.S. Census Bureau, 2010).

Although the divorce rate is higher than it was before no-fault divorce laws were enacted in the 1970s, the rates decreased starting in 2010 to 1.89 new marriages to 1 divorce, compared to 2.05 to 1 in 2000 (see Figure 7.3). The 2 to 1 U.S. divorce ratio commonly is misinterpreted. It means in a given year, for every two new marriages, one will fail. The ratio does not include previously existing marriages. Furthermore, the ratio for first-time marriages decreased a bit (Centers for Disease Control and Prevention, 2005; "Fifty Percent," 2012).

One may not see families as healthy today because families are adapting to increased economic demands, changed standards of living, and more flexible gender/ sex expectations. Yet these very transitions enable families to thrive.

Figure 7.3   Divorce Trends, 1960-2009. Rates per 1,000 of total population.

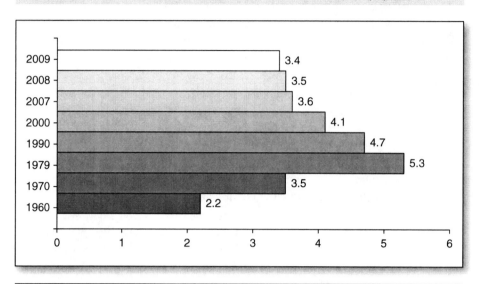

Source: Centers for Disease Control and Prevention. (2011). Births, marriage, divorces, and deaths: Provisional data for 2009. *National Vital Statistics Reports* 58(25). Retrieved from www.cdc.gov/nchs/fastats/divorce.htm.

In *Unfinished Revolution: How a New Generation Is Reshaping Family, Work, and Gender in America*, sociologist Kathleen Gerson (2010) randomly sampled 120 people ages 18 to 32 living in New York, who grew up in different parts of the United States, with diverse race, ethnicity, social class, sexual orientation, and family background. She interviewed each one, asking for a family life history. She found, across a wide variety of family-of-origin experiences, participants wanted parents to provide emotional and economic support. The structure of the family was basically irrelevant. Regarding the participants' expectations for their future family life, the young adults expressed hope and concern. The concerns were largely tied to gender expectations, as they wanted long-lasting egalitarian relationships but were concerned about balancing work and family demands. For example, most of the women wanted to be autonomous and self-reliant and saw employment as essential for their well-being. Many of the men were concerned about how sharing parenting and domestic tasks might negatively affect their careers. Gerson (2010) argues for a focus on family as a process, not a structure. The process that seemed to work best for participants was one in which their parents were able to demonstrate gender flexibility and adjust to families' changing challenges over time. Gerson (2010) recommends gender flexibility as a way for families to prepare for and adapt to 21st-century uncertainties:

> Most young women and men do not see the sexes as opposites who possess different capacities and occupy different planets. They reject a forced choice between personal autonomy and lasting commitment, preferring a relationship and a vision of the self that honors both. (p. 190)

More rigid parental behaviors may leave families ill prepared to cope with unexpected contingencies.

In a review of research on gender and sexual orientation in families, Walsh (2012) argues the new norm is pluralistic family structures. Families are one important place where tolerance of diversity can be taught and lived. More flexible gender roles and teaching gender tolerance can help families be more adaptable to cultural *and* individual needs.

Communicating in Families

In this section, we explore how traditional gender norms are expressed and challenged in families, focusing on three types of interaction: parent-child, children's, and couple. We end with a discussion of how violence is institutionalized in families in the form of domestic violence.

Parent-Child Communication

Even before children are born, parents influence their gender identity. Sociologist Emily Kane (2009) found in interviews with 42 women and men that most knew what sex they wanted their child to be and why:

> African American, working-class, heterosexual father: I always wanted a son, someone that would respect me the most, and that would be a male, since I am a male. . . . I wanted to teach my son to play basketball. I wanted to teach my son to play baseball, and so forth.

> White upper/middle-class, lesbian mother: I envisioned that a daughter would be sweet, a great companion in old age. . . . We would do things together, a lot of girl time. . . . A girl would never forget your birthday, would be much more emotionally connected. (p. 372)

Most participants preferred boys, and the parents' comments suggest the sex of their child will influence how they interact with their child and the type of relationships they will seek to build. Before the child is even born, they are "rehearsing for potential interactions," and gender/sex seems central to those interactions (Kane, 2009, p. 378).

Parental models for children's gendered identities are particularly powerful because of children's extensive dependency. Social learning theory suggests children learn by observing and imitating others and by being rewarded for gender behaviors that are consistent with their sex and punished for those that are not (Bandura, 2002). Based on the findings that follow, we argue social learning does not always have to induce compliance with binary gender roles. Learning is contextual (Addis, Mansfield, & Syzdek, 2010).

Communication scholars Mark Morman and Kory Floyd (2006a, 2006b) report that fathers today are generally more affectionate with sons than fathers in previous generations and that both parties value physical affection in the relationship, at least until adolescence. Other intersecting identities may also influence how parents model more than gender/sex alone. Black feminist scholar Patricia Hill Collins (1994) describes an alternative form of motherhood evident among those who must prepare children to face discrimination. Although many (mostly upper-class Whites) might think of mothers as gentle souls who provide unconditional love and protective nurturing, others (many working-class people and African Americans) might think of mothers as the people who gave them the strength and ability to handle life's hard knocks.

Although most research suggests parents teach gender norms through nonconscious, routine forms of interaction, such as dads roughhousing and moms baking, parents may also consciously work to gender/sex their child. In Kane's (2006) study, parents, regardless of race, ethnicity, sexual orientation, or whether they were single or dual parenting, preferred to encourage their children toward activities culturally seen as masculine. They reported "enjoying dressing their daughters in sports themed clothing, as well as buying them toy cars, trucks, trains, and building toys. Some described their efforts to encourage . . . what they considered traditionally male activities such as t-ball, football, fishing, and learning to use tools" (pp. 156–157). Fathers especially wanted their daughters to be athletic. An African American, working-class, heterosexual father said, "I don't want her just to color and play with dolls, I want her to be athletic" (p. 157).

In contrast, although 21 of the 42 parents praised their son's abilities in domestic chores and being nurturing and empathic, most did so with a counterbalance to assure he was not too soft, such as reprimanding sons who cried frequently. Boys' desire to own or play with Barbie was particularly troublesome to most, especially heterosexual fathers. Even parents who said they personally were more open to such behaviors expressed concern that their sons would be teased and labeled homosexual. One White, heterosexual, middle-class mother whose son wanted a Barbie explained, "I would ask him, 'What do you want for your birthday' . . . and he always kept saying Barbie. . . . So we compromised, we got him a NASCAR Barbie" (Kane, 2006, p. 161). Lesbian/gay parents expressed similar concerns but for different reasons—fear of mistreatment of their child by others.

Parents believe their choices will help steer their children in gendered and sexually oriented ways and that gender is not simply a matter of allowing some natural identity to emerge. One also can infer that parents realize that girls who adopt traditional masculine behaviors will raise their social status, but boys who adopt feminine behaviors risk losing social status. The parents were not trying to maintain binary gender differences for boy and girl children as one might expect. They were devaluing many activities and characteristics associated with girls, whether they had girl or boy children. A White, middle-class, heterosexual father said of his son,

> If [he] were to be gay, it would not make me happy at all. I would probably see that as a failure as a dad . . . because I'm raising him to be a boy, a man I don't want him to be a little "quiffy" thing, you know. . . . It's probably my own insecurities more than anything. I guess it won't ruin his life. (Kane, 2006, p. 163)

This comment demonstrates that parent-child communication affects parents' gender identity too. Parenting seems to encourage some adults to become more restrictive in their own gender performance. Once they realize they are role models and need to set an example that will help their children fit in socially, some seem to become less flexible in their own gender performance: for example, fathers become careful not to cry in front of their children, mothers become conscious of what color clothing they buy their children (lavender and pink for girls, blue and green for boys; Kane, 2012). An alternative example comes from parents with children who resist normative cisgender expectations.

Psychologist Diane Ehrensaft (2011), director of the Bay Area Youth Gender Acceptance Project in California, writes,

> In the feedback loop between parent and child [interaction and influence], the transgender or gender nonconforming child may be shaping the parent far more than the parent is shaping the child. The shaping begins with a child who is presenting the original kernel of the true gender self that existed at birth, whether as a result of genetics, biochemistry, prenatal environment, or some yet to be explained phenomenon. (p. 536)

She suggests some parents change and transform to provide their child the love and support needed to overcome adversities. They do this through time and work: coming to their own gender authenticity and by recognizing their child has an identity separate from theirs. Parents who do not do this may adhere to rigid gendered expectations for themselves as parents and for their child, enabling bullying and sexual harassment toward the child inside and outside the home.

Children's Communication

Children, too, play an active role in constructing gendered/sexed identities in the family (Ehrensaft, 2011; Kane, 2012; Malpas & Lev, 2011). Young children search for cues for appropriate gender/sex behavior: Who should they seek for comfort when hurt? Who should they play with? Who can they roughhouse with? According to gender schema theory, children selectively choose stimuli that seem consistent with their gender identity. Parents tend to give children gender-specific toys, and children tend to choose gender-specific toys once they learn their prescribed gender identity and which toys are gender/sex appropriate (Eliot, 2009a). In other words, children gender/sex themselves.

Siblings and birth order also seem to influence gender identities, with younger siblings modeling older siblings' gendered behaviors. Girls who have older brothers have been found to show more masculine identities than girls without siblings or with other sisters. Boys with older sisters have been found to show more feminine identities than those without or those with older brothers (Eliot, 2009a).

Couple Communication

Perhaps as testament to the powerful ideology of romantic relationships, heterosexual marriage is the most studied type of interpersonal relationship. Two topics are prominent in the literature: domestic labor and conflict communication.

Domestic labor. The issue of domestic labor recurs in discussions of gender/sex in family communication because domestic labor not only produces household goods and services but also produces gender (Coltrane, 1989; Hochschild, 2003;

Shelton & John, 1996). Historically, men's sex role was to be a good financial provider. But as more wives entered the paid labor force from the 1950s on, the necessary, unpaid, and often unrecognized duties at home fell into question. Who would do the housework and child care? Until very recently, the overwhelming answer for heterosexual homes has been women. As a financial provider, men could choose and/or negotiate tasks with their spouse. Imbalanced housework distribution between men and women has been one of the clearest indicators of the continuing influence of the nuclear family norm and its inequitable gender roles.

Gender/Sex Distribution of Household Work

For Women
Housework* hours per week went from 32 in 1965 to 19 in 2000.
Child care** hours per week declined from 10 to 8½ from 1965 to 1975 but
    rose after 1985 to 13 hours a week, where it remained as of 2010.
Total of 32 hours of work at home on top of full-time employment

For Men
Housework* hours per week went from 4 hours in 1965 to 10 hours in 1985
    and remains there.
Child care** hours were stable at 2½ hours per week from 1965 to 1985 but
    increased by 2000 to 7 hours per week.
Total of 17 hours of work at home on top of full-time employment
*(housework = cleaning, cooking, food shopping, lawn care, in addition to managing the family, purchasing goods and services, and so on)
**(child care = feeding, clothing, bathing, making and keeping doctor's
    appointments, helping with homework, playing, reading, and maintaining
    relations with extended family such as grandparents)

(Bianchi, Raley, & Casper, 2012; U.S. Census Bureau, 2010)

Gender/sex distribution of household work is closer to being balanced than before, but even surveys that recognize men's contributions in the home still a show a difference of 15 hours. Surveys consistently show women tend to do more unpaid work in the home. One way couples have sought increased balance is by lowering standards and simplifying tasks to cut the number of hours spent doing housework. Women and men have stepped up the hours devoted to child care. Men tend to be more involved in their children's lives than in previous generations.

Conflict communication. Local bookstores' shelves of self-help books and women's magazines reveal communication problems in marriage are to be feared (instead of seen as a normal result of interdependent lives). Because the advice targets women, it positions them as responsible for addressing marital problems. These expectations are largely based on assumptions of binary innate gender differences. The book title that has made this assumption most vivid is *Men Are From Mars, Women Are From Venus* by John Gray (1992). Gray has since written 12 other books with title variations such as *Why Mars and Venus Collide, Mars and Venus in Love, Mars and Venus on a Date, Mars and Venus in the Bedroom,* in addition to his high-dollar workshops. Gray enjoys popularity despite the fact that family therapists and communication scholars have declared his advice directly contradicts findings of marriage and family research, feminist theory, and principles underlying the "best practices" of the counseling field (Zimmerman, Haddock, & McGeorge, 2001, p. 55; Wood, 2002).

Interpersonal communication scholars and marital therapists see conflicts in long-term relationships as inevitable, based on the degree and types of interdependence (Baxter, 2010; Kelley et al., 1983). Researchers have focused on a particularly ineffective pattern of marital conflict called the **demand/withdrawal pattern** in which the partner who most wants a change demands (through complaints, criticisms, or other forms of pressure), and the one who does not want change resists (by withdrawing in some way, such as changing the topic, eye avoidance, or leaving the room), resulting in a failure to resolve the conflict (Papp, Kouros, & Cummings, 2009). One behavior triggers the other and vice versa. For example, if Jo wants Casey to stop playing the video game and talk, Casey does not want to, Casey withdraws from Jo, and Jo makes more demands. Repeatedly researchers have found wives tend to demand (i.e., for closeness), and husbands tend to withdraw (i.e., for independence; Christensen, Eldridge, Catta-Preta, Lim, & Santagata, 2006; Gottman, 1994; Walker, 1999). These findings have been linked to traditional gender roles. The two-culture theory suggests the woman demands because her relationship orientation is toward talk and the man withdraws because he is socialized to value unilateral problem solving. Men prefer to fix problems alone, and if a problem cannot be repaired, men will not see value in discussion (Tannen, 1990).

There are several problems with this explanation. First, the person who raises the topic tends to be the demander regardless of gender/sex in heterosexual and same-sex couples (Baucom, Snyder, & Gordon, 2009; Holley, Sturm, & Levinson, 2010; Papp et al., 2009). Second, parents and children display this pattern as well, with parents demanding more than children, regardless of the gender/sex of the parent (Caughlin & Ramey, 2005). Third, couples in distressed relationships over time seem to lock into stereotypic binary gender roles of wife demanding, husband withdrawing, even when they are not presently in conflict (Eldridge, Sevier, Jones, Arkins, & Christensen, 2007). That is, people adhere to rigid binary roles when there is stress in the relationship, and, once adopted, these roles are difficult to change. Regardless of gender/sex, relationship type, and which partner plays which role, falling into a habit of demand/withdraw can lead to negative emotions, lower levels of conflict resolution, spousal depression, and domestic violence (Papp et al., 2009).

Domestic Violence

It is a common assumption that most violence, particularly sexual violence, is perpetrated by a male stranger lurking in dark shadows at night to attack a female. This assumption is false. A person who inflicts interpersonal violence is usually someone who is known, such as a romantic partner or a family member. Intimate violence is the most common form of violence against women in the United States; 28% to 50% of women experience physical, mental, emotional, and/or verbal abuse from an intimate partner (Catalano, 2012). About four in five reported victims of intimate-partner violence are female; men are less likely to report or file charges (Catalano, 2012).

We want to make clear that a focus on individual seemingly random acts of violence is insufficient to understand domestic violence. The pervasiveness of violence in intimate relationships, and specifically in families, indicates it is a common part of this institution, hence the term **domestic violence**: physical, psychological, and/or sexual abuse within a couple or family unit.

The institution of family enables violence because it obscures and denies that violence occurs there. In the United States, people assume the primary function of family is to create a home (a welcoming, protective, loving, intimate environment). When violence occurs in the home, family members and communities often deny its existence. Public discussions about domestic violence tend to focus on extreme forms and consider individuals' psychological illnesses the primary causes of violence, making it more difficult to recognize the roles of gender and power in perpetuating violence (Harris, Palazzolo, & Savage, 2012).

Violence exists in all forms of intimate relationships. Gay and lesbian couples report being victims of violence, as do siblings, grandparents, and especially children. Here we focus on couple violence as tied to gender/sex, making clear not all couple violence is the same.

At least three types of couple violence exist. Most early research focused on wife battering from husbands abusing their power and seeking to control. Also known as intimate terrorism, Kelly and Johnson (2008) have renamed it **coercive controlling violence**: forms of violence where a pattern of multiple strategies is used to seek power and control over the other person. Communication scholar Michael Johnson (2006) suggests this type of violence is fed by institutional influences. The abuse is tied to traditional gender expectations that men should be the head of the household, leading men who feel they are not meeting this expectation to perform their masculinity through dominance and control. The physical abuse is generally accompanied with verbal and emotional abuse, destroying the partner's self-esteem with repeated messages such as "No one else would have you," "You are worthless," "You are ugly," "What would you do without me?"—all comments that boost the speaker's self-esteem by derogating the partner.

Coercive controlling violence has been tied to the demand/withdraw conflict pattern, which tends to worsen over time. Except once a partner's violence escalates, it is more likely the man or abuser who demands and the woman or victim who withdraws to avoid further abuse (Olson, 2002). The rigidity of the demand/withdrawal cycle helps to maintain control and abuse.

Johnson (2006) argues the cultural rhetoric of romance discussed previously plays a pervasive role in coercive controlling violence. Communication scholar Julia Wood (2001) discovered this link between abuse and romantic myths when interviewing women from abusive relationships who were strongly invested in predominant heterosexual gender expectations and fairy-tale notions of romance. Many spoke of failing in their responsibilities as women to care for their partners, or they insisted the abuse was out of character for the Prince Charming who had originally swept them off their feet. They would not leave the relationships because they felt they needed men to feel complete.

Coercive controlling violence should not be understood as an aberration in an otherwise well-functioning gendered family institution. Instead, it ought to be seen as a possible outcome of the cultural gendered/sexed pressures brought to bear on families.

A second type of domestic violence is **violent resistance**: a person tries to protect herself or himself by resisting the other's abuse. The resistance situation that receives the most media attention is women who murder their partners. In a study of women on trial for, or convicted of, attacking their intimate partner, they report frequent violent attacks from their partner, and most murders were not preplanned but took place during an attack from their partner (Ferraro, 2006). Donileen Loseke and Demie Kurz (2005) suggest the following:

> Men's violence toward women and women's violence toward men are not the same, because these acts occur within the historical, cultural, political, economic and psychological contexts of gender.... This gendered context includes the history of tolerance of men's violence toward women that continues to be taught and reinforced in social institutions such as sports and fraternities. It includes the normalization of violence against women in heterosexual romantic relationships. (pp. 84–85)

Coercive controlling violence and violent resistance are not the result of inherent sex differences but of socialization practices that tend to socialize some men into a form of masculinity that sees violence as a solution to problems.

The third type of domestic violence is the most common form of aggression: **situational couple violence**. This type of violence is perpetrated by both partners in heterosexual or same-sex relations, married or cohabitating. It is not typically tied to relationship-wide patterns of control and coercion. Either partner is likely to initiate the violence in specific situations, such as observing one's partner flirting with another person or stress due to finances or child concerns. The violence typically happens with less frequency within a particular relationship, and partners are not afraid of each other as in coercive controlling violence (Kelly & Johnson, 2008).

Not all domestic partner violence is the same. These distinctions are important because they prevent readers from overgeneralizing claims such as only men abuse or women are violent only when abused. Men do tend to inflict more serious physical injuries when they are violent and participate in all the listed forms of domestic violence more than women. Violence is inflicted on women and other men (Kelly & Johnson, 2008).

Flexible and Diverse Family Structures Today

You may have noticed we avoid using the term *the family*, except in reference to the institution and related ideology of the nuclear family. Instead we refer to families. *The* family suggests only one model of family exists, when in fact a wide variety of family structures exists within and across cultures. The highly respected academic journal previously named *Journal of Marriage and the Family* changed its name in 2001 to the *Journal of Marriage and Family* to better recognize the diversity of actual families (inside cover).

We conclude by offering examples of the less studied and acknowledged diverse family processes (and structures) thriving today. We are not attempting to replace one ideology (nuclear family) with another or suggesting alternate family structures are perfect. We offer these examples to illustrate the variety of ways in which gender/sex is being constructed and changed within diverse families and how more flexible gendered communication is actually at the center of helping families thrive.

Singles

Contrary to popular assumptions, a large number of childfree singles and single parents (widowed, divorced, or never married) live in the United States. The ideology of the nuclear family declares them inadequate, as lacking, due to the romantic expectation for adults to be coupled. Today, given the increasingly delayed age of first marriage, U.S. women now spend more years of their adult lives unmarried than married (DePaulo & Trimberger, 2008). Although it continues to be more acceptable for men to delay commitment or remain single, single women and men experience gender discipline when they are labeled unwanted, abnormal, selfish, homosexual, or socially inept (DePaulo, 2006). People without children are commonly called child*less*, rather than child*free*, as if not having children signals a lack (Morrell, 1994).

When singles do have children, critics worry the children will miss out on the important social learning the other parent might provide. They fear boys raised by women may become effeminate and girls raised by men may become tomboys. This concern is overstated for three reasons. First, sometimes being raised by a single parent is better than being raised in an abusive or neglectful structure. Second, single parents, like coparents, usually have a network of family and friends to help. Third, all men do not father in the same way, and all women do not mother in the same way.

Regardless of parental status, research suggests singles play multiple important roles in the larger society. In interviews with 43 single, middle-class women, one researcher found that across race, ethnicity, and sexual orientation, most of the women struggled with the cultural expectation that they must marry and have children, even if they were satisfied in their single lives (Trimberger, 2005). They felt the pressure to conform, yet the researcher observed strength in the single women's lives. Furthermore, when commitments are delayed, the strength and stability of the marriage and family are better.

In a review of research on singles, Bella DePaulo (2012) stressed the need to reframe the way society thinks about singles. Most are not without family, and research is needed to recognize the variety of ways single adults are contributing members of families. They may have families of choice as in friendships, they have parents, siblings, sometimes children, nieces, nephews, and many model for their families more flexibly gendered identities. Most have important, long-term relationships. They are less likely to settle for a relationship that is not healthy, and they have the skills of being autonomous and connected.

Engaged Fatherhood

If the norm has been for fathers to play more emotionally distant, wage-earning roles, then an alternative is for fathers to play more interpersonally active, emotionally engaged roles in the day-to-day caretaking of their children and other family members. Wide variances in fathering have always existed, and researchers continue to find more evidence of fathers playing central roles in child rearing (Cabrera & Tamis-LeMonda, 2013; Dienhart, 1998), but the myth of the distant, wage-earning father persists. Thus, the predominant cultural terministic screen about fatherhood as removed and detached must change.

The reality is that many men *are* primary caregivers. A 2010 U.S. Census Bureau report shows nearly 3 million men report being single fathers, up from 393,000 in 1970. A growing body of research documents men's increased efforts at engaged parenting. The benefits of engaged fathers are many, not only for children and mothers but also for fathers. In a review of research, communication scholars William Doherty and John Beaton (2004) found a positive relationship between involved parenting and a father's psychological well-being, confidence, and self-esteem.

Although fathering research is now being conducted, much of it, like the research on mothers, has focused on White, middle-class fathers who are primarily secondary caretakers and playmates for their children. Research on noncustodial divorced fathers, regardless of ethnic background, has shown an even more limited nurturing role. Compounding negative portrayals of fathers of color is the stereotype of Black fathers as irresponsible (which ignores the economic and educational disadvantages faced by many who are trying to provide for families) and the machismo, dictatorial image of Asian and Hispanic men (which makes it difficult for them to be seen as nurturing in the home).

Law professor Nancy Dowd (2000) argues that when researchers examine the roles fathers play, they must do so from an intersectional perspective:

Men's identities as fathers do not exist in isolation from their identities as men. Indeed, that broader masculine identity arguably poses the most difficult challenge to a redefined and differently lived fatherhood. . . . As long as masculinity is defined in opposition to femininity, and requires devaluing and stigmatizing things labeled feminine, men will be blocked from or conflicted by learning from female role models. The learning and valuing of nurture [*sic*] is blocked by misogyny and homophobia. . . . It is also challenged by the embrace of violence as a part of masculinity, a value or trait antithetical to nurture and care. (pp. 181–182)

Dowd points out that because being economic providers is how men prove their masculinity, "Black men are denied the means to be men in traditional terms" (p. 75). Thus, noninvolvement of fathers may be tied to social class. Poor men, regardless of race, ethnicity, or sexual orientation, have a more difficult time being involved in parenting. As long as men are expected to be the primary wage earners in the home, their ability to share parenting will be limited. Thus, if people want to seriously reconsider fatherhood, they also must reconsider motherhood and work (Dowd, 2000).

For example, Swedish parental insurance guarantees parents 480 days to take care of an infant, 390 of which are fully paid. Most dual-parent homes are choosing to split this time in some way. In interviews and observations with 20 gay and heterosexual, middle- and working-class fathers, one researcher suggests they are constructing new ideals of fathering. The fathers are not just sharing the more rewarding tasks (e.g., rocking or playing with a child) but the jobs of cleaning up diapers, cleaning bottles, and caring for the child. They were not comfortable talking about their role as "fathering," instead preferring "parenting." This does not mean they denied their masculinity but rather were redefining their masculine identities, placing more priority on their family life and seeking a balance between work and family. However, this arrangement is easier for middle-class and older fathers (Johansson, 2011).

Same-Sex Parents

Most of the research on nonheterosexual couples focuses on gay and lesbian families. They are gaining social acceptance due to legalization of same-sex marriage, the increased number of couples who are public, and the increased number of children being raised by gay and lesbian couples (Pew Research, 2010; Walsh, 2012). A substantial amount of research has examined whether having gay or lesbian parents negatively affects children's gender identity development. In a review of this research, Letitia Peplau and Kristin Beals (2004) reported the following:

There is no evidence that the children of gay and lesbian parents differ systematically from children of heterosexual parents. . . . No significant differences have been found in psychological well-being, self-esteem, behavioral problems, intelligence, cognitive abilities, or peer relations. . . . There is no evidence that the children of gay or lesbian parents are confused or uncertain about their gender identity. (p. 242)

Walsh (2012) concurs: "A large body of research over two decades has clearly documented that children raised by lesbian and gay parents fare as well as those reared by heterosexual parents in relationship-quality, psychological well-being, and social adjustment" (p. 14; see also Wainright & Patterson, 2008). In a quantitative study, researchers found children of same-sex couples faired equally well in quality of life (Geldern et al., 2012).

One of the common criticisms of same-sex couples is that they will raise their children to be homosexual, which suggests that sexual orientation is a teachable choice. Existing research shows that the majority of children from lesbian and gay parents grow up to identify as heterosexual, just like most children from heterosexual parents (Patterson, 2000).

Raising Transgender/Transsexual Children

Kristen Norwood (2012) and Melissa MacNish and Marissa Gold-Peifer (2011) studied how families adjust to gender nonconformity in their child. Both studies showed parents navigate complex tensions between accepting and loving their child and protecting their child from external social rejections. Lev and Malpas (2011) shared their experiences as family therapists facilitating support groups for such families. In one case, a mother clarified how the gender disciplining of her child also gender disciplined her:

> "The hardest part is not my relationship with my daughter and her fluidity, but it is having everyone, my family, the outside world, school, everyone scrutinize my parenting. I feel watched and always on the fault line. I feel bullied as a parent who loves my child for who she is. But I know she is going to grow up and I will be in her life. She will want to be with us because we have believed in her." (p. 5)

Many parents struggle to comprehend transgender identity, especially when it is a part of their family, but love can induce adaptation. For example, a father described as "a gruff man with an 8th grade education" agreed to attend a clinical support group. Here is what happened:

> "How do I raise a son without a penis?" he whimpered. He readily came into therapy and shared an experience he'd had at a construction site with "a woman . . . a person . . . a girl who looked like a guy." He watched his friends make jokes about her, and he said with anger in his voice, "That could be my child they are making fun of. Until this happened to us, I never would've understood. I would've laughed too . . . but now I understand when I see people on the street, who are, you know, queer in some way, I am the first person to defend them. . . . This has changed me." (p. 7)

Empathy, seeing others as fully human, may be the most important lesson this father learned.

The key for these families was becoming more flexible by accepting diverse gender identities, using more flexible interaction styles, employing more sensitive communication to respect the child's identity (e.g., proper pronoun usage), and providing a sense of stability for the child and the whole family through the communication of love and support.

Conclusion

The father just quoted summarized this chapter's lesson: "Talking about gender and sexuality will not only help families like us, families with a gay or gender-variant child. It will free everyone from having to think in such narrow ways. It will free us all from fear" (Lev & Malpas, 2011, p. 6). The importance of gender flexibility is a key research finding across studies and is important because "families who move beyond the limits of traditional gender are more able to respond to contemporary life challenges. . . . Children benefit developmentally when gender stereotypes are challenged and more possibilities are open to fit their needs and preferences" (Knudson-Martin, 2012, p. 340). Instead of forcing boys to shoot Nerf guns and girls to coddle baby dolls, parents can encourage more fluid gender roles and challenge stereotypes in their home by allowing children's imagination to run wild. We conclude by offering some suggestions for adults who want to encourage a full range of children's potentials.

> ## Subtle Way Adults Can Encourage Gender Flexibility
>
> Model flexible gender/sex behaviors—parents should take turns cooking or fixing the car.
>
> Be aware of what you model—in criticizing their own bodies, parents may be modeling unhealthy behaviors.
>
> Provide diverse gendered/sexed experiences—encourage a child to play sports and participate in theater; encourage a variety of playmates, rather than only same-sex playmates.
>
> Buy gender-inclusive toys to develop skills and creativity.
>
> Monitor your interruptions.
>
> Stop behaviors of bullying and other dominance patterns.
>
> Promote gender/sex equality through values, rules, and norms.
>
> Teach thoughtfulness—avoid talk that perpetuates "boys will be boys" or "girls should be doormats."
>
> Compliment a range of attributes—recognize all of a child's strengths, not just those that are gender specific. Instead, compliment children for being inquisitive, fearless, caring, and creative.
>
> (Adapted from Forbeswoman, 2012;
> Knudson-Martin, 2012)

In this chapter, we trace how family as a social institution, through the cultural ideology of the traditional nuclear family, constructs and maintains gendered/sexed identities of difference and inequality. The importance of the family becomes especially vivid when examining the prevalence of gendered/sexed violence and norms that contribute to it. As research better documents the diverse ways individuals construct families across cultures, families may be better able to create the good homes they are expected to provide.

KEY CONCEPTS

coercive controlling
    violence   156

demand/withdrawal
    pattern   155

domestic violence   156

family   143

gender role scripts   147

gender/sex roles   143

heteronormativity   145

nuclear family   144

situational couple
    violence   157

violent resistance   157

DISCUSSION QUESTIONS

1. What evidences do the authors give to illustrate Haddock et al.'s (2003) claim that "families and gender are so intertwined that it is impossible to understand one without reference to the other. Families are not merely influenced by gender; rather families are *organized* by gender" (p. 304).

2. Does studying family as a social institution affect the way you reflect on your own family experience? If so, how?

3. How does family construct and constrain gender?

4. Why are friendships and dating included in a chapter on the family as a social institution?

CHAPTER 8

Education

E ven when discussing the reading habits of U.S. schoolchildren, the meta-phor of gender wars rears its ugly head, as in an essay in *World: Today's News/Christian Views'* book section titled "Gender Wars: A New Survey Traces the Divide Between Elementary Boys' and Girls' Reading Tastes" (Olasky, 2008). As you might expect, there really is no war, and the author vastly overstates the gender divide given the results of Renaissance Learning's survey. Renaissance Learning provides a snapshot of what kids read every year, and the divide in 2012 is no bigger than it was in 2008. In their report, the most read books by first graders, boys *and* girls, were Dr. Seuss's *Green Eggs and Ham* and *The Foot Book*; by second graders, boys *and* girls—*Green Eggs and Ham* and Doreen Cronin's *Click, Clack, Moo: Cows That Type*; by third through sixth graders, boys *and* girls—Jeff Kinney's *Diary of a Wimpy Kid: The Ugly Truth*; by seventh graders, boys *and* girls—*Diary* and S. E. Hinton's *The Outsiders*; by eighth graders, boys *and* girls—*Outsiders* and *The Hunger Games*. You get the picture. There are more similarities than differences in boys' and girls' reading habits. Although some of this may have had to do with assignments from school, the report covered more than that.

Interestingly, in the report, novelist Ellen Hopkins points out, "The most fre-quently challenged books for the past three years" covered the following topics: "Sexuality. Gender identity. Physical, mental, and sexual abuse. Drugs. Race and racism. Religion. Diversity. The same issues that are being scrubbed or excised from schools, textbooks, discussions and, should certain special interests succeed, our society as a whole" (Renaissance Learning, 2012, p. 59).

We open with this example to highlight two points. First, the education of chil-dren is not a war over gender. Children's commonalities are greater than their dif-ferences. However, this does not mean gender/sex is not an issue in education. Education genders children, and the institution of education itself is gendered. Second, what students learn is something over which public debate occurs. Interestingly, even though sex, gender, race, violence, and diversity significantly affect social structures, these topics' inclusion in the curriculum is often challenged.

Joan Swann (2003), a British professor in education and language studies, explains the relationship among gender, communication, and education: "Insofar as gender is 'done' in educational settings it is done, to a large extent, through language. And insofar as language is gendered in educational settings, this will affect girls' and boys' development as 'schooled subjects,' in their experiences of education, and what they get out of it." (p. 624). To unpack the relationship between gender in communication and education, we examine how communication in and about the institution of education is gendered/sexed. In particular, we explore the history of education and its curriculum. We then look at the specific topics of classroom interaction, Title IX, performance gaps, peer pressure and bullying, and higher education. We end with a discussion of what emancipatory education might look like.

Education Is a Gendered Institution

When children cross the threshold of the classroom in preschool, they enter a social institution charged with their education for the next 12 years (and hopefully more). Once U.S. children enter the first grade, they usually spend an average of 7 hours a day, 5 days a week in a formal education institution. Those who graduate from high school have had a minimum of 12 years of formal educational influence during their most formative psychological, physical, moral, and intellectual developmental period.

Education is one of the most important influences on one's life, and a good education can contribute to raised income, career options, health, and quality of life. However, education is not only about imparting information and developing skills; it is a major socializing agent. Education influences identity formation, self-esteem, one's aspirations, determination, and more. Education has never been just about imparting some neutral information; implicit in what you learn are the values and biases of the culture.

The institution of education is a creator and keeper of socially sanctioned and respected knowledge. This is perhaps the most pervasive influence of education, as it legitimizes what is recognized as knowledge and who is given access to that knowledge. To make visible how education is gendered, we first offer a bit of history and then an assessment of curricula.

Education's History: Gendered/Sexed, Raced, and Classed

Education is an institution with the potential to be a great equalizer—a promoter of individual growth—but much of its history has been about being the great divider (Ruane & Cerulo, 2008). For the majority if its history, education has been the bastion of White male privilege. The history of U.S. education goes back to the early 1800s, to British public schools that taught wealthy boys how to be ruling-class men, preparing them for leadership in the armed services and business. This British model of education became the basis for schools in formerly colonized countries such as Australia, New Zealand, Canada, India, South Africa, and the United States. Thus, U.S. public education originally was intended exclusively for White, upper-class boys. African American slaves in the United States were prohibited from learning to read, as a way of controlling them (although many still learned to read with a Bible). Not until the early 1900s did poor people and racial/ethnic minority persons obtain education, particularly past the eighth grade. Public education—education for all—did not become the norm until the mid-1900s.

During the Victorian era, opponents to women's education believed their bodies could not withstand the rigors of education. Advances in theories of blood circulation had scientists believing that if women used their brains too much, it would divert blood from their wombs. Additionally, the stress of study might cause them to stop menstruating and become barren and unmarriageable (Minnich, 1998). Only White women from wealthy families could obtain higher education before the 1900s, and even they were discouraged from taking courses in what were considered the masculine domains of business, science, and mathematics. Colleges for women were usually finishing schools, focused on domestic skills to make a woman a good wife for a successful husband.

Fearing the specter of coeducation, in 1873, Dr. Edward H. Clarke warned that "identical education of the two sexes is a crime before God and humanity, that physiology protests against, and that experience weeps over" (p. 127). A few years later, scientist R. R. Coleman warned college women:

> Women beware. You are on the brink of destruction: . . . you are attempting to cultivate your mind . . . you are beginning to spend your mornings in study . . . you are exerting your understanding to learn Greek, and solve propositions in Euclid. Beware!! Science pronounces that the woman who studies is lost. (as cited in Ehrenereich & English, 2005, p. 141)

Educators also worried that coeducation would emasculate college curriculum by presenting it at a slower pace and simplifying it for women. It was thought that working side by side with girls would feminize boys. Critics not only worried boys would become effeminate; they worried boys would become gay (Kimmel, 2012a; Minnich, 1998).

As more women sought higher education in the early 1900s, women's colleges formed, following the highly successful model of Black colleges of the South. However, the majors and career options for women remained largely gendered. Faculty, parents, future employers, and students themselves believed the appropriate career options for women were secretary, teacher, and nurse (not all of which required college degrees). Furthermore, a woman's marital status determined if she could work outside the home at all. Up until the 1950s, in many states, women who were grade school teachers were forcibly "retired" when they married. The assumption was that they had a male provider and should let someone else have a paying job. Men were largely barred from these professions (because the professions were below them), and lower pay discouraged men from pursuing nontraditional gender/sex careers. These norms were strong up to the 1980s and still linger (Minnich, 1998).

Race and ethnicity also play a role in the history of education. The great migration of European immigrants into the United States in the early 1900s finally propelled the establishment of coeducational public education from kindergarten to 12th grade. The government created public schools to assimilate the recent immigrants into the English language and U.S. values (Andersen, 2011). Despite the push for assimilation of immigrants, schools in the South remained racially segregated until forced to integrate after, in 1954, the Supreme Court ruled in *Brown v. Board of Education* that separate schools are never equal in quality.

The debates over coeducation continue, with some arguing for a return to same-sex education, especially in primary and middle school. Advocates believe single-sex schools help counter underachievement, low self-esteem, drugs, teen pregnancy, and gang violence (NASSPE, 2006a, 2006b). But does segregated education trigger improvements? Liz Crowley, the principal of a predominantly Black urban grade school with a successful single-sex program said, "I don't think you can just put kids in a gender specific classroom and expect to see results" (quoted in Campbell, 2006, p. 3A). A closer look at same-sex classes shows they use a combination of improved teaching strategies that would help coeducational schools as well: tighter learning communities where the child stays with the same teacher for multiple years, more engaged parents, smaller class sizes, uniforms, opportunities for a wider variety of activities, and ways to assess one's gender identity beyond attractiveness to the other sex (Sadker & Zittleman, 2005). Finally, sex-segregated education divides students by sex; it does not take into account gender or sexual orientation, all of which may affect a child's degree of comfort in a same-sex educational program.

Curriculum: Gendered, Raced, Classed, and Heterosexist

When you crossed that preschool threshold, you probably did not think your experience would be affected by your gender/sex. Few do, but it is. How does this happen? While not all agree, many education researchers argue the curriculum is gendered masculine. It is not intentional but rather a **hidden curriculum**: norms, values, and beliefs as a byproduct of education that people often fail to question.

Consider what you learned in school. For example, history tends to be told as a series of battles where men play all the roles. How is it possible that so many White men played important roles in U.S. history but other groups did not? People know who the founding fathers are, but were there no founding mothers? Where are the contributions and struggles of Native Americans, African Americans, Hispanics, people with disabilities, and people who are LGBTQ? When people in these marginalized groups are noted, they tend to be presented as the exceptional one of their group or this part of their identity is hidden. For example, most people did not know the handsome and famous actor Rock Hudson was gay until he died in 1985 and are only now exploring evidence that President Abraham Lincoln had gay relations prior to his presidency (Morris, 2009). As a quick thought exercise, see if you can identify the following people and their contributions to the topic listed.

Topic	White Men	Women and People of Color
Abolition of slavery	Abraham Lincoln	Frederick Douglass, Maria Miller Stewart, Harriet Tubman, Sojourner Truth
U.S. revolution	George Washington, John Adams	Abigail Adams, Deborah Sampson Ganet, Margaret Corbin
Civil rights	John F. Kennedy, Lyndon Baynes Johnson	Rev. Martin Luther King, Jr., Fannie Lou Hamer, Thurgood Marshall, Ella Baker, Septima Poinsette Clark

Curriculum is gendered in terms of what is taught and to whom. Home economics traditionally is seen as feminine, whereas shop/auto mechanics is seen as masculine, even though students can take either course. Literature and language arts classes are associated with expressiveness, emotion, and relationships—in short, femininity. They are a part of the humanities and have been described as expressive and subjective. Social sciences linked to the humanities are called "soft" sciences. In contrast, math, technology, business, and science have traditionally been described as rigorous and objective—"hard" sciences. If these descriptions remind you of female and male anatomy, the similarity is not a misperception (Alcoff & Potter, 1993).

The hidden curriculum of education makes clear that a critical gender analysis must go further than simply comparing individual women and men for possible differences in educational experiences. A critical gender analysis of communication in and about education explores how society conceives of and pursues truth and knowledge. Furthermore, what gets taught to students as truth and knowledge reflects predominant cultural values.

A salient example of this process of knowledge construction took place in 2010, when the Texas Board of Education voted to approve new guidelines for social studies curriculum in elementary, middle, and high schools. Rather than selecting already written textbooks, the board told the expert authors what would and would not be included in the textbooks the state chose to endorse. These dictates affect more than one state. As the second largest state in the textbook market (California is first), Texas has major bargaining power, and what they do influences the remaining 48 states' textbook options and selections. The following are some of the changes made law until 2020. As you read through these changes, consider the hidden curriculum. What are some of the norms, values, and beliefs embedded in these changes?

- Eliminating the history of the Ku Klux Klan in Texas
- Excluding names of the Tejanos who died defending the Alamo
- Reinterpreting Thomas Jefferson's intent regarding the separation of church and state

- Incorrectly vindicating McCarthy for the 1950s arrests of celebrities charged as communists
- Focusing on the positive values of capitalism and equating it with free enterprise
- Making light of the need for the human rights movements in the 1960s
- Not including women and people of color (e.g., in a list of Congressional Medal of Honor recipients, the lone female recipient Mary Edwards Walker is not included)
- Including conservative, antifeminist author Phyllis Schlafly as a key contributor to society but excluding names of women who helped seek the right to vote in 1920 or Title IX in 1972
- Ignoring Dorothea Dix, Clara Barton, the Grimke sisters, and other abolitionists in general, even though their work helped raise consciousness to end slavery
- Naming many White women who contributed to Texas history but not African American or Mexican/Hispanic women

This rewriting of the curriculum is an example of abuse of institutional power. U.S. Education Secretary Arne Duncan said at one of the board meetings, "We do a disservice to children when we shield them from the truth, just because some people think it is painful or doesn't fit with their particular views" (as cited in "Texas Board," 2010). Clearly, much of what has been given the status of knowledge in the United States is the product of White, Western, capitalist, masculine viewpoints.

As the example of Texas illustrates, textbooks are important. Researchers comparing five seventh-grade life science books did not find overt sexism, but there were subtle forms of sexism in language choices and images used and few examples of activities that might motivate girls (Potter & Rosser, 2006). Another study of 15 college-level educational psychology textbooks used to train future teachers showed no gender/sex stereotypes in portrayals, with one sad exception. The books contained negative portrayals of boy students as troublemakers in the classroom (Yanowitz & Weathers, 2004).

Even the sciences, which are considered objective, are influenced by cultural biases. In a classic study, feminist scholar Inge K. Broverman and colleagues (1970) asked 79 therapists to define the psychological characteristics of three variations: a healthy adult person, a healthy adult man, and a healthy adult woman. Their replies described the healthy man and healthy adult almost identically as active, independent, adventurous, and logical. The healthy woman, by contrast, was described as dependent, emotional, subjective, passive, and illogical, characteristics ascribed to an "unhealthy" adult. The findings suggest women were in a double bind; an active, logical, and independent woman would be sick under the definitions used by the respondents. Until this study, mental health was defined according to stereotypical masculine qualities. These sexist assumptions were then passed on in college courses, medical schools, and in clinicians' assessments of patients.

This hidden curriculum has real effects. Even though statistically women and girls outnumber men and boys at every level of education,

> a gender gap persists in various dimensions of the schooling experiences. A hidden curriculum in schools is part of the gender socialization that produces different educational outcomes for women and men. Women become segregated into particular fields of education and still fall behind in education that leads to careers in math and science. (Andersen, 2011, p. 323)

The hidden curriculum, combined with gendered classroom interactions, creates differential education effects for women and men, Whites and people of color, and rich and poor.

Classroom Interactions

If gender is improvisation within a scene of constraint, then schools are one of the primary stages on which actors interact. Sociologist Margaret Andersen (2011) describes schools as "the stage where society's roles—roles defined by gender, class, race, sexuality, and age—are played out" (p. 304). Children are cast in particular roles and guided toward some subjects and discouraged from developing positive attitudes and skills in other subjects. Teachers do not set out to treat boys and girls differently, just as they don't set out to treat children differently because of race or ethnicity, but teachers' worldviews are influenced by the dominant culture. Although most teacher education programs now include some form of diversity awareness, Sadker and Silber's (2007) review of curriculum revealed that gender is largely missing.

No other social institution promotes as constantly the notion that girls and boys are different as education. Education seems to organize many of its activities along the sex binary. Common practices include teachers dividing the class by sex to enter and exit their classrooms, to eat lunch, and during educational and extracurricular activities. Extensive research on communicative interactions in classrooms has identified a range of ways gender/sex and other bases for inequality are sustained and how they can be challenged.

**Subtle Ways Teachers
Reinforce Binary and Unequal Differences**

- Naming—referring to the class as "boys and girls" (where does the transgender child stand?)
- Referencing—knowing and using some groups of children's names more than others

(Continued)

(Continued)

- Attention—calling on some student groups more than others
- Negative reinforcement—noticing when some children do things wrong but not right
- Grouping—as in "girls against boys"
- Expecting—as in expecting boys to not like to read; girls to struggle with math
- Unequal rules—allowing some children to shout out answers and rewarding others for taking their turn
- Competition—not collaboration as the predominant motivator
- Complimenting—for gender stereotypic behaviors, when girls are quiet and polite and when boys exert physical masculinity
- Calling out—as in asking a minority student to speak for all people of color, LGBTQ, disabled

Subtle Ways Teachers Can Challenge Binary and Unequal Difference

- Avoid generalizing—as in "you boys," "you girls," or even "your people"
- Time—giving the most valued commodity a teacher has to offer, one-on-one time with a student
- Wait time—giving students adequate time to answer a question, not rushing them
- Diversity in examples—offering examples that reflect multiple students' identities

(Extracted from Sadker, 2002; Sadker & Sadker, 1994; Sadker & Silber, 2007; Spencer, Porche, & Tolman, 2003; Swain, 2005)

Whether meaning to or not, teachers and administrators make gender/sex distinctions a central part of children's identities. If it is not acceptable to intentionally segregate children by race, why is it acceptable to segregate by sex? Although (one hopes) teachers would never ask all the students of color to stand in a line against one wall and the White students to stand against another, many do not think twice about segregating girls and boys this way. Nor would teachers punish all members of a racial group just because a few misbehaved. Unfortunately, it is not uncommon for all the boys or all the girls to be punished because of the behaviors of a few (Kramer, 2005; Kimmel, 2012a).

Adults often assume that children have same-sex preferences for friends, whether they do or not, and plan activities accordingly (Frawley, 2005). Competitions are commonly organized as girls against boys. The practice is cultural; it is not based on sound pedagogical learning practices. No evidence proves that segregated gender/sex competition in school activities, such as spelling bees and math quizzes, yields any positive educational, social, or psychological results. Such practices encourage girls and boys to see each other not only as different but as opponents (Sadker & Zittleman, 2005).

Title IX

Although interpersonal interactions and the hidden curriculum mark education as gendered/sexed, the possibility for institutional change exists. Educational sex equity has been helped most by the passage of Title IX of the Education Amendments Act of 1972. This legislation made it illegal for any federally funded educational program to discriminate on the basis of sex. It declares, "No person in the United States shall, on the basis of sex, be excluded from participation in, be denied the benefits of, or be subjected to discrimination under any education program or activity receiving Federal financial assistance" (20 U.S.C. § 1681).

Although most think of Title IX only in relation to sports, it governs all educational practices. Although full sports equity has not been achieved due to the complexities involved in implementation (such as providing an equivalent to men's football teams for women sports), the goal is that qualified athletes should receive the same scholarship awards at a given institution and have equally good equipment, schedules, tutoring, and coaches. In addition, Title IX promises all students the right to education without bullying, sexual harassment, and other threats of violence. Monitored by the Department of Justice, universities in particular are held accountable for rigorous, effective student affairs policies and procedures should an assault occur.

For 40 years, schools (from kindergarten to graduate) that receive federal funding have worked to meet this mandate. It is inducing the United States to be more inclusive of gender, as well as race, ethnicity, class, and sexual orientation (Hanson, Guilfoy, & Pillai, 2009). Researchers report the law has changed sports, other extracurricular opportunities, and student conduct and that these changes have effects far beyond the institution of education (Hanson et al., 2009). Title IX is playing an essential role in a nationwide cultural shift toward more flexible gender roles whereby people have more socially sanctioned options available in how they live their lives. The long-term effects of Title IX became clear in the 2012 Olympics.

1900: women first participate in the Olympics

1972: Title IX became law; women represented 21% of the U.S. Olympic team (84 of 400)

2012: for the first time in history, women represented 50.7% of the U.S. Olympic team (269 of 530).

Analysts believe this rise in women's participation is a direct result of Title IX (although the tipping over of the 50% mark in 2012 may be partially attributable to the men's soccer team not qualifying).

Source: Whiteside, Kelly. (2012, July 11). Women majority on Team USA. *USA Today,* A1.

Performance Gaps

In the last 25 years, many educators and popular authors have fed the widespread belief of sex-based performance gaps in education. The most prominent belief is that girls lack the biological brain tendencies to excel in math and science. This was dismissed for four reasons. First, females adequately trained do equally well as males on items measuring spatial ability (Newcombe, Mathason, & Terlecki, 2002). Second, in a statistical meta-analysis of studies claiming boys' superiority in math, Hyde (2007) found the differences were far overstated. In fact, girls and boys perform very similarly in completing math problems. Third, the results depend on the context. Multiple types of math skills were not taken into account when making this claim. In an analysis of national testing of 15-year-olds, gender/sex differences emerged only in some math-related skills, not all, and the differences found were not strong (Liu & Wilson, 2009). Fourth, the differences cannot be biological given girls have increasingly improved in national testing over the last decade.

The challenge for girls and women in science is not ability but bias and stereotype threat. Faculty bias still exists at the university level and can subtly affect women students' degree of support in the programs and hiring opportunities after graduation. In one study, 127 science faculty at research-intensive universities reviewed application materials randomly assigned a male or female name. Women and men faculty rated the application identified as male higher than an identical application identified as female and offered male candidates a higher starting pay and more career mentoring. Faculty also gave less support to women students (Handelsman, Moss-Racusin, Dovidio, Brescoll, & Graham, 2012).

When claims of performance gaps are made, they often create the very gap they claim to describe. Given stereotype threat, students internalize negative gender stereotypes about their ability to learn a subject, and their performance suffers (Good et al., 2008). Where might this stereotype come from? When the talking Barbie was marketed in 1992, some of the first words she uttered included "Math is hard!" Fortunately, nearly 800 million consumers objected, and subsequent talking Barbies did not make that comment (Lord, 1994). The message, however, was evidence of the common belief that girls cannot do math, and the unspoken message was that boys do math well.

Other pressures influence underperformance for boys. Kimmel (2012a) argues that boys are doing poorly in school because it is not okay for boys to like reading and do well in school. In fact, he reports that homophobia is used to discipline boys who excel, especially in reading and language. The ability to excel is described by students as, "That's so gay" (p. 212). Getting good grades is not considered cool, especially for boys. Masculinity has traditionally been defined as brawn, not brain, and education is seen as a passive, feminine activity (Connell, 2000; Francis & Skelton, 2005).

Peer Pressure, Bullying, and Harassment

Adolescents tend to experience intense **peer pressure** to conform to the norms of the group they want to be a part of (Swain, 2005). Peer groups have as much, if not more, influence on adolescents' gender identities than do parents. Boys who conform too much to school expectations instead of group expectations get labeled *goody boy*, *brownnoser, teacher's pet, wimp, sissy, girly girl,* or *fag.* Students in grade school through high school report the words *gay* and *fag* are the most commonly used, particularly among boys to bully others. Homosexuality is seen as a threat to masculinity, and so the person using the term against others is attempting to distance himself from it (Connell, 2000; Swain, 2005). Boys get the message that they should perform masculinity at all costs, so they repress emotions and act tough.

C. J. Pascoe (2011) found boys make it difficult for other boys to be successful in school given the culture of harassment. He observed student interactions in a suburban, working-class high school in north central California from 2003 to 2004. Both girls and boys knew "fag was the worst epithet one guy could direct at another" (p. 468), and the boys claimed that dislike of fags was just a part of what it means to be a guy. One student in the study explained what might earn a boy the epithet of "fag": "Anything . . . literally, anything. Like you were trying to turn a wrench the wrong way, 'dude, you're a fag.' Even if a piece of meat drops out of your sandwich, 'you fag!'" (p. 468). Although anything could trigger this discourse, it had a clear racialized component. White masculinity means one is not supposed to care about clothes while African American boys who are a part of hip-hop culture are not afraid to show they care about their dress. Thus, White boys racialize *fag* to include hip-hop groups. A racialized "fag discourse" hurts boys by rigidly enforcing masculinity with the threat of homosexuality.

Heteronormativity is a central component of peer pressure. As children enter middle and high school, having a girlfriend or boyfriend of the other sex becomes a means to gain status. Jon Swain (2005) points out that "having" a girlfriend is simply a continuation of efforts to declare one's heterosexuality (p. 223). Attitudes toward school and students' identities tied to sexuality and gender/sex become conflated. Sometimes, these attitudes manifest themselves in bullying.

Bullying is "repeated negative events, which over time are directed at special individuals and which are carried out by one or several other people who are stronger than the victim" (Aluede, 2008, p. 152). It is systematic verbal, physical, and/or cyber harassment of other individuals. Usually older children bully younger or physically smaller children, and boys bully girls and effeminate boys.

Statistics on Bullying

- Nearly 33% of middle and high school students report being bullied.
- One out of 9 teens reports bullying others.
- Twenty-eight percent of K–12 students report experiencing bullying at school.
- Six percent of K–12 students report being cyberbullied.
- Boys and girls are bullied and report being bullied.
- Just over 61% of LGBT youth felt unsafe at school because of their sexual orientation.
- Nearly 85% of LGBT youth were verbally harassed about their sexual orientation.
- Just over 40% of LGBT youth were physically harassed.

(Bartkiewicz, Diaz, Greytak, & Kosciw, 2009;
The Gay, Lesbian & Straight Education Network, 2011;
National Center for Education Statistics, 2010)

Since the 1999 shooting of students at Columbine High School in Colorado, students' mistreatment of each other has received greater public attention given that the male students at Columbine who murdered their peers were reportedly retaliating against others' bullying. Since then, many public schools have adopted a zero-tolerance policy on bullying. What used to be considered bad behavior is now recognized as a criminal act. Sadly, bullying is so widespread that communities attempting to create laws and school policies against bullying struggle to define it.

Boys are not the only ones who bully or harass. Girls bully, too. Researchers find that female forms of harassment tend be less physical, relying more on mean-spirited words and actions of exclusion. Journalist Leora Tanenbaum (2000) wrote about her own experience of being labeled a slut in school and interviewed 50 other girls and women from around the country who had been targeted as sluts during junior or senior high school. The participants had nothing in common except that male and female peers had sexually stigmatized them. The reasons for the abuse were multiple: being a social outcast, developing breasts earlier than one's peers, or being the target of revenge. Tanenbaum found that such verbal abuse ruins social reputations, hurts self-concept, affects academic performance, leads to sexual promiscuity and experimenting with drugs, and sets one up to be a target of rape. Girls' and women's participation in this name calling should not be surprising. Just as boys and men are pressured to prove their masculinity and heterosexuality, girls are pressured to view each other as competition for male attention, which leads to insider cliques and bullying.

At college and K–12 levels, students say they do not bother reporting bullying because it is considered a normal part of school. On the McGrath Training Systems website for educators, author Mary Jo McGrath (2007) noted, "Bullying and ridiculing behaviors are often precursors to full-blown sexual harassment or acts of extreme aggression in either the child who is doing the taunting and bullying or in the child who is persistently bullied. It's all part of a continuum of violence" (n.p.).

In college, statistics on sexual harassment and violence make clear education is not free from institutionalized violence. In 2006, the American Association of University Women conducted a national survey to examine sexual harassment at the college level. Results show 62% of all college students report being harassed in some way, including having sexual rumors spread about them, being forced into unwanted physical contact (from ostensibly accidental touching to rape), enduring sexual comments, and being spied on. Female and male students were nearly equally likely to be sexually harassed on campus. Females were more likely to be the target of sexual jokes, comments, gestures, and looks. Males were more likely to be called gay or a homophobic name.

Many men and even more women said the harassment was emotionally disturbing and damaged their educations and college experiences. The female students said they were likely to change their behavior as a result of the harassment, for example, avoiding a particular location on campus. They also found it harder to concentrate on their studies and harder to sleep at night. Lesbian, gay, bisexual, and transgender students were more likely to experience harassment than heterosexual students and were more troubled by it. Female as well as male students were more likely to be harassed by men than by women. The students said the harassment happens everywhere: in classrooms, in residence halls, at parties and bars, and from peers and university staff.

Gender/Sex in Higher Education

The phrase "the feminization of higher education" has been showing up in the popular press for the last decade to describe the trend in which more young women than men, across race and ethnicity, are entering college and completing degrees (e.g., Pollard, 2011, par. 2).

Does this mean social equality is being achieved? While it is good news that more women are earning degrees, this does not mean they are earning more money when completing their degrees. One estimate shows U.S. women still earn 82.2% of what men earn (The Institute for Women's Policy Research, 2012). The pay disparity is in part due to women being socialized and academically advised to choose majors that pay less. Career choices are still heavily influenced by gender roles and expectations. Women still tend to choose college degrees in service professions such as social work, nursing, and teaching; men still tend to choose degrees in business and the sciences (Mullen, 2010; Norén, 2012). In addition, gender/sex plays an important role in higher education in two other places: the professoriate and sexual violence.

Table 8.1 Race and Sex in Higher Education Statistics

Bachelors Degrees Granted in 2009-10 by Race/ethnicity			
Race/ethnicity	*Share of US Population*	*Share of Degrees Earned*	*Gender/Sex Gap in Degrees Earned**
Asian	4%	7%	10%
White	60%	71%	12%
American Indian	1%	1%	22%
Black	15%	10%	32%
Hispanic	18%	9%	22%

*Women earned more degrees in every racial/ethnic category.

Data: US Dept of Education, National Education Statistics (2011) "Table 300".

Source: Norén, 2012. Retrieved from http://thesocietypages.org/graphicsociology/2012/09/04/race-and-gender-in-higher-education.

Higher Education Employment

The university professorship traditionally has been considered a male position, and men continue to dominate this profession, especially at doctoral institutions. In 2011–2012, women represented 45.5% of the faculty at bachelor's institutions, 46.1% at master's institutions, and 38.1% at doctoral institutions (AAUP, 2012). Women and minority faculty continue to have a much more difficult time getting hired, being evaluated positively by students and administrators, and receiving promotion, particularly at the more elite schools or in male-dominated academic fields (Haag, 2005; Kerber, 2005). Women and minority faculty tend to be evaluated more harshly than White men faculty. They tend to be more closely observed and are more likely to have to prove their competence to receive a positive evaluation, whereas men are likely to be perceived competent at the outset and may only have to demonstrate incompetence before receiving negative evaluations (Haag, 2005). Women are more likely to be judged by actual accomplishments, and men are more likely to be judged on their promise (Wilson, 2004). Students, too, tend to more harshly evaluate female faculty, particularly African American women faculty. They are more often challenged and viewed negatively, regardless of their teaching performance (Turner, 2003).

Michael Messner (2004) points out that being a professor continues to be gendered masculine. Therefore, if a male teacher acts masculine, he becomes a better professor; however, if a female teacher acts feminine, she may have a more difficult time being seen as a good professor. Messner found women faculty are judged first on how well they perform femininity and then on their teaching—which creates contradictory expectations that are difficult to fulfill. This has negative consequences for women and men faculty perceived as feminine.

College students' choices of their best and worst professors suggested similarly that gender expectations influence students' judgments of teachers. In a study of 220 students at a public university, this was particularly true of male students with female professors. Male students emphasized the female professor's interpersonal skills, especially that she be approachable. Males rated a female professor as worst, not for her lack of knowledge on the subject but for her classroom interaction style, particularly seeming closed-minded. It should be noted that male and female professors were equally likely to be chosen by all students as a worst professor (Basow, Phelan, & Capotosto, 2006).

Sexual Violence on College Campuses

Sexual assault and its threat remains one of the barriers to gender equality on college campuses. Women are most often the reported victim. They are more likely to be raped than women the same age not in college, and 25% of college-age women have been victims of rape (Fisher, Cullen, & Turner, 2000, as reported in Sampson,

2011). Jackson Katz (2010), a national gender violence educator who works with U.S. college campuses and military groups, argues that the predominant culture's definition of masculinity as aggressive, virile, and dominant perpetuates violence against women, LGBTQ persons, and other men. Educating students and faculty to recognize and support alternative and diverse forms of masculinity is at the heart of preventing violence. Although sexual violence occurs in all institutions, it is particularly prevalent on college campuses given their hypersexualized and alcohol-soaked culture.

For example, in the fall of 2011, a survey was circulated among members of the Sigma Phi Epsilon Fraternity at the University of Vermont to get to know the 45 brothers better. It started with seemingly innocent questions asking for name, major, and favorite memory and then asked, "If I could rape someone, who would it be?" (Hartmann, 2011, par. 1). While the full survey or its results were never disclosed, the fraternity was put on suspension and required to cease all activities. Ten months later, the school's investigation concluded the fraternity was not responsible for the survey. It was the act of one person who was disciplined. The fraternity suspension was lifted (McGilvery, 2012).

In the original university response, the incident was punished due to its rape-promoting banter. That type of banter has been reported in previous research with college-age men (e.g., Gilmore, 1995), and it contributes to a campus climate in which research shows sexually assaulted victims typically know their attacker and do not usually report him. It is usually a classmate, friend, boyfriend, ex-boyfriend, or other acquaintance (in that order, Sampson, 2011). There are many reasons for not reporting sexual violence:

- Embarrassment and shame
- Fear of publicity
- Fear of reprisal from assailant
- Fear of social isolation from the assailant's friends
- Fear that the police will not believe them
- Fear that the prosecutor will not believe them or will not bring charges
- Self-blame for drinking or using drugs before the rape
- Self-blame for being alone with the assailant, perhaps in one's own or the assailant's residence
- Mistrust of the campus judicial system
- Fear that their family will find out
- Not realizing it is a crime (Sampson, 2011)

A contributing factor to sexual violence in college contexts is the pervasive abuse of alcohol. Leading researchers on alcohol and sexual assault report that in over three-quarters of college rapes, the offender, the victim, or both were drinking (Sampson, 2011). Alcohol is a normative part of college culture, and it tends to make hooking up with an acquaintance easier by relaxing inhibitions. *Hooking up* infers both parties are willing. However, when alcohol is involved, it is more difficult to distinguish hooking up from assault (Eshbaugh & Gute, 2008). When sexual aggressors abuse alcohol they reduce perceived responsibility for their actions and increase the blame on their victim.

This link between drinking and sexual assault is addressed in progressive campus policies that require verbal consent for consensual sex and note that if a person is incapacitated, that person cannot say yes. Consider this statement from the University of Northern Iowa Student Sexual Misconduct Policy (2011):

Article I—Sexual Misconduct

The University prohibits sexual misconduct in any form. Sexual misconduct is a broad term encompassing any unwelcome behavior of a sexual nature that is committed without consent or by force, intimidation, coercion, or manipulation. Sexual misconduct can occur between persons of the same or different sex.

For the purposes of this policy, consent is defined as a freely and affirmatively communicated willingness to participate in sexual activity, expressed either by words or clear, unambiguous actions. It is the responsibility of the initiator of the sexual activity to ensure he or she has the other person's consent to engage in sexual activity. Consent must be present throughout the sexual activity by all parties involved. At any time, a participant can communicate that he or she no longer consents to continuing the activity. Consent may never be obtained through the use of force, coercion, intimidation, or manipulation or if the victim is mentally or physically disabled or incapacitated, including through the use of drugs or alcohol.

Consent cannot be assumed because of the existence of a dating relationship between the persons involved or due to the existence of a previous sexual relationship between the persons. The perpetrator or victim's use of alcohol or other drugs does not diminish the perpetrator's responsibility. (par. 5–7)

Emancipatory Education

Education more than any other institution has the potential to level the playing field, to help each child advance, but, as critics suggest, it is a long way from accomplishing this goal (Ruane & Cerulo, 2008). For education to be a truly egalitarian institution, people must embrace **emancipatory education**: educational practices that seek to challenge accepted categories, unexamined norms, and repressive practices.

Bias in education, particularly bias tied to gender/sex, race, ethnicity, sexual orientation, and class, must be eliminated. Bias can limit students' ambitions and accomplishments, affecting them throughout life. Specifically addressing the bias tied to gender/sex, educator Timothy Frawley (2005) notes that "polarized approaches to education fail to recognize a middle ground for children who are not strongly gender-typed as masculine or feminine. The aim should be to not only stop labeling children as such, but to also accept and encourage androgynous behavior for both" (p. 222). Similarly, education researcher Jane Rolland Martin (1991) calls for "a gender-sensitive model of an educated person" that does not fall into the simplistic trap of biological determinism and false dichotomies (p. 10). What is a **gender-sensitive model**? It is more than focusing on individual learning styles and needs. Although an individual focus sounds good in theory, it does not address the underlying structural barriers in education tied to racism, sexism, classism, and homophobia.

A gender-sensitive model is more than single-sex education, which is, at best, a temporary response to a larger cultural misconception. Even advocates of single-sex education acknowledge that boys and girls need to learn to work together. Gender-sensitive education can be achieved only if one addresses the entire learning environment. Educators must pay attention to what is on the shelves and walls of schools, making sure they send inclusive, nonstereotypical messages. Schools also must provide opportunities for girls and boys to play together safely at recess. The gender-sensitive in-class techniques proposed by educator Tamara Grogan (2003) focus on practical ways teachers can create more inclusive classrooms. For example, rather than letting students gravitate to race, class, and single-sex groups, teachers can have students line up or group according to birthdates, favorite foods, or interests.

This does not mean that girls can never be grouped together to work or that teachers must police same-sex friendships. There is value in same-sex learning and interacting, but creating a community that includes gender/sex, race, class, and sexual-orientation diversity enhances education. Strict gender/sex divisions are oppressive and harmful to all children.

So, how does one know when attention to gender liberates rather than constrains? A distinction between *gender-specific* and *gender-relevant* educational programs is helpful (Connell, 2000). Most of the existing changes in education and curriculum have embraced a **gender-specific model** that targets only one sex. In contrast, a **gender-relevant model** includes girls *and* boys, as it attempts to make the gendered dimension of social life and education a part of the discussion. Educators directly address stereotypical assumptions as a part of the lesson, be it reading, writing, math, or science. R. W. Connell (2000) describes the benefits of a gender-relevant approach:

> The symbolic gendering of knowledge, the distinction between "boys' subjects" and "girls' subjects" and the unbalancing of curriculum that follows, require a gender-relevant not gender-specific response—a broad re-design of curriculum, timetable, division of labour among teachers, etc. The definition of masculinities in peer-group life, and the creation of hierarchies of masculinity, is a process that involves girls as well as boys. It can hardly be addressed with one of these groups in isolation from the other. (pp. 168–169)

Connell argues for coeducational programs in which the construction of students' critical gendered lenses is a part of the educational curriculum.

Another approach to gender-sensitive and gender-relevant education focuses on teaching styles. Teaching methods themselves contribute to liberatory or oppressive educational experiences. Brazilian educator Paulo Freire (1972) argues that the traditional lecture-based instruction style can be oppressive, particularly to groups already marginalized and silenced. He describes the lecture as a "banking" model of teaching, in which the teacher's role is to "fill" students' brains with information, and the students' role is simply to "store the deposits" (p. 63).

The alternative is **connected teaching** (hooks, 1994), which suggests that learning is more accessible when topics are concretely related to learners' individual life experiences rather than taught in abstract ways, isolated from context. Connected teaching requires teachers to provide examples to which students can relate, to share the ways in which they themselves connect to the material, to be more flexible with their teaching styles, and to be less controlling. It also requires teachers to share control over the learning process by being willing to engage in the learning moment with students rather than simply using the classroom as a place to report what one knows. Author and educator bell hooks (1994) explains that it requires instructors to make themselves vulnerable in the classroom and to make uncertainty and diversity of opinions acceptable parts of the learning process, and it requires students and instructors to explain or defend their ideas. The instructor works together with the students to construct knowledge through interaction. The ultimate goal is to learn how to learn, which requires recognizing the complexity of class members' identities.

Education professor David Sadker (2002) argues schools should cherish individual differences because "gender stereotypes shortchange all of us" (p. 238). He criticizes the labeling of a "war against boys," when educators and researchers are trying to address a history of male entitlement in schools (p. 235). If there is to be a war, it should challenge gender stereotypes and open up opportunities for all students to explore their individual strengths and identities. Education should teach students to appreciate diversity, not fear it.

The final alternative emerges from global educational programs that focus on girls in countries that deny them access to education. The United Nations (UN) and many nongovernmental organizations (NGOs) have long recognized the intersecting, systemic influences of gender/sex oppressions in education, family, poverty, health, and other social factors that contribute to human rights and livable lives. When persons are illiterate, they are more likely to be poor and uneducated, to have poor health and limited access to paid work, to be more susceptible to violence from others, and to have a shorter life expectancy. Countries in South Asia, for example, "account for the largest numbers of poor people in the world and have the highest number of children who do not attend school—46 million, more than half of whom are girls" (Subrahmanian, 2005, p. vii). Because of economic limitations and cultural traditions, girls usually are the last to be placed in schools and the first to be removed. South Asian girls' barriers to education include cultural biases such as son preference; cultural beliefs about women's appropriate roles that keep girls working at home; lack of gender/sex–sensitive infrastructure, such as latrines; unfriendly school environments; lack of community involvement to ensure girls' safety at school; lack of positive role models for girls; practices relating to early marriage, such as dowries; weak legal frameworks that do not implement free primary education or enforce child labor legislation; and labor market discrimination, which offers low returns on women's education (Subrahmanian, 2005).

In the last several decades, international organizations have focused on the plight of women and children, particularly in poor regions of the world, as represented by the UN Platform for Action, adopted at the 1995 Fourth World Conference on Women in Beijing. When organizations invest in girls' and women's literacy and education, they invest in entire families and communities. Consequently, the UN has targeted girls' and women's education for improvement. The New Millennium Development Goals include to "promote gender equality and empower women" and to "eliminate gender disparity in primary and secondary education, preferably by 2005, and in all levels of education no later than 2015" (Millenium Campaign, 2004).

This recognition of the unique oppressions of girls and women in education worldwide provides a fuller picture of the challenges regarding gender/sex and education. It also provides an educational model that attends to intersecting, systemic influences of gender/sex oppressions across social institutions, a model the U.S. education system may find useful.

Ultimately, each person must demand an education. Philosopher Adrienne Rich (1977), in a lecture at Douglass College, explains, "You who are students . . . cannot afford to think of being here to receive an education; you will do much better to think of yourselves as being here to claim one" (p. 608). You do not need to rely on teachers or peers to receive an emancipatory education. You can

> demand to be taken seriously so that you can also go on taking yourself seriously. This means seeking out criticism, recognizing that the most affirming thing anyone can do for you is demand that you push yourself further, show you the range of what you *can* do. . . . It means assuming your share of responsibility for what happens in the classroom. (p. 611)

Conclusion

Education is composed of communicative practices—lectures, books, activities—that teach students to perform gender. Detailed analysis of educational practices demonstrates the gendered/sexed elements of education, including who is educating whom, about what, in what way, and for what purpose. Educators and those being educated have an opportunity and responsibility to think about how the classroom can be a microcosm for multiple social inequalities *and* for social change.

KEY CONCEPTS

bullying   175

connected teaching   182

emancipatory education   180

gender-relevant model   181

gender-sensitive model   181

gender-specific model   181

hidden curriculum   168

peer pressure   174

DISCUSSION QUESTIONS

1. Do your own review of "Rate My Professor" (or a similar online tool). Do you see indicators that professors are being assessed according to binary gender expectations and stereotypes, heterosexism, racism, and/or ableism?

2. Find out the number of women, men, White, and racial or ethnic minority tenure-track faculty versus adjunct temporary faculty on your campus. How many of these groups are in higher administration on your campus? What do the results suggest about the gendered/sexed and raced climate for faculty on your campus? How might this affect your educational experience outside and inside the classroom?

3. What are some ways in which the institution of education has constructed and constrained gender? Can you offer examples of any of these from your own educational experiences?

4. How has bullying and sexual harassment affected your educational experience or that of others you know?

CHAPTER 9

Work

I n the summer of 2012, a cover story in *The Atlantic* magazine catalyzed a national conversation about work–life balance. The author, Anne-Marie Slaughter, wrote a story titled "Why Women Still Can't Have It All." Slaughter is a Princeton University professor of politics and international affairs, former dean of Princeton's Woodrow Wilson School of Public and International Affairs, former director of policy planning at the U.S. State Department from 2009 to 2011, and the mother of two teenage boys. The story attracted over 1.2 million readers within two weeks after publication. It broke every online record for the magazine; it was the most read article on the website and the most "liked" *Atlantic* essay, with almost 200,000 likes on Facebook (Boyle, 2012; "Can Women," 2012).

In the story, Slaughter asked why women are still woefully underrepresented in boardrooms, executive positions, and at the top levels of business and government. Slaughter's central observation was that "juggling high-level government work with the needs of two teenage boys was not possible"—women like her ("highly educated, well-off women who are privileged enough to have choices in the first place" [p. 89]) could not have it all, *all* being defined as achieving success at the highest levels of her profession and being available as a parent whenever she was most needed (p. 86). Her explanation was that given the way work is structured, creating work-life balance was impossible. If Slaughter, as an example of the most elite, could not find a way to stay on the fast track to occupational success, what could that say about the rest of the workforce?

The reaction to her essay was immediate, raising questions about what it means to "have it all" and how a State Department position like hers would have challenged a man to balance work and family commitments just as much ("*The Atlantic's*," 2012). Journalist Kate Bolick (2012) observes that "seeking out a more balanced life isn't just a women's issue, it's a human issue, and we'd *all*—men and women—be a lot better off if we addressed (or at least legislated) the issue that way" (par. 2). It is also important to note that Slaughter's solution was not to leave paid work completely but to leave government and return to her full-time tenured teaching position at Princeton and her 50-gigs-a-year speaking schedule.

A month later, another woman sparked discussions about work-life balance. Marissa Mayer was hired by Yahoo for its CEO post and then publicly announced her pregnancy, explaining, "My maternity leave will be a few weeks long and I'll work throughout it" (quoted in Sellers, 2012, par. 10). Reaction was swift and ranged from scoffing dismissals of her plans to questioning whether she could do her job as the parent of a newborn. While Mayer's story was front-page news, it is telling that a similar situation was not. Two months after Larry Page became CEO at Google, it was announced he was expecting his second child. In his case, "there were no follow-up headlines, no social media debates, no loud conversations about how he could lead an Internet giant and still be a father" (Petrecca, 2012, p. A1). These stories demonstrate the persistent challenge of work-life balance, one faced not only by women but also by men.

To explore gender in communication about work and at work, we first discuss how work is a gendered institution: how the relative value of one's work is gendered/sexed, how work is structured, and even how the way work is defined is gendered/sexed. Second, we explore how communication at work is intersectionally gendered: particularly in terms of emotion, power, and leadership at work; in terms of the double oppressions of African American women at work; and with regard to sexual harassment as normative violence at work. Quite simply, "workplace interactions are important" because "the workplace is a crucial site for the reproduction of gender inequality" (C. Connell, 2010, p. 32).

Work Is a Gendered/Sexed Institution

Workplaces are locations where both work and gender/sex are done. Scholars have noted that in workplaces, "'Doing gender' is entrenched in organizational practices and communicated to workers in a multitude of ways. . . . Gender dynamics are enacted in organizations . . . because the same norms and expectations are present as they are in other venues of daily life" (Carlson & Crawford, 2011, p. 360). Workplaces are never just about doing work because they are populated with people doing gender. Evidence that gender/sex matters at work can be found in pay statistics.

Gendered/Sexed Wage Disparity

Inequality based on sex (and exacerbated by race, nationality, and relation to the globalizing economy) is undeniable. Globally, according to research conducted for the United Nations Development Fund for Women, a "[sex] gap in earnings exists across almost all employment categories" (Chen, Vanek, Lund, & Heintz, 2005, p. 3); in 2008, the average wage gap worldwide was 17% ("UN Women," n.d.). Contributing to this imbalance is the fact that women tend to bear responsibility for unpaid household work, and often women are restricted to home-based employment, further limiting their earnings (Chen et al., 2005).

Structural inequalities in earnings are found in the United States as well. The Institute for Women's Policy Research (2012) found that during 2011, women, across positions, make 82.2% of men's earnings (p. 1). This adds up across a lifetime of earning (see Figure 9.1). The Center for American Progress explains,

> Because of this gap women working full time are able to afford less education, housing, transportation, food, and health care for themselves and their families than their male counterparts. As a result women and female-headed households are more likely to be in poverty and less likely to have health insurance. The pay gap translates into a significant economic disadvantage for women and their families, especially when nearly two-thirds (63.9 percent) of women are now either the primary breadwinner or a co-breadwinner. (Separa, 2012, par. 3)

What does this gap look like?

Although some contest the size of the pay gap, most everyone admits one exists. Even the most conservative analysis recognizes at least a 5% pay gap across all jobs (Kolesnikova & Liu, 2011). And when specific professions are analyzed, the differences become vivid. A recent report by the U.S. General Accounting Office (2010) found that "female managers earned 81 cents for every dollar earned by male managers in 2007" (p. 3) even adjusted for other characteristics such as age, hours worked, race, location, education level, and whether there were dependent children.

When specific professions are analyzed, the dynamics of the cause become clear. Sociology professor Janice F. Madden analyzed the pay gap in brokerage firms, one of the jobs where the pay gap is largest with women earning only about two-thirds as much as men. Because pay in such a position is commission based, many argue that the pay gap merely reflects performance. However, this is not what Madden found. Instead, she identified a "performance-support bias": "Differences in management's discretionary assignments of sales opportunities, and not in sales capacities, account for the gender pay gap among stockbrokers in these two firms" she studied (Madden, 2012, p. 4). A wage gap also persists among doctors. Even after a study took into account "differences in specialty, institutional characteristics, academic productivity, academic rank, work hours, and other factors," the

Figure 9.1 Gender Pay Gap

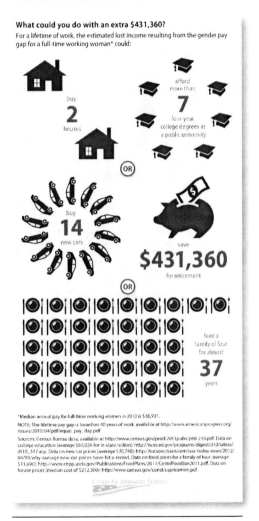

Source: This material was created by the Center for American Progress (www.americanprogress.org) and is sourced from the article *Infographic: The Gender Pay Gap* by Matt Separa.

researchers still found that men earned over $12,000 a year more than women (which would accumulate to over $350,000 over a lifetime; Jagsi et al., 2012).

Some research ties the wage gap to communication practices. Linda Babcock and Sara Laschever (2007) found that women's reluctance to initiate and directly negotiate their initial salary offer directly contributes to the salary gap between women and men (p. 6). As the title of their book points out, "women don't ask"—for salary, for work opportunities, for perks. In fact, communication may influence whether one receives a job offer given "assertive women are more likely to be hired" (Basow, 2008, p. 22).

In a follow-up study, Bowles, Babcock, and Lai (2007) found that evaluators "penalized female candidates more than male candidates for initiating negotiations" regarding pay (pp. 84, 99). They also explored why women and men might be more or less willing to negotiate for pay. They found that "gender differences in the propensity to initiate negotiations may be motivated by social incentives as opposed to individual differences" (p. 85). Basically, women recognized they face greater social costs for negotiating than men. Thus, they choose not to negotiate because they perceive they will be penalized, not because they are personally unwilling or unable to negotiate. In fact, in the experiment, the negative judgment of evaluators was 5.5 times greater for women regardless of whether their request was simple or assertive (p. 91). What these studies make clear is that individual changes alone are insufficient. The solution is not that individual women should negotiate. Instead, an institutional correction is needed: The social environment of work needs to change (p. 100).

The fact that work institutions maintain, and are sites of, gender inequality is well established. However, this leaves unanswered the question as to *how* work produces these inequalities. Scholars identify two interrelated ways in which organizations are gendered: organizational structure and microcommunication.

Gendered/Sexed Organizational Structure and Microcommunication

Sociologist Joan Acker pioneered the study of how work is gendered, particularly through its organizational structure. Her research and theorizing make clear that "organizational structure is not gender neutral" (Acker, 1990, p. 139). She writes,

> To say that an organization . . . is gendered means that advantage and disadvantage, exploitation and coercion, action and emotion, meaning and identity, are patterned through and in terms of a distinction between male and female, masculine and feminine. Gender is not an addition to ongoing processes, conceived as gender neutral. Rather, it is an integral part of those processes, which cannot be properly understood without an analysis of gender. (Acker, 1990, p. 146)

Acker calls for a systematic theory of gender and organizations. Her five reasons for attention to gender and organizations are the sex segregation of work, including which work is paid and which is unpaid; income and status inequality between women and men and how this is created through organizational structure; how organizations invent and reproduce cultural images of sex and gender; the way in which gender, particularly masculinity, is the product of organizational processes; and the need to make organizations more democratic and more supportive of humane goals. Communication is central to how these five intersecting processes intertwine gender with power, control, and dominance.

Dennis Mumby (2001), a critical organizational theorist, has definitively declared, "It is impossible to study and theorize adequately about organizational power without addressing its gendered character" (p. 609). But studying organizational structure is not enough. Studying communication is essential because "communication produces, not merely expresses, the realities of organization. . . . Organizational reality is not constructed spontaneously or consensually; negotiating meaning is a political process that is both constrained by and constitutive of power structures" (Ashcraft & Mumby, 2004, p. xviii). Work by **critical organizational communication** scholars (e.g., Ashcraft & Mumby, 2004; Buzzanell, 2000; Calás & Smircich, 2001; Trethewey, 2001) has begun to correct one of the "great blind spots, and errors" of organizational theory: the assumption that organizations are gender neutral (Rothschild & Davies, 1994, p. 583). Their research examines communication on a range of levels, from an individual's "engrained personal communication habits" to daily interactions, to the form of an organization, to the social narratives about work (Ashcraft & Mumby, 2004, p. 28).

Daily practices, which often appear insignificant when viewed as isolated instances, accumulate to create masculine gendered work organizations. Organizational communication scholar Patrice Buzzanell (2000) urges people to be aware of how "organization members 'do gender' . . . in the course of their mundane, everyday organization practices" (p. 4). It is not just superiors telling subordinates what to do but the communication between co-workers, as well as the structure of work itself, that genders the workplace setting. Who talks to whom in the hallway, and about what, genders those involved. Work also is gendered/sexed in the way people and cultures define work.

The Definition of Work Is Gendered/Sexed/Nationalized

From culture to culture and from time to time, the meaning and significance of work shifts. For example, in capitalist societies, economies have shifted from agrarian to industrial and now to service oriented and information based. Because work is embedded in a larger economic structure, such as capitalism, it is difficult for those living in the predominant culture to realize the meaning is not universal. This is why it is important to locate the discussion of gender in work in the macrostructure of cultural economies. In the United States, work is considered a characteristic of what makes Americans American. "What do you do?" is one of the first questions many people ask when getting to know each other, and they are not asking about what one does with family, or to learn, or to be entertained; instead, the question is about the wage-earning work one does. The prominence of the question is indicative of how U.S. people tend to define identity by the work they do.

The way a culture's economy is structured exposes much about what is valued in that culture. Whether good or bad, **capitalism** depends on creating and maintaining a culture where people value materialism and purchasing power. Work is how people in the culture gain purchasing power and the status that comes with that. The very definition of work then contains cultural ideologies. In the United States, the predominant ideology is that hard work pays off. People who work hard will be rewarded with job security, financial independence, and a better quality of life. This cultural ideology seems to persist even in the face of economic downturns (e.g., recessions) that individual workers cannot control, increased hours of mandatory work, and people living in poverty regardless of how hard they work in the midst of what is a highly developed country. Minimal-paying jobs held by poor women and men of color drive the capitalistic economy by providing processed foods, clothing, and other consumer products, but they do not provide enough for workers to do more than minimally survive (Ehrenreich, 2001; Mawdsley, 2007).

In the United States, if people are asked to define work, they will most likely define it as paid work *outside* the home. "Working mothers" are those women with young children who *also* work outside the home for a wage. Of course, if you were to ask a mother who does not have a wage-paying job that requires her to leave the home, "Do you work?" the answer ought to be a resounding, "Yes!" Child rearing is work, but because it is not paid, people do not think of it as work (Daniels, 1987). Revealingly, a term exists to name *working mother*, but *working father* sounds odd. It is expected that men continue to work at wage labor after the birth of their children. "Stay-at-home dads" seem to be anomalous, although their numbers are growing. As of 2012, of the 24.7 million men part of a heterosexual married couple with children under 18, 176,000 (up from 98,000 in 2005) are stay-at-home fathers (which is around .7%) and 15% of single parents are men (U.S. Census Bureau, 2012a). The number is higher among non-nuclear family forms. Among male same-sex couples, 26% include one stay-at-home parent, which is 1% higher than the percentage of stay-at-home mothers in heterosexual married couples and 4% higher than for female couples (Bellafante, 2004).

Who Should Work (Outside the Home) Is Gendered/Sexed

Work outside the home as a legitimating ideology also is evident in recent debates over welfare reform. Many women and men parents work and so place their children in day care or seek the help of extended family. While women who work outside the home are criticized for placing their children in day care, poor women who have had to rely on welfare if they remain home to care for young children are considered bad mothers because they do not work: "The only women for whom wage work is an unambivalently assigned social responsibility are welfare mothers" (Mink, 1995, pp. 180–181). Only women who seek assistance through government programs are encouraged to work; for mothers who have other sources of economic stability, work is at best perceived as a temporary indulgence or, at worst, a discouraged activity.

By blaming individual women for not being "good mothers" social problems become personalized and attention is deflected away from systemic solutions. The cultural practice of defining women as mothers first (or only), not as people forced to make difficult decisions within cultural restraints, is a systemic problem that needs to be addressed.

This expectation is particularly dismissive of African American women's lives, where there is a history of being single parents, earning more than their husbands, and needing to help support extended family. Additionally, "for generations black women have viewed work as a means for elevating not only their own status as women, but also as a crucial force in elevating their family, extended family and their entire race" (Clemetson, 2006, p. G1).

A critical gendered lens directed at organizational communication focuses attention on work-family dilemmas not as individual problems or private choices but as "social arrangements over which individual women and men have only limited control" and thus redirects researchers away from blaming individuals and toward "understanding the larger social contexts in which personal choices and strategies are crafted" (Gerson, 2004, p. 164).

Occupations Are Gendered/Sexed Privileged

Many professions are sex segregated (e.g., men tend to be firefighters, women tend to be nurses). Predominantly male occupations possess more social value, as indicated by more pay, prestige, authority, and opportunities for advancement. Numerous studies demonstrate that if an occupation is female dominated, it tends to carry less prestige, authority, and autonomy. Even in part-time work, people (usually young men) who mow and care for lawns tend to be paid more than people who babysit children (usually young women). See Table 9.1, "Gender/Sex Work Segregation and Wage Disparities," for more examples.

Table 9.1   Gender/Sex Work Segregation and Wage Disparities

Occupation	Total Population Employed in This Occupation	Percentage of Female Employees	Median Salary, Female	Median Salary, Male
Registered nurses	2,843,000	91.1%	$53,768	$56,212
Maids and housekeeping cleaners	1,407,000	89.0%	$20,384	$24,596
Elementary and middle school teachers	2,813,000	81.8%	$48,516	$53,144
High school teachers	1,221,000	57.0%	$51,428	$54,548
Physicians and surgeons	872,000	32.3%	$79,404	$100,620
Police and sheriff's patrol officers	714,000	13.0%	$48,776	$49,296
Construction laborers	1,267,000	2.7%	No data available	$30,524

The total U.S. population 16 years of age and older employed in 2010 when these statistics were compiled was 139,064,000. Of that number, 47.2% were female. (U.S. Bureau of Labor Statistics, 2011; U.S. Census Bureau, 2012a.)

Workplace Organization Is Gendered/Sexed

In the 1970s, scholars began to recognize how the structure of organizations, rather than the individual characteristics of women and men, generated gender differences (Kanter, 1977). Organizations ostensibly are structured around the abstract worker—a bodiless, sexless, emotionless worker who does not procreate. However, Acker (1990) explains, "It is the man's body, its sexuality, minimal responsibility in procreation, and conventional control of emotions that pervades work and organizational processes"; in contrast, "women's bodies are ruled out of order, or sexualized and objectified, in work organizations" (p. 152). Martin (2003) confirms that doing gender in organizational work settings continues to constrain women because how men and women socially construct each other at work affects their work experiences, and this tends to impair women workers' identities and confidence (p. 343). In arguing this, Martin is careful to note that "multiple masculinities and femininities exist, and people practice, and are held accountable to specific kinds depending on their bodies (health, attractiveness), class, race/ethnicity, religion, sexual orientation, age, nation, and other social statuses" (p. 355).

How the structure of work—both paid labor and housework—is gendered becomes most evident in **work-family tensions**. The institutions of work and family generate tensions, causing many people to feel they must choose one over the other. These choices are gendered, raced, and classed.

The conflict between work and family in the United States was made evident by sociologist Arlie Hochschild (1997). Her study found that the rapidly increasing time stress in U.S. culture induces more persons to choose work over family because of the rewards work promises. These pressures could be recalibrated. Work and home *could* be structured to mutually support each other. For example, in Nordic countries, work pay continues even during parental leave; benefits provided at the birth of a child are reduced if both parents do not take time off work; and parental leave is nontransferable, thus prompting both parents to take time off. Lawmakers in Nordic countries have structured work benefits to challenge the pattern whereby women carry disproportionate responsibility in child rearing (Moss & Deven, 1999). Unfortunately, U.S. family leave is not structured this way, meaning the tensions between work and family persist, leading to the very challenges the Slaughter essay with which we opened the chapter outlines.

This reality contributed to the passage of the Pregnancy Discrimination Act of 1978 and the Family Medical Leave Act of 1993 (the latter allowing women and men up to 12 weeks of unpaid leave for pregnancy, personal, or family reasons). These U.S. laws are meant to create conditions whereby people affected by pregnancy and caregiving are not penalized and are able to return to their jobs after a leave. Although both of these laws are necessary and significant, they demonstrate that legal change alone is not sufficient to create equality; a change in the communication about an issue also is necessary. A law can be enacted in hopes of creating more gender/sex equality, but until communication surrounding the issue changes, the law's effect is incomplete.

In the case of work and family, a vocabulary that recognizes the complex ways in which women experience parenthood has not yet been developed. Lori Peterson and Terrance Albrecht (1999) found that in discussions of work and women's childbearing processes, maternity leave was interpreted as a *benefit* (something that would be a bonus or a business's choice and not a guaranteed right), and pregnancy was interpreted as a *disability*. This means that even with legal protections and leave policies in place, work's male-centered structure continues to present challenges to women about to be parents. A study done by organizational communication scholars Patrice M. Buzzanell and Meina Liu (2005) confirms that the work-family culture and supervisory relationships played a key role in determining the degree to which women were satisfied with a company's leave policy and, hence, were able and willing to return to work after childbirth. The law alone did not make the difference in their work lives; it was the specific supervisor's approach to the law that made the difference.

A Vivid Illustration: Transgender Workers' Experience

In case you are not yet convinced that work is gendered and sexed, consider the experience of workers who transition from one sex to another while working. In a study of their work experiences, sociologist Catherine Connell (2010) found that "transgender workers who transitioned on the job described changes in their employers' assumptions about their abilities" (p. 47). The person is the same person; the only thing that changes is the sex designation. Yet, that alone is enough to trigger different treatment from their employers.

The pattern in the treatment is telling. In an extensive study, sociologist Kristen Schilt (2011) found "transwomen are more likely to face workplace barriers than transmen" (p. 133). Transwomen, in interviews, told stories of resistance to their transition while transmen told stories of support. Becoming a woman was resisted while becoming a man was praised. This also translated into different judgments of work products. Transmen interviewed reported "an increase in allocation of resources such as respect, authority, and in some cases, financial resources," influenced by "race, height, perceived sexuality, and masculine embodiment" (Tesene, 2012, p. 677). In contrast, transwomen told stories of superiors questioning their abilities after their transition. The conclusion is clear: "The workplace is not a gender-neutral location that equitably rewards workers based on their individual merits . . . but rather 'a central site for the creation and reproduction of gender differences and gender inequality' (C.L. Williams 1995, 15)" (Schilt, 2011, pp. 132–133).

Gendered/Sexed Communication in the Workplace

Many books and articles identify ostensible differences between women's and men's communication strategies in the workplace (e.g., Claes, 2006; Tannen, 1994b). However, much communication in the workplace characterized as feminine actually tends to be practiced by men as much as, if not more than, by women. Differences emerge not in the actual practice of communication but in others' interpretation of it. Recent research makes clear that "gender differences in actual communication and leadership behaviors are slight, although expectations of gender differences are strong. The situations that remain most problematic for women are the ones in strongly male-dominated or culturally masculine organizations" (Basow, 2008, p. 27). Thus, the reality is not that women and men communicate differently but that they are assessed differently because people impose gendered expectations on them, and these expectations benefit some and disadvantage others. For example, "when men are seen in a positive light for adopting feminine strategies, women will not receive the same evaluation" (Mullany, 2007, p. 47). This is demonstrated particularly in relation to emotional expression in the workplace.

The differences in expectation and assessment are especially true regarding women's emotional expression because "the same actions can be evaluated very differently depending on whether they are enacted by a man or woman manager" (Mullany, 2007, p. 47). For the most part, the expression of **emotions** at work is considered inappropriate. Men (and women) are expected not to cry or to show fear, sadness, or joy; it is more appropriate, however, for men to show anger. Ultimately, though, it is impossible to compare and contrast women's and men's emotions because emotions considered organizationally appropriate when expressed by a man tend to be perceived as inappropriate when expressed by a woman (Hearn, 1993; Martin, 2006).

If one studies activities rather than emotional expression, it appears that men engage in practices that are stereotypically attributed to women more than to men, such as "wasting time talking to coworkers, pretending to like people they dislike, making decisions based on affect rather than 'objective' evidence, and ignoring rules in favor of particularistic sentiments. . . . When women coworkers socialize, they waste time; when men coworkers socialize, they advance their careers" (Martin, 2003, p. 358). The one distinction is that men tend to do some communicative behaviors differently from women. "Peacocking" and other self-promoting behaviors, in particular, were directed only at other men: "The audience(s) to whom/that [*sic*] men hold themselves accountable at work relative to gender[/sex] is . . . primarily other men" (p. 358). In other words, the differences claimed by some to exist do not exist, and the differences that do exist tend not to be recognized as distinctive masculine behavior because the work institution is gendered masculine, and so the behavior appears neutral.

These subtle practices highlight how mechanisms of exclusion and discrimination are not always readily apparent, even if they are demonstrably present. As Martin (2003) explains, "Men need not invent schemes for excluding women from daily work processes in order for women to experience exclusion. As men engage in gendering practices consistent with institutionalized norms and stereotypes of masculinity, they nonetheless create social closure and oppression" (p. 360). For this reason, the insights offered by communication studies become important. The following is an example from Martin's research.

> Maria [Systems Analyst, Latina, age 35]: I would talk to my boss about a problem, just to think it through. . . . I found out my boss was taking my problem to his boss and they were solving it for me. I did not like this. This was not what I had asked my boss to do. I felt he meant well. . . . But this was not what

I meant or wanted to happen. I wanted to have his ear and thoughts in working through the problem myself. So I told my boss, "Don't do this to me. When I come to you to discuss something, that's [all] I want. Don't solve the problem for me, OK?" If he solves my problems, this will make me look like I can't solve my problems. (Martin, 2006, p. 263)

Maria's boss was perhaps unconsciously performing his own gendered masculinity to fix the computer problem and imposing unfair assumptions about his employee's technical abilities as a woman. Close analysis of micro-organizational communication dynamics can enable one to trace, and thus challenge, the gendered norms of interaction in work settings (Martin, 2006).

African American Women and Work

Patricia S. Parker (2003) has provided an exhaustive review of the literature on African American women and how they experience control (and exercise resistance and create empowerment) in raced, gendered, and classed work contexts. Parker highlights the way in which race, gender/sex, and class "structure communicative practices in everyday organizational life—such as hiring and recruitment rituals, interaction patterns, and symbolic processes—that contribute to African American women's continued subordination and oppression in the U.S. labor market" (p. 258). What is important to note is that African American women face this subordination not just from White men but also from White women (Parker, 2003, p. 271; for research on Hispanic women, see Calás, 1992; for research on working-class women, see Gregg, 1993).

Work practices that maintain and create subordination are not always overt, like quid pro quo sexual harassment, but can be more subtle, located in "ordinary, daily procedures and decisions" (Parker, 2003, pp. 264, 261), such as who is asked to do which type of tasks. Racism and sexism are not located in individuals' prejudices but in political practices. Studies of African American women and work make clear that their experiences of subordination at work begin in school, when counselors and teachers tend to steer them away from particular work aspirations (Parker, 2003). The problems African American women face are intensified at the time of job entry and then exacerbated with job advancement (or the lack thereof). Summarizing the research, Parker (2003) concludes that "research on African American women's work experiences reveals the persistent structuring of organizational divisions along race, gender[/sex], and class lines that occurs through power-based communicative practices" (p. 268). How African American women are talked to and talked about influences the types of work they and others consider suitable for African American women.

Our attention to how institutional structures of work affect African American women differently than White American women should make clear that a critical gendered lens applied to the institution of work does not generate a simple list of different experiences for women and men. One should be attentive to the differences among women and men as well as to the similarities between women and men.

Paid Care Work

Historically, women have tended to be the primary caregivers to small children, and women of color have often been hired by White women to be caregivers. Job segregation not only occurs across sex lines but also across race lines within sex. Again, an intersectional approach enables one to see ways in which systemic inequalities manifest themselves. As a paradigmatic example, "Black women's initial overrepresentation in domestic service reflects the intersections of race, gender, and class—the idea that Blacks are best suited for servitude, that women belong in the private sphere of the home, and that work done in the home does not deserve significant economic reward" (Harvey, 2005, p. 791). With the globalization of the economy, this dynamic has been extended to cover not only Black women but also Filipina women in Canada (Welsh, Carr, MacQuarrie, & Huntley, 2006) and Latina immigrants in the United States (Hondagneu-Sotelo & Avila, 1997).

Sociologist Mignon Duffy (2005) speaks directly to this issue in an essay analyzing how **paid care work** is segregated along race, class, and sex lines. We would add age, with young and old women being valued less, paid less, and more often hired as care workers. Duffy analyzes jobs that would be considered part of reproductive labor, such as domestic service, health care, child care, teaching, food preparation, and cleaning and building services. Her analysis was situated within broader research that establishes the U.S. labor market as "stratified, segmented into various sectors that provide workers with grossly unequal wage levels and access to opportunities for advancement" (p. 71). This stratification is neither race nor sex neutral, because "interlocking systems of gender and racial oppression act to concentrate women and people of color in those occupations that are lower paying and lower status" (p. 71). Even within care labor, stratification can be found in which White women assume the public face of care work, populating those jobs that call for the most interaction with others, that are most professionalized, and that pay more. In contrast, "women of color are disproportionately represented in the 'dirty, back-room' jobs such as maids and kitchen workers" (p. 72).

Violence, Gender/Sex, and Work: Sexual Harassment

Perhaps the issue that makes most evident the power relations present in work is workplace aggression. Research has found that "workplace aggression and violence . . . does not affect men and women equally" (Magley, Gallus, & Bunk, 2010, p. 423). In a meta-analysis of 57 empirical studies, M. Sandy Hershcovis and colleagues (2007) found men tended to be more aggressive at work than women. Men are more likely to engage in physical and psychological aggression, view aggression as acceptable behavior, and seek revenge (Magley et al., 2010, p. 431). Institutionalized violence—how violence becomes normalized through institutional processes—deserves attention. In the workplace, the normalization of violence most clearly takes the form of **sexual harassment**, or repeated, unwanted verbal or nonverbal communication of a sexual nature (for broad considerations of violence and organizations, see Hearn, 1994).

The naming of sexual harassment and the creation of legal redress for those who experience it have done much to counter gendered/sexed violence in the workplace. However, even with the evolutions in law and the raising of public consciousness about harassment, sexual harassment persists. The U.S. Equal Employment Opportunity Commission (2012) reports that in fiscal year 2011, women filed 83.7% of the 11,364 charges of sexual harassment. Still, many instances of sexual harassment are never reported to the EEOC. In the United States, 13% to 31% of men and 40% to 75% of women have been sexually harassed by others in the workplace (McDonald, 2012). Although some examples exist of women harassing men, men harassing men, and women harassing women, by far the most predominant form of harassment is men harassing women (McDonald, 2012).

The law recognizes two types of sexual harassment. **Quid pro quo**, pressures to provide sexual favors in exchange for job security, and a **hostile work environment**, meaning behaviors create a negative culture where work becomes impossible. It is difficult to develop a consensus of recognizable behaviors that constitute sexual harassment, at least between most women and men. Women tend to define more acts as constituting harassment and are more likely to perceive coercion in a particular situation, whereas masculine men are more likely to blame the person harassed instead of empathizing with that person (Quinn, 2002).

To explore this disjuncture, sociologist Beth A. Quinn (2002) studied "**girl watching**," a form of harassment that tends to be labeled as such by women but is defined as play by men who engage in it. In the activity, the woman being watched may be unaware, although other women may not be. Thus, it seems that the target of the action may not be the particular woman being watched but may be other men and, indirectly, other women in the organization. When Quinn asked sexual harassers and those harassed what it meant to them, she found that girl watching functions as a form of gendered play among the men, as "both a source of fun and a mechanism by which gendered identities, group boundaries, and power relations are (re)produced" (p. 393). It is a form of play that bolsters masculinity by being premised on "a studied lack of empathy with the feminine other" (p. 391). In fact, watching targets the watched woman as a game piece, an object, rather than another player. The other players are men. Quinn (2002) outlines the complex dynamics of femininity, masculinity, sexuality, and competence implicated in girl watching:

> The gaze demonstrates their right, as men, to sexually evaluate women. Through the gaze, the targeted woman is reduced to a sexual object, contradicting her other identities, such as that of a competent worker or leader. . . . Calling attention to a woman's gendered sexuality can function to exclude recognition of her competence, rationality, trustworthiness, and even humanity. In contrast, the overt recognition of a man's heterosexuality is normally compatible with other aspects of his identity; indeed, it is often required . . . because being seen as sexual has different consequences for women and men. (p. 392)

Quinn demonstrates that sexual joking and girl watching is "a common way for heterosexual men to establish intimacy among themselves" (p. 394). This begs the question, why do some men base their bonding on the sexual objectification of women?

In a culture of hegemonic masculinity, men become men by performing their virility in front of other men. When asked what "being a man" entailed, the people Quinn interviewed indicated that it involves "notions of strength (if not in muscle, then in character and job performance), dominance, and a marked sexuality, overflowing and uncontrollable to some degree and natural to the male 'species'" (p. 394). One way for men to perform uncontrollable sexuality is through girl watching.

Most interesting in Quinn's study is that when pushed to look at girl watching from a woman's perspective, the men who claimed not to see the act as constituting a hostile work environment *did* understand the harm. Thus, Quinn concludes that differences between men and women "in interpreting sexual harassment stem not so much from men's not getting it . . . but from a . . . lack of motivation to identify with women's experiences" (p. 397). Men who have learned to perform masculinity *correctly* must not demonstrate empathy; thus, they fail to see harassing behaviors from the perspective of the other. This means that sexual harassment is an example not only of one man exerting power over one woman but of how masculinity itself is premised on a relation of dominance of men over women. This, of course, has important implications for training programs about sexual harassment. It is not enough simply to inform people about actions that constitute sexual harassment. It also is necessary to challenge prevailing notions of masculinity that discourage empathy in men.

Absent from the general statistics about harassment is the way race intersects with sex in harassing behaviors. Communication researchers Brian K. Richardson and Juandalynn Taylor (2009) explain that "women of color experience sexual harassment at the intersection of race and gender" (p. 249). In their study, African American women reported they "faced sexual harassment that was often based upon racial stereotypes or was carried out by powerful cultures (White males) at the expense of marginalized cultures. Such events support the notion that sexual harassment experiences are often intertwined with racial discrimination" (p. 265). Not only did race influence the form of harassment, but it also limited the women's range of responses to it. African American women often chose not to report the harassment because "speaking out was made difficult by concerns over fulfilling stereotypes of being 'overly emotional' or 'angry' minority women. In fact, at least one participant quit her job rather than fulfill the stereotype of the angry Black woman" (pp. 265–266).

In a study of Canadian women, researchers sought to determine how diverse women understood harassment (Welsh et al., 2006). They conducted focus group research with Black women; Filipinas working as part of the Live-In Caregiver Program; White women in unionized, male-dominated manufacturing settings; and mixed-race women employed by the federal government. They found that race and citizenship played a significant role in how women defined harassment. White women's definitions were most similar to the legal definition. In contrast, the Black women and Filipinas tended to not label harassing behaviors *sexual* harassment, in part because the behaviors could not be distinguished from harassment on account of race and/or citizenship status.

Finally, it is important to turn a gendered lens on sexual harassment laws themselves. Given sexual harassment laws tend to presume heteronormativity, they tend only to envision men harassing women (or occasionally women harassing men). This makes the law blind to cases of same-sex gender harassment, wherein people are harassed because their gender does not match the expectations attached to their sex. In other words, sexual harassment is not something men do to women because they are women but something that people do to other people to maintain strict gender/sex binary norms and inequalities.

Conceiving of sexual harassment as an attempt to maintain gender norms enables one to recognize the harassment of masculine women and feminine men by women and men. Law professor Francisco Valdes (1995) argues the belief that gender discrimination is a woman's issue only makes the law blind to the fact that women could harass men for being feminine. Similarly, because gender and sexual orientation are conflated, many assume that feminine men are gay and harass them on the basis of a falsely attributed sexuality. This makes it difficult for straight, feminine men to receive redress, because their harassers will say they harassed not because of sex but because of sexual orientation—and limited protections exist for harassment based on orientation. The complexity of the issue of sexual harassment makes clear why it is important to apply a critical gender analysis. It also provides a fascinating example to explore how the discourse of law structures social understandings of sex, gender, and orientation.

Work as Liberation and Locations of Empowerment

As we note in other chapters, a description of institutions solely as locations of subordination is incomplete. They also are locations of resistance. To resist generally requires more than a one-time effort and using individual and collaborative agency (Allen, 1996, also see 1995, 1998). Resistance is more than a strategy; it is a way of rethinking, renaming, and remaking the world. Organizational scholar Patricia Buzzanell (2000) urges people to "focus more on the ways that people incorporate resistant thinking and behaving into their identities and interactions. Resistance takes many forms" (p. 260).

For example, to balance work-life demands, many African American women have been found to develop communities of "*othermothers* and *fictive kin* to help each other with balancing work and family" (Parker, 2003, p. 268). Parker (2003) identifies five forms of resistance and empowerment that individuals, in this case African American women, use: "a) developing and using voice, b) being self-defined, c) being self-determined, d) connecting to and building community, and e) seeking spirituality and regeneration" through spiritual growth and church support (p. 280). Many Latina immigrants are redefining *mother* to mean "wage earner" as they leave their own children in order to earn money caring for others' children (Hondagneu-Sotelo & Avila, 1997). Some women in the United States codified forms of legal redress in the 1960s to use against sexual harassers. Even as power dynamics in the institution of work constrain people's options, resistance is possible.

Knowing one's options can both protect one's own self-esteem and also create potential solutions. When one confronts an instance where work has been gendered/sexed, as when a man is discouraged from pursuing a profession that traditionally has been populated by women, understanding that such job segregation can be challenged may enable him to pursue his career dreams. And, when enough people follow this man's lead, more pervasive changes in the nature of work are possible. For women pursuing work outside the home, the reality is that even as work can constrain, it also "provides women with the same rewards that it has historically offered men, including a degree of economic independence and enhanced self-esteem" (Gerson, 2004, p. 166).

A society's understandings of gender/sex, race, and class are not static. Norms can be altered—sometimes quite subtly or even unintentionally and sometimes quite overtly and very intentionally. How gender is institutionalized makes clear that this practice finds its persistence and stability in its institutionalization. However, gender also is "dynamic, emergent, local, variable, and shifting" (Martin, 2003, p. 351).

Conclusion

Work is something virtually every person does, whether it is paid or unpaid (such as housework or yard work), and if one does not work that in itself is a basis for judgment. Work can be extremely rewarding, and people can consider their jobs a core part of their identities. However, work also can be extremely dehumanizing, something done only as a way of earning money to pay for the necessities of life.

Work as an institution both genders and is gendered. The jobs people do, people's interactions with others at work, and law and discourse all influence the performance of gender/sex. In turn, gender/sex influences how people understand work and its relation to family, identity, and culture. The tensions and intersections between work and family, work and leisure, and work and law can be improved only if one overtly considers gender as part of that mix.

Work as a gendered/sexed institution can only be opened to all if the gendered/sexed reality of work is recognized. Interestingly, despite all the statistical evidence about pay gaps, differential opportunity for advancement, sexual harassment, and job segregation, college students still tend to believe they will face no discrimination once they enter the workplace. In a study of 1,373 college students taking business courses at a public southeastern university, the researchers report that

> college students fail to perceive that gender discrimination might affect their own careers or the careers of women in business. . . . Almost 90% of all student respondents reported that their opportunities for advancement, networking, mentoring, and pay would not be affected by their gender. Similarly, 90% of students perceived that women would not have fewer opportunities for networking and mentoring because of their gender. Moreover, 75% believed that women would not face pay disparity, and 60% believed that gender would present no obstacle to women in the workplace. (Sipe, Johnson, & Fisher, 2009, p. 344)

These findings are particularly troubling because awareness of and knowledge about the way work is gendered, sexed, raced, and compulsorily heterosexual are necessary to minimize the effects of workplace discrimination. If one does not expect to find work gendered/sexed and then experiences discrimination, the effects on self-esteem tend to be greater and the ability to seek ways to productively counter these effects is lessened. It is extremely difficult to resist unequal treatment if one is unwilling to recognize it exists.

KEY CONCEPTS

capitalism   190

critical organizational
   communication   189

emotions   194

girl watching   197

hostile work
   environment   197

paid care work   196

quid pro quo   197

sexual harassment   196

work-family tensions   192

DISCUSSION QUESTIONS

1. The authors state that discriminatory gender constructions based on sex and race are manifest in the institution of work, perhaps more than any other institution. What evidence do you find of this in the chapter or in your personal observations?

2. Often, when women who are primary caregivers use day care, they are seen as bad mothers.
   - Why is it that putting a child in day care does not make a man a bad father?
   - Discuss how this gives insight into the existence of double standards.
   - Does motherhood influence women's identity differently than fatherhood influences men's identity? If so, how? If not, why?

3. Apply Acker's (1990) five reasons why gender in organizations should be studied by identifying examples in this chapter to illustrate each reason. What does this reveal?

4. What does it mean to say that the institution of work should be studied in the larger context of capitalism and consumerism? What is gained from this analysis? What questions remain?

CHAPTER 10

Religion

I n the summer of 2012, gender, sex, and religion entered the public consciousness from a rather surprising source: Catholic nuns. The Leadership Conference of Women Religious (LCWR), the organization that represents about 80% of U.S. nuns, found itself under close scrutiny by the Vatican. Because the Vatican believed U.S. nuns had strayed from Catholic doctrinal teachings, it scheduled an apostolic visit. After three years of visiting 400 religious institutes in the United States, Mother Mary Clare Millea reported that the "enduring reality" of U.S. women religious was "one of fidelity, joy, and hope" (as cited in Apostolic Visitation, 2012, p. 1). However, when she submitted her report to the Congregation of the Doctrine of the Faith, it responded that U.S. nuns are pushing "radical feminist themes incompatible with the Catholic faith" because the LCWR mission focused on social justice rather than taking an overt public stand against abortion, euthanasia, homosexuality, same-sex marriage, and the ordination of women (Congregatio Pro Doctrina Fidei, 2012, p. 3). The Vatican called for a complete reform of the group. In response, Sister Beth Rindler described the divergent view of U.S. nuns as a gender issue: "The church in Rome believes in the patrimony of God. But we believe that God created men and women equally. That's where we clash" (as cited in Nadeau, 2012, par. 6). Despite the LCWR's claim that the Vatican's accusations were unsubstantiated, the Vatican decided that "for the next five years, the LCWR will effectively be under Vatican receivership," meaning the men in the hierarchy will determine how women religious practice the gospel (Winfield, 2012, par. 14).

Although internal disputes within the Catholic Church might typically pass under the radar of public attention, this did not. During July, Network (a national Catholic social justice lobby) sponsored a nine-state "Nuns on the Bus" tour, during which time a group of nuns met with Republican legislators who supported deep spending cuts in social programs proposed by Representative Paul Ryan's (R-WI) budget, a budget the nuns believe "harms people who are already suffering" (Nuns on the Bus, 2012, par. 1). As Sister Simone Campbell (2012) explained,

We remain committed to Gospel values: healing the sick, feeding the hungry, welcoming the immigrant.

> Some might prefer that we sit down and keep quiet. Instead, we just finished a nine-state bus tour to highlight the critical work Catholic sisters do in leading anti-poverty initiatives and calling attention to a Republican budget that the U.S. Conference of Catholic Bishops has criticized as failing a moral test. (par. 1–2)

Between the tour and media coverage of the Vatican response to the LCWR, the issue rose to public consciousness. Stories appeared in the *New York Times*, *Washington Post*, and *Philadelphia Enquirer* and on CNN, MSNBC, CBS, and NPR. *The Colbert Report* even covered the controversy with a segment on "Radical Feminist Nuns" and interviews with Sister Simone airing on June 11 and December 13, 2012.

Figure 10.1   Sister Simone Campbell, June 18, 2012, in Ames, Iowa, on the first day of the Nuns on the Bus tour.

Source: AP Photo/Charlie Neibergall

As this example should make clear, religious institutions participate in the construction of sex, gender, and sexuality. Regardless of whether one is examining the general functioning of religion or a specific religious tradition, using a critical gendered lens enables one to understand more about how gender intersects with religious identity and how religion influences the construction of gender.

We examine how the communication of religion as a social institution constructs, constrains, and liberates gender. First, the messages of religious institutions influence sex roles of both women and men. Second, religious institutions' messages about gender delimit acceptable forms of sexuality; thus, the study of religion is central to understanding the construction of and intersections among sex, gender, and sexuality. Third, religious institutions can empower as much as they constrain. But before delving into an analysis of religion, we first want to offer a few thoughts about why it is important to talk about religion, even though it is not an easy thing to discuss given how closely many people hold their faith.

Why Study Religion, Gender, and Communication?

In 2008, the Pew Forum on Religion and Public Life, one of the most respected U.S. polling groups, conducted a survey to examine religious affiliations in the United States. It outlined the general breakdown of people into religions: 84% of people describe themselves as belonging to an organized religion, leaving 16% unaffiliated (Pew Forum, 2008, p. 5). Here is the breakdown among specific religions:

Figure 10.2 Religious Affiliations in the United States

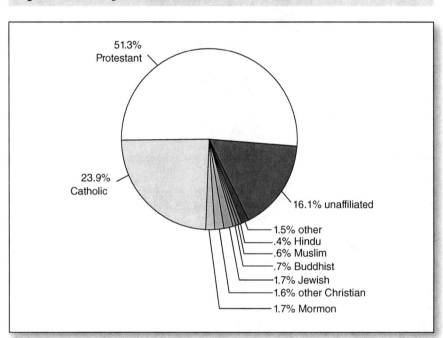

Source: Based on Pew Forum on Religion and Public Life. (2008, Feburary). *U.S. Religious Landscape Survey.* Washington, D.C. Retrieved from http://religions.pewforum.org/reports#

Contrast this to global religious distribution: 33% Christian; 21% Muslim; 14% Hindu; 6% each indigenous religions, Chinese traditional religions, and Buddhist; 0.36% Sikh; 0.22% Jewish; and 16% nonreligious (Adherents.com, 2007).

Although Christian religions are the majority in the United States, globally they are not (see Figure 10.3). However, because this textbook focuses on gender in communication in the United States, most of our discussion will focus on Christianity.

When we refer to **institutionalized religion**, we want to make clear we are referencing the institutions that mediate people's relations with a higher power or divinity, not a person's personal relationship with that power, which is typically referred to as **spirituality** (Klassen, 2003). Clearly, spirituality and religion are intertwined insofar as religion influences a person's spirituality. However, one can be spiritual without participating in an institutionalized religion.

This distinction between spirituality and religion is a Western artifact and makes little sense when discussing South and East Asian religious practices. In many Asian

Figure 10.3   Religious Affiliations Globally

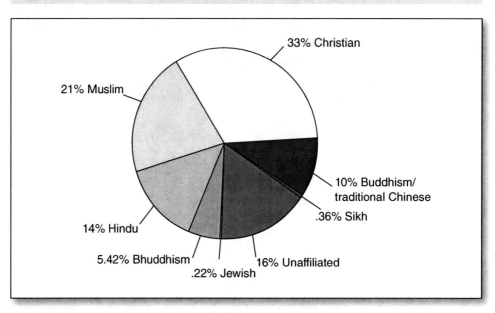

Source: Based on Pew Forum on Religion and Public Life. (2008, Feburary). *U.S. Religious Landscape Survey.* Washington, D.C. Retrieved from http://religions.pewforum.org/reports#

cultures, one is not religious because one belongs to a particular church, temple, or shrine but because one lives in the culture. In China, Confucianism influences under-standings of morality; in Japan, people practice ancestor worship (Dorman, 2006); and in Taiwan, the prevailing religion does not have a specific name but is composed of "beliefs, rituals and organizations that deeply permeate the secular life of the indi-vidual and society" (Yang, Thornton, & Fricke, 2000, p. 121). Spirituality is infused throughout the culture in every daily practice and is not split off into a formal religion (Narayanan, 2003).

Thus, when we describe religion as an institution, we are speaking from a Western perspective. Our examples presume that religion can be distinguished from the broader culture, even as we recognize that religion influences the broader culture. This is not to discredit our insights into how religion functions but to point out why a more extensive discussion of the religious practices of South and East Asia is missing from this text and to make clear that many of our points would not explain those practices.

Because a person's religion is based on faith, a belief in a higher, infallible power, analyzing religion as an institution might cause discomfort. However, religion can be analyzed as one of many institutions of cultural influence, and religions' messages inform how people are sexed and gendered. Influential postcolonialist theorist Gayatri Spivak (2004) explained, "Religion in this sense is the ritual markers of how we worship and how we inscribe ourselves in sexual difference" (p. 104). Religion informs not only people's personal relationships with their god(s) but also people's relationships with their gender/sex.

Religion and Sex Roles

Religious institutions communicate a number of messages about gender and sex. Religions invite men and women to participate in different ways, provide guidance on how to relate as women and men, and define what it means to be a good man or a good woman. Religion clearly is an important source of information on how to do gender and how to be a sex.

Gender, Sex, and Religiosity

As with other assessments of gender and sex, many people operate under the fallacious assumption that women and men experience religion differently. In fact, most studies of sex/gender and religion that assume women are "more religious" than men (Preston, 2003) link religious activity to sex and not to gender identity. Like most assumptions about difference, this one does not survive close scrutiny. The statistical evidence comparing women's and men's religious activity is compelling—but the numbers alone do not explain what the numbers mean. While numerically more women than men participate in religion, one's gender orientation is the variable that most determines one's level of religiousness, not one's sex. Women who tend toward more masculine gender orientations tend to be less religious, and men who are more feminine in their orientations tend to be more religious. Obviously, because of social pressures for women to be feminine, it makes sense that a correlation between sex and religiosity might appear, but one must remember that the intervening variable of gender orientation, not sex, is *the* influential factor.

Research bears this out. Leslie J. Francis (2005), a psychology of religion expert, studied almost 500 English women and men in their 60s and 70s. She had all participants complete the Bem Sex Role Inventory and the Francis Scale of Attitude toward Christianity. Francis found "the data demonstrated that psychological femininity is key to individual differences in religiosity . . . within the sexes and that, after taking gender role orientation into account, biological sex conveyed no additional predictive power in respect of individual differences in religiosity" (p. 179). This study is a vivid example of why researchers need to carefully think about sex and gender as distinct and not conflate them when researching. Here gender (not sex) does influence religiosity, a relationship many other studies miss because they look at sex as the only key variable.

Sex and Institutional Religious Power

Although there is no compelling evidence that one sex is more religious than another, sex does affect the role one can play in religious institutions. One can argue that religious institutions are gendered/sexed insofar as they tend to assign relatively rigid roles according to one's sex. In other words, who is allowed to communicate for (and sometimes to) a religious deity is sometimes determined by sex. In Roman Catholic and Eastern Orthodox churches, women cannot be ordained as priests, and the Southern Baptist Convention in 2000 announced that only men could serve as pastors. In Islam, women cannot serve as imams. Even in the Christian churches in which women can be ordained, they tend to serve as assistant or associate pastors, not senior pastors. When a woman does ascend to a position of power, it can spark controversy, as demonstrated by the 2006 election of Bishop Katherine Jefferts Schori to lead the U.S. church in the Anglican Communion ("Presiding Bishop," 2012). Although there was widespread support by most U.S. Episcopal churches of the ordination of women, conservative dioceses, such as the Diocese of Fort Worth, asked for an alternative Primatial oversight in order to not be under Schori's leadership (Episcopal Diocese of Fort Worth, 2007).

Perhaps the best way to understand how institutionalized forms of religion have delimited gender/sex roles is to explore two of the dominant religions, Christianity and Islam. The history of antipathy between these two religions (as embodied in the Roman Catholic Crusades to capture the Holy Land from Muslims from the 11th through the 13th centuries) might make one think they have little in common. However, religious scholars have noted the ways in which these two religions share much when it comes to understanding women's and men's roles.

Religion scholar Elina Vuola (2002) analyzed how much Christian and Islamic fundamentalisms share. She explains that the rise of both forms has been "accompanied by a vigorous promotion and enforcement of gender roles whose explicit intent entails the subordination of women" (p. 175). In particular, she notes how Western Christianity (as represented by the Vatican) and Islam (as represented by some Muslim states) have begun to cooperate on a wide range of issues concerning women's political and social rights, reproductive freedoms, and women's roles in their religious traditions. She finds that "Judaism, Christianity and Islam have more in common in their image of women (and sexuality) than they have differences" (p. 183). Thus, the Vatican and Islamic states have worked together against progressive changes to protect women's human rights on the international and national levels. At the international level, the Vatican has aligned with Muslim nations to attempt to block progressive language on reproductive and sexual rights in the Beijing Platform for Action on Women's Rights (Petchesky, 1997).

However, for Vuola (2002), this is not an argument for forsaking religion. Instead, it is an argument for understanding how religion constructs gender and for women and men to play a more conscious role in thinking through religion and how it influences people's understandings of themselves. Religion informs many people's identities. Thus, "women are not going to—nor do they have to—give up their cultural, political and religious traditions simply because they are used against them" (p. 191).

Complementarians and Egalitarians

In many ways, the religious struggles over sex and gender are about the relationship between men and women. Are they equal in God's eyes, or are they meant to be complementary to one another, with God giving men authority over women? In her work on gender and religion, Carolyn James (2011) described the two worldviews:

> [C]omplementarians believe the Bible establishes male authority over women, making male leadership the biblical standard. According to this view, God calls women to submit to male leadership and take up supportive roles to their husbands and to male leaders in the church. The complementarian jury is split over whether this includes the public sphere. **Egalitarians** believe that leadership is not determined by gender but by the gifting and calling of the Holy Spirit, and that God calls all believers to submit to one another. At the heart of the debate is whether or not God has placed limits on what women can or cannot do in the home and in the church, although the discussion inevitably bleeds into other spheres of life. (pp. 154–155)

Regardless of the religion, the complementarians versus egalitarians argument seems to emerge. Consider the Roman Catholic Church's "Letter to the Bishops of the Catholic Church on the Collaboration of Men and Women in the Church and in the World" (Ratzinger, 2004; for a full text of the letter, see www.wf-f.org/CDF-LetteronCollaboration.html). The letter was written by then Cardinal Joseph Ratzinger, who served as Pope Benedict XVI from April 19, 2005, to February 28, 2013. The letter was offered as a definitive statement of men's and women's roles in the Church and the world. The introduction explains that the letter was written because the "Church is called today to address certain currents of thought which are often at variance with the authentic advancements of women" (sec. 1), ways of thinking that tend to emphasize "conditions of subordination in order to give rise to antagonism" and to deny natural differences between the sexes (sec. 2).

Sister Joan Chittister, O.S.B., (2004) notes how the letter both empowers and constrains. The letter is progressive in its call that the institution of work needs to be altered to recognize the demands working mothers face and in its celebration of values traditionally associated with women, values that embrace an orientation toward others. The letter recognizes those values can be found in women as well as men.

The letter also constrains. First, it embraces a theory of sex and gender that adopts a binary understanding of sex. Second, the letter posits feminism as an adversary of the Church and in the process tends to treat feminism and its theories as a monolithic whole, which the diversity of theories in this text ought to make clear is not an accurate description. Third, the letter conflates sex and gender to the extent that it sees women as the sole repository of feminine values, even as it recognizes that men might be able to participate in those values. Fourth, women's role is consigned to two sexual locations: A woman is either a mother or a virgin. Finally, even though the letter encourages a form of active collaboration between women and men and seeks to move away from a metaphor of battle as descriptive of the relationship between the sexes, the letter almost exclusively focuses on what women should do and spends little to no time on what men should do. Theology professor Edward Collins Vacek (2005) explains that the letter is "not really about collaboration," for it "scarcely mentions the myriad ways men and women collaborate" (p. 159).

Muscular Christianity

Scholars who study how gender, sex, and religion intersect have found that "there were distinctive patterns of men's spiritual experience" (Bradstock, Gill, Hogan, & Morgan, 2000, p. 2). This research into muscular Christianity explores how Christian religions gendered men with particular forms of masculinity. **Muscular Christianity** was "defined simply as a Christian commitment to health and manliness" (Putney, 2001, p. 11) premised on the belief that an association existed between "physical strength, religious certainty, and the ability to shape and control the world around oneself" (Hall, 1994, p. 7). Although its roots go back to the Bible, muscular Christianity did not emerge as a dominant theme until the 1850s, when it appeared as a term describing a popular novel of the day, Charles Kingsley's *Two Years Ago* (1857). The concept would emerge in England and quickly travel to the United States.

The muscular Christianity movement sought to make Protestant Christianity masculine but faced resistance from evangelical Protestant churches who at that point were particularly enamored of feminine iconography such that by the 1850s, they were "channeling much of their energy into praising such stereotypically 'female' traits as nurturance, refinement, and sensitivity" (Putney, 2001, p. 24). The feminization of Protestant religions could be found in "an altered rhetorical style for preaching, popular depictions of the divine, and the increased presence and influence of women in Christian sects" (Maddux, 2012, p. 44). In response, muscular Christians glorified such "stereotypically 'male' traits as strength, courage, and endurance" (Putney, 2001, p. 24) as they sought to "masculinize the rhetorical style of preaching, popular images of Jesus, and the leadership and membership of the churches" (Maddux, 2012, p. 44).

Muscular Christianity also faced resistance from the Puritan tradition that viewed sport as a "sinful diversion" because "exercising one's muscles for no particular end except health struck many Protestants in the mid-nineteenth century as an immoral waste of time" (Putney, 2001, pp. 20, 24). One found salvation through work, and sport was viewed as play. Thus, for U.S. Protestants during the antebellum period, organized sports were an abomination. In fact, in his book exploring the rise of muscular Christianity in the United States, Clifford Putney (2001) cites Washington Gladden (Congregational church pastor, leader of the Social Gospel movement, and Progressive movement member), who grew up in the 1840s thinking, "If I became a Christian it would be wrong for me to play ball" (p. 20).

The push for more muscular forms of religion emerged in the late 1800s in the United States as a response to the insecurities and fears many men faced during an age in which change overwhelmed them. The United States had just survived the Civil War, women in increasing numbers were working, and the nation was industrializing. As Donald E. Hall (1994) explains in his book on muscular Christianity, "The broad strokes in the discourse of the muscular Christians were reactions to threats posed by a world growing ever more confusing and fragmented. . . . Muscular Christianity was an attempt to assert control over a world that had seemingly gone mad" (p. 9). Muscular Christianity not only gendered White, Protestant, native, male U.S. citizens, but it also functioned as a location to discipline, through caricature, the bodies of lower-class, Irish, and non-European men. The struggle was not only over how particular male bodies would act in the world but also over "social, national, and religious bodies," for which the male body functioned as a metaphor (Hall, 1994, p. 8). The male body is a site for struggle, because it serves "as a paradigm and metaphor for male-dominated culture and society" (p. 6).

During the 1880s and through the 1920s in the United States, a number of factors influenced the willingness to accept muscular Christianity. First, Protestant church leaders as well as secular reformers were worried about the church becoming feminized as women came to outnumber men in church attendance and also began to assume more leadership positions. Communication scholar Kristy Maddux (2012) argues that "the movement for muscular Christianity was aimed at least in part to winning men back to the churches" (p. 49). Second, depopulation of the rural areas and the increasingly urbanized population meant that men could not be assured of physical activity doing farm work. Legitimizing physical activity for nonwork-related tasks helped some men maintain their physical masculinity and their religious identity. The two were no longer in conflict. Third, the influx of Catholic immigrants began to threaten the dominance of Protestantism. The U.S. Protestant establishment "entertained fears of well-bred but overeducated weaklings succumbing before muscular immigrant hordes" (Putney, 2001, p. 31). And fourth, the emergence of the modern woman (meaning working woman) worried male church leaders. From 1900 to 1920, the number of women working in white-collar jobs increased threefold (Putney, 2001).

For an example of feminine and muscular Christianity in conflict, see Kristy Maddux's (2012) analysis of Aimee Semple McPherson, in which she argues the following:

McPherson attracted controversy because she persisted with a feminized preaching style long after that style had proved threatening to Christianity and after it had suffered rebuke from the proponents of masculine, or muscular, Christianity. Unlike her contemporaries Billy Sunday and Paul Rader, whose sermons boasted of their athletic exploits, McPherson performed the feminized style of evangelical preaching, drawing upon its emotional and embodied conventions, and she innovated feminized personae, including the servant and the bride. Her critics, in turn, derided her for being a deceptive temptress who preyed upon her listeners' emotional vulnerabilities. (p. 60)

(Continued)

(Continued)

Figure 10.4 Aimee Semple McPherson delivering a sermon at the Spreckels Organ Pavilion during the 1935 Exposition, San Diego

Figure 10.5 Billy Sunday, 1917

Figure 10.6 Paul Rader, 1922

Source: San Diego History Center

Source: Library of Congress

Source: Library of Congress

Figure 10.7 Tim Tebow seen here "Tebowing," or taking a knee to pray

Source: Wikimedia Commons/Clemed

Given this history, it becomes clear that the centrality of sports to U.S. hegemonic masculinity is tied to religion. Muscular Christianity and its secular counterpart of the strenuous life (as advocated by Theodore Roosevelt) would dominate social life at the turn of the 19th century and into the 20th. Even though its prominence waned in the years after World War I (1914–1918) because many thought muscular Christianity had fanned the flames of war, its effects persisted. Although the movement lost some of its intellectual influence, "paeans to health and manliness continued to emanate both from the mainline churches and from best-selling authors" (Putney, 2001, p. 200). The recent resurgence of muscular Christianity among the Promise Keepers and the Fellowship of Christian Athletes indicates that the connection between religion and masculine identity is not a thing of the past. As the popularity of Tim Tebow demonstrates, one can be a muscular Christian; religiosity is consistent with masculinity. His act of "Tebowing," taking a knee to pray, has become a cultural phenomenon.

Religion and Sexuality

Not only do institutionalized religions make overt pronouncements about gender/sex, they also offer teachings about sexuality. As religions structure understandings of sex and gender, they grapple with understandings of sexuality, of what is and is not acceptable. Many people's condemnation of homosexuality is informed by religious beliefs. Despite many religious traditions' rejection of homosexuality, people of faith struggle to find ways to reconcile their faith and their sexuality. DignityUSA works toward respect and justice for all gay, lesbian, bisexual, and transgender persons in the Catholic Church (www.dignityusa.org). Queer Jihad (www.well.com/user/queerjhd) provides a location for lesbian, gay, and queer Muslims to work through issues of homosexuality in Islam. The documentary *Trembling Before G-d* (DuBowski, 2003) portrays the stories of lesbian and gay Hasidic and Orthodox Jews who seek to reconcile their love of faith with their homosexuality.

Of course, the religious teachings on sexuality do not affect only those who participate in a particular religion. As the recent U.S. debates over same-sex marriage demonstrate, religion enters into the secular world, informing which unions receive civil recognition. In other words, if one wants to understand how gender, sex, and sexuality are political issues, one must attend to the role religion plays in defining gender/sex/sexuality and the role that sexuality plays in drawing the lines between what is a religious issue and what is a secular public issue.

Religion as Liberation and Locations of Empowerment

Religion, like all social institutions, constructs and is constructed by gender/sex and is a location of both subordination and empowerment. This complexity highlights the need to understand the relationship between spiritual equality and social equality. Religion is one location in which people find validation of their intrinsic worth as human beings. Most religions declare **spiritual equality** before their supreme deity. For example, in Christianity many cite Paul: "There is neither Jew nor Greek, there is neither slave nor free person, there is not male and female; for you are all one in Christ Jesus" (Galatians 3:28, New American Standard Version). In Islam, it is believed that both women and men are capable of knowledge, and "seeking knowledge is an obligation for every Muslim man and woman" ("Understanding Islam," n.d., question 11). Also, in the Qur'an, men and women's requirements and responsibilities are described as equal and parallel. These examples raise the question of how spiritual equality before God's eyes intersects with social equality. How do people reconcile the spiritual equality of all people with the institutional and social inequality of some people?

Even when religious institutions dictate rigid sexualities and gender roles, individuals still find empowerment and fulfillment in their religious traditions.

We take seriously the fact that people, particularly people of color in the United States, see religion as creatively productive in their lives and as a safe haven and site of resistance to broader social injustices. Although the institution of religion is important in structuring people's understanding of who they are and where they fit in the universe, religion (perhaps more than any other institution) also highlights how "institutions are constituted and reconstituted by embodied agents" (Martin, 2004, p. 1257). Religion is as much about people's daily practices of religion as it is about scripture and belief systems.

To explore diverse expressions of religion, one can study the communication about and of religion in the form of "religious experiences, texts, transcriptions of interviews, personal accounts, rituals, or religious communities," as well as images of divinity and the documents declared definitive by church leaders (Thie, 1994, p. 232). When expansive forms of religious communication are studied, it becomes clear that "religions and divinities are more than a source of violence; . . . religions are also a source of resistance, hope, and struggle" (p. 232). So, we now want to turn to three distinct instances where people have negotiated gender, sex, religion, and empowerment.

African Americans and Religion

Although religious appeals have been used to outline strict gender roles, and scriptural grounds have been used to justify women's and minorities' social inequality (see Gaffney, 1990), religion also has long played a significant role in people's liberation. Maria Miller Stewart (1803–1879), the African American woman who was the first woman to speak to a mixed-sex audience, argued that she had been called by God to speak against the evil of slavery. Even though she knew she would face extreme opposition to speaking in public—and she did—she cited her faith in God and her belief that she was doing God's work as authorization for her entry into the public sphere (Sells, 1993).

Spirituality and religion play a central role in much African American women's rhetoric (Pennington, 2003). Sojourner Truth (circa 1797–1883), Harriet Tubman (1820–1913), and Fannie Lou Hamer (1917–1977) provide archetypal examples. All of them cited their spirituality as enabling and motivating them to take incredible risks as social activists—respectively, as an abolitionist, a conductor on the Underground Railroad, and a voting rights activist. For them, the institution of their church provided a location for the development of a powerful spirituality, a spirituality that is "not merely a system of religious beliefs similar to logical systems of ideas" but rather "comprises articles of faith that provide a conceptual framework for living everyday life" (Collins, 1998, p. 245).

Not only does religion function as a powerful motivating force for individuals, it also functions to create a sense of group worth and community. In the antebellum United States, slaves' singing of spirituals constituted an act of resistance for all slaves, male and female, insofar as the songs "constituted themselves as members of a valued community, as fully human in their desire and ability to create, as chosen for special notice by God, and as capable of acting on their own behalf" (Sanger, 1995, p. 190). During the civil rights movement (1955–1965), the Christian churches attended by African Americans played a vital role in their struggle for employment and voting rights, not only organizationally but also philosophically (Chappell, 2004).

Even as religion motivated those who struggled for civil rights, gender continued to define the roles played by women and men, consigning women to serve invisible (though essential) leadership roles in the movement at the grassroots level (such as directing the choirs or organizing community meals) placing them as a vital bridge between the movement and potential constituents (McNair Barnett, 1993; Robnett, 1996).

In pointing out the role religion played for African Americans, one should not infer that it played no role for Whites. In fact, White women who became involved in the civil rights movement seemed to do so not as a result of direct experiences of oppression (such as those inflicted on African Americans) but because of feelings of empathy informed by their religious beliefs (Irons, 1998).

Those who have studied the role of religion in the civil rights movement have concluded that "one cannot understand Black women's ability to cope, or their activity to ensure liberation and empowerment, without addressing their religious and spiritual heritages, beliefs, and practices" (Klassen, 2003, par. 11). Thus, when studying the public rhetoric, organizational relations, and interpersonal expressions of African American women activists, it is important to identify those places in which religion offers a motivation and basis from which to resist social injustice.

Veiling Practices

Veiling practices have both religious and secular significance, are used by men and women as well as by Christians and Muslims, and have been misread by the West. Veiling practices provide an excellent example of how religion is a site of resistance and emancipation but also can be used as a justification for subordination.

Veiling practices provide a paradigmatic example of bodily, or nonverbal, communication. Fadwa El Guindi (1999), an anthropologist who revolutionized the study of covering practices, explains that "veiling is . . . a language that communicates social and cultural messages" (p. xii). A critical gendered lens, attentive to issues of intersectionality and colonialism, embraces the role of the world traveler (rather than the arrogant perceiver) and can avoid the error of many Western critics who view the veil as "a sign of women's backwardness, subordination, and oppression" (p. 3). World travelers recognize the complexity of cultural practices, the way in which their own cultures veil (or impose a dress code), and that many Islamic women wear the veil as a form of empowerment.

A world traveler should note how the term *veil* is problematic. It is the lone word English-speaking peoples use to describe a vast range of clothing options.

El Guindi (1999) explains that Arabic has no single linguistic referent for the veil. Because the practice differs among groups, cultures, and times, multiple words exist: "*burqu', abayah, tarhah, burnus, jilbab, jellabah, hayik, milayah, gallabiyyah, dishdasha, gargush, gina', mungub, lithma, yashmik, habarah, izer*" (p. 7). Each type can be differentiated by whether it is a face cover, a head cover, or a body cover. This linguistic subtlety contrasts to the "indiscriminate, monolithic, and ambiguous" Western term *veil* (p. 7). El Guindi reminds analysts that each form of covering reveals, conceals, and communicates differently.

Within Arabic, the multiple terms distinguish among these subtle differences, whereas in English the single term obscures the complexity of body-covering practices. In Afghanistan, women (were forced to under the Taliban but now might choose to) cover their bodies and faces with the burqu'; in Iran women (choose to but are sometimes forced to) wear the *chador*, which covers the body but leaves the face free; and women from Indonesia choose to wear the *hijab* (which covers the hair and neck but leaves the face revealed) even when living in the United States because it is part of their identities. Despite this complexity, those in the West obsessively critique the harem (another misunderstood concept), polygamy, and the veil, all of which have been held to be "synonymous with female weakness and oppression" (El Guindi, 1999, p. 10).

What might explain the West's misreading of the veil? In reality, the veil has a longer history in Christian traditions (where it is associated with living secluded from worldly life and sex) than in Islam. Most images of the Virgin Mary show her wearing a headscarf much like a hijab, and Catholic women were required to wear head coverings to church until the 1960s. The narrow interpretation of Islamic covering practices may be more informed by Christianity's interpretation of the practice than by the meaning of the Islamic practice.

Although the practice of veiling has religious connections, the links are not unique to Islam (many Christian women veil their faces during wedding ceremonies), and not all practices have religious foundations. At the time of Islam's rise in the 7th century, veiling was already practiced by many cultures in the Eastern Mediterranean and the Middle East (Cichocki, 2004). Even though the burqu', due to media coverage of the Taliban in Afghanistan, is perceived to be an expression of Islam, it actually is part of a secular tradition (El Guindi, 2005a, p. 262). It was imposed not as part of religious expression (given that face coverings are prohibited by Islam in the most sacred spaces of worship and during pilgrimages to Mecca) but as part of a culture in a particular country at a particular time.

Additionally, body covering practices are embraced by women and men. The contemporary dress code for Muslim men and women is to "wear full-length gallabiyyas (jilbab in standard Arabic), loose fitting to conceal body contours, in solid austere colors made of opaque fabric. They lower their gaze in cross-sex public interaction and refrain from body or dress decoration or colors that draw attention to their bodies" (El Guindi, 2005b; "The Dress," par. 1). Researchers who examine only women's clothing practices fail to notice that the standards of dress expected of women *and* men call for a deemphasis of the body. It would be unfair to read dress standards calling for head and body coverings as evidence of women's oppression. This becomes even more evident when women's political uses of the veil are recognized.

Veiling did not take on its overt political dimensions until the 19th century, "when European powers justified the colonial project by claiming to rescue Muslim women from the oppression of savage faith, most readily visible in the practices of veiling and seclusion" (Cichocki, 2004, p. 51). Interestingly, at the same time that colonial powers were seeking to save Muslim women from Muslim men, no one was calling for the rescue of Catholic nuns who also wore veils (in the form of the habit) and lived in the seclusion of their convents. As colonized nations began to fight against colonial powers, veils became a form of resistance. Women donned the veil to protest Westernization and modernization's pressure on women to adopt revealing clothing.

In 1936, Iran's Shah Reza Pahlavi's embrace of Westernization included banning women from wearing the chador. His impetus for this move was his belief that women served best as decorative accessories to men. In response, even women who considered themselves modern began wearing the chador to protest the Shah's regime. When the Shah's son was eventually overthrown in 1979, the Ayotollah Khomeini then required women to wear the chador, causing many women who had worn it as a form of resistance now to protest against it. The garment is not the problem; the mandate to wear it or not to wear it is the problem. The veil is "a complex symbol: female emancipation can be denoted by either wearing it or removing it; the veil can acquire both secular and religious meaning in that it either denotes resistance to colonization, or ties with the Islamic tradition" (Cichocki, 2004, p. 49).

Egypt presents a similar pattern. In mid-1970s Cairo, young, urban, female college students began veiling themselves from head to toe in contrast to the more Western forms of dress favored by their parents. As Islamic movements have grown, "dress has played a pivotal symbolic, ritual and political role in this dynamic phenomenon. The new vocabulary and dress style embodies a moral/behavioral code. Islam has struggled to position itself vis-a-vis the Islamic veil" (El Guindi, 2005b, "The Veil," par. 2). Quite simply, the "Islamizing of life politics and resistance" as represented by young women's wearing of veils "is directly related to the colonial/imperial assault on Arabs and Muslims" (par. 2). Women veiled as a way to renew traditional cultural beliefs of reserve and restraint and as a response to pressures from Western materialism, consumerism, and commercialism. Even though the Egyptian government tried to resist women's move to veil (universities banned veils), courts eventually threw out the prohibitions.

Our point in providing so much detail on veiling practices is to make clear how the practices of non-Western cultures often are misread. El Guindi (2005b) highlights the missteps those interested in gender, sex, and religion should avoid. When Christian people filter their understanding of a non-Christian culture through their own religious tradition, "efforts to understand the Middle East have resulted in distorted perspectives about Islamic constructions of gender, space, and sexuality" ("Two Notions of Gender," par. 1). Western European society's understanding of the relationship between the domestic (private) and the public is distinct from Arab and Islamic society's understanding. The West's understanding of piety as separate from worldliness and sexuality results in a focus on seclusion and virginity, missing the nuances of Islamic conceptions of space and privacy as they pertain to veiling.

It also is important to recognize the specific meanings of the veil for women living in the United States. In an ethnographic study of 13 Muslim women living in the United States who used veiling practices, Rachel Droogsma (2007) found they saw six major functions for the veil: "defining Muslim identity, functioning as a behavior check, resisting sexual objectification, affording more respect, preserving intimate relationships, and providing a source of freedom" (p. 301). The women reported that wearing the hijab was important because it enabled them to bond with other Muslims, please God, and take control of their bodies. In many ways, the women saw Western dress practices as far more oppressive than the hijab, which gave them a measure of agency; they could control who saw their bodies. Participants also pointed out how some very revered women of the Christian faith (nuns and the Virgin Mary) covered their bodies in a similar way (p. 307).

In case you think misreadings of the veil have no effect, consider how Western misinterpretations of non-Western traditions have real effects. Communication studies scholars Kevin Ayotte and Mary Husain (2005) demonstrate why it is even more important to make sure the presuppositions of one religious tradition are not imposed on other traditions' practices. They analyze how the burqu' was used in portrayals of Afghan women to present them as slaves in need of rescue by the West. They track how "the image of the Afghan woman shrouded in the burqa has played a leading role in various public arguments seeking to justify U.S. military intervention in Afghanistan following the 9/11 attacks" (p. 113). Prior to September 11, President Bush never commented on the repressive conditions under which Afghan women lived. However, after September 11, the administration "launched a new initiative to publicize the brutal treatment of Afghan women and girls by the Taliban regime. Events include meetings with women leaders, a Saturday radio address by First Lady Laura Bush (2001), and release of a U.S. State Department report on gender apartheid by Secretary of State Colin Powell" ("Bush Administration," 2001). Two official statements were made by Bush, including his December 12, 2001, remarks on signing the Afghan Women and Children Relief Act of 2001. In 2002, Bush included longer commentary about Afghan women in four separate statements (G. Bush, 2001–2002).

Administration comments and media coverage provided a justification for military intervention in Afghanistan. Ayotte and Husain explain that "collapsing differences among Muslim women through the use of the burqa as a generalized symbol of female oppression performs a colonizing function" and hence justified a military engagement in Afghanistan (p. 118). Unfortunately, such a justification may have resulted in an engagement that did more harm to those it was meant to help. First, demonization of the burqu' diverts attention from the fact that the garment was mandated. The issue is not the burqu' but the lack of freedom of choice. Second, the demonization of the burqu' denies the possibility that women might choose to wear it.

The result is that many U.S. citizens now believe that because Afghan women are unveiled, they are free. This ignores how Afghan women continue to face enormous structural and physical violence.

Rereading the History of Women Religious

One of the ways people have attempted to reappropriate religion is to reread its history. In most religions, men have held institutionalized power and hence have been the ones with the authority to interpret key religious texts. However, women have long sought to make clear the central role played by women in religion. Religious communication scholar Helen Sterk (1989) examines the ways women are represented in the Bible. She argues that most (male) religious authorities typically focus on women's limited roles as wives, slaves, or mothers of important men. However, this particular understanding of women's role in the Christian tradition is not an accurate representation of what is in the Bible. In part, translations have created artificial limits for women's roles. For example, *anthropos* was long translated as *man*, rather than as *humanity*, which is more accurate. Additionally, numerous stories in which women play important roles, such as the stories of Rahab, Jael, Deborah, Esther, Mary Magdalene, Martha, Joanna, and Susanna, could be highlighted. However, these more expansive readings of women's roles have been constrained in Christian religious traditions. In turn, these religious traditions then inform the secular roles allowed to women and men.

Sterk's point is not that the Bible is sexist but that society's sexism has led to interpretations of the Bible that ignore women's presence. Sterk argues that women's centrality to the Christian tradition is easy to find in Scripture. It also is easy to find in practice.

Within Catholicism, women played a significant role, writing on issues of morality and doctrine. In medieval times, a life in service to the Church was the only option for women who wanted to live a life of the mind. Hildegard of Bingen (1098–1179), a 12th-century German nun, spoke to the life of women in *Scivias*, her major religious work (1151/1152/1990). In the 13th century, Hadewijch, a Flemish mystic, joined the Beguines, a group of devout women who lived "a life of apostolic poverty and contemplation without taking vows as nuns" (Hart in Hadewijch, 1980, p. 3). Catherine of Sienna (1347–1380), an Italian nun of the Dominican order, was one of two women to be granted the title of Doctor of the Roman Catholic Church. Julian of Norwich (1342–1423), an English nun, wrote about the spiritual problems encountered between the soul and God (1393/1978).

Later, Sor Juana Inés de la Cruz (1651–1695), a Mexican nun, was a poet and theological writer. Following the distribution of one of her essays, a bishop chastised her. Her response, *La Respuesta* (1701/1987), is a defense of women's rights to education and culture, presaging the demands of the U.S. first-wave women's movement by almost a century. The writings of these women all demonstrate that despite constraints, women were drawn to religious traditions and found locations of resistance within them.

Conclusion

Religious institutions construct the gender of their own members through doctrinal declarations, historical narratives, and intersections with other dominant institutions. Religion informs how people understand *man* and *woman*, delimits acceptable sexual practices, and is inextricably linked with race and nationality. Religion also informs people's understandings of the gender of those of other faiths through misreadings of verbal and nonverbal practices such as veiling. A gendered lens attentive to issues of intersectionality and informed by a world traveler ethic can offer a nuanced understanding of religious communication.

Even as religion constructs, and in the process constrains expression of, people's sex, gender, and sexuality, it also provides a location from which people can engage in resistance. Religion is not solely an institution of constraint; it empowers. In religion's celebration of grace and the inherent worth of humanity, it reassures those whose humanity has been denied by others that they are blessed. The complexity of religion makes clear why continued scholarship on the intersections of religion, sex, gender, sexuality, race, and nationality are warranted.

Sterk (2010) outlines seven areas for future research in the area of gender and religion in communication:

First, where do gender constructions intersect with particular faith communities? . . .

Second, what gendered communication principles, practices, and structures do various religious groups bring to life? . . .

Third, how do various uses of language either empower or constrain people's full humanity within religious traditions? . . .

Fourth, what sorts of constructions of masculinity and masculine communication practices are enhanced by various religious traditions? . . .

Fifth, how do race, gender, and faith come together? . . .

Sixth, how do faith, sexual identity, and communication come together? . . .

And seventh, how do race, sexual identity and faith come together? (pp. 212–213)

We hope that this chapter encourages you to keep asking these questions and provides you some foundational ideas to begin formulating answers to them. As Sterk (2010) explains, asking and answering these questions "matters because if we care about human beings and their flourishing and God's presence and love as shown in the whole panoply of religions, we will care about how individuals flourish spiritually due to the communication they create and experience" (p. 213).

KEY CONCEPTS

complementarians   209

egalitarians   209

institutionalized religion   205

muscular Christianity   210

spiritual equality   213

spirituality   205

veiling practices   215

DISCUSSION QUESTIONS

1. Why is it necessary to understand relationships between spiritual equality and social equality?

2. What "gendered communication principles, practices, and structures" of religion construct and constrain gender?

3. What are some ways in which religion has liberated and/or empowered persons or groups?

4. Using the critical gendered lens of a world traveler, how might you compare some of your own religious traditions to the traditions of other faiths?

CHAPTER 11

Media

The commercial entertainment media you watch (and play) is not real. The Hunger Games have not occurred, Master Chief John-117 is not fighting the Covenant, vampires and werewolves do not roam the forests of Washington, and Voldemort's horcruxes were not destroyed by the dynamic quartet from Gryffindor (remember Neville and the snake?). Even reality television is not real: Producers artificially construct scenarios (have you ever had to survive on a deserted island with a group of other—usually very attractive—people?), manipulate footage, show events out of sequence, and use creative editing to make people seem to say the opposite of what they did. Yet viewers often forget that everything they see on television, in magazines, and on their computer screens has been manipulated, particularly if the image is of a woman's body.

In 2009, Ralph Lauren was ridiculed for a Photoshop "fail" when it slimmed down already thin supermodel Filippa Hamilton. Others saw this image as about more than just bad editing. For a comparison of the overly photoshopped photo to a less photoshopped photo, see http://wxrt.cbslocal.com/2011/07/06/doctors-to-fashion-no-more-photoshop-fails/.

In 2011, the American Medical Association (AMA) denounced the use of alterations of models' images. In a policy statement, the AMA explained, "Such alterations can contribute to unrealistic expectations of appropriate body image—especially among impressionable children and adolescents. A large body of literature links exposure to media-propagated images of unrealistic body image to eating disorders and other child and adolescent health problems" (par. 5). In explaining the policy, a spokesperson likely referred to the Ralph Lauren image when she said, "In one image, a model's waist was slimmed so severely, her head appeared to be wider than her waist. We must stop exposing impressionable children and teenagers to advertisements portraying models with body types attainable only with the help of photo editing software" (AMA, 2011, par. 6). Although media images are not real, they have real effects on how people perceive sex and gender.

Female beauty is just one example of media power over gender. Beauty norms change, and a driving force in that change is media, from Renaissance paintings (see Figure 11.1), to computer-generated images of the perfect thigh in Christian Dior's advertisements for cellulite control (Bordo, 1997b; see Figure 11.2), to the perfect woman in the digitally idealized Lara Croft (Herbst, 2004; see Figure 11.3).

Figure 11.1   Tintoretto's *Susanna and the Elders*, c. 1555–1556

Source: © Corbis

Figure 11.2   Christian Dior advertisement, 1994

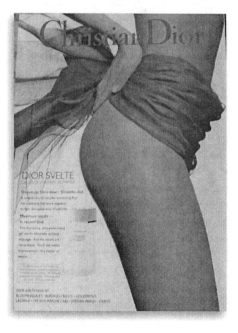

Figure 11.3   Lara Croft, digital star of the *Tomb Raider* video games

Source: © Joe Bird/Alamy

Because people often think of media products as merely entertainment or artistic expression, they forget that media play an ideological role too. As social learning theory points out, human beings learn by watching others, and this includes watching characters on television or in the movies. Communication scholar Bonnie Dow's (1996) insight about television is true of all media forms; they are "simultaneously, a commodity, an art form, and an important ideological forum for public discourse about social issues and social change" (p. xi). In this chapter, we hope to turn your critical gendered lens on the media you watch and use.

Rigorous academic analysis of media's ideological function might seem to condemn or destroy the pleasure one feels when watching a movie or reading a lifestyle magazine. That is not our goal. Instead, it is to encourage you to develop critical consciousness about media even as you take pleasure from it and to use that critical consciousness as the basis for political action. Philosophy professor Susan Bordo (1997b) points out, "Cultural criticism clears a space in which we can stand back and survey a scene that we are normally engaged in living in, not thinking about" (p. 14). Media criticism is not about dismissing people's personal choices and pleasures; it is about "preserving consciousness of the larger context in which our personal choices occur, so that we will be better informed about their potential consequences, for ourselves as well as for others" (p. 16). Is your decision about what to wear really a personal choice, or is it a response to the larger cultural context that determines some fashion choices are acceptable and others are not? Without the ability to see the external influences on what you think of as your personal choices, you lose the ability to analyze, challenge, and change institutionalized power.

To explore the interactions between media and gender, we first examine what media are and how they work. Second, we explore the gaze people use to watch media. Third, we note that whom media show, and who use which forms of media, is sexed and gendered, as well as raced and aged. Fourth, we explore two examples of how media sex and gender people. Broad trends in media include the sexualization of women (and increasingly of younger girls) and the resecuring of men's masculinity.

Defining Media and How They Function

Media are ubiquitous in contemporary U.S. society: prints, paintings, television, movies, radio, newspapers, comics, comix, novels, zines, magazines, CDs, MP3s, podcasts, video games, blogs, videos, and Tweets, to name just a few. Note that our list of media includes forms that fall outside the scope of commercial mass media. A variety of forms and content exists, as well as different economic types, including mass advertising communication and specialized communication that may be noncommercial or subsidized (Budd, Entman, & Steinman, 1990). Also note that we talk about plural *media* and avoid the term *the media*. Media are not a monolith; no such thing as "the media" operates as a single, unified, controlling entity. Instead, media compose a complex set of production and consumption practices. Thus, the gender representations found in one medium can respond to gender representations in another. For example, the Guerrilla Girls zap actions use the pop-art medium of posters to criticize the absence of women from the high culture medium of major New York art museums and galleries (Demo, 2000).

Although media contain conflicting discourses, it is useful to recognize the existence of culture industries to draw attention to the way popular culture mirrors industrial factory processes, creating standardized goods for consumption (Horkheimer & Adorno, 1972). Media function as culture industries as they convey messages that generate demand for specific products; media influence how people dress, what they eat, what they look like, the games they play, the music they listen to, and the entertainment they watch. Media convey these messages in two ways: first, in the message content of the television shows, magazine articles, news items, music, and movies and, second, in the advertising that surrounds these messages.

Advertisements would not dominate commercial media in the way they do unless they worked: creating demand within consumers for products. To give a sense of how much is spent on advertising, consider the following statistics from 2010 (see Table 11.1):

Table 11.1   Selected Examples of Amount Spent on Advertising in 2010

Corporation	Amount Spent on Advertising
Bank of America	$1.9 billion
Walmart	$2.5 billion
Verizon	$2.5 billion
Ford	$3.9 billion
General Motors	$4.2 billion

Source: Data from Laya, 2011.

Advertisers spend this amount of money on advertising because they know it generates demand for their products. Shows, magazines, or papers that do not receive advertising dollars do not circulate for long.

Writing about diverse media presents difficulties for textbook writers. First, it is particularly difficult to keep examples fresh; media products are ephemeral. Shows, actors, and musicians popular one year are not the next. Many books written in the early 2000s focus on Britney Spears, whose record-breaking sales and pop icon status made her worthy of study. Now, she is more often the butt of jokes (*Glee*'s "*Britney*/Brittany" episode excepted). Second, for every example that illustrates a point, you are likely to think of a counterexample—demonstrating that popular culture and its media of transmission present "inescapable levels of *contradiction*" (Gauntlett, 2002, p. 255, italics in original). These contradictions temper the power of media to exert absolute control over gender/sex identities. Like other institutions, even as media reiterate norms concerning gender, media also enable people to work the weaknesses in the norms and challenge common assumptions. English professor Sherrie A. Inness (2004) notes that "action chick" characters—such as

Lara Croft of *Lara Croft, Tomb Raider*; Buffy of *Buffy the Vampire Slayer*; Xena of *Xena: Warrior Princess*; Aeryn Sun of *Farscape*; and (we would add) Zoe Washburne of *Firefly* and Katniss Everdeen of *The Hunger Games*—"can be rooted in stereotyped female roles but can simultaneously challenge such images" (p. 6). Despite these contradictions within and across media forms, dominant messages do emerge to support hegemonic constructions of gender, especially as the consumption of visual media becomes a central part of your daily life.

Mitchell Stephens (1998), in *The Rise of the Image, the Fall of the Word*, argues that the most recent shift in communication, particularly in more economically privileged countries, is from the word to the image, such that "most of the world's inhabitants are now devoting about half their leisure time to an activity that did not exist two generations ago"—watching television (p. 7). In the United States, most people spend at least 2.8 hours a day watching TV (U.S. Bureau of Labor Statistics, 2012), and 96.7% of households have at least one television set (Stelter, 2011). The ubiquity of mediated images from television, movies, and music videos "are perhaps the most powerful familiarizing influences shaping our contemporary society" (Westerfelhaus & Brookey, 2004, p. 305). Media scholars believe that just as religion, and then science, outlined how people should behave and be, "mass entertainment now performs a similar normative role in our media-saturated society" by providing myths, or recurrent story structures, through which human beings understand who they are and where they fit in a social order (p. 305). Given the explosion of visual media, this chapter primarily focuses on them.

Part of the video revolution is the digital revolution. As of 2012, 76.7% of households had at least one computer (U.S. Census Bureau, 2012b). For a small taste of how quickly the digital revolution has impacted media, consider the following time line:

Late 1980s: e-mail became privatized and commercially available.

Early 1990s: cell phones became widely used when they became small enough to fit in a pocket.

Mid-1990s: the Internet emerged when the U.S. government allowed the commercialization of the networking technologies that enable worldwide participation.

August 1996: Google is launched.

1997: Dreamweaver launched its initial version, allowing people to construct their own websites.

2001: Wikipedia is launched.

2002: Blogs became popular due to software making them easy to create.

2003: MySpace is founded.

2004: Facebook is founded.

2005: YouTube is founded.

2006: Twitter is created.

What makes the Internet different from other media forms is that its users have access to inexpensive two-way mediated communication in which they can be media producers as well as consumers. Users can create their own mediated forms (YouTube videos, blogs, Twitter feeds, webpages) in a context with its own unique and constantly evolving norms for communication (Manago, Graham, Greenfield, & Salimkhan, 2008). With this new context comes increased opportunities for users to seek inclusion, construct and promote their desired identities, make social comparisons to others, network beyond geographic boundaries, organize group actions, create expression, and create and play group games (Manago et al., 2008; Zhao, Grasmuck, & Martin, 2008). The noncentralized nature of the Internet also provides opportunities for rallying hate groups, consumer targeting, and new forms of gendered violence such as sexting and violently misogynist games. Researchers continue to find gender and sexuality are predominant issues in cybercommunication, particularly for teens and young adults (Manago et al., 2008).

Media Hegemony or Polysemy

The concept of **hegemony** is particularly useful when discussing media power. One way the predominant social group can make its beliefs appear to be common sense is through media representations that shape the cognitive structures through which people perceive and evaluate social reality (Dow, 1996). However, this hegemonic system is not all-powerful. It must be maintained, repeated, reinforced, and modified in order to respond to and overcome the forms that oppose it. Thus, "hegemony, rather than assuming an all powerful, closed text, presumes the possibility of resistance and opposition" (Dow, 1996, p. 14). Media maintain hegemonic understandings of gender even as they create gaps and fissures in representations of gender.

Most of the debate about media is about the precise scope of their power. One side, represented by the work of Theodor Adorno (1991) and the Frankfurt School, argues that mass media have considerable power (or a hegemonic hold) over people as they "churn out products which keep the audience blandly entertained, but passive, helping to maintain the status quo by encouraging conformity and diminishing the scope of resistance" (Gauntlett, 2002, p. 41). Media create false consciousness, making people believe they exert control over what they view (and what they think about what they view) when in reality they have little or no control. The other side, represented by the work of John Fiske (1987) and cultural studies, argues that people do not consume media offerings mindlessly but instead actively and creatively engage with them, "using 'guerilla' tactics to reinterpret media texts to suit their own purposes" (Gauntlett, 2002, p. 41). These varied purposes are possible because, Fiske believes, media message are **polysemous**, or open to a range of different interpretations at different times. Meaning is not determined by the media providers but created individually by each person.

The best explanation of media power is somewhere between these two extremes. Clearly, pervasive media messages have an effect, particularly in the U.S. consumer culture. However, it also is clear that people can resist media influence if they are critical media consumers. Thus, it would be counterproductive for us to side exclusively with the media hegemony side of the debate if we want to enable you to be creative and productive contributors to the public discourse in which media participate. Like British media scholar David Gauntlett, we believe that "it seems preferable to assume that people are thoughtful and creative beings, in control of their own lives—not least of all because that is how most people surely see themselves" (p. 111). However, it also is true that people's level of thoughtfulness and creativity is influenced by their education (formal and otherwise).

Media Polyvalence

Fiske may be correct that textual polysemy exists, but the range and richness of the possible meanings depend on the ability of audiences to produce them. Additionally, media texts cannot be all things to all people, because media foreground some interpretations as preferred. Celeste Condit (1989) argues that instead of the concept of polysemy (having a multitude of meanings), researchers should use **polyvalence** (having a multitude of valuations): "Polyvalence occurs when audience members share understandings of the denotations of a text but disagree about the valuation of these denotations to such a degree that they produce notably different interpretations" (p. 106). For example, when looking at a an advertisement aired during Super Bowl halftime, viewers may agree that it links the consumption of beer to the performance of masculinity but disagree on whether that performance of masculinity is one that should be encouraged.

Oppositional interpretations of mainstream media texts are influenced by the social context; some contexts provide more opportunities and training for resistant readings. One social factor that influences the reception of messages is peer groups. In a study of girls at two middle schools, one predominantly White and the other predominantly Mexican American and African American, journalism professor Meenakshi Gigi Durham (1999) found that "girls *on their own* may be somewhat more able to critically examine and deconstruct media messages than in the peer group context" (p. 210, italics in original). Oppositional readings of texts are constrained by the social structures reproduced in peer groups: "The peer group was shown to be a training ground where girls learned to use the mass media to acquire the skills of ideal femininity," although sometimes rejections of these norms could be voiced (p. 212). Thus, when cultural studies researchers claim that mediated messages are polysemous, they may be ignoring the fact that media consumption and interpretation often are a group activity, not an individual one.

Different people at any given time also have different resources available for resistance and must expend more or less effort to construct resistant readings. It is easy to "acquire the codes necessary for preferred readings"; however, "the acquisition of codes for negotiated or oppositional readings is more difficult and less common" (Dow, 1996, p. 13), and transforming those readings into political action is the most difficult and least common of all. Because the acquisition of such codes requires work, one consequence is "the tendency of such burdens to silence viewers" (Condit, 1989, p. 109).

Think about how you look at magazines (especially those focused on fashion and men's health). What can you say about the images in them? If the only language (or code) you have is one that enables you to compare the relative attractiveness of the models, that is a very limited code that operates within hegemonic understandings. It measure people's worth only in terms of their appearance. But you can develop a more nuanced code.

To enable an oppositional reaction to mediated texts, it is important to understand how the way people look at media has been structured in a particular way. Perhaps more important than the content of media is the way you look at it. Can you see when some content (some people) are missing? Can you see when the content induces you to value some things over others?

The Gaze(s)

Two parallel lines of research emerged in the 1970s to explain how visual media gender the practice of watching, create a legitimating gender ideology, and influence gender identity. The first theory focuses on the way media position audiences. The second theory uses psychoanalysis to explain how cinema's form spoke exclusively to a male spectator.

Ways of Seeing

In the 1970s, the British Broadcasting Company aired a television series titled *Ways of Seeing*. A book by the same name soon followed. John Berger's *Ways of Seeing* (1972) argues that in European art, from the Renaissance onward, men were the presumed viewers (because they were the presumed purchasers; p. 64). In one of the book's most quoted passages, Berger describes how artistic representations construct an image of men and women:

> *Men act* and *women appear.* Men look at women. Women watch themselves being looked at. This determines not only most relations between men and women but also the relation of women to themselves. The surveyor of woman in herself is male: the surveyed female. Thus she turns herself into an object— and most particularly an object of vision: a sight. (p. 47)

The presumed sex of the viewer is male, and even when the viewer is female she views herself through men's eyes. Thus, when a woman assesses her body, she does so not from the perspective of another woman (or from her own perspective) but from the perspective of a man. Berger's observation is quite similar to the point made by objectification theory: Women are seen as objects—things to be looked at rather than people who can act.

In case you do not believe that men long were presumed the "'ideal' spectator," try this experiment: Examine an image of a traditional nude and imagine replacing the image of a woman with the image of a man (see Figures 11.4 and 11.5). How do you perceive the female form? How do you perceive the male form?

Figure 11.4 *Reclining Bacchante*, Trutat, 1844

Source: Catalogue officiel illustré de l'Exposition centennale de l'art français de 1800 à 1889 (1900) www.archive.org/stream/catalogueofficiel00expo#page/66/mode/2up

Now, try this experiment with contemporary images. Look at a women's fashion magazine and imagine men's bodies were posed in the same way.

The oddity of men's bodies posed in the same way as women's also is highlighted by images appearing online, including young men mimicking the position of young women in their Facebook photos and fantasy author Jim Hines re-creating the images of fantasy novels on his blog (see Figure 11.6).

As one final example, consider the following image by artist Kevin Bolk, which challenges the different ways the bodies of male and female comic book super-heroes are presented. In the drawing, he parodies the poster for the superhero movie *The Avengers* by placing the male superheroes in the same sexualized pose that female superhero Black Widow adopts in the original movie poster (see Figure 11.7).

Berger's point is that the way the body is positioned, whether in paintings or in advertisements, employs a series of codes that audiences can read, even though they may not be conscious of them.

Communication professor Sut Jhally, in his video *Codes of Gender* (2009), refers to Berger's work in his analysis of contemporary advertising. Jhally explains

Figure 11.5 *Vanity*, Hans Memling, 1485

Source: Musée des Beaux-Arts, Strasbourg
Source: www.kfki.hu

Figure 11.6 Fantasy author Jim Hines re-creates the poses of young women featured on the book covers of fantasy novels.

Source: © jimchines.com

Figure 11.7 Kevin Bolk's reimagining of the poster for *The Avengers*

Source: © kevinbolk.com

how mass mediated images construct an understanding of gender in which feminine women are physically passive and ineffective and masculine men are physically active and capable. Using the writings of sociologist Erving Goffman (1979), Jhally seeks to "make visible what seems to be invisible" (p. 4). He enables people to read the codes of gender as they are performed by bodies by enabling them to see how media present men's and women's bodies (see Table 11.2).

Table 11.2 How People Read Codes of Gender

	Male	Female
Whole-body posture	More often shown standing and moving	More often shown lying down
Head	Straight and positioned directly at the camera	Tilted at an angle or looking away from the camera
Eyes	Focused and watching the world around them	Not paying attention, spaced out
Hands	Controlling and assertive; hands use the objects to do something; men touch others	Passive and controlled by environment; objects rest in them; women touch themselves
Legs	Legs are straight, in motion, or solidly planted	Knees are bent so that the body is tilted and off-center; legs are crossed or women hold one of their feet
Performance of age	Mature and manly	Infantile, shown snuggling into men; women presented as looking like girls, and girls presented looking like women

As a quick exercise, find a copy of a recent fashion or men's magazine (e.g., *Elle, Mademoiselle, Vogue, Maxim, GQ*). Look at the images and see if you read them differently now that you have a new way to decode them.

Berger's insights also can help explain images people post of themselves on social media. In a study about presentation of self, researchers asked 23 college students to discuss their use of MySpace (Manago et al., 2008). The researchers found that men's portrayals followed "stereotypical norms of masculinity in which playboys embody strength and power and that women portray themselves as attractive and affiliative" (p. 453). In other words, men presented themselves as doing, while women presented themselves as appearing. A woman offered, "Girls tend to put a lot of pretty pictures of themselves and their best friends" (p. 453); a man shared, "I have Godfather, Scarface, power figures and cool people that I want to be seen as" (p. 454). Why this difference in presentation? One woman explained, "Girls . . . want pretty pictures of themselves online, you know? And I see guys doing it, and it's just like ok, you should be playing sports somewhere, not sitting taking pictures of yourself" (p. 454). While it is acceptable for women to present themselves as objects of the gaze, it is not acceptable for men to do the same. In referring to why he does not post pretty pictures, a man said, "People would probably think you're gay or something, honestly" (p. 454). People engage in practices of gazing, and those practices, in turn, influence how they present themselves. Women have internalized a male gaze and engage in self-objectification while men believe they should always be the gazers and to be gazed upon threatens one's heterosexuality.

Berger's insights are useful insofar as they encourage those studying media to think about the ways audiences look. However, his work has limits. First, it explains ways of looking unique to Western art traditions. In a cross-cultural study of advertising (Frith, Shaw, & Chang, 2005), the authors argue that one reason why Western women's bodies are sexually objectified but Asian women's bodies are not is the Western art tradition. In contrast to Western art, "displaying the female body has not been the tradition in Chinese art" (p. 65). Thus, "traditions of 'gaze' may very well have developed differently in the East and the West" (p. 65).

Second, Berger's book predates important changes in the way men's bodies are presented in advertising. From Robert Mapplethorpe's art photography to Abercrombie & Fitch's advertising, men's bodies are increasingly on display. Susan Bordo (1999) explores how recent advertising images of men create gender tensions, stating that "men are not supposed to enjoy being surveyed *period*. It's feminine to be on display" (p. 173, italics in original). However, images of men that have appeared since the 1990s, particularly in Calvin Klein underwear advertisements, do present men as on display. Such ads have led to an evolution in masculinity's meaning. Consistent with Berger, Bordo argues that "to be so passively dependent on the gaze of another person for one's sense of self-worth is incompatible with being a real man"; thus, "men and women are socially sanctioned to deal with the gaze of the Other in different ways" (pp. 172–173). Yet, as Jhally's analysis points out, it is still mostly women's bodies presented as ineffective, inactive, and to be surveyed.

Third, "Berger's opposition of 'acting' and 'appearing,' . . . is something of a false duality—and always has been" because women's appearance involves immense action: "It takes time, energy, creativity, dedication. It can *hurt*" (Bordo, 1999, pp. 220–221). However, the fiction that appearance is act-free persists. Few stars admit their bodies have been surgically sculpted, and most magazine readers gleefully engage in the willing suspension of disbelief, accepting pictures as perfect reflections of the models even as most should be aware that virtually every image appearing in fashion magazines has been digitally altered.

The Gaze

At the same time Berger's series and book appeared, media theorist Laura Mulvey (1975) published what would become one of the most frequently cited essays in media studies. Using psychoanalytic theory, Mulvey posits that cinema not only highlights woman's to-be-looked-at-ness but actually builds the way woman is to be looked at into the film itself. The way the camera, the audience, and the male character (with whom all spectators—male and female—identify) look at women reinforces the male as active and the female as passive. For Mulvey, the cinematic gaze is male. Mulvey's criticism applies to all mainstream cinema, and she believes the only way to avoid the dominance of the male gaze is through avant-garde film that undermines the system of representation.

Mulvey's theory is criticized because she identifies a single, universal gaze. She assumed that there was only one White male gaze and that no possibility for a female or a non-White gaze existed. Others would challenge this, arguing that female (Gamman & Marshment, 1989; Kaplan, 1983) and transgender (Halberstam, 2005) gazes are possible, that people can read against the grain of the male gaze (de Lauretis, 1984; Walters, 1995), and that the focus of psychoanalysis on sexual difference as the fundamental organizing principle of human subjectivity was misplaced in light of the centrality of race to identity (DiPiero, 2002). Mulvey also assumed a lone media text directly and unilaterally affected the spectator at the moment of consumption, ignoring that multiple factors simultaneously influence the spectator, such as socialization, education, other texts, and peer pressure. The most trenchant criticism of Mulvey is provided by bell hooks (1992): "Feminist film theory rooted in an ahistorical psychoanalytic framework that privileges sexual difference actively suppresses recognition of race, reenacting and mirroring the erasure of black womanhood that occurs in films, silencing any discussion of racial difference—of racialized sexual difference" (p. 123).

Not only can multiple gazes exist, but Brenda Cooper (2000) argues that one can find a rejection of the dominant male gaze even in mainstream Hollywood films. Cooper argues that *Thelma & Louise* (1991) encourages viewers to identify not with the males on the screen but with the female figures who actively mock and challenge patriarchal conventions. Cooper's analysis is bolstered by her earlier study (1999) of spectator responses, which found that men and women saw the film differently. Men tended to see the film as an example of unjustified male bashing (perhaps because they identified with the men in the film, few of whom were sympathetic), and women tended to see it as a commentary on women's marginalized social position (because they identified with the women in the film). Cooper's study illustrates Condit's point about polyvalence; male and female audiences' readings were polyvalent.

Despite the criticisms of Mulvey, her recognition of the gendered pleasures of the gaze continues to spark research. *Signs*, the premiere journal of feminist scholarship, devoted an entire special issue to feminist theories of visual culture. Every essay made clear the importance of intersectionality to understanding how the gaze operates. In order to answer the question, "How do I look?" one must think about "gender . . . as inextricably entwined (embodied, experienced, thought, and imagined) with other aspects of identity, including race and ethnicity, nationality, sexual orientation, and class" (Doyle & Jones, 2006, p. 608). In particular, Eve Oishi (2006) offers a theory of perverse spectatorship, which calls for attention to "the infinitely oblique and circuitous routes through which identification passes" (p. 649). Of course, being able to read or watch against the grain (to be perverse) requires being able to identify the grain, and that requires that one be able to identify the hegemonic preferred readings and offer an oppositional interpretation of them.

An Oppositional Gaze

To be an active participant in media discourse about gender, instead of a passive recipient of it, one must possess a vocabulary with which to critically discuss the content and the gaze. One cannot engage in creative readings of media unless one knows such readings are necessary and possible. In her book on race and representation, bell hooks labels this an **oppositional gaze**.

Although hooks's *Black Looks* (1992) focuses mostly on race, her arguments apply to gender, sex, and sexual orientation as well. She argues that discussions of race need to expand beyond debates about good and bad representations to address the issue of standpoint. She asks, "From what political perspective do we dream, look, create, and take action?" (p. 4). Media's positioning of the audience is not determinative as long as audiences are conscious of media's attempt to position them. Audience members can reposition themselves. African Americans can refuse to look through White eyes. Women can refuse to look through men's eyes. LGBTQ people can refuse to look through heterosexual eyes. All people can learn to look through each other's eyes. A number of elements compose an oppositional gaze.

First, to embrace an oppositional gaze, one must "consider the perspective from which we look, vigilantly asking ourselves who do we identify with, whose image do we love" (hooks, 1992, p. 6). Even though hooks's call to action targets Blacks as an audience, hers is a call to all people. She challenges Blacks to unlearn their cherishing of hateful images of themselves. She challenges Whites, as "the many non-black people who produce images and critical narratives about blackness and black people," to "interrogate their perspective"; otherwise, "they may simply recreate the imperial gaze—the look that seeks to dominate, subjugate, and colonize" (p. 7). Our point in highlighting one's positioning in relation to media is to encourage those with privilege to recognize that privilege. This does not mean, however, that one needs to identify as a victim (p. 14). Instead, it means one should ask to whom and for whom this media representation speaks. When one enjoys mediated depictions of gendered/ sexed violence, with whom is one identifying—the perpetrator or the victim?

Second, one must recognize the degree to which she or he participates in culture. People are not merely passive audiences for media messages and images. Bordo (1997b) explains, "Unless one recognizes one's own enmeshment in culture, one is in no position to theorize about that culture or its effects on others" (p. 13). Recognizing the way in which people are "culture makers as well as culture consumers" enables each person to act to transform the culture (p. 15). Remember, we chose to not write about an all-powerful *the media*. Instead, we chose to write about *media* and the ways each person participates in the institution as both recipient and creator. However, we also chose to speak of media as an institution to highlight the way in which it is social and economic and creates hegemonic messages that require work to read from an oppositional perspective. Personal choices about gender are not sufficient to change the gendered institution of media, nor do personal cultural choices necessarily translate into political action in the public sphere.

Our point in highlighting individual agency in relation to media representations is not to imply that each person individually controls the effect of media.

An institutional focus makes clear that even those choices considered the most personal are influenced by larger social forces. Do you wear makeup or not? Do you seek to develop muscles or not? Do you wear jeans or not? Like Bordo (1997b), our call for critical consciousness is meant to celebrate "those choices that are undertaken in full consciousness that they are not only about 'creating' our own individual lives but constructing the landscape of our culture" (p. 16). A person's embrace of cosmetic and fashion industry beauty ideals influences not only that person's body but others' bodies as well. Bordo explains, "Each of us shapes the culture we live in every moment of our lives, not only in our more public activities but also in our most intimate gestures and personal relationships, for example, in the way we model attitudes toward beauty, aging, perfection, and so on for our children, friends, students, lovers, colleagues" (p. 16).

Third, an oppositional gaze necessarily moves from social critique to political action. The goal in examining popular culture is not just to critique the image but to transform the image, to create alternatives, to find images that subvert, and to pose critical alternatives that move people beyond thinking merely about good or bad images. Cultural criticism becomes just another pastime if not linked to institutional change.

Fourth, an oppositional gaze is conscious of the way in which contemporary media engage in **commodification**—the selling of cultural, sexual, or gender difference in a way that supports institutionalized discrimination. For hooks (1992), one must recognize when presentations of ethnicity are not signs of inclusiveness but the production of "colorful ethnicity for the white consumer appetite that makes it possible for blackness to be commodified in unprecedented ways, and for whites to appropriate black culture without interrogating whiteness or showing concern for the displeasure of blacks" (p. 154). Some rap music videos demonstrate how particular representations of Black gender/sex are sold to White youth, often by White corporations for the benefit of White shareholders (Yousman, 2003). Rap videos, particularly those marketed to suburban White youth, present Black men and dark-skinned Black women as hypersexualized. Young White men's consumption of rap music and their embrace of the nonverbal and linguistic customs of hip-hop culture is not a sign of cultural inclusiveness, because this commodification of Blackness maintains an "ideology that is consistent with an acceptance of White economic, political and social supremacy" (p. 386). White youth obsession with Black culture is not a sign of progressive social change but rather a form of consuming the other because "the particular nature of the images that White youth are consuming—images of Black youth who are violent or hostile, often unemployed and/or involved in criminal practices—may in fact reinforce, rather than challenge, the tendency of White youth" to support institutionalized racism (p. 387).

An oppositional gaze enables you to see not everyone is equally represented in media; in commercial television and news, White men tend to predominate while people of color and women are underrepresented. An oppositional gaze also enables recognition of the way people are represented. Media representations are not only a reflection of social reality but also actively construct it. This chapter focuses on two of those representations: femininity as hypersexualized and masculinity as in crisis.

Who Is Represented in Media

Women are underrepresented in U.S. media, regardless of the form. Representations of male characters far outnumber women in children's books, news, television shows, film, and video games. Whites also outnumber people of color in media representations. Even in the realm of social media, where people produce as well as consume, representational differences emerge.

Researchers examined 5,618 U.S. children's books (Caldecott Award winners, Little Golden Books, and books listed in the Children's Catalog) published from 1900 to 2000 (McCabe, Fairchild, Grauerholz, Pescosolido, & Tope, 2011). Overall, they found that male characters outnumbered female characters two to one and appeared 1.6 times more often as lead characters. Male characters appeared in 100% of all books, while "no more than 33 percent of books published in a year contain central characters who are adult women or female animals" (pp. 208–209). Sadly, although the balance in representation did improve somewhat toward the end of the century for human characters, it did not improve for animal characters, with males outnumbering females two to one. Such a finding is important because "the disparities . . . point to the symbolic annihilation of women and girls, and particularly female animals, in twentieth-century children's literature, suggesting to children that these characters are less important than their male counterparts" (p. 218).

In the news arena for 2011, women were only 21.7% of the guests on Sunday morning public affairs shows, 39.9% of the local television news workforce, and 22% of the local radio news workforce (Yi & Dearfield, 2012). The election of 2012 provides a particularly vivid illustration of women's absence in the news (see Figure 11.8). Extensive attention was paid to the "gender gap" (really a sex gap) in men's and women's support of Barack Obama and Mitt Romney, with Gallup polling declaring the "20-point gender gap is the largest Gallup has measured in a presidential election since it began compiling the vote by major subgroups in 1952" (Jones, 2012, par. 1). However, even as it became clear women would play a deciding role in the election, they did not figure prominently in news coverage of it or the issues that most directly affected them.

Women also are underrepresented in entertainment media. On television, women are only 41% of all fictional characters (a decline of 2 points from the 2007–2008 season with its historic high of 43%; Yi & Dearfield, 2012). In an analysis of the 100 top-grossing films from 2007 to 2009, "women represented only one-third of speaking characters across all three years. . . . Only about one in six (16.8%) films depicted 'gender balance' (women in 45–54.9% of speaking roles)" (p. 9).

Minorities too are underrepresented in media. In a content analysis of samples representing eight week-long periods of prime-time television shown from 2000 to 2008, the researcher found the appearance of Black characters had actually declined toward the end of the time period while the representation of other minority groups and Hispanics continued to be "nearly invisible" (Signorielli, 2009, p. 324).

Figure 11.8 Gender Gap in the 2012 Election Coverage

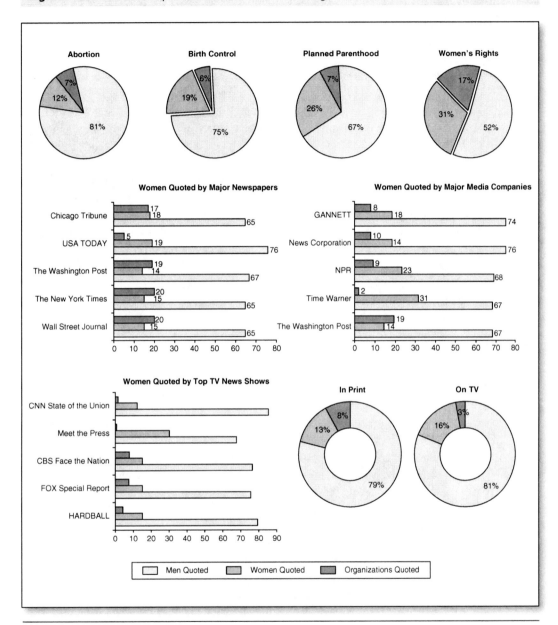

Source: © 4thEstate.net

This decline in the representation of African Americans is startling given that their representation actually reflected their proportion of the population in the 1970s and 1980s. The troubling conclusion is that prime-time programming "was less diverse at the end of the first decade of the 21st century than it was earlier in the decade"; and, even when parity was approached mid-decade, "it was a representation of segregation and isolation, particularly for Black women" because when Black characters did appear, it often was in all-Black situation comedies, with 60% of Black women characters appearing in that type of show (Signorielli, 2009, p. 334).

Video games also underrepresent women and minorities. One study analyzed 150 games from across nine platforms. The researchers found "a systematic over-representation of males, white[s] and adults and a systematic under-representation of females, Hispanics, Native Americans, children and the elderly" (Williams, Martins, Consalvo, & Ivory, 2009, p. 815). The most popular games tended to be the least representative. Even when underrepresented groups were present, they were usually only in secondary roles. Such underrepresentation is a problem because it "makes those groups seem less visible, while social identity theory additionally suggests that they will be seen as less important" (p. 829). Even though these are only games, they are communication media that influence how people see the world.

Race and sex also play a role in social networking sites (SNS). Although the invention of a technology that allows individuals to create and publish material of their choice might appear to be inclusive of race, gender, sex, sexual orientation, age, disability, and national origin, it is not. Some recent findings illustrate the need for an intersectional approach when understanding the relative presence (or absence) of identities online:

- Economic and social resources create inequitable access to the Internet around the world, regardless of gender/sex (Selwyn, 2004).
- Age continues to play a central role, with teenagers and young adults leading the way in usage.
- Race and gender intersect, with African American boys using Internet technology the least and African American girls using it most. White and African American boys played games more and girls used cell phones more (Jackson et al., 2008).
- Hispanic college students have been underrepresented in Internet research; what exists suggests they do not rely on it as much as other groups for socializing (Jones, Johnson-Yale, Millermaier, & Pérez, 2009).
- Personality and gender together influence the degree of SNS participation. Generally, women and men with more outgoing, open personalities participate more on SNS. Men who are not as open tend to play games more; women who are not as open tend to use instant messaging more than social networking sites (Muscannell & Guadangno, 2011).

Understanding usage, however, does not necessarily mean one understands online presence. When creating an online persona on a blog, in a multiuser online game, or on Facebook, you need not present your sex, gender, race, or sexuality as you perform it in the bricks and mortar world. Because of this, many argue that the Internet is race-free. Communication scholar Lisa Nakamura (2008) questions the belief that the

Internet can or ought to be raceless; we also interrogate the idea that it should be considered sexless. Two questions must be addressed: Is the Internet raceless and sexless? Should the Internet be raceless and sexless? Nakamura answers no to both questions in regard to race. We answer no to both questions in regard to sex.

Race is present on the Net. First, online race is presumed White, and there are "incentives for minorities to opt for default whiteness online" (Nakamura, 2005, p. 531). Second, race is commodified through identity tourism, wherein, for example, White men take on the gender persona of Asian men and women. Nakamura notes how many chat sites present themselves as race-free (meaning one should not overtly talk about one's race lest one be perceived divisive), yet the avatars (icons used to represent the users) are clearly raced. This mixing of virtual and material presence becomes clear in video games.

In a study of the virtual game world *Second Life*, researchers found women and people of color were present as avatars, but they received more harassment in the forms of name calling, misogynist comments on women's portly or small-breasted bodies, and refusal to interact with them. Players were significantly less likely to help a dark-skinned avatar (Eastwick & Gardner, 2008). The issue is not only whether women and people of color are not present but also how they are portrayed. Sociologist Eve Shapiro found many dark-skinned avatars lack facial details compared to White avatars, and the availability of skin colors, clothing, and gestures that fit appropriately for larger bodies are just not available: "In a social space not bound by real-life bodily limitations, people are working very hard to reproduce hegemonic bodies" (Shapiro, 2010, p. 122). This example makes clear it is as important to study *how* people are represented as it is to understand *who* is represented.

How People Are Represented

A nearly infinite range of themes can be explored relating to media and gender. We have chosen to write about two broad themes that cross a variety of media forms, including magazines, television shows, advertisements, movies, and video games: the hypersexualization of women and girls and the need for masculinity to be resecured.

Sexualization of Women

In 2007, the American Psychological Association commissioned a task force to report on the sexualization of girls. Contrasting it to healthy sexuality, the task force defined **sexualization** as occurring when

- a person's value comes only from his or her sexual appeal or behavior, to the exclusion of other characteristics;
- a person is held to a standard that equates physical attractiveness (narrowly defined) with being sexy;

- a person is sexually objectified—that is, made into a thing for others' sexual use, rather than seen as a person with the capacity for independent action and decision making; and/or
- sexuality is inappropriately imposed upon a person. (p. 1)

Examples include "dolls wearing black leather miniskirts, feather boas, and thigh-high boots," thongs for 7- to 10-year-olds, and child beauty pageants (p. 1). Textiles and apparel scholar Annette Lynch (2012) adds to the list: "midriff marketing," sexy Halloween costumes, T-shirts sold for teens at Walmart in 2007 saying "Some call it stalking—I call it love," and T-shirts sold at Next for 5- to 6-year-olds saying "So many boys, so little time" (p. 62).

The sexualization of culture is driven by increased depictions of sexuality on television. After reviewing 1,154 programs, researchers found that from 1998 to 2005, the percentage of shows with sexual content increased from 56% to 70% and with sexual behavior increased from 23% to 35%; for prime-time shows, 77% had sexual content (Kunkel, Eyal, Finnerty, Biely, & Donnerstein, 2005). However, when one looks more closely at the data, it becomes clear that men's and women's bodies are not sexualized in the same way or to the same extent.

For years, cultural critics have noted that regardless of the media form, one thing holds constant: Women are presented as sexual objects. The male gaze persists, where women are treated as objects of desire, rather than as agents of action. The Media Education Foundation's video *Dreamworlds II* (Jhally, 1995) educates viewers about sexual imagery in music videos, and the video *Killing Us Softly 4* (Kilbourne & Jhally, 2010) focuses on advertising's images of women. A study of the 100 top-grossing films from 2007 to 2009 found "in many cases women film characters were 'hyper-sexualized.' In all three years, female characters were more likely than males to wear sexy clothing, more likely to be depicted partially nude, and to be referred to as attractive" (Yi & Dearfield, 2012, p. 9). Table 11.3 shows the statistical breakdown for 2009. Although both men and women are sexualized, women are sexualized 3 to 5 times more often than men.

Even in media targeted at women that claim to transgress against stereotypes, sexualization is common. The magazine *Cosmopolitan*, in the form most people

Table 11.3   Sexualization of Female and Male Movie Characters in 2009

Percentage Shown	Female	Male
In sexy attire	25.8	4.7
Partially nude	23.6	7.4
Referred to as attractive	10.9	2.5

Source: Data from Yi & Dearfield, 2012, p. 9.

now recognize, was launched in 1964 in the United States by Helen Gurley Brown when she took over its editorship. When launched, the magazine had an explicit sexual agenda, "for *Cosmo* was playing *Playboy* at its own game, seeing sexual pleasure as important, and suggesting that women were entitled to it. *Cosmo*'s assertion of women's right to enjoy sex, and to talk about it, was quite radical" (Gauntlett, 2002, p. 53). However, the femininity of *Cosmo* is a particular one—a heterosexual one. Fashion magazines offer a limited range of femininity. Women's magazines may be playful in their approach to makeup and clothing, but "they would never encourage women to step outside their carefully imagined boundaries of the 'sexy,' the 'stylish' and the 'fashionable'" (p. 206). A hegemonic message is presented: A woman's self-worth is influenced by her looks, clothes, and accessories.

The sexualization of women also occurs in men's magazines. In a study of magazines targeted at young men in Great Britain, called "lads' mags," researchers found they were "normalizing extreme sexist views by presenting those views in a mainstream context" (Horvath, Hegarty, Tyler, & Mansfield, 2012, p. 454). The researchers came to this conclusion after performing two different studies. In one, they gave 90 young men "derogatory quotes about women drawn from recent lads' mags, and from interviews with convicted rapists"; the young men identified more with the quotes when they were attributed to the magazines, even when they actually came from rapists. In the second study, the researchers asked 40 young women and men to identify the source of derogatory quotes about women; they "could not reliably judge the source of those same quotes." Even though the people studied generally indicated they saw lads' mags' statements as "normal" and rapists' comments as "extreme," they could not tell the difference between the two. In fact, "they categorized quotes from both sources as derogatory with equal frequency" (p. 454).

In presenting their results, Peter Hegerty explained their studies "tell us that there is an overlap in the content of the legitimations that rapists use to legitimate their violence against women and the kinds of things that are said about women in lads' mags. . . . And at the same time, they show us that when those things are attributed to lads' mags that they're easier for young men to identify with" ("Are Sex," 2011, video). Miranda Horvath warned,

> These magazines support the legitimisation of sexist attitudes and behaviours and need to be more responsible about their portrayal of women, both in words and images. They give the appearance that sexism is acceptable and normal—when really it should be rejected and challenged. Rapists try to justify their actions, suggesting that women lead men on, or want sex even when they say no, and there is clearly something wrong when people feel the sort of language used in a lads' mag could have come from a convicted rapist. ("Are Sex," 2011, par. 9)

Men's magazines often are criticized for sexually objectifying women. This study makes clear exactly how problematic that objectification is. How men's magazines talk about women is not all that different from how rapists talk about their victims.

Sexualization occurs not just to women's bodies, but increasingly it is affecting younger girls as well. Girls as young as 6 years old have started to judge themselves in relation to their sexual attractiveness. In one study, which used sexualized and nonsexualized dolls as prompts, "girls overwhelmingly chose the sexualized doll over the non-sexualized doll for their ideal self and as popular" (Starr & Ferguson, 2012, p. 463). The conclusion? "Young girls overwhelmingly demonstrate a sexualized view of their desired selves and equate sexiness with popularity" (p. 473).

Given a child from 6 to 11 years of age watches a weekly average of 28 hours of media (television, movies, video games), with 22 hours of that devoted to television watching, there is "increasing evidence that exposure to sexual content on television is a significant contributor to many aspects of young people's sexual knowledge, beliefs, expectations, attitudes, and behaviors" (Kunkel et al., 2005, p. 57). But television is not the sole explanation. Starr and Ferguson's study found it was not television alone that determined whether 6-year-old girls self-sexualized; instead, it was "the *interaction* between media hours and maternal self-objectification that creates vulnerability for early sexualization—daughters with high media consumption whose mothers have a more objectified view of their bodies are at greater risk for equating sexiness with popularity" (Starr & Ferguson, 2012, p. 472).

This study supports two of our earlier points. First, an oppositional gaze is necessary. The good news is that when parents (mothers in this study) teach their children to view media from a critical perspective, the effects of sexualization can be lessened (Starr & Ferguson, 2012, p. 472). Second, perceiving one's body as an agent of action, and not just as an object of the gaze, can lessen self-sexualization. The researchers found that girls enrolled in dance class did not sexualize themselves as much, perhaps indicating they had a different relation to their bodies (p. 473).

Researchers also studied adolescent girls to see what relationship existed between watching "sexually objectifying music television, primetime television programs, fashion magazines, and social networking sites" to determine whether there was a relationship between that viewing and "the internalization of beauty ideals, self-objectification, and body surveillance" (Vandenbosch & Eggermont, 2012, p. 870). The researchers found a relationship: "Our results suggested that exposure to sexually objectifying media is related to the internalization of beauty ideals, self-objectification, and body surveillance for a younger sample as well" (p. 884). This worried the researchers because "even 'small' increases in self-objectification can cause fundamental changes in an individual's self-image. . . . Girls with higher levels of internalization, self-objectification, and body surveillance may construct a more objectified self image," and over years those small increases from repeated exposure to media accrue (p. 884).

Even in the seemingly mundane medium of novels, sexualization occurs. Researchers analyzed books from the June and July 2008 *New York Times* Best Sellers List for Children's Books, which includes picture, middle-school, and young-adult books. The study found the 40 books contained 452 acts of sexual content and books aimed at girls were more likely to contain sexual content than those for boys (Callister et al., 2012, p. 483). Even with the 452 instances of sexual content, contraception (condoms) was mentioned only four times, no discussion of safe sex occurred, and the consequences of sex were mentioned only nine times. This is troubling given "consumption of popular adolescent literature may influence adolescent perceptions of what constitutes normative teen behavior" (pp. 477–478).

Even though many commentators focus on media representations of femininity as the primary place in which women are socialized to body image ideals, "the degree to which this message is internalized varies depending on factors such as race, nationality, and sexual orientation" (Harvey, 2005, p. 796). Although all women may be held to beauty standards, the standard is not the same for all women. Intercultural media researchers Katherine Frith, Ping Shaw, and Hong Cheng (2005) examine how beauty is constructed in magazine advertising. Using cross-cultural analysis, they compared advertisements in magazines published in Singapore, Taiwan, and the United States. Overall, magazines in Taiwan and Singapore were dominated by ads for facial beauty products, and U.S. ads focused on clothing. They also found that women and their bodies were more sexualized in the U.S. advertisements than in the Asian advertisements. They concluded that the charge that advertising presents women as sex objects is not a universal phenomenon. Interestingly, though, when an advertisement appearing in an Asian magazine did sexualize a woman, the model usually appeared White.

The prevalence of the sexual objectification of women has so dominated media, it should be unsurprising that people self-objectify when they become producers of mediated messages. Sexting, "the sending or receiving of sexually-explicit or sexually-suggestive images or video via a cell phone" (Hinduja & Patchin, 2010, p. 1), is one example of the practice of self-objectification. With advances in digital technology, people can now take pictures of themselves and distribute them (although, when initially sent, people may not think they are participating in a mass medium, it is important to remember that anything sent over the Internet can be distributed to a mass audience). One example illustrates how such images circulate. Two female high school students took a picture of themselves. Although the 16-year-old deleted the image from her own phone, her friend sent it to another friend, who sent it to a football player, who sent it to the team, from where it was sent to the entire senior class and ended up being so widely distributed that a print of the image was left in her vice principal's mailbox (Joffe-Walt, 2009).

A 2008 study by the National Campaign to Prevent Teen and Unplanned Pregnancy and CosmoGirl.com found 20% of teens ages 13–19 and 30% of young adults ages 20–26 had posted or sent nude or seminude pictures of themselves. In a 2010 survey of 4,400 students ages 11–18, boys admitted to sending seminaked photos of themselves more than girls, and boys were by far the most frequent recipient of such mail (Hinduja & Patchin, 2010). In another survey of 948 high school students in Texas, girls were 55.9% of the participants in sexting. All the studies suggest sexting tends to be indicative of teens' sexual activity and potentially risky behaviors (Temple et al., 2012).

Sexting is part of the media culture. Communication researcher Hugh Curnutt (2012) believes teens, and especially girls, sext "as a kind of remediation in which the libidinal focus of the media industry is internalized and reproduced by its consumers" (p. 355). In other words, the sexualization initially presented in media outlets (television, film, music videos) is internalized by teens who then seek to outwardly re-present it in their images of themselves. They see how media represent sexuality and copy them through sexting. If the primary image one sees of women is sexualized, then the most likely way to self-represent is through a sexualized image.

"Masculinity in Crisis"

During the 2010 Super Bowl, a series of advertisements aired that raised some interesting issues about masculinity. The advertisements shared a common theme: Men's masculinity was in crisis and needed to be reasserted (Green & Van Oort, 2013). Even an advertising agency took notice, remarking,

> The Superbowl has long been one of man's last havens of masculinity—beer in hand, buddies, football, munchies. . . . Even here, in the bastion of masculinity, utter gender confusion and questions surrounding what it means to "be a man" are surfacing. (Katherine, 2010, par. 1)

Dodge advertised its Charger by showing close-ups of beleaguered men's faces as a voiceover intoned, "I will be civil to your mother. I will put the seat down . . . I will carry your lip balm. I will watch your vampire TV shows with you . . . and because I do this, [vroom] I will drive the car I want to drive. Charger: Man's last stand." In a Dockers ad, a motley group of pantless men in styleless shirts and tighty whities march across a field singing, "I wear no pants." The end of the ad provides a solution: "Calling all men. It is time to wear the pants." In an advertisement for FloTV, Jason is shown standing forlornly in the lingerie department holding shopping bags with a red lace bra over his shoulder while his girlfriend browses. The narrator explains that we have an "injury report": Jason's "girlfriend has removed his spine, rendering him incapable of watching the game." The solution: "Get yourself a FloTV personal television . . . so that now live sports goes where you go. Change out of that skirt Jason." These ads all told a similar story: Men's masculinity was under attack and consuming the right product would resecure it. (The ads can all be seen on YouTube by searching for Dodge Charger Super Bowl 2010, Dockers 2010 SuperBowl, and flo-tv-spineless.)

For an interesting example of how new digital media enable people to critically respond to media messages, see "Woman's Last Stand: Dodge Charger Commercial Spoof" (www.youtube.com/watch?v=ou5Ens-qNRc). Filmmaker MacKenzie Fegan parodied the original advertisement, offering a political intervention into consumer culture.

Why might masculinity need to be resecured? Whether one believes it is the recession's impact on men's self-image (Olopade, 2010) or a broader cultural questioning of masculinity, most agree: masculinity is in flux. In his study of men's magazines, Gauntlett (2002) argues that whether in the United States or United Kingdom, "the magazines really show men to be *insecure* and *confused* in the modern world, and seeking help and *reassurance*, even if this is (slightly) suppressed by a veneer of irony and heterosexual lust" (p. 167). Gauntlett believes the discourses of masculinity in these contemporary magazines are distinctive because they recognize that masculinity is a social construction, not a cultural given. He believes the subject matter of "today's magazines for men are *all about* the social construction of masculinity" (p. 170).

Masculinity is the subject matter because social forces have destabilized masculinity. Previously,

men didn't need lifestyle magazines because it was obvious what a man was, and what a man should do. . . . It is only in the modern climate, in which we are all aware of the many choices available to us, and are also aware of the feminist critique of traditional masculinity, and the fact that gender roles can and do change, that men have started to need magazines about how to be a man today. (p. 170)

Reassertions of traditional masculinity appear across media as a response to a perceived fear of its erosion. But just because masculinity may be in flux does not mean there is not a form of masculinity with normative force.

Media representations are one location where hegemonic masculinity is identifiable, particularly in relation to sports coverage. In his analysis of baseball star Nolan Ryan, Nick Trujillo (1991) identifies five defining characteristics of **U.S. hegemonic masculinity**:

1. power means physical force and control;

2. occupational achievement;

3. familial patriarchy, in which the man is the breadwinner;

4. symbolized by the frontiersman and the outdoorsman; and

5. heterosexual.

Although this masculinity may be hegemonic, it does not deny the existence of nonhegemonic forms. For example, hip-hop offers forms of Black masculinity to which even some Whites aspire (H. Gray, 1995; Smith, 2002).

Media representations of ideal men are important because they present an image to which other men can aspire. In relation to men and media, media scholar Robert Hanke (1998) explains that "hegemonic masculinity is won not only through coercion but through consent, even though there is never complete consensus" (p. 190). People *want* to participate in the socially sanctioned and idealized notions of masculinity. A discussion of a media-created "crisis in masculinity" adds to the conversation by recognizing that additional pressures have been placed on men to be manly by overperforming a very particular type of masculinity.

In their review of discussions of masculinity across media forms, communication scholars Karen Ashcraft and Lisa Flores (2003) believe that "U.S. representations of manhood converge on the claim that masculinity is in the midst of crisis" (p. 2). Whether masculinity is, in fact, in crisis is not the issue. Media present masculinity as in crisis, and actions are called for to reclaim it. When masculinity "figures itself as in crisis and figures white men as vulnerable to attack," it can "justify the constant securing of its borders" (Dickinson & Anderson, 2004, p. 290).

Just as muscular Christianity was a response to the perceived effeminization of men at the end the 19th century, much popular culture at the turn of the 20th century is a response to the "imminent collapse of the corporate man, over-civilized and emasculated by allied obligations to work and women. To rebuild this haggard creature," movies such as *Fight Club* (1999) and *In the Company of Men* (1997) turn to what Ashcraft and Flores label a "'civilized/primitive' masculinity, embodied by the hardened white man who finds healing in wounds" (p. 2). Men employ physical and psychological violence (their primitive side) to maintain or recapture their masculinity even in the world of business (their civilized side).

An analysis of fictional men in fictional movies seems like a strange place to discover what it means to be a "real" man; however, one can study masculinity not only by studying actual men but also by studying discourses about masculinity found in popular culture. The purpose of media analysis is not to determine whether the media representations are empirically accurate but to explore how such representations shape the social imagination. Regardless, "accomplishing gender necessarily entails performance, whether improvised in the mundane moments of everyday life or memorialized on screen for countless witnesses" (Ashcraft & Flores, 2003, p. 3).

In their analysis, Ashcraft and Flores (2003) pay particular attention to the way in which masculinity, like femininity, is "not a stable or unified phenomenon; its meanings shift over time and in relation to culture, context, and person," and it also "is inevitably raced and classed" (p. 3). They note that when hegemonic masculinity is discussed, authors often are referring to hegemonic *White* masculinity, even though race is not overtly mentioned; U.S. hegemonic masculinity is raced White. This is part of the power of hegemonic White masculinity: It "co-opts discourses of race, class, and sexuality without deposing its white, heterosexual, and middle-class footing" (p. 4).

Fight Club also illustrates how media forms criticized by religious and social conservatives actually may support, instead of undermine, the heteronormative ideal. Robert Westerfelhaus and Robert Alan Brookey's (2004) analysis of *Fight Club* explores how heteronormative values are pervasive even though the film is "self-consciously irreverent and seemingly antireligious" (p. 321). *Fight Club* initially celebrates the homosocial relationship between narrator Jack (Edward Norton) and Tyler (Brad Pitt) through subtextual eroticism, which is part of the film's theme of rebellion, but that relationship ultimately is violently rejected.

Even as the film mocks many social institutions, it reinforces heteronormativity, a key component of hegemonic masculinity.

How masculinity as physical power is marketed to men becomes clear when one compares men's bodies in men's magazines to those in women's. Researchers have found "the ideal male body marketed to men is more muscular than the ideal male body marketed to women" (Frederick, Fessler, & Haselton, 2005, p. 81). Remember G.I. Joe's ever-expanding biceps? Men are increasingly influenced by body image aspirations; like women's, men's body norms have changed across time (Bordo, 1999).

Primitive masculinity expressed through violence is a staple in video games as well. The video game culture predominantly portrays a hypermasculinity (Kimmel, 2012a). One can understand video games as an example of an attempt to secure masculinity by overperforming it. In a comprehensive review of video games, media scholars Richard Campbell, Chris Martin, and Bettina Fabos (2013) conclude that video gaming is a field dominated by White men as the creators, producers, actors, and players, and the adventures created in the games are those of violence, power, domination, and misogyny. Although women now make up 47% of players (Entertainment Software Association, 2012), games are dominated by male characters that conform to social stereotypes about masculine domination and aggression. Some of the hypermasculinized characteristics in the most violent ("mature audience") genre of games are the following:

- Combat with guns and every other type of weapon imaginable is featured.
- The action is intentionally violent.
- The storyline is a dark fantasy or horror.
- Players take on villainous roles (e.g., serial killers, gun-wielding assassins, underworld criminals out for revenge).
- Players earn points by killing or hurting as many others as possible.
- Human characters are predominantly White men and (rarely) women.
- Women do not exist in most games.
- The women portrayed tend to be scantily dressed even if they enact aggression; others are the target of abuse, rape, and murder. (Campbell, Martin, & Fabos, 2013)

Grand Theft Auto demonstrates the disturbing way women are treated in the games. The player is encouraged to rape a prostitute in a stolen car and then kill her, as if this is just what a guy does on a Saturday night. In another game trilogy, *God of War*, the setting is Ancient Greece, the women have little or no clothing, and the only way a man advances in the game is to have sex with the women who cross his path. The women's roles are limited to either running for their lives or seducing the hero. In one of the most bloody, violent trilogies, *Gears of War*, women were introduced in the last adventure, but whether they are equal competitors is yet to be determined. These are the type of messages that make the games particularly misogynistic.

Unfortunately, virtual violence seeps into the material world. Media representations of violence are *one* of the ways gendered violence is normalized in U.S. culture.

Reviews of the research on gaming indicate it leads to aggression and violence in children and adults (e.g., Doğan, 2006; Kierkegaard, 2008). Media images of hegemonic masculinity present violence as the answer to problems: If someone kills a man's family, his solution is to kill them even more violently, as in *Mad Max* (1979), *The Patriot* (2000), or *The Punisher* (2004).

Conclusion

The creativity and artistry involved in media creations open spaces for creative performances of gender—within limits. Even as Hollywood is condemned for failing to live up to traditional family values, most dominant media images reinforce the gender binary of heteronormativity. However, even though the politics of much media are regressive, most people take pleasure in going to movies, reading novels, perusing magazines, playing video games, and surfing the web. The danger is not that people do these things but that they often do them uncritically. Audiences act as though they are passive recipients of media, not active participants in culture. The more you realize that you can *talk back* to the screen, the page, or the picture, the more you are not merely buying a commodity. The more you become an engaged member of the cultural conversation, the more you learn to employ an oppositional gaze. Condit (1989) explains that audience's complex relationship to media "is a consequence of the fact that humans, in their inherent character as audiences, are inevitably situated in a communication *system*, of which they are a part, and hence have some influence within, but by which they are also influenced" (p. 120). This chapter should make clear the ways in which people can engage in the active and dynamic practice of resistant readings of media. People can use "media texts to serve their own interests in unpredictable ways" (Dow & Condit, 2005, p. 457).

Although creative uses of media are important, an institutional approach to media also makes clear they may be insufficient. First, media are ephemeral, making them a "fragile basis for lasting social change" (Dow, 2001, p. 137). Second, changes in representation do not necessarily translate into changes in policy (Budd et al., 1990). Although we believe that images, texts, and messages matter, we also want to clarify the limits of personalized politics; institutional-level change is required, and heightened consciousness of media images of women and men, masculinity and femininity, Whiteness and otherness does little if it is not translated into political action.

KEY CONCEPTS

commodification 237	polysemous 228	the gaze 230
hegemony 228	polyvalence 229	U.S. hegemonic masculinity 247
oppositional gaze 236	sexualization 241	ways of seeing 230

DISCUSSION QUESTIONS

1. The next time you watch a television show or movie, keep a record of
   - the characters with whom you identify
   - the characters you want to emulate or be
   - the characters you find attractive

   What does this tell you about your gaze? Through whose eyes are you watching? Using an oppositional gaze, what might you see differently?

2. The next time you watch TV, go to a movie, play a video game, or read a magazine, count the number of times characters are sexualized. How many times are women and men presented in a way that makes sexuality their primary attribute? Are there examples of women characters whose sexuality is completely irrelevant to their identity? Are there examples of men?

3. What messages do the media you read and watch give you about masculinity? Is masculinity secure and certain? Is it something natural? Is it something that can be maintained only through action? If so, what actions must be taken?

4. Can you think of ways in which individual agency (or gender) is commodified and sold?

   *Why is it that buying a soft drink, one that thousands of others buy as well, is a sign of your individuality? Are you really "a pepper" if everyone around you is a pepper too?

   *Have you really "come a long way, baby" because you smoke a cigarette?

   *Are you really an iconoclastic participant in the X-culture because you "Do the Dew"?

CHAPTER 12

One Last Look Through a Critical Gendered Lens

During 2012's holiday season, 13-year-old McKenna Pope wanted to buy her younger brother a toy he requested, an Easy Bake oven, which used to come in teal, yellow, silver, and blue (the latter color the one in which one of your authors cooked some fabulous cakes). After shopping with her parents for the oven, she realized no boys were pictured on the packaging and the oven came in a pink and purple floral print only, sending the message "only girls play with it" ("Hasbro," 2012). Pope posted a video on YouTube ("Hasbro," 2012) and wrote the following petition on Change.org:

> We . . . found it quite appalling that boys are not featured in packaging or pro-motional materials for Easy Bake Ovens—this toy my brother's always dreamed about. And the oven comes in gender-specific hues: purple and pink.
>
> I feel that this sends a clear message: women cook, men work. . . .
>
> I want my brother to know that it's not "wrong" for him to want to be a chef, that it's okay to go against what society believes to be appropriate. (Pope, 2012, par. 3–4)

After more than 45,000 signatures and much media coverage (stories appeared on ABC, CNN, MSNBC, and NPR and in the Associated Press, the *Los Angeles Times*, the *Washington Post*, and numerous local papers), Hasbro responded that they were producing a silver and black model of the oven and will change their packaging so the toy is marketed to girls *and* boys.

This example illustrates a number of themes in this book. Binary gender/sex differences are reinforced through communication. Seemingly innocent practices (like color coding) really affect children's perceptions of themselves and others. Institutional communication, recirculated by media, maintains the gender/sex binary. But the good news is that people talk back against these restrictive norms.

A 13-year-old girl, using only communication (a petition and a YouTube video), asked for change. She challenged the binary and succeeded. So, if she could find a way to see beyond the binary and make a place in the world where her brother would not feel "wrong," what can you do?

Using your critical gendered lens, you can

- recognize the drawbacks of the gender differences approach;
- embrace an oppositional gaze that enables you to see when people of a particular sex, gender, race, class, and/or religion are left out, missing, or unrecognized; and
- make interventions in the world—intrapersonally, interpersonally, and publicly—that make the world work (and cook) for everyone.

The long-dominant differences approach to gender in communication reinforces the gender/sex binary. It assumes there are only two sexes (male and female), which are opposites. It also assumes there are only two genders (masculine and feminine) and men are masculine and women are feminine, and the more you are of one, the less you are of the other. Embedded within this gender/sex binary is heteronormativity. Everyone is presumed heterosexual, and if one violates this presumption, then intense questions are raised about one's gender, and if one violates presumptions about one's gender, then questions are raised about one's sexual orientation. Many problems plague a differences approach. A focus on differences between women and men

- ignores the vast array of similarities among people;
- ignores the existence of intersex and transgender people;
- assumes that sex determines gender; and
- ignores the differences among women and among men and thus fails to accurately account for the importance of issues such as race, class, religion, and nationality.

Perhaps most importantly, a differences approach tends to ignore the issue of power and its offspring, violence. When one simply assumes men and women are different, then one too easily explains away power inequalities as the natural outcome of differences. We hope you realize that understanding gender in communication is nowhere near as simple as identifying differences. In fact, accepting a heteronormative gender/sex binary is more likely to induce you to commit errors when you assess communicative exchanges. Accordingly, we have not offered a list of differences between women's and men's communication.

It would simply be wrong, a categorical error, to talk about gender in communication by talking about differences between women's and men's communication patterns. The most up-to-date research demonstrates that looking for gender differences in communication by studying women as one group and men as another yields no meaningful results. Even though many tend to believe that men (as men) and women (as women) communicate differently, "the literature shows unstable, context-specific, relatively small, and variable effects" (Dow & Condit, 2005, p. 453). According to meta-analyses of research on gender in communication, biological sex accounts for "a miniscule 1% of the variance in communication behaviors" (p. 453). *One percent.* Biological sex is not the determining element; rather, gender role characteristics and expectations are. It would be a waste of time to devote an entire book to explaining only 1% of communicative actions.

Further complicating one's understanding of gender/sex in communication is the fact that gender is not an isolable component of a person's identity. Identity is intersectional. Your performance of gender is inextricably influenced by your race, ethnicity, class, sex, sexual orientation, physical ability, nationality, religion, education, work status, family, citizenship status, and every other identity ingredient that makes up who you are. A book about gender in communication is necessarily about much more than gender.

Gender communication scholar John Sloop (2005) writes in his review of research on sex, race, class, and gender, "A gender/sexuality project that avoids questions of, say, class and race, not only reinforces the larger material and economic ways in which class and racial borders are reinforced and delimited, but also provides a critique of gender/sexuality issues that has limited explanatory power" (p. 326). Our goal is to make clear that one cannot understand gender unless one also understands the complexity of each person's identity, the influences of institutions upon gender, and how questions of power are woven throughout. If one examines gender diversity using a critical gendered lens, many more subtleties and complexities emerge, justifying the scope of this book.

Despite the complexities and fluidities of identity, many institutions are still structured around identity categories as if each were permanently fixed, unproblematically identifiable, and easily distinguished. For this reason, even though gender is highly interdependent with other identity ingredients, it still is useful as a category of analysis when trying to understand the dynamics of communication.

By tending to violence throughout this book, we make clear that differences are rarely innocent cultural constructions. Instead, these constructions (e.g., man, woman, Black, White, rich, poor, citizen, noncitizen, physically able, disabled) have consequences. These consequences become clearest when one tracks issues such as rape, domestic violence, poverty, and genocide. Our point is not that men and masculinity are the cause of all society's ills. Instead, hegemonic masculinity and the normalization of violence as a solution to problems contribute to those ills.

We realize that our approach to understanding gender in communication is complex. We also realize that accounting for complexity is not easy. However, we do not consider this a drawback. We would rather be overly complex to get you thinking about gender diversity than overly simple and risk ignoring important variables that influence human communication. Human beings are wonderfully complex, and so it makes sense that the identity ingredient of gender would be, too. Gender communication scholars Bonnie Dow and Celeste Condit (2005) make this clear: "Sex and gender are not simply variables deserving incorporation in equations, but are complex factors that require careful, sustained attention to their formation and to the nonsimple ways in which they play out in human communication" (p. 454).

We have tried to highlight moments of emancipation and liberation, as well as moments of oppression and subordination. Although institutional structures and social power create inequalities, those inequalities do not persist unchallenged. Despite grinding poverty, people live full lives. Despite oppression and subordination, people find ways to creatively express themselves. Despite constant threats of violence, people resist. In many cases, acts of resistance use the very gender structures meant to subordinate. These acts of resistance are not without consequence, but for many the risk of backlash is not enough to deter them from finding ways to have livable lives. Of course, for many, accommodation is the selected path by which they find ways to live with the demands social institutions place upon them.

Although many gender scholars are criticized (if not condemned) for denying that differences exist, we believe this criticism is based on a misunderstanding of our (and others') argument. In recognizing gender diversity, we are not denying differences between women and men. Instead, we highlight the diversity that exists between women, between men, and between all people. There are not two genders that neatly correspond to two sexes. Instead, a multiplicity of genders exists, genders that intersect with, influence, and are influenced by the vast array of other identity ingredients. Gender is constructed through institutional, interpersonal, and public discourse, and these constructions demand and maintain expectations of gender differentiation. Thus, we do not reject difference but account for far more differences, and far more similarities, than people usually think about. Our goal is not to deny the existence of gender/sex; rather, it is to open up possibilities for more genders and sexes. We simply reject the notion that the differences can be understood solely as differences between women and men and that differences exist solely within individual women and individual men.

Because we operate from a perspective of gender diversity, we also want to make clear that all people have at their disposal a range of communication strategies, even though those strategies may not always neatly fit within the gender identity one typically performs. Adaptability and flexibility are the marks of a good communicator. The same is true when one considers gender in communication: Gender flexibility is good. Different contexts, different interpersonal relationships, and different times in a person's life will call for different gendered styles of communication.

As important as personal choices about gender performance are, and as much as we want to empower people to exercise agency in their communication choices about gender, we also want to make clear that those choices exist in larger social and institutional structures. Choice is never totally free of external constraints. Some choices are more valued and more validated than others, such as choosing to have children in a traditional, heterosexual marriage. Some choices are easier to make because people recognize their possibility, such as men's choices to be firefighters and women's to be nurses. Some choices are not seen as choices, because they participate in hegemonic patterns and practices, such as women's wearing of skirts and men's wearing of pants. Some choices are devalued or condemned, such as the choice of a woman to be childfree or a man's choice to be the primary care-giver to young children. Some choices seem impossible, such as the choice of women in the 1900s to speak publicly. Some choices are highlighted as choices, as people flaunting something, such as the choice of men to dress in skirts or the choice of same-sex couples to kiss in public. For these reasons, one cannot discuss personal choices about gender in communication without also discussing the public politics of sex and gender.

A critical gendered lens is necessary to study public communication about gender and to study institutions that construct and maintain gender/sex. Attention to how media messages reinforce gender/sex is necessary. Understanding how communication patterns about work gender particular groups is essential. Exploring how public statements about religion define what it means to be (only) a man or a woman is important. Analysis of what gets to be considered a family helps one understand who gets to be considered fully human. Analysis of public discourse about education enables one to track the ways stereotypes about gender/sex are maintained.

Personal gender/sex politics, although essential and important, are not the whole story. Personal choices matter. But political choices matter, too, and one should not lose sight of them. Gender in communication is not just about interpersonal relationships but also about larger social structures and the way they interact with the realities of people's personal lives. It *does* matter who does the dishes, cleans the toilet, takes out the trash, and changes diapers. It also matters what the minimum wage is—or what an economically privileged person pays another to perform this labor.

We hope that we have provided you with the skills to ask the complicated questions, to ask whether a pattern exists along gender or sex lines, to ask why people do things the way they do, to ask whether something can be changed, to ask for something to change, to ask whether gender alone really explains it all. Sex privilege exists, and race privilege exists, but class privilege can complicate both. More than sex difference, power seems to be one of the most important analytical categories. For example, in the capitalist, consumerist society of the contemporary United States, power means money. In the United States, a rich White woman often holds more power than a poor Black man. A rich Hispanic man often holds more power than a poor White man. However, statistically there are many more rich White men in the United States than any other category of rich people. Research on gender in communication must take into account race, class, citizenship, sexuality, and religion as well as the specific context if it is to say anything meaningful about the human condition.

Gender/sex is about real lives. Everyone faces real consequences if people do not recognize and resist the intensification of hegemomic masculinity and hyperfemininity. We hope you can help create a future in which the people around you—friends, family, acquaintances, co-workers, children—will be freer to be themselves without fear of harm. It will take everyone—women and men and intersexed people, queer and straight, cisgender and transgender, young and old, Whites and people of color—working (and cooking) together.

DISCUSSION QUESTIONS

1. Review the book and select four theories, concepts, images, or findings that are most helpful in creating your critical gendered lens. Be able to explain your choices.

2. A friend who knows you took a course on gender in communication inquires, "What did you learn? Why can't women and men communicate?" How would you answer the person's question? What problems do you see with the perspective inferred by the person's question?

3. What does it mean to recognize gender diversity and not focus on gender differences in the study of gender in communication? How does a gender diversity approach help you to consider the topic from a global perspective?

4. Consider McKenna Pope's protest of Hasbro's Easy Bake Oven advertising. Can you identify a simple act of social justice you could do relating to gender/sex, race, ethnicity, class, physical ability, body size, age, or sexual orientation in communication? What would it take for you to implement this action?

References

We have taken some liberties with APA reference style. To help readers see the contributions of both women and men to our subject, we have included first names of authors where known. Although we recognize the artificiality of sex distinctions and the complexity of identity, we also realize that no matter how artificial, identity categories matter. M. Jacqui Alexander and Chandra Talpade Mohanty (1997) note that even as postmodernist theories attempt to pluralize and dissolve "the stability and analytic utility of the categories race, class, gender, and sexuality . . . the relations of domination and subordination that are named and articulated through the processes of racism and racialization still exist, and they still require analytic and political specification and engagement" (p. xvii).

Abbasi, Jennifer. (2012, July 17). Why 6-year-old girls want to be sexy (study). *Huff Post Parents*. Retrieved from www.huffingtonpost.com/2012/07/17/6-year-old-girls-sexy_n_1679088.html

Ablow, Keith. (2011, April 11). *J. Crew plants the seeds for gender identity.* FoxNews.com. Retrieved from www.foxnews.com/health/2011/04/11/j-crew-plants-seeds-gender-identity

Acker, Joan. (1990, June). Hierarchies, jobs, bodies: A theory of gendered organizations. *Gender & Society, 4*(2), 139–158.

Adams, Josh. (2009). Marked difference: Tattooing and its association with deviance in the United States. *Deviant Behavior, 30,* 266–292.

Addis, Michael E., Mansfield, Abigail K., & Syzdek, Matthew R. (2010). Is "masculinity" a problem? Framing the effects of gendered social learning in men. *Psychology of Men & Masculinity, 11*(2), 77–90.

Adherents.com. (2007). *Major religions of the world ranked by number of adherents.* Retrieved from www.adherents.com/Religions_By_Adherents.html

Adorno, Theodor W. (1991). *The culture industry: Selected essays on mass culture.* London: Routledge.

Agbese, Aje-Ori. (2003, Spring). Maintaining power in the face of political, economic and social discrimination: The tale of Nigerian women. *Women and Language, 26*(1), 18–26.

Alcoff, Linda. (1995). The problem of speaking for others. In Judith Roof & Robyn Weigman (Eds.), *Who can speak? Authority and critical identity* (pp. 97–119). Urbana: University of Illinois Press.

Alcoff, Linda, & Potter, Elizabeth. (Eds.). (1993). *Feminist epistemologies*. New York: Routledge.

Alexander, M. Jacqui, & Mohanty, Chandra Talpade. (Eds.). (1997). Introduction: Genealogies, legacies, movements. In *Feminist genealogies, colonial legacies, democratic futures* (pp. xiii–xlii). New York: Routledge.

Allen, Brenda J. (1995). "Diversity" and organizational communication. *Journal of Applied Communication Research, 23,* 143–155.

Allen, Brenda J. (1996). Feminist standpoint theory: A Black woman's (re)view of organizational socialization. *Communication Studies, 47*(4), 257–271.

Allen, Brenda J. (1998). Black womanhood and feminist standpoints. *Management Communication Quarterly, 11,* 575–586.

Aluede, Oyaziwo. (2008). A review of the extent, nature, characteristics and effects of bullying behavior in schools. *Journal of Instructional Psychology, 35*(2), 151–158.

American Association of University Professors. (2012). *Annual report on the economic status of the profession, 2011–12.* Washington, DC: AAUP.

American Association of University Women. (2006). *Drawing the line: Sexual harassment on campus.* Washington, DC: Author.

American Medical Association. (2011, June 21). AMA adopts new policies at annual meeting. Retrieved from www.ama-assn.org/ama/pub/news/news/a11-new-policies.page

American Psychiatric Association. (2000). *Diagnostic and statistical manual of mental disorders* (4th ed., text rev.). Washington, DC: Author.

American Psychiatric Association. (2012). *Diagnostic and statistical manual of mental disorders. DSM-5 Development.* Retrieved from www.dsm5.0rg/Pages/Default.aspx

American Psychological Association. (2007). *Report of the APA task force on the sexualization of girls.* Washington, DC: Author. Retrieved from www.apa.org/pi/women/programs/girls/report-full.pdf

Andersen, Margaret L., with Witham, Dana Hysock. (2011). *Thinking about women: Sociological perspectives on sex and gender* (9th ed.). Boston: Pearson Education, Allyn & Bacon.

Anderson, Kelli. (2012, May 7). How athletic participation brought dreams to life. *Sports Illustrated,* p. 49.

Anderson, Kristin J., & Leaper, Campbell. (1998, August). Meta-analyses of gender effects on conversational interruption: Why, what, when, where, and how. *Sex Roles, 39*(3–4), 225–252.

Angier, Natalie. (1999). *Woman: An intimate geography.* New York: Anchor Books.

Ankney, Davison C. (1992). Sex differences in relative brain size: The mismeasure of woman, too? *Intelligence, 16*(3/4), 329–336.

An open letter from Black women to the SlutWalk. (2011, September 23). *The Huffington Post.* Retrieved from www.huffingtonpost.com/susan-brison/slutwalk-black-women_b_980215.html

Anzaldúa, Gloria. (1987). *Borderlands/La Frontera: The new Mestiza.* San Francisco: Aunt Lute Books.

Anzaldúa, Gloria. (1990). Bridge, drawbridge, sandbar or island: Lesbians-of-Color *hacienda alianzas*. In Lisa Albrecht & Rose M. Brewer (Eds.), *Bridges of power: Women's multicultural alliances* (pp. 216–231). Philadelphia: New Society Publishers.

Apostolic Visitation of Institutes of Women Religious in the United States. (2012, January 9). *Apostolic visitation closes with final report submission* [Press release].

Apple, R. W., Jr. (2001, October 15). A nation challenged: News analysis: Nature of foe is obstacle in appealing for sacrifice. *New York Times,* p. B1.

Archer, John. (2006). Testosterone and human aggression: An evaluation of the challenge hypothesis. *Neuroscience and Biobehavioral Reviews, 30*(3), 319–345. doi:10.1016/j.neubiorev.2004.12.007

Ardener, Edwin. (1973). *Some outstanding problems in the analysis of events.* Paper presented at the meeting of the Association of Social Anthropologists' decennial conference, Oxford. Later published in Malcom Chapman (Ed.), *The voice of prophecy and other essays/Edwin Ardener* (pp. 105–108). Oxford, England: Basil Blackwell.

Ardener, Shirley. (2005). Ardener's "muted groups": The genesis of an idea and its praxis. *Women and Language, 28*(2), 50–54.

Ardila, Alfredo, Rosselli, Monica, Matute, Esmerelda, & Inozemtseva, Olga. (2011). Gender differences in cognitive development. *Developmental Psychology, 47*(4), 984–990.

Are sex offenders and lads' mags using the same language? (2011, December 6). University of Surrey. Retrieved from www.surrey.ac.uk/mediacentre/press/2011/69535_are_sex_offenders_and_lads_mags_using_the_same_language.htm

Aries, Elizabeth. (2006). Sex differences in interaction: A reexamination. In Kathryn Dindia & Daniel J. Canary (Eds.), *Sex differences and similarities in communication* (2nd ed., pp. 21–36). Mahwah, NJ: Erlbaum.

Armstrong, Jeannette. (1990). Words. In The Telling It Book Collective (Ed.), *Telling it: Women and language across cultures* (pp. 23–30). Vancouver, British Columbia, Canada: Press Gang.

As G.I. Joe bulks up, concern for the 98-pound weakling. (1999, May 30). *New York Times,* p. 2.

Ashcraft, Karen Lee, & Flores, Lisa A. (2003, January). "Slaves with white collars": Persistent performances of masculinity in crisis. *Text and Performance Quarterly, 23*(1), 1–29.

Ashcraft, Karen Lee, & Mumby, Dennis K. (2004). *Reworking gender: A feminist communicology of organization.* Thousand Oaks, CA: Sage.

Atkinson, Michael. (2002). Pretty in pink: Conformity, resistance, and negotiation in women's tattooing. *Sex Roles, 47*(2), 219–235.

The *Atlantic*'s 'Women can't have it all' manifesto: The backlash. (2012, June 26). *The Week.* Retrieved from http://theweek.com/article/index/229808/the-atlantics-women-cant-have-it-all-manifesto-the-backlash

Ayotte, Kevin, & Husain, Mary E. (2005, Fall). Securing Afghan women: Neocolonialism, epistemic violence, and the rhetoric of the veil. *NWSA Journal, 17*(3), 112–133.

Babcock, Linda, & Laschever, Sara. (2007). *Women don't ask: The high cost of avoiding negotiation—and positive strategies for change.* New York: Bantam Dell.

Bandura, Albert. (2002). Social cognitive theory of mass communication. In Jennings Bryant & Dolf Zillman (Eds.), *Media effects: Advances in theory and research* (2nd ed., pp. 121–153). Mahwah, NJ: Erlbaum.

Bandura, Albert, & Walters, Richard H. (1963). *Social learning and personality development.* New York: Holt, Rinehart & Winston.

Barnett, Rosalind, & Rivers, Caryl. (2004). *Same difference: How gender myths are hurting our relationships, our children, and our jobs.* New York: Basic Books.

Bartkiewicz, Mark J., Diaz, Elizabeth M., Greytak, Emily, & Kosciw, Joseph G. (2009). *The 2009 national school climate survey: The experiences of lesbian, gay, bisexual, and transgender youth in our nation's schools.* GLSEN. Retrieved from www.glsen.org/cgi-bin/iowa/all/news/record/2624.html

Bartky, Sandra Lee. (1990). *Femininity and domination: Studies in the phenomenology of oppression.* New York: Routledge.

Basow, Susan A. (2008). Speaking in a "man's world": Gender differences in communication styles. In Michele A. Paludi (Ed.), *The psychology of women at work: Challenges and solutions for our female workforce* (pp. 15–30). Westport, CN: Praeger.

Basow, Susan A., Phelan, Julie E., & Capotosto, Laura. (2006). Gender patterns in college students' choices of their best and worst professors. *Psychology of Women Quarterly, 30,* 25–35.

Bate, Barbara. (1988). *Communication and the sexes.* Prospect Heights, IL: Waveland.

Baucom, Donald H., Snyder, Douglas K., & Gordon, Kristina Coop. (2009). *Helping couples get past the affair: A clinician's guide.* New York: Guilford Press.

Baugh, John. (2003). Linguistic profiling. In Sinfree Makoni, Geneva Smitherman, Arnetha F. Ball, & Arthur K. Spears (Eds.), *Black linguistics: Language, society, and politics in Africa and the Americas* (pp. 155–168). London: Routledge.

Baugh, John. (2007). Linguistic contributions to the advancement of racial justice within and beyond the African diaspora. *Language & Linguistics Compass, 1*(4), 331–349.

Baxter, Judith. (2007). *Positioning gender in discourse: A feminist methodology.* Basingstoke, Hampshire, England: Palgrave, Macmillan.

Baxter, Judith, & Wallace, Kieran. (2009). Outside in-group and out-group identities? Constructing male solidarity and female exclusion in UK builders' talk. *Discourse & Society, 20,* 411–429.

Baxter, Leslie A. (2010). The dialogue of marriage. *Journal of Family Theory & Review, 2,* 370–387.

Baxter, Leslie A. (2011). *Voicing relationships: A dialogic perspective.* Thousand Oaks, CA: Sage.

BBC. (2009, March 6). What would a real life Barbie look like? *BBC News Magazine.* Retrieved from http://news.bbc.co.uk/2/hi/uknews/magazine/7920962.stm.

Becker, Anne E., Burwell, Rebecca A., Herzog, David B., Hamburg, Paul, & Gilman, Stephen E. (2002). Eating behaviours and attitudes following prolonged exposure to television among ethnic Fijian adolescent girls. *The British Journal of Psychiatry, 180,* 509–514.

Begley, Sharon, & Murr, Andrew. (1995, March 27). Gray matters. *Newsweek,* pp. 48–54.

Bell, Elizabeth, Haas, Lynda, & Sells, Laura. (Eds.). (2008). *From mouse to mermaid: The politics of film, gender, and culture.* South Bend: Indiana University Press.

Bell, Leslie C. (2004). Psychoanalytic theories of gender. In Alice H. Eagly, Anne E. Beall, & Robert J. Sternberg, (Eds.), *The psychology of gender* (2nd ed., pp. 145–168). New York: Guilford Press.

Bellafante, Ginia. (2004, January 12). Two fathers, with one happy to stay at home. *The New York Times,* p. 1.

Bem, Sandra. (1974). The measurement of psychological androgyny. *Journal of Counseling and Clinical Psychology, 42,* 155–162.

Bennett, Jeffrey. (2008). Passing, protesting, and the arts of resistance: Infiltrating the ritual space of blood donation. *Quarterly Journal of Speech, 94,* 23–43. doi:10.1080/00335630701790818

Berger, John. (1972). *Ways of seeing.* London: Penguin Books.

Berlant, Lauren, & Warner, Michael. (1995, May). What does queer theory teach us about X? *PMLA, 110*(3), 343–349.

Bianchi, Suzanne M., Raley, Sara B., & Casper, Lynne M. (2012). Changing American families in the 21st century. In Patricia Noller & Gery C. Karantzas (Eds.), *The Wiley-Blackwell handbook of couples and family relationships* (pp. 36–47). West Sussex, England: John Wiley & Sons.

Bizzell, Patricia. (2010). Chastity warrants for women public speakers in nineteenth-century American fiction. *Rhetoric Society Quarterly, 40*(4), 385–401.

Blackless, Melanie, Charuvastra, Anthony, Derryck, Amanda, Fausto-Sterling, Anne, Lauzanne, Karl, & Lee, Ellen. (2000). How sexually dimorphic are we? Review and synthesis. *American Journal of Human Biology, 12,* 151–166.

Blakey, M. L. (1999). Scientific racism and the biological concept of race. *Literature and Psychology, 45,* 29–43.

Bleske-Rechek, April, Somers, Erin, Micke, Cierra, Erickson, Leah, Matteson, Lindsay, Stocco, Corey, Schumacher, Brittany, & Ritchie, Laura. (2012). Benefit or burden? Attraction in cross-sex friendship. *Journal of Social and Personal Relationships, 29*(5), 569–596.

Blustain, Sarah. (2000, November). The new gender wars. *Psychology Today, 33,* 42.

Boddice, Rob. (2011). The manly mind? Revisiting the Victorian 'sex in brain' debates. *Gender & History, 23*(2), 321–340.

Bolick, Kate. (2012, June 28). Single people deserve work-life balance, too [Blog post]. *The Atlantic.* Retrieved from www.theatlantic.com/business/archive/2012/06/single-people-deserve-work-life-balance-too/259071

Bordo, Susan. (1997a). Anorexia nervosa: Psychopathology and the crystallization of culture. In Carole Counihan & Penny Van Esterik (Eds.), *Food and culture: A reader* (pp. 226–250). New York: Routledge.

Bordo, Susan. (1997b). *Twilight zones: The hidden life of cultural images from Plato to O.J.* Berkeley: University of California Press.

Bordo, Susan. (1999). *The male body: A new look at men in public and private.* New York: Farrar, Straus & Giroux.

Bordo, Susan. (2003). *Unbearable weight: Feminism, western culture, and the body* (10th anniversary edition). Berkeley: University of California Press.

Bosher, Monroe. (1996, September 6). *Gender Wars review.* Gamespot. Retrieved from www.gamespot.com/gender-wars/reviews/gender-wars-review-2536230

Botta, Renee A. (2006). The mirror of television: A comparison of Black and White adolescents' body images. *Journal of Communication, 50*(3), 144–159.

Bowles, Hannah Riley, Babcock, Linda, & Lai, Lei. (2007). Social incentives for gender differences in the propensity to initiate negotiations: Sometimes it does hurt to ask. *Organizational Behavior and Human Decision Processes, 103,* 84–103.

Boyd, Emily M., Reynolds, John R., Tillman, Kathryn Harker, & Martin, Patricia Yancey. (2010). Adolescent girls' race/ethnic status, identities, and drive for thinness. *Social Science Research, 40,* 667–684.

Boyle, Katherine. (2012, June 24). *Atlantic* magazine story goes viral, and women have something to say about having "it all." *The Washington Post.* Retrieved from www.washingtonpost.com/lifestyle/style/atlantic-story-on-whether-women-could-have-it-all/2012/06/24/gJQAihWQ0V_story_1.html

Bradstock, Andrew, Gill, Sean, Hogan, Anne, & Morgan, Sue. (Eds.). (2000). *Masculinity and spirituality in Victorian culture.* New York: St. Martin's Press.

Brannon, Linda. (2011). *Gender: Psychological perspectives* (6th ed.). Boston: Pearson Education.

Braunberger, Christine. (2000). Revolting bodies: The monster beauty of tattooed women. *NWSA Journal, 12*(2), 1–23.

Britton, Dana M. (1999). Cat fights and gang fights: Preference for work in a male-dominated organization. *The Sociological Quarterly, 40*(3), 455–474.

Brod, Harry. (1987). The case for men's studies. In Harry Brod (Ed.), *The making of masculinities: The new men's studies* (pp. 39–62). Boston: Allen & Unwin.

Brooks, Meredith, & Peiken, Shelly. (1997). *Bitch* [Music lyrics]. Retrieved from www.musicfanclubs.org/meredithbrooks/bitc.html

Broverman, Inge K., Broverman, Donald M., Clarkson, Frank E., Rosenkrantz, Paul S., & Vogel, Susan R. (1970). Sex-role stereotypes and clinical judgments of mental health. *Journal of Counseling and Clinical Psychology, 34*(1), 1–7.

Brown, Erin R. (2011, April 8). *J. Crew pushes transgendered child propaganda.* Culture and Media Institute. Retrieved from www.mrc.org/cmi/articles/2011/JCREW_Pushes_Transgendered_Child_Propaganda_.html

Brown, Penelope, & Levinson, Stephen. (1978). Universals in language usage: Politeness phenomenon. In Esther N. Goody (Ed.), *Questions and politeness* (pp. 56–89). Cambridge, England: Cambridge University Press.

Brown, Penelope, & Levinson, Stephen. (1987). *Politeness: Some universals in language usage.* Cambridge, England: Cambridge University Press.

Brumbaugh, Claudia C., & Wood, Dustin. (2009, June). Using revealed mate preferences to evaluate market force and differential preference explanations for mate selection. *Journal of Personality & Social Psychology, 96*(6), 1226–1244.

Brummett, Barry. (1976). Some implications of "process" or "intersubjectivity": Postmodern rhetoric. *Philosophy & Rhetoric, 9*(1), 21–51.

Buchanan, Pat. (1992, August 17). *Remarks by Republican presidential candidate Pat Buchanan.* Republican National Convention. Retrieved from www.buchanan.org/pa-92–0817-rnc.html

Buchbinder, David. (2013). *Studying men and masculinities.* London: Routledge.

Budd, Mike, Entman, Robert M., & Steinman, Clay. (1990, June). The affirmative character of U.S. cultural studies. *Critical Studies in Mass Communication, 7*(2), 169–184.

Burke, Kenneth. (1966). *Language as symbolic action: Essays on life, literature, and method.* Berkeley: University of California Press.

Burke, Kenneth. (1969). *A rhetoric of motives.* Berkeley: University of California Press.

Burleson, Brant R., & Kunkel, Adrianne. (2006). Revisiting the different cultures thesis: An assessment of sex differences and similarities in supportive communication. In Kathryn Dindia & Dan J. Canary (Eds.), *Sex differences and similarities in communication* (2nd ed., pp. 137–160). Mahwah, NJ: Erlbaum.

Bush administration publicizes plight of Afghan women. (2001, November 16). Feminist Daily News Wire. Retrieved from www.feminist.org/news/newsbyte/uswirestory.asp?id=5948

Bush, George W. (2001–2002). *Weekly compilation of presidential documents.* Retrieved from www.frwebgate.access.gpo.gov/cgi-bin/multidb.cgi

Bush, Laura. (2001, November 17). *Radio address by Laura Bush to the nation.* Retrieved from www.whitehouse.gov/news/releases/2001/11/20011117.html

Butler, Judith. (1990a). *Gender trouble: Feminism and the subversion of identity.* New York: Routledge.

Butler, Judith. (1990b). Performative acts and gender constitution: An essay in phenomenology and feminist theory. In Sue-Ellen Case (Ed.), *Performing feminisms: Feminist critical theory and theatre* (pp. 270–282). Baltimore: John Hopkins University Press.

Butler, Judith. (1991). Imitation and gender insubordination. In Diana Fuss (Ed.), *Inside/out: Lesbian theories, gay theories* (pp. 13–31). New York: Routledge.

Butler, Judith. (1992). Contingent foundations: Feminism and the question of "postmodernism." In Judith Butler & Joan W. Scott (Eds.), *Feminists theorize the political* (pp. 3–21). New York: Routledge.

Butler, Judith. (1993). *Bodies that matter: On the discursive limits of "sex."* New York: Routledge.

Butler, Judith. (1997). *Excitable speech: A politics of the performative.* New York: Routledge.

Butler, Judith. (2004). *Undoing gender.* New York: Routledge.

Buzzanell, Patrice M. (Ed.). (2000). *Rethinking organizational and managerial communication from feminist perspectives.* Thousand Oaks, CA: Sage.

Buzzanell, Patrice M., & Liu, Meina. (2005, February). Struggling with maternity leave policies and practices: A poststructuralist feminist analysis of gendered organizing. *Journal of Applied Communication Research, 33*(1), 1–25.

Buzzanell, Patrice M., Sterk, Helen, & Turner, Lynn H. (Eds.). (2004). *Gender in applied communication contexts.* Thousand Oaks, CA: Sage.

Byne, William M. (2005). Why we cannot conclude sexual orientation is a biological phenomenon. In J. Kenneth Davidson & Nelwyn B. Moore (Eds.), *Speaking of sexuality* (2nd ed., pp. 245–248). Los Angeles: Roxbury.

Cabrera, Natasha J., & Tamis-LeMonda, Catherine S. (2013). *Handbook of father involvement: Multidisciplinary perspectives* (2nd ed.). New York: Taylor & Francis.

Cahill, Larry. (2005, May). His brain, her brain. *Scientific American, 292*(5), 40–47.

Caiazza, Amy. (2005). Don't bowl at night: Gender, safety, and civic participation. *Signs, 30*(2), 1607–1631.

Calafell, Bernadette Marie. (2004). Disrupting the dichotomy: "Yo soy Chincana/o?" in the New Latina/o South. *The Communication Review, 7,* 175–204.

Calás, Marta B. (1992). An/other silent voice? Representing "Hispanic woman" in organizational texts. In Albert J. Mills & Peta Tancred (Eds.), *Gendering organizational analysis* (pp. 201–221). Newbury Park, CA: Sage.

Calás, Marta B., & Smircich, Linda. (2001). From "the woman's" point of view: Feminist approaches to organization studies. In Stewart R. Clegg, Cynthia Hardy, & Walter N. Nord (Eds.), *Handbook of organization studies* (pp. 218–257). Thousand Oaks, CA: Sage.

Callister, Mark, Coyne, Sarah M., Stern, Lessa A., Stockdale, Laura, Miller, Malinda J., & Wells, Brian M. (2012). A content analysis of the prevalence and portrayal of sexual activity in adolescent literature. *Journal of Sex Research, 49*(5), 477–486.

Cameron, Deborah. (1995). Rethinking language and gender studies: Some issues for the 1990s. In Sara Mills (Ed.), *Language and gender: Interdisciplinary perspectives* (pp. 31–44). London: Longman.

Cameron, Deborah. (1997). Performing gender identity: Young men's talk and the construction of heterosexual masculinity. In Sally Johnson & Ulrike Hanna Meinhof (Eds.), *Language and masculinity* (pp. 47–64). Oxford, England: Basil Blackwell.

Cameron, Deborah. (1998). Lost in translation: Non-sexist language. In Deborah Cameron (Ed.), *The feminist critique of language* (2nd ed., pp. 155–163). New York: Routledge.

Campbell, Anne. (1993). *Men, women and aggression.* New York: Basic Books.

Campbell, Karlyn Kohrs. (1973, February). The rhetoric of women's liberation: An oxymoron. *Quarterly Journal of Speech, 59,* 74–86.

Campbell, Karlyn Kohrs. (1989). *Man cannot speak for her* (Volumes 1 and 2). Westport, CT: Praeger.

Campbell, Karlyn Kohrs. (2005). Agency: Promiscuous and protean. *Communication and Critical/Cultural Studies, 2*(1), 1–19.

Campbell, Lynn. (2006, August 7). Waterloo's "experiment." *The Des Moines Register,* pp. 1A, 3A.

Campbell, Richard, Martin, Christopher R., & Fabos, Bettina. (2013). *Media and culture: An introduction to mass communication* (8th ed.). Boston: Bedford/St. Martin's.

Campbell, Sister Simone. (2012, July 2). Nuns on the Bus sister: Women religions respond to real-world struggles. *National Catholic Reporter.* Retrieved from http://ncronline.org/news/women-religious/nuns-bus-sister-women-religious-respond-real-world-struggles

Canary, Daniel J., & Hause, Kimberley S. (1993, Spring). Is there any reason to research sex differences in communication? *Communication Quarterly, 41*(2), 129–144.

Cancian, Francesca M. (1989). Love and the rise of capitalism. In Barbara J. Risman & Pepper Schwartz (Eds.), *Gender in intimate relationships* (pp. 12–25). Belmont, CA: Wadsworth.

Can women have it all? (2012, September). *The Atlantic, 310*(2), 16.

Caplan, Paula J., & Caplan, Jeremy, B. (1999). *Thinking critically about research on sex and gender* (2nd ed.). New York: Longman.

Carbaugh, Dan. (2002). "I can't do that!" But I "can actually see around corners": American Indian students and the study of public "communication." In Judith N. Martin, Thomas K. Nakayama, & Lisa N. Flores (Eds.), *Readings in intercultural communication: Experiences and contexts* (pp. 138–149). Boston: McGraw-Hill.

Carlson, Jessica H., & Crawford, Mary. (2011, July). Perceptions of relational practices in the workplace. *Gender, Work and Organization, 18*(4), 359–376.

Carroll, Janell L. (2005). *Sexuality now.* Belmont, CA: Wadsworth.

Catalano, Shannan. (2012, November). *Special report: Intimate partner violence, 1993–2010.* U. S. Department of Justice, Office of Justice Programs. Retrieved from www.bjs.gov/index.cfm?ty=pbdetail&iid=4536

Caughlin, John P., & Ramey, Mary E. (2005). The demand/withdraw pattern of communication in parent-adolescent dyads. *Personal Relationships, 12,* 337–355.

Centers for Disease Control and Prevention. (2005, May 3). Births, marriages, divorces, and deaths: Provisional data for November 2004. *National Vital Statistics Reports, 53*(19).

Chappell, David. (2004). *A stone of hope: Prophetic religion and the death of Jim Crow.* Chapel Hill: University of North Carolina Press.

Chen, Martha, Vanek, Joann, Lund, Francie, & Heintz, James. (2005). *Progress of the world's women 2005: Women, work and poverty.* New York: United Nations Development Fund for Women.

Chittister, Joan Sr., OSB. (2004, August 13). To the 'experts in humanity': Since when did women become the problem? [Electronic version]. *National Catholic Reporter, 40*(36), 7.

Chodorow, Nancy. (1978). *The reproduction of mothering: Psychoanalysis and the sociology of gender.* Berkeley: University of California Press.

Chow, Irene Hau-Siu, & Ding, Daniel Z. Q. (2002). Moral judgement and conflict handling styles among Chinese in Hong Kong and PRC. *The Journal of Management Development, 21*(9), 666–679.

Christensen, Andrew, Eldridge, Kathleen, Catta-Preta, Adrianna Bokal, Lim, Veronica, & Santagata, Rossella. (2006). Cross-cultural consistency of the demand-withdraw interaction pattern in couples. *Journal of Marriage and Family, 68,* 1029–1044.

Cichocki, Nina. (2004, November). Veils, poems, guns, and martyrs: Four themes of Muslim women's experiences in Shirin Neshat's photographic work. *Thirdspace, 4*(1). Retrieved from www.iiav.nl/ezines/web/Thirdspace/2004/N01/thirdspace/4_1_Cichocki.htm

Claes, Marie-Therese. (2006). Women, men and management style. In Paula J. Dubeck & Dana Dunn (Eds.), *Workplace/women's place: An anthology* (3rd ed., pp. 83–87). Los Angeles: Roxbury.

Clarke, Edward H. (1873). *Sex in education.* Boston: J. R. Osgood.

Clemetson, Lynette. (2006, February 9). Work vs. family, complicated by race. *The New York Times,* p. G1.

Cloud, Dana L. (1998, Fall). The rhetoric of "family values": Scapegoating, utopia, and the privatization of social responsibility. *Western Journal of Communication, 62*(4), 387–419.

Cloud, Dana L. (2004). "To veil the threat of terror": Afghan women and the "clash of civilizations" in the imagery of the U.S. war on terrorism. *Quarterly Journal of Speech, 90*(3), 285–306.

Coates, Jennifer. (1996). *Women talk: Conversations between women friends.* Oxford, England: Basil Blackwell.

Coates, Jennifer. (1997). One-at-a-time: The organization of men's talk. In Sally Johnson & Ulrike Hanna Meinhof (Eds.), *Language and masculinity* (pp. 107–129). Oxford, England: Basil Blackwell.

Coates, Jennifer. (2003). *Men talk: Stories in the making of masculinities.* Malden, MA: Basil Blackwell.

Coates, Jennifer. (2004). Women, men, and language: A sociolinguistic account of gender differences in language. London: Pearson Education.

Cohn, D'Vera, Passel, Jeffrey, Wang, Wendy, & Livingston, Gretchen. (2011). *Barely half of U.S. adults are married—a record low*. Pew Research Center. Retrieved from www .pewsocialtrends.org/2011/12/14/barely-half-of-u-s-adults-are-married-a-record-low

Colbert, Stephen (Anchor), & Silverman, Allison (Executive Producer). (2012, June 11). *The Colbert report* [Television broadcast]. Retrieved from www.colbertnation.com/ the-colbert-report-videos/415111/june-11-2012/radical-feminist-nuns

Collins, Patricia Hill. (1994). Shifting the center: Race, class, and feminist theorizing about motherhood. In Donna Bassin, Margaret Honey, & Maryle Mahrer Kaplan (Eds.), *Representations of motherhood* (pp. 56–74). New Haven, CT: Yale University Press.

Collins, Patricia Hill. (1998). *Fighting words: Black women and the search for justice*. Minneapolis: University of Minnesota Press.

Coltrane, Scott. (1989). Household labor and the routine production of gender. *Social Problems, 36*, 473–490.

The compact edition of the Oxford English dictionary. (1971). Glasgow, Scotland: Oxford University Press.

Condit, Celeste Michelle. (1989, June). The rhetorical limits of polysemy. *Critical Studies in Mass Communication, 6*(2), 103–122.

Condit, Celeste Michelle. (1992). Post-Burke: Transcending the sub-stance of dramatism. *Quarterly Journal of Speech, 78*(3), 349–355.

Condit, Celeste Michelle. (1998). Gender diversity: A theory of communication for the post-modern era. In Judith S. Trent (Ed.), *Communication: Views from the helm for the 21st century* (pp. 177–183). Boston: Allyn & Bacon.

Congregatio Pro Doctrina Fidei. (2012). Doctrinal Assessment of the Leadership Conference of Women Religious. Retreived from www.usccb.org/about/doctrine/doctrinal-assess ment-for-lcwr.cfm

Connell, Catherine. (2010). Doing gender, or redoing gender? Learning from the workplace experiences of transpeople. *Gender & Society, 24*(1), 31–55.

Connell, R. W. (1995). *Masculinities*. Berkeley: University of California Press.

Connell, R. W. (2000). *The men and the boys*. Berkeley: University of California Press.

Connell, R. W., & Messerschmidt, James W. (2005, December). Hegemonic masculinity: Rethinking the concept. *Gender & Society, 19*, 829–859.

Coontz, Stephanie. (1992). *The way we never were: American families and the nostalgia trap*. New York: Basic Books.

Coontz, Stephanie. (1997). *The way we really are: Coming to terms with America's changing family*. New York: Basic Books.

Coontz, Stephanie. (2006). *Marriage, a history: From obedience to intimacy, or how love conquered marriage*. New York: Penguin.

Cooper, Brenda. (1999, March). The relevancy and gender identity in spectators' interpretations of *Thelma & Louise*. *Critical Studies in Mass Communication, 16*(1), 20–41.

Cooper, Brenda. (2000, Fall). "Chick flicks" as feminist texts: The appropriation of the male gaze in *Thelma & Louise*. *Women's Studies in Communication, 23*(3), 277–306.

Crawford, Mary. (1995). *Talking difference: On gender and language*. London: Sage.

Crawford, Mary, & Fox, Annie. (2007). From sex to gender and back again: Co-optation of a feminist language reform. *Feminism & Psychology, 17*, 481–486.

Crenshaw, Kimberlé. (1989). Demarginalizing the intersection of race and sex: A Black feminist critique of antidiscrimination doctrine, feminist theory and antiracist politics. *University of Chicago Legal Forum*, 139–167.

Crenson, Matthew A., & Ginsberg, Benjamin. (2002). *Downsizing democracy: How America sidelined its citizens and privatized its public*. Baltimore: Johns Hopkins University Press.

Curnutt, Hugh. (2012). Flashing your phone: Sexting and the remediation of teen sexuality. *Communication Quarterly, 60*(3), 353–369.

Dabbs, James McBride, & Dabbs, Mary Godwin. (2001). *Heroes, rogues, & lovers: Testosterone and behavior*. New York: McGraw-Hill.

Daly, Mary. (1987). *Websters' first new intergalactic wickedary of the English language*. Boston: Beacon Press.

Daniels, Arlene Kaplan. (1987). Invisible work. *Social Problems, 34*(5), 403–415.

Davis, Kathy. (2008). Intersectionality as buzzword: A sociology of science perspective on what makes a feminist theory successful. *Feminist Theory, 9*, 67–84. doi:10.1177/1464700108086364

de Beauvoir, Simone. (2011). *The Second Sex* (Trans. Constance Border & Shelia Malovany-Chevallier). New York: Vintage Books. (Original work published 1949)

De Fina, Anna, Schiffrin, Deborah, & Bamberg, Michael. (2006). Introduction. In Anna DeFina, Deborah Schiffrin, & Michael Bamberg (Eds.), *Discourse and identity* (pp. 1–23). Cambridge, England: Cambridge University Press.

DeFrancisco, Victoria. (1991). The sounds of silence: How men silence women in marital relations. *Discourse and Society, 2*(4), 413–424.

DeFrancisco, Victoria. (1997). Gender, power, and practice: Or putting your politics where your mouth is. In Ruth Wodak (Ed.), *Gender, discourse, and ideology* (pp. 37–56). London: Sage.

DeFrancisco, Victoria, & O'Connor, Penny. (1995). A feminist critique of self-help books on heterosexual romance: Read 'em and weep. *Women's Studies in Communication, 18*(2), 217–227.

DeGenova, Mary Kay, Stinnett, Nick, & Stinnett, Nancy. (2011). *Intimate relationships, marriage & families* (8th ed.). New York: McGraw Hill.

de la Cruz, Sor Juana Inés. (1987). *La Respuesta*. In *A woman of genius* (Margaret Sayers Peden, Trans.). Salisbury, CT: Lime Rick Press. (Original work published 1701)

de Lauretis, Teresa. (1984). *Alice doesn't: Feminism, semiotics, cinema*. London: MacMillan.

Demo, Anne Teresa. (2000, Spring). The Guerrilla Girls' comic politics of subversion. *Women's Studies in Communication, 23*(2), 133–156.

DePaulo, Bella. (2006). *Singled out: How singles are stereotyped, stigmatized, and ignored, and still live happily ever after*. New York: St. Martin's Griffin.

DePaulo, Bella. (2012). Singles, no children: Who is your family? In Anita L. Vangelisti (Ed.), *The Routledge handbook of family communication* (2nd ed., pp. 190–204). New York: Routledge.

DePaulo, Bella, & Trimberger E. Kay. (2008). Single women. *Sociologists for Women in Society Fact Sheet*. Retrieved from www.socwomen.org/web/images/stories/resources/fact_sheets/fact_win2008-single.pdf

Deutsch, Francine M. (2007). Undoing gender. *Gender & Society, 21*(1), 106–127.

Dickinson, Greg, & Anderson, Karrin Vasby. (2004, September). Fallen: O. J. Simpson, Hillary Rodham Clinton, and the re-centering of white patriarchy. *Communication and Critical/Cultural Studies, 1*(3), 271–296.

Dienhart, Anna. (1998). *Reshaping fatherhood: The social construction of shared parenting*. San Francisco: Sage.

Dindia, Kathryn. (2006). Men are from North Dakota, women are from South Dakota. In Kathryn Dindia & Daniel J. Canary (Eds.), *Sex differences and similarities in communication* (2nd ed., pp. 3–20). Mahwah, NJ: Erlbaum.

Dindia, Kathryn, & Allen, M. (1992). Sex differences in self-disclosure: A meta-analysis. *Psychological Bulletin, 112*, 106–124.

Dindia, Kathryn, & Canary, Dan. (2006). *Sex differences and similarities in communication* (2nd ed.). Mahwah, NJ: Erlbaum.

Dines, Gail, & Murphy, Wendy J. (2011, May 8). SlutWalk is not sexual liberation. *The Guardian,* p. 25. Retrieved from www.guardian.co.uk/commentisfree/2011/may/08/slutwalk-not-sexual-liberation

DiPiero, Thomas. (2002). *White men aren't.* Durham, NC: Duke University Press.

Disch, Estelle. (2009). *Reconstructing gender: A multicultural anthology* (5th ed.). Boston: McGraw-Hill.

Doğan, Filiz Öztütüncü. (2006). Video games and children: Violence in video games. *New/Yeni Symposium Journal, 44*(4), 161–164. Retrieved from www.yenisymposium.net

Doherty, William J., & Beaton, John M. (2004). Mothers and fathers parenting together. In Anita L. Vangelisti (Ed.), *Handbook of family communication* (pp. 269–286). Mahwah, NJ: Erlbaum.

Dorman, Benjamin. (2006, Winter). Tokyo's Dr. Phil. *Religion in the News, 8*(3), pp. 20–21, 26.

Do Rozario, Rebecca-Anne C. (2004). The princess and the Magic Kingdom: Beyond nostalgia, the function of the Disney princess. *Women's Studies in Communication, 27*(1), 34–59.

Douglas, Delia. (2002). To be young, gifted, black and female: A meditation on the cultural politics at play in representations of Venus and Serena Williams. *Sociology of Sport Online, 5*(2). Retrieved from http://physed.otago.ac.nz/sosol/v5i2/v5i2_3.html

Dow, Bonnie J. (1996). *Prime-time feminism.* Philadelphia: University of Pennsylvania Press.

Dow, Bonnie J. (2001, June). *Ellen,* television, and the politics of gay and lesbian visibility. *Critical Studies in Media Communication, 18*(2), 123–140.

Dow, Bonnie J. (2003). Feminism, Miss America, and media mythology. *Rhetoric & Public Affairs, 6,* 127–149.

Dow, Bonnie J., & Condit, Celeste. (2005, September). The state of the art in feminist scholarship in communication. *Journal of Communication, 55*(3), 448–478.

Dowd, Nancy E. (2000). *Redefining fatherhood.* New York: New York University Press.

Doyle, Jennifer, & Jones, Amelia. (2006). Introduction: New feminist theories of visual culture. *Signs, 31*(3), 607–615.

Droogsma, Rachel Anderson. (2007, August). Redefining hijab: American Muslim women's standpoints on veiling. *Journal of Applied Communication Research, 35*(3), 294–319.

Dubois, Diane, Serbin, Lisa, & Derbyshire, Alison. (1998). Toddlers' intermodal and verbal knowledge about gender. *Merrill-Palmer Quarterly, 44,* 338–351.

DuBowski, Sandi Simcha (Director/Producer). (2003). *Trembling before G-d* [Documentary]. Israel: Simcha Leib Productions and Turbulent Arts, presented in Association with Keshet Broadcasting Ltd.

Duffy, Mignon. (2005, February). Reproducing labor inequalities: Challenges for feminists conceptualizing care at the intersections of gender, race, and class. *Gender & Society, 19*(1), 66–82.

Durham, Meenakshi Gigi. (1999, Summer). Girls, media, and the negotiation of sexuality: A study of race, class, and gender in adolescent peer groups. *Journalism and Mass Communication Quarterly, 76*(2), 193–216.

Dworkin, Andrea, & MacKinnon, Catharine A. (1988). *Pornography & civil rights: A new day for women's equality.* Minneapolis, MN: Organizing Against Pornography.

Eagly, Alice H., & Koenig, Anne M. (2006). Social role theory of sex differences and similarities: Implication for prosocial behavior. In Kathryn Dindia & Daniel J. Canary (Eds.), *Sex differences and similarities in communication* (2nd ed., pp. 3–20). Mahwah, NJ: Erlbaum.

Earp, Brian D. (2012, Spring). The extinction of masculine generics. *Journal for Communication and Culture, 2*(1), 4–19.

Eastwick, Paul W., & Gardner, Wendi, L. (2008). Is it a game? Evidence for social influence in the virtual world. *Social Influence, 4*(1), 18–32.

Eckert, Penelope, & McConnell-Ginet, Sally. (1992). Communities of practice: Where language, gender and power all live. In Kira Hall, Mary Bucholtz, & Birch Manwomon, (Eds.), *Locating power, proceedings of the 2nd Berkeley Woman and Language Conference* (pp. 89–99). Berkeley, CA: BWLG.

Eckert, Penelope, & McConnell-Ginet, Sally. (1999). New generalizations and explanations in language and gender research. *Language in Society, 28,* 185–201.

Eckert, Penelope, & McConnell-Ginet, Sally. (2011). Communities of practice: Where language, gender, and power all live. In Jennifer Coates & Pia Pichler (Eds.), *Language and gender: A reader* (2nd ed., pp. 573–582). West Sussex, England: John Wiley-Blackwell.

Education Amendments of 1972, 20 U.S.C. § 1681–1688 (1972).

Edwards, Renee, & Hamilton, Mark A. (2004, April). You need to understand my gender role: An empirical test of Tannen's model of gender and communication. *Sex Roles: A Journal of Research, 50*(7–8), 491–505.

Ehrenreich, Barbara. (1990). Are you the middle-class? In Margaret L. Andersen & Patricia Hill Collins (Eds.), *Race, class and gender: An anthology* (pp. 100–109). Belmont, CA: Wadsworth.

Ehrenreich, Barbara. (2001). *Nickel and dimed: On (not) getting by in America.* New York: Holt.

Ehrenreich, Barbara, & English, Dierdre. (2005). *For her own good: Two centuries of the experts' advice to women.* New York: Anchor.

Ehrensaft, Diane. (2011). Boys will be girls, girls will be boys: Children affect parents as parents affect children in gender nonconformity. *Psychoanalytic Psychology, 28*(4), 528–548.

Eide, Elisabeth. (2010). Strategic essentialism and ethnification. *Nordicom Review, 31,* 63–78.

Eldridge, K. A., Sevier, M., Jones, J., Atkins, D. C., & Christensen, A. (2007). Demand-withdraw communication in severely distressed, moderately distressed, and nondistressed couples: Rigidity and polarity during relationship and personal problem discussions. *Journal of Family Psychology, 21,* 218–226.

Elgin, Suzette Haden. (2000). *Native tongue.* New York: The Feminist Press at City University of New York. (Original work published 1984)

Elgin, Suzette Haden. (2002a). *The Judas rose: Native tongue II.* New York: The Feminist Press at City University of New York. (Original work published 1987)

Elgin, Suzette Haden. (2002b). *Earthsong: Native tongue III.* New York: The Feminist Press at City University of New York. (Original work published 1993)

El Guindi, Fadwa. (1999). *Veil: Modesty, privacy, and resistance.* New York: Berg.

El Guindi, Fadwa. (2005a). Confronting hegemony, resisting occupation. In Faye V. Harrison (Ed.), *Resisting racism and xenophobia: Global perspectives on race, gender and human rights* (pp. 251–268). New York: AltaMira Press.

El Guindi, Fadwa. (2005b, June). Gendered resistance, feminist veiling, Islamic feminism [Electronic version]. *Ahfad Journal, 22*(1), 53–78.

Elias, Marilyn. (1992, August 3). Difference seen in brains of gay men. *USA Today,* p. 8D.

Eliot, Lise. (2009a). *Pink brain, blue brain: How small differences grow into troublesome gaps and what we can do about it.* Boston: Houghton Mifflin Harcourt.

Eliot, Lise. (2009b, September 8). Girl brain, boy brain? *Scientific American.* Retrieved from www.scientificamerican.com/article.cfm?id=girl-brain-boy-brain

Emens, Elizabeth F. (2007). Changing name changing: Framing rules and the future of marital names. *The University of Chicago Law Review, 74*(3), 761–863.

Enck-Wanzer, Suzanne Marie. (2009). All's fair in love and sport: Black masculinity and domestic violence in the news. *Communication & Critical/Cultural Studies, 6,* 1–18. doi:10.1080/14791420802632087

Enloe, Cynthia. (1989). *Bananas, beaches, and bases: Making feminist sense of international politics.* Berkley: University of California Press.

Ensler, Eve. (2000). *The vagina monologues: V-day edition.* New York: Villard.

Entertainment Software Assocation. (2012). *Essential facts about the computer and video game industry.* Retrieved from www.theesa.com/facts/gameplayer.asp

Entman, Robert M., & Rojecki, Andrew. (2001). *The black image in the white mind.* Chicago: University of Chicago Press.

The Episcopal Diocese of Fort Worth. (2007, May 16). *Diocese reaffirms pursuit of APO* [Press release]. Forth Worth, TX: Author.

Eshbaugh, Elaine M., & Gute, Gary. (2008). Hookups and sexual regret among college women. *Journal of Social Psychology, 148*(1), 1–10.

Fabj, Valeria. (1993). Motherhood as political voice: The rhetoric of the Mothers of Plaza de Mayo. *Communication Studies, 44,* 1–18.

Fausto-Sterling, Anne. (1992). *Myths of gender: Biological theories about women and men* (2nd ed.). New York: Basic Books.

Fausto-Sterling, Anne. (1993). The five sexes. *Sciences, 33*(2), 20–25.

Fausto-Sterling, Anne. (2000). *Sexing the body: Gender politics and the construction of sexuality.* New York: Basic Books.

Felski, Rita. (2006). "Because it is beautiful": New feminist perspectives on beauty. *Feminist Theory, 7*(2), 273–282.

Ferguson, Christopher J., Munoz, Monica E., Contreras, Sandra, & Velasquez, Kristina. (2011). Mirror mirror on the wall: Peer competition, television influences, and body image dissatisfaction. *Journal of Social and Clinical Psychology, 30*(5), 458–483.

Ferns, Ilse. (2000, September). Moral development during adolescence: A cross-cultural study. (South Africa). *Dissertation Abstracts International: Section B: The Sciences and Engineering, 61*(3-B), 1670.

Ferraro, Kathleen J. (2006). *Neither angels nor demons: Women, crime and victimization.* Boston: Northeastern University Press.

Fikkan, Janna L., & Rothblum, Esther D. (2012). Is fat a feminist issue? Exploring the gendered nature of weight bias. *Sex Roles, 66*(9–10), 575–592.

Fifty percent of American marriages are ending in divorce—Fiction! (2012). TruthOrFiction.com. Retrieved from www.truthorfiction.com/rumors/d/divorce.htm

Finch, Jenny, with Ann Killio (2011). *Throw like a girl: How to dream big and believe in yourself.* Chicago: Triumph Books.

Fine, Cordielia. (2010). *Delusions of gender: How our minds, society, and neurosexism create difference.* New York: W. W. Norton.

Fisher, Bonnie S., Cullen, Francis T., & Turner, Michael G. (2000). *The sexual victimization of college women.* Washington, DC: National Institute of Justice.

Fisher, Jill A. (2002). Tattooing the body, marking culture. *Body & Society, 6*(4), 91–107.

Fishman, Pamela. (1978). Interaction: The work women do. *Social Problems, 25,* 397–406.

Fiske, John. (1987). *Television culture.* New York: Methuen.

Flores, Lisa A. (1996, May). Creating discursive space through a rhetoric of difference: Chicana feminists craft a homeland. *Quarterly Journal of Speech, 82,* 142–156.

Foner, Nancy, & Fredrickson, George M. (Eds.). (2005). *Not just black and white: Historical and contemporary perspectives on immigration, race and ethnicity in the United States.* New York: Russell Sage Foundation.

Forbeswoman. (2012, June 28). 7 ways you're hurting your daughter's future. *Forbes.* Retrieved from www.forbes.com/sites/learnvest/2012/06/28/7-ways-youre-hurting-your-daughters-future

Forth, Christopher, E. (2008). *Masculinity in the modern west: Gender, civilization and the body.* New York: Palgrave MacMillan.

Foucault, Michel. (1980). *Power/knowledge* (Colin Gordon, L. Marshall, J. Mephan, & K. Soper, Trans.). New York: Pantheon.

Francis, Becky, & Skelton, Christine. (2005). *Reassessing gender and achievement: Questioning contemporary key debates.* London: Routledge.

Francis, Leslie J. (2005). Gender role orientation and attitude toward Christianity: A study among older men and women in the United Kingdom. *Journal of Psychology and Theology, 33*(3), 179–186.

Frassanito, Paolo, & Pettorini, Benedetta. (2008). Pink and blue: The color of gender. *Child's Nervous System, 24*(8), 881–882.

Frawley, Timothy. (2005). Gender bias in the classroom: Current controversies and implications for teachers. *Childhood Education, 81*(4), 221–228.

Frederick, David A., Fessler, Daniel M. T., & Haselton, Martie G. (2005). Do representations of male muscularity differ in men's and women's magazines? *Body Image, 2,* 81–86.

Fredrickson, Barbara L., & Roberts, Tomi-Ann. (1997). Objectification theory: Toward understanding women's lived experiences and mental health risks. *Psychology of Women Quarterly, 21,* 173–206.

Freeman, Sue J. M., & Bourque, Susan C. (2001). Leadership and power: New conceptions. In Sue J. M. Freeman, Susan C. Bourque, & Christine M. Shelton (Eds.), *Women on power: Leadership redefined* (pp. 3–24). Boston: Northeastern University Press.

Freire, Paulo. (1972). *Pedagogy of the oppressed.* London: Penguin.

Freud, Sigmund. (1975). *Three essays on the theory of sexuality.* New York: Basic Books.

Friedan, Betty. (1963). *The feminine mystique.* New York: Dell.

Frisch, Hannah, L. (1977). Sex stereotypes in adult-infant play. *Child Development, 48,* 1671–1675.

Frith, Katherine, Shaw, Ping, & Cheng, Hong. (2005, March). The construction of beauty: A cross-cultural analysis of women's magazine advertising. *Journal of Communication, 55*(1), 56–70.

Fulghum, Robert. (2004). *All I really need to know I learned in kindergarten* (15th ed.). New York: Ballantine Books.

Gaffney, Edward McGlynn, Jr. (1990). Politics without brackets on religious convictions: Michael Perry and Bruce Ackerman on neutrality. *Tulane Law Review, 64,* 1143–1194.

Gamman, Lorraine, & Marshment, Margaret. (Eds.). (1989). *The female gaze: Women as viewers of popular culture.* Seattle, WA: The Real Comet Press.

Gauntlett, David. (2002). *Media, gender and identity.* London: Routledge.

The Gay, Lesbian & Straight Education Network. (2011). *2011 National School Climate Survey: LBGT youth face pervasive, but decreasing levels of harassment.* Retrieved from www.glsen.org/cgi-bin/iowa/all/library/record/2897.html?state=research&type=research

Gelderen, Loes van, Bos, Henny M. W., Gartrell, Nanette, Hermanns, Jo, & Perrin, Ellen C. (2012). Quality of life of adolescents raised from birth by lesbian mothers: The US national longitudinal family study. *Journal of Developmental Behavior Pediatrics, 33*(1), 17–23.

Gergen, Kenneth J. (1994). *Realities and relationships: Soundings in social construction.* Cambridge, MA: Harvard University Press.

Gerschick, Thomas J., & Miller, Adam Stephen. (2004). Coming to terms: Masculinity and physical disability. In Michael S. Kimmel & Michael A. Messner (Eds.), *Men's lives* (6th ed.). Boston: Allyn & Bacon.

Gerson, Kathleen. (2004, August). Understanding work and family through a gendered lens. *Community, Work and Family, 7*(2), 163–178.

Gerson, Kathleen. (2010). *The unfinished revolution: How a new generation is reshaping family, work and gender in America.* Oxford, England: Oxford University Press.

Gherovici, Patricia. (2010). *Please select your gender: From the invention of hysteria to the democratizing of transgenderism.* New York: Routledge.

Gibson-Davis, Christina M. 2011. Mothers but not wives: The increasing lag between non-marital births and marriage. *Journal of Marriage and Family, 73,* 1–15.

Giffney, Noreen. (2004). Denormatizing queer theory: More than (simply) lesbian and gay studies. *Feminist Theory, 5*(1), 73–78.

Gill, Rosalind, Henwood, Karen, & McLean, Carl. (2005). Body projects and the regulation of normative masculinity. *Body & Society, 11*(1), 37–62.

Gillespie, Dair L., & Leffler, Ann. (1983). Theories of nonverbal behavior: A critical review of proxemics research. In Randall Collins (Ed.), *Sociological theory* (pp. 120–154). San Francisco: Jossey-Bass.

Gilligan, Carol. (1982). *In a different voice: Psychological theory and women's development.* Cambridge, MA: Harvard University Press.

Gilmore, Sean. (1995). Sports sex: A theory of sexual aggression. In Helen Sterk & Lynn Turner (Eds.), *Difference that makes a difference: Examining research assumptions in gender issues.* Westport, CT: Greenwood.

GLAAD. (n.d.). *GLADD's transgender resources.* Retrieved from www.glaad.org/transgender?gclid=CKn_9b7th64CFU2b7QodHDkT4Q

Glenn, Evelyn Nakano (2008). Yearning for lightness. *Gender & Society, 22,* 281–302.

Goffman, Erving. (1963). *Behavior in public places: Notes on the social organization of gatherings.* New York: Free Press.

Goffman, Erving. (1979). *Gender advertisements.* New York: Harper & Row.

Goldsmith, Daena J., & Fulfs, Patricia A. (1999). You just don't have the evidence: An analysis of claims and evidence in Deborah Tannen's *You just don't understand.* In Michael E. Roloff (Ed.), *Communication yearbook* (Vol. 22, pp. 1–49). Thousand Oaks, CA: Sage.

Good, Catherine, Aronson, Joshua, & Harder, Jayne Ann. (2008). Problems in the pipeline: Stereotype threat and women's achievement in higher-level math courses. *Journal of Applied Development Psychology, 29,* 17–28.

Goodwin, Marjorie Harness. (2006). *The hidden life of girls: Games of stance, status, and exclusion.* Oxford, England: Blackwell.

Gottman, John, M. (1994). *What predicts divorce? The relationship between marital processes and marital outcomes.* Hillsdale, NJ: Erlbaum.

Grabe, Shelly, & Hyde, Janet Shibley. (2006). Ethnicity and body dissatisfaction among women in the United States: A meta-analysis. *Psychological Bulletin, 132*(4), 622–640.

Grabe, Shelly, Hyde, Janet Shibley, & Lindberg, Sara M. (2007). Body objectification and depression in adolescents: The role of gender, shame and rumination. *Psychology of Women Quarterly, 31,* 164–175.

Gramsci, Antonio, Rosenthal, Raymond, & Rosengarten, Frank. (1993). *Letters from prison.* New York: Columbia University Press.

Gray, Herman. (1995). Black masculinity and visual culture. *Callaloo, 18*(2), 401–405.

Gray, John. (1992). *Men are from Mars, women are from Venus: A practical guide for improving communication and getting what you want in your relationship.* New York: HarperCollins.

Gray, John. (2012). *Mars Venus.* Retrieved from www.marsvenus.com/john-gray-mars-venus.htm

Green, Kyle, & Van Oort, Madison. (2013, Spring). "We wear no pants": Selling the crisis of masculinity in the 2010 Super Bowl commercials. *Signs, 38*(3), 695–719.

Greenberg, Julie A. (1999, Summer). Defining male and female: Intersexuality and the collision between law and biology. *Arizona Law Review, 41,* 265–328.

Greenberg, Julie, A. (2012). *Intersexuality and the law: Why sex matters.* New York: New York University Press.

Gregg, Nina. (1993). Politics of identity/politics of location: Women workers organizing in a postmodern world. *Women's Studies in Communication, 16*(1), 1–33.

Grogan, Tamara. (2003). *Boys and girls together: Improving gender relationships in K–6 classrooms.* Greenfield, MA: Northeast Foundation for Children.

Guerrero, Laura K. (2012). *Interpersonal communication.* Boston: Pearson.

Guerrilla Girls. (1995). *Confessions of the Guerrilla Girls.* New York: HarperPerennial.

Gunning, Isabelle R. (1997). Arrogant perception, world traveling, and multicultural feminism: The case of female genital surgeries. In Adrien Katherine Wing (Ed.), *Critical race feminism: A reader* (pp. 352–360). New York: New York University Press.

Haag, Pamela. (2005, February 11). Navigating the new subtleties of sex-discrimination cases in academe. *The Chronicle of Higher Education, 51*(23), B20.

Hackman, Heather. W. (2012). Teaching LBGTQI issues in higher education: An interdependent framework. *Diversity & Democracy: Civic Learning for Shared Futures, 15*(1), 2–4.

Haddock, Shelley A., Zimmerman, Toni Schindler, & Lyness, Kevin P. (2003). Changing gender norms: Transitional dilemmas. In Froma Walsh (Ed.), *Normal family processes: Growing diversity and complexity* (3rd ed., pp. 301–336). New York: Guilford Press.

Hadewijch. (1980). *The complete works* (Mother Columba Hart, O.S.B., Trans.). New York: Paulist Press. (Original work published ca. mid-1200s)

Halberstam, Judith. (1998). *Female masculinity.* Durham, NC: Duke University Press.

Halberstam, Judith. (2005). *In a queer time & place.* New York: New York University Press.

Hall, Donald E. (Ed.). (1994). *Muscular Christianity: Embodying the Victorian age.* Cambridge, England: Cambridge University Press.

Hall, Edward T. (1966). *The hidden dimension.* New York: Doubleday.

Hall, Judith, Coates, Erik J., & LeBeau, Lavonia Smith (2005). Nonverbal behavior and the vertical dimension of social relations: A meta-analysis. *Psychological Bulletin, 131*(6), 898–924.

Hall, Kira. (2000). Performativity. *Journal of Linguistic Anthropology, 9*(1–2), 184–187.

Hall, Kira. (2009). Boys' talk: Hindi, moustaches and masculinity in New Delhi. In Pia Pichler & Eva Eppler (Eds.), *Gender and spoken interaction* (pp. 139–162). New York: Palgrave Macmillan.

Hall, Stuart. (1993). Encoding, decoding. In Simon During (Ed.), *The cultural studies reader* (pp. 90–103). London: Routledge.

Hamilton, Laura, Geist, Claudia, & Powell, Brian. (2011). Marital name change as a window into gender attitudes. *Gender & Society, 25,* 145–175.

Handelsman, Jo, Moss-Racusin, Corinne A., Dovidio, John F., Brescoll, Victoria L., & Graham, Mark J. (2012, September 17). *Science faculty's subtle gender biases favor male students.* Proceedings of the National Academy of Sciences of the United States of America. Retrieved from www.helmholtz-muenchen.de/fileadmin/GLEICHSTELLUNG/PDF/Science_facultys_subtle_gender_biases_favor.pdf

Hanke, Robert. (1998, May). Theorizing masculinity with/in the media. *Communication Theory, 8*(2), 183–203.

Hanson, Katherine, Guilfoy, Vivian, & Pillai, Santá. (2009). *More than Title IX: How equity in education has shaped the nation.* Lanham, MD: Rowman & Littlefield.

Harding, Sandra. (1995). Subjectivity, experience, and knowledge: An epistemology from/for Rainbow Coalition politics. In Judith Roof & Robyn Weigman (Eds.), *Who can speak? Authority and critical identity* (pp. 120–136). Urbana: University of Illinois Press.

Harris, Angela. (1997). Race and essentialism in feminist legal theory. In Adrien Katherine Wing (Ed.), *Critical race feminism: A reader* (pp. 11–26). New York: New York University Press.

Harris, Judith. (2003, December 7). If shoe won't fit, fix the foot? Popular surgery raises concern. *The New York Times,* pp. A1, A36.

Harris, Kate Lockwood, Palazzolo, Kellie E., & Savage, Matthew, W. (2012). "I'm not sexist, but . . .": How ideological dilemmas reinforce sexism in talk about intimate partner violence. *Discourse & Society, 23*(6), 643–656.

Hartley, Cecilia. (2001). Letting ourselves go: Making room for the fat body in feminist scholarship. In Jana Evans Braziel & Kathleen LeBesco (Eds.), *Bodies out of bounds: Fatness and transgression* (pp. 60–73). Berkeley: University of California Press.

Hartmann, Margaret. (2011, December 14). *Frat suspended after disturbing rape survey.* Jezebel. Retrieved from http://jezebel.com/5867922/frat-suspended-after-disturbing-rapey-survey-to members

Harvey, Adia M. (2005, December). Becoming entrepreneurs: Intersections of race, class, and gender at the Black beauty salon. *Gender & Society, 19*(6), 789–808.

Hasbro: Feature boys in the packaging of the Easy-Bake Oven [YouTube video]. (2012, November 30). Retrieved from www.youtube.com/watch?v=zHESKyxrxJM

Hearn, Jeff. (1993). Emotive subjects: Organizational men, organizational masculinities and the (de)construction of "emotions." In Stephen Fineman (Ed.), *Emotion in organizations* (pp. 142–166). London: Sage.

Hearn, Jeff. (1994). The organization(s) of violence: Men, gender relations, organizations, and violences. *Human Relations, 47,* 731–754.

Hegde, Radha Sarma. (1995). Recipes for change: Weekly help for Indian women. *Women's Studies in Communication, 18*(2), 177–188.

Henley, Nancy. (1977). *Body politics: Power, sex, and nonverbal communication.* Englewood Cliffs, NJ: Prentice Hall.

Henley, Nancy. (1995). Body politics revisited: What do we know today? In Pamela J. Kalbfleisch & Michael J. Cody (Eds.), *Gender, power and communication in human relationships* (pp. 27–61). Hillsdale, NJ: Erlbaum.

Henley, Nancy, & Kramarae, Cheris. (1991). Gender, power, and miscommunication. In Nikolas Coupland, Howard Giles, & John M. Wiemann (Eds.), *"Miscommunication" and problematic talk* (pp. 18–43). Newbury Park, CA: Sage.

Hennessy, Rosemary. (1995). Subjects, knowledges, . . . and all the rest: Speaking for what. In Judith Roof & Robyn Weigman (Eds.), *Who can speak? Authority and critical identity* (pp. 137–150). Urbana: University of Illinois Press.

Henson v. City of Dundee, 682 F.2d at 902 (11th Cir. 1982).

Herbst, Claudia. (2004). Lara's lethal and loaded mission: Transposing reproduction and destruction. In Sherrie A. Inness (Ed.), *Action chicks: New images of tough women in popular culture* (pp. 21–46). New York: Palgrave MacMillan.

Hermans, Erno J., Ramsey, Nick F., & van Honk, Jack. (2008). Exogenous testosterone enhances responsiveness to social threat in the neural circuitry of social aggression in humans. *Journal of Biological Psychiatry, 63,* 263–270. doi:10.1016/j.biopsych.2007.05.013

Hershcovis, M. Sandy, Turner, Nick, Barling, Julian, Arnold, Kara A., Dupré, Kathryne E., Inness, Michelle, LeBlanc, Manon Mireille, & Sivanathan, Niro. (2007). Predicting workplace aggression: A meta-analysis. *Journal of Applied Psychology, 92*(1), 228–238.

Hildegard of Bingen. (1990). *Scivias* (Mother Columba Hart & Jane Bishop, Trans.). New York: Paulist Press. (Original work published ca. 1151/1152)

Hinde, Robert A. (2005). A suggested structure for a science of relationships. *Personal Relationships, 2*(1), 1–15.

Hinduja, Sameer, & Patchin, Justin W. (2010). *Sexting: A brief guide for educators and parents.* Cyberbullying Research Center. Retrieved from *www.cyberbullying.us/Sexting_Fact_Sheet.pdf*

Hines, Caitlin. (1999). Rebaking the pie: The woman as dessert metaphor. In Mary Bucholtz, A. C. Liang, & Laurel A. Sutton (Eds.), *Reinventing identities: The gendered self in discourse* (pp. 145–162). New York: Oxford University Press.

Hochschild, Arlie Russell. (1997). *The time bind: When work becomes home and home becomes work.* New York: Henry Holt.

Hochschild, Arlie Russell. (2003). *The second shift* (2nd ed.). New York: Avon Books.

Hoerl, Kristen, & Casey, Kelly. (2010). The post-nuclear family and the depoliticization of unplanned pregnancy in *Knocked Up, Juno,* and *Waitress. Communication & Critical/Cultural Studies, 7,* 360–380. doi:10.1080/14791420.2010.523432

Hoerrner, Keisha L. (1996). Gender roles in Disney films: Analyzing behaviors from Snow White to Simba. *Women's Studies in Communication, 19*(2), 213–228.

Holley, Sarah R., Sturm, Virginia E., & Levinson, Robert W. (2010). Exploring the basis for gender differences in the demand-withdraw pattern. *Journal of Homosexuality, 57,* 666–684.

Holmes, Janet. (1997). Story-telling in New Zealand women's and men's talk. In Ruth Wodak (Ed.), *Gender and discourse* (pp. 263–293). London: Sage.

Holmstrom, Amanda J. (2009). Sex and gender similarities and differences in communication values in same-sex and cross-sex friendships. *Communication Quarterly, 57*(2), 224–238.

Hondagneu-Sotelo, Pierette, & Avila, Ernestine. (1997, October). "I'm here but I'm there": The meanings of Latina transitional motherhood [Electronic version]. *Gender & Society, 11*(5), 548–569.

hooks, bell. (1989). *Talking back: Thinking feminist, thinking black.* Boston: South End Press.

hooks, bell. (1992). *Black looks: Race and representation.* Boston: South End Press.

hooks, bell. (1994). *Teaching to transgress: Education as the practice of freedom.* New York: Routledge.

Hoover, Stewart M., Clark, Lynn Schofield, & Alters, Diane F. (2004). *Media, home and family.* New York: Routledge.

Horkheimer, Max, & Adorno, Theodor W. (1972). *Dialectic of enlightenment* (John Cumming, Trans.). New York: Herder and Herder.

Horney, Karen. (1967). The flight from womanhood. In Karen Horney (Ed.), *Feminine Psychology* (pp. 54–70). New York: W. W. Norton. (Reprinted from *The International Journal of Psycho-Analysis,* pp. 324–339, by Karen Horney, 1926)

Horvath, Miranda A., Hegarty, Peter, Tyler, Suzannah, & Mansfield, Sophie. (2012, November). "Lights on at the end of the party": Are lads' mags mainstreaming dangerous sexism? *British Journal of Psychology, 103*(4), 454–471.

Horwitz, Linda Diane. (1998). *Transforming appearance into rhetorical argument: Rhetorical criticism of public speeches of Barbara Jordan, Lucy Parsons, and Angela Y. Davis.* Unpublished doctoral dissertation, Northwestern University, Evanston, IL.

Houston, Marsha. (2000). Multiple perspectives: African American women conceive their talk. *Women and Language, 23*(1), 11–17.

Houston, Marsha. (2004). When Black women talk with White women: Why the dialogues are difficult. In Alberto Gonzalez, Marsha Houston, & Victoria Chen (Eds.), *Our voices: Essays in culture, ethnicity, and communication* (4th ed., pp. 119–125). Los Angeles: Roxbury.

Hunt, Lynn. (Ed.). (1993). *The invention of pornography.* New York: Zone Books.

Hyde, Janet Shibley. (2005). The gender similarities hypothesis. *American Psychologist, 60*(6), 581–592.

Hyde, Janet Shibley. (2007). New directions in the study of gender similarities and differences. *Current Directions in Psychological Science, 16*(5), 259–263.

Ingoldsby, Bron B., & Smith, Suzanna. (Eds.). (2006). *Families in multicultural perspective* (2nd ed.). New York: Guilford Press.

Ingraham, Chrys. (2008). *White weddings: Romancing heterosexuality in popular culture* (2nd ed.). New York: Routledge.

Inness, Sherrie A. (Ed.). (2004). *Action chicks: New images of tough women in popular culture.* New York: Palgrave MacMillan.

Institute for Women's Policy Research. (2012, April). *The gender wage gap by occupation* [Fact sheet]. IWPR #C350a

Irons, Jenny. (1998). The shaping of activist recruitment and participation: A study of women in the Mississippi civil rights movement. *Gender & Society, 12*(6), 692–709.

Ivy, Diana. (2011). *GenderSpeak: Personal effectiveness in gender communication* (5th ed.). Boston: Allyn & Bacon.

Jackson, Linda A., Zhao, Yong, Kolenic III, Anthony, Fitzgerald, Hiram E., Harold, Rena, & Von Eye, Alexander. (2008). Race, gender, and information technology use: The new digital divide. *CyberPsychology & Behavior, 11*(4), 437–442.

Jackson, Ronald L. II, & Dangerfield, Celnisha L. (2003). Defining Black masculinity as cultural property: Toward an identity negotiation paradigm. In Larry A. Samovar & Richard E. Porter (Eds.), *Intercultural communication: A reader* (pp. 120–130). Belmont, CA: Wadsworth.

Jagsi, Reshma, Griffith, Kent A., Stewart, Abigail, Sambuco, Dana, DeCastro, Rochelle, & Ubel, Peter A. (2012). Gender differences in the salaries of physician researchers. *JAMA, 307*(22), 2410–2417.

James, Carolyn Custis. (2011). *Half the church: Recapturing God's global vision for women.* Grand Rapids, MI: Zondervan.

James, Susan Donaldson. (2011, April 13). *J. Crew ad with boy's pink toenails creates stir.* ABCNews.Health. Retrieved from http://abcnews.go.com/Health/crew-ad-boy-painting-toenails-pink-stirs-transgender/story?id=13358903

Jhally, Sut. (Producer/Writer/Editor). (1995). *DreamWorlds II* [Motion picture]. (Available from Media Education Foundation, 26 Center Street, Northampton, MA 01060)

Jhally, Sut. (Producer/Writer/Editor). (2009). *Codes of gender* [Motion picture]. (Available from Media Education Foundation, 26 Center Street, Northampton, MA 01060)

Joffe-Walt, Chana. (2009, March 11). *"Sexting": A disturbing new teen trend?* All Things Considered. Retrieved from www.npr.org/templates/story/story.php?storyId=101735230

Johansson, Thomas. (2011). Fatherhood in transition: Paternity leave and changing masculinities. *Journal of Family Communication, 11*(3), 165–180.

Johnson, Fern. (1996). Friendship among women: Closeness in dialogue. In Julia T. Wood (Ed.), *Gendered relationships: A reader* (pp. 79–94). Mountain View, CA: Mayfield.

Johnson, Jessica. (2010, March 2). "Cool pose culture" hurts young black men. *Online Athens Banner-Herald.* Retrieved from http://onlineathens.com/stories/030210/opi_569412104 .shtml

Johnson, Michael P. (2006). Gendered communication and intimate partner violence. In Bonnie J. Dow & Julia T. Wood (Eds.), *The Sage handbook of gender and communication* (pp. 71–87). Thousand Oaks, CA: Sage.

Johnson, Michelle Kirtley, Weaver, James B. III., Watson, Kittie W., & Barker, Larry B. (2000). Listening styles: Biological or psychological differences. *International Journal of Listening, 14,* 32–46.

Jones, Jeffrey M. (2012, November 9). *Gender gap in 2012 vote is largest in Gallup history.* Gallup.com. Retrieved from www.gallup.com/poll/158588/gender-gap-2012-vote-largest-gallup-history.aspx

Jones, Steve, Johnson-Yale, Camille, Millermaier, Sarah, & Pérez, Francisco S. (2009). U.S. college students' Internet use: Race, gender and digital divides. *Journal of Computer-Mediated Communication, 14,* 244–264.

Jordan-Zachery, Julia S. (2007). Am I a Black woman or a woman who is Black? A few thoughts on the meaning of intersectionality. *Politics & Gender, 3,* 254–263. doi:10.1017/S1743923X07000074

Journal of Marriage and the Family. (2001). Inside cover. *63*(1).

Julian of Norwich. (1978). *Showings* (Edmund Colledge, O. S. A. & James Walsh, S. J., Trans.). New York: Paulist Press. (Original work published ca. 1393)

Kachru, Braj B. (Ed.). (1982). *The other tongue: English across cultures.* Oxford, England: Pergamon Press.

Kane, Emily W. (2006). "No way my boys are going to be like that!" Parents' responses to children's gender nonconformity. *Gender & Society, 20*(2), 149–176.

Kane, Emily W. (2009). "I wanted a soul mate": Gendered anticipation and frameworks of accountability in parents' preferences for sons and daughters. *Symbolic Interaction, 32*(4), 372–389.

Kane, Emily W. (2012). *The gender trap: Parents and the pitfalls of raising boys and girls.* New York: New York University Press.

Kanter, Rosabeth Moss. (1977). *Men and women of the corporation.* New York: Basic Books.

Kaplan, E. Ann. (1983). Is the gaze male? In Ann Snitow, Christine Stansell, & Sharon Thompson (Eds.), *Powers of desire: The politics of sexuality* (pp. 309–327). New York: Monthly Review Press.

Kapur, Ratna. (2012). Pink chaddis and SlutWalk couture: The postcolonial politics of feminism lite. *Feminist Legal Studies, 20,* 1–20.

Karraker, Meg Wilkes, & Grochowski, Janet R. (2012). *Families with futures: Family studies into the 21st century* (2nd ed.). New York: Routledge.

Katherine. (2010, February 8). *Masculinity in crisis: Superbowl ads reveal changing gender identities.* Sparxoo.com. Retrieved from http://sparxoo.com/2010/02/08/masculinity-in-crisis-superbowl-ads-reveal-changing-gender-identities

Katz, Jackson. (2003). *Wrestling with manhood: Boys, bullying and battering* [Videotape]. Northampton, MA: Media Education Foundation.

Katz, Jackson. (2010). It's the masculinity, stupid: A cultural studies analysis of media, the presidency, and pedagogy. In Z. Leonardo (Ed.), *Handbook of cultural politics and education* (pp. 477–507). Rotterdam, The Netherlands: Sense Publishers.

Katzman, Melanie A., Hermans, Karin M. E., Van Hoeken, Daphne, & Hoek, Hans W. (2004). Not your typical "island woman": Anorexia nervosa is reported only in subcultures in Curacao. *Culture, Medicine, and Psychiatry, 28,* 463–492.

Keith, Genevieve Amaris. (2009). *Hailing gender: The rhetorical actions of greeting cards.* Unpublished master's thesis, George Washington University, Washington, DC. Retrieved from http://gradworks.umi.com/14/64/1464059.html

Kellerman, Kathy. (1992). Communication: Inherently strategic and primarily automatic. *Communication Monographs, 59,* 288–300.

Kelley, Harold H., Berscheid, Ellen, Christensen, Andrew, Harvey, John H., Huston, Ted L., Levinger, George, McClintock, Evie, Peplau, Letitia Anne, & Peterson, Donald R. (1983). *Close relationships.* New York: W. H. Freeman.

Kelly, Joan B., & Johnson, Michael P. (2008). Differentiation among types of intimate partner violence: Research update and implications for interventions. *Family Court Review, 46*(3), 476–499.

Kennedy, Randall. (2002). *Nigger: The strange career of a troublesome word.* New York: Pantheon Books.

Kerber, Linda K. (2005, March 18). We must make the academic workplace more humane and equitable. *The Chronicle of Higher Education,* pp. B6–B9.

Khan, Anber Younnus, & Kamal, Anila. (2010). Exploring reactions to invasion of personal space in university students. *Journal of Behavioural Sciences, 20*(2), 80–99.

Kierkegaard, Patrick. (2008). Video games and aggression. *International Journal of Liability and Scientific Enquiry, 1*(4), 411–417.

Kikoski, John F., & Kikoski, Catherine Kano. (1999). *Reflexive communication in the culturally diverse workplace.* Westport, CT: Praeger.

Kilbourne, Jean (Creator), & Jhally, Sut (Director, Editor, Producer). (2010). *Still killing us softly 4* [Motion picture]. (Available from Media Education Foundation, 26 Center Street, Northampton, MA 01060)

Kim, Susanna. (2011, March 23). *U.S. couples spend an average of 27,000 on weddings in 2011.* ABC Good Morning America. Retrieved from http://abcnews.go.com/Business/top-expensive-areas-married/story?id=15980519

Kimmel, Michael, S. (2008). *Guyland: The perilous world where boys become men.* New York: Harper Collins.

Kimmel, Michael S. (2012a). *The gendered society* (5th ed.). New York: Oxford University Press.

Kimmel, Michael S. (2012b). *Manhood in America: A cultural history* (3rd ed.). New York: Oxford Press.

Kingsley, Charles. (1857). *Two years ago.* Cambridge, England: Macmillan.

Kirtley, Michelle D., & Weaver, James B. III. (Fall, 1999). Exploring the impact of gender role self-perception on communication style. *Women's Studies in Communication, 22*(2), 190–204.

Kissling, Elizabeth Arveda. (1991). Street harassment: The language of sexual terrorism. *Discourse and Society, 2*(4), 451–460.

Kitzinger, Celia. (2005). Heteronormativity in action: Reproducing the heterosexual nuclear family in after-hours medical calls. *Social Problems, 52*(4), 477–498.

Kitzinger, Celia. (2008). Conversation analysis: Technical matters for gender research. In Kate Harrington, Lia Litosseliti, Helen Sauntson, & Jane Sunderland (Eds.), *Gender and language research methodologies* (pp. 119–138). New York: Palgrave MacMillan.

Kivel, Paul. (2002). *Uprooting racism: How White people can work for racial justice* (Rev. ed.). Gabriola Island, British Columbia, Canada: New Society Publishers.

Klassen, Chris. (2003, November). Confronting the gap: Why religion needs to be given more attention in women's studies. *Thirdspace: A Journal for Emerging Feminist Scholars, 3*(1). Retrieved from www.thirdspace.ca/articles/klassen.htm

Knudson-Martin, Carmen. (2012). Changing gender norms in families and society: Toward equality and complexities. In Froma Walsh (Ed.), *Normal family processes: Growing diversity and complexity* (pp. 324–346). New York: Guilford Press.

Kochman, Thomas. (1990). Force fields in Black and White. In Donald Carbaugh (Ed.), *Cultural communication in intercultural contact* (pp. 193–194). Hillsdale, NJ: Erlbaum.

Kohlberg, Lawrence. (1966). A cognitive-developmental analysis of children's sex-role concepts and attitudes. In Eleanor E. Maccoby (Ed.), *The development of sex differences* (pp. 82–173). Stanford, CA: Stanford University Press.

Kolesnikova, Natalia, & Liu, Yang. (2011, October). Gender wage gap may be much smaller than most think. *The Regional Economist,* 14–15.

Kopelman, R. E., Shea-Van Fossen, R. J., Paraskevas, E., Lawter, L., & Prottas, D. J. (2009). The bride is keeping her name: A 35-year retrospective analysis of trends and correlates. *Social Behavior and Personality, 37*(5), 687–700.

Kosut, Mary. (2006). An ironic fad: The commodification and consumption of tattoos. *The Journal of Popular Culture, 39*(6), 1035–1048.

Kowal, Donna M. (1996). *The public advocacy of Emma Goldman: An anarcho-feminist stance on human rights.* Unpublished doctoral dissertation, University of Pittsburgh.

Kowal, Donna M. (2000). One cause, two paths: Militant vs. adjustive strategies in the British and American women's suffrage movements. *Communication Quarterly, 48,* 240–255.

Kowalczyk, Liz. (2001, September 28). Patriotic purchasing. Americans are being urged to spend, but analysts doubt the strategy will have an impact in the long run. *The Boston Globe,* p. C1.

Kramarae, Cheris. (1981). *Women and men speaking: Frameworks for analysis.* Rowley, MA: Newbury House.

Kramarae, Cheris. (1992). Harassment and everyday life. In Lana Rakow (Ed.), *Women making meaning: New feminist directions in communication* (pp. 100–120). New York: Routledge.

Kramarae, Cheris, & Treichler, Paula A. (1992). *Amazons, bluestockings and crones: A feminist dictionary* (2nd ed.). London: Pandora Press.

Kramer, Laura. (2005). *The sociology of gender: A brief introduction* (2nd ed.). Los Angeles: Roxbury.

Kreimer, Susan. (2011). More kids hospitalized for eating disorders: Better programs urged for those affected; a growing number are boys, young men. *H&HN Hospitals & Health Networks, 85*(3), 18. Retrieved from www.hhnmag.com/hhnmag/jsp/articledisplay.jsp?dcrpath=HHNMAG/Article/data/03MAR2011/0311HHN_Inbox_clinicalcare&domain=HHNMAG

Kroløkke, Charlotte, & Sørensen, Anne Scott. (2006). *Gender communication theories and analyses: From silence to performance.* Thousand Oaks, CA: Sage.

Kunkel, Dale, Eyal, Keren, Finnerty, Keli, Biely, Erica, & Donnerstein, Edward. (2005, November). *Sex on TV 4.* A Kaiser Family Foundation report. Menlo Park, CA. Retrieved from *www.kff.org/entmedia/upload/sex-on-tv-4-full-report.pdf*

Kwan, Samantha. (2010). Navigating public spaces: Gender, race, and body privilege in everyday life. *Feminist Formations, 22*(2), 144–166.

Lacan, Jacques. (1998). *The four fundamental concepts of psychoanalysis. The seminar of Jacques Lacan, Book 11.* (1st American ed.). New York: W. W. Norton.

Lacroix, Celeste. (2004). Images of animated others: The Orientalization of Disney's cartoon heroines from *The Little Mermaid* to *The Hunchback of Notre Dame. Popular Communication, 2*(4), 213–229.

Lakoff, George, & Johnson, Mark. (1980). *Metaphors we live by.* Chicago: University of Chicago Press.

Lakoff, Robin. (1975). *Language and woman's place.* New York: Harper & Row.

Laner, Mary Riege, & Ventrone, Nicole A. (2000). Dating scripts revisited. *Journal of Family Issues, 21,* 488–500.

Langman, Lauren. (2008). Punk, porn and resistance: Carnivalization and the body in popular culture. *Current Sociology, 56*(4), 657–677.

Lawrence, Charles R. III. (1993). If he hollers let him go: Regulating racist speech on campus. In Mari J. Matsuda et al. (Eds.), *Words that wound* (pp. 53–88). Boulder. CO: Westview Press.

Laya, Patricia. (2011, June 6). *Do you pay enough for advertising?* Business Insider. Retrieved from www.businessinsider.com/corporations-ad-spending-2011-6?op=1

Leaper, Campbell, & Robnett, Rachael D. (2011). Women are more likely than men to use tentative language, aren't they? A meta-analysis testing for gender differences and moderators. *Psychology of Women Quarterly, 35*(1), 129–142.

Lee, Emily S. (2011). The epistemology of the question of authenticity, in place of strategic essentialism. *Hypatia, 26*(2), 258–279.

Lee, Lin-Lee. (2004). Pure persuasion: A case study of *Nüshu* or "women's script" discourses. *Quarterly Journal of Speech, 90,* 403–421.

Lennard, Natasha. (2012, December 27). *Transgender no longer a medical disorder.* Salon. com. Retrieved from www.salon.com/2012/12/27/transgender_no_longer_a_medical_ disorder

Lev, Arlene Istar, & Malpas, Jean. (2011). Exploring gender and sexuality in couples and families. In Arlene Istar Lev & Jean Malpas (Eds.), *At the edge: Exploring gender and sexuality in couples and families. AFTA Monograph Series, 7* (pp. 2–8). Washington, DC: American Family Therapy Academy.

Levin, Diane E., & Kilbourne, Jean. (2009). *So sexy so soon: The new sexualized childhood and what parents can do to protect their kids.* New York: Ballantine Books.

Li, Eric P. H., Min, Hyun Jeong, Belk, Russell W., Kimura, Junko, & Bahl, Shalini. (2008). Skin lightening and beauty in four Asian cultures. *Advances in Consumer Research, 35,* 444–449.

Liu, Ou Lydia, & Wilson, Mark. (2009). Gender differences in large-scale math assessments: PISA trend 2000–2003. *Applied Measurement in Education, 22*(2), 164–184.

Livia, Anna, & Hall, Kira. (1997). "It's a girl!" Bringing performativity back to linguistics. In Anna Livia & Kira Hall (Eds.), *Queerly phrased: Language, gender, and sexuality* (pp. 3–20). New York: Oxford University Press.

Livingston, Jennifer. (2012, October 2). *CBS WKBT News anchor's on-air response to viewer calling her fat* [YouTube video]. Retrieved from www.youtube.com/ watch?v=rUOpqd0rQSo

Long, Jeffrey C., & Kittles, Rick A. (2003). Human genetic diversity and the nonexistence of biological races. *Human Biology, 75*(4), 449–471.

Lorber, Judith. (1994). *Paradoxes of gender.* New Haven, CT: Yale University Press.

Lorber, Judith, & Martin, Patricia Yancy. (2011). The socially constructed body: Insights from feminist theory. In Peter Kivisto (Ed.), *Illuminating social life: Classical and contemporary theory revisited* (5th ed., pp. 279–304). Thousand Oaks, CA: Sage.

Lorber, Judith, & Moore, Lisa Jean. (2007). *Gendered bodies: Feminist perspectives.* Los Angeles: Roxbury.

Lord, M. G. (1994). *The unauthorized biography of a real doll.* New York: William Morrow.

Lorde, Audre. (1984). *Sister outsider.* Trumansberg, NY: The Crossing Press.

Loseke, Donileen R., & Kurz, Demie. (2005). Men's violence toward women is the serious social problem. In Donileen R. Loseke, Richard J. Gelles, & Mary M. Cavanaugh (Eds.), *Current controversies on family violence* (pp. 79–95). Thousand Oaks, CA: Sage.

Low, Setha M. (2003). Embodied space(s): Anthropological theories of body, space, and culture. *Space and Culture, 6*(9), 9–18.

LSA Resolution on the Oakland "Ebonics" Issue. (1997, July 1). Approved by members attending the 71st Annual Business Meeting, Chicago, Illinois, January 3, 1997; adopted by LSA membership in a mail ballot, July 1, 1997. Retrieved from https://lsadc.org/info/lsa-res-ebonics.cfm

Lynch, Annette. (1999). *Dress, gender, and cultural change: Asian American and African American rites of passage.* Oxford, England: Berg.

Lynch, Annette. (2012). *Porn chic: Exploring the contours of raunch eroticism.* New York: Berg.

MacNish, Melissa, & Gold-Peifer, Marissa. (2011). Families in transition: Supporting families of transgender youth. In Arlene Istar Lev & Jean Malpas (Eds.), *At the edge: Exploring gender and sexuality in couples and families. AFTA Monograph Series, 7* (pp. 34–42). Washington, DC: American Family Therapy Academy.

Madden, Janice. (2012). *Performance-support bias and the gender pay gap among stockbrokers.* PSC Working Paper Series, PSC 12–04. Retreived from repository.upenn.edu/psc_working_papers/35

Maddux, Kristy. (2012). The feminized gospel: Aimee Semple McPherson and the gendered performance of Christianity. *Women's Studies in Communication, 35,* 42–67.

Magley, Vivki J., Gallus, Jessica A., & Bunk, Jennifer A. (2010). The gendered nature of workplace mistreatment. In J. C. Chrisler & D. R. McCreary (Eds.), *Handbook of gender research in psychology* (pp. 423–441). New York: Springer.

Majors, Richard. (2001). The cool pose, how Black men present themselves as a spectacle of self-expression and agency, by adopting the cool pose. In Stephen M. Whitehead & Frank J. Barrett (Eds.), *The masculinities reader* (pp. 209–218). Cambridge, England: Polity Press.

Majors, Richard, & Billson, Janet Mancini. (1992). *Cool pose: The dilemmas of Blackmanhood in America.* New York: Lexington Books.

Malpas, Jean, & Lev, Arlene I. (2011). *At the edge: Exploring gender and sexuality in couples and families.* Washington, DC: American Family Therapy Academy.

Maltz, Daniel N., & Borker, Ruth. (1982). A cultural approach to male-female miscommunication. In John J. Gumperz (Ed.), *Language and social identity* (pp. 196–216). Cambridge, England: Cambridge University Press.

Manago, Adriana M., Graham, Michael B., Greenfield, Patricia M., & Salimkhan, Goldie. (2008). Self-presentation and gender on MySpace. *Journal of Applied Developmental Psychology, 29,* 446–458.

Mansbridge, Jane. (1998). Feminism and democracy. In Anne Phillips (Ed.), *Feminism & politics* (pp. 142–158). New York: Oxford University Press.

Maracle, Lee. (1989, Spring). Moving over. *Trivia: A Journal of Ideas, 14*(Part II), 9–12.

Mare, Lesley Di, & Waldron, Vincent R. (2006). Researching gendered communication in Japan and the United states: Current limitations and alternative approaches. In Kathryn Dindia & Dan J. Canary (Eds.), *Sex differences and similarities in communication* (2nd ed., pp. 195–218). Mahwah, NJ: Erlbaum.

Martin, Jane Roland. (1991). The contradiction and the challenge of the educated woman. *Women's Studies Quarterly, 19*(1–2), 6–27.

Martin, Judith N., & Nakayama, Thomas K. (2004). *Intercultural communication in contexts* (3rd ed.). Boston: McGraw-Hill.

Martin, Patricia Yancey. (2003). "Said and done" versus "saying and doing": Gendering practices, practicing gender at work. *Gender & Society, 17*(3), 342–366.

Martin, Patricia Yancey. (2004, June). Gender as social institution. *Social Forces, 82*(4), 1249–1273.

Martin, Patricia Yancey. (2006). Practising gender at work: Further thoughts on reflexivity. *Gender, Work and Organization, 13*(3), 254–276.

Martyna, Wendy. (1980a). Beyond the "he/man" approach: The case for nonsexist language. *Signs, 5,* 482–493.

Martyna, Wendy. (1980b). The psychology of the generic masculine. In Sally McConnell-Ginet, Ruth Borker, & Nelly Furman (Eds.), *Women and language in literature and society* (pp. 69–78). New York: Praeger.

Martyna, Wendy. (1983). Beyond the he/man approach: The case for nonsexist language. In Barrie Thorne, Cheris Kramarae, & Nancy Henley (Eds.), *Language, gender, and society* (pp. 25–37). Rowley, MA: Newbury House.

Mascaro, Lisa. (2012, September 27). Todd Akin says McCaskill debated like a "wildcat," not as "ladylike." *Chicago Tribune.* Retrieved from www.chicagotribune.com/news/politics now/la-pn-todd-akin-mccaskill-ladylike-20120927,0,3070998.story

Mast, Marianne Schmid, & Sczesny, Sabine. (2010). Gender, power, and nonverbal behavior. In Joan C. Chrisler & Donald R. McCreary (Eds.), *Handbook of gender research in psychology* (pp. 411–425). New York: Springer.

Matsuda, Mari. J. (1993). Public response to racist speech: Considering the victim's story. In Mari J. Matsuda, Charles R. Lawrence III, Richard Delgado, & Kimberlè Williams Crenshaw (Eds.), *Words that wound* (pp. 17–51). Boulder, CO: Westview Press.

Matsuda, Mari J., Lawrence, Charles R. III, Delgado, Richard, & Crenshaw, Kimberlè Williams. (Eds.). (1993). *Words that wound.* Boulder, CO: Westview Press.

Matthews, Glenna R. (1992). *The rise of public woman: Woman's power and woman's place in the United States, 1630–1970.* New York: Oxford University Press.

Mawdsley, Emma. (2007). The millennium challenge account: Neo-liberalism, poverty and security. *Review of International Economy, 14*(3), 487–509.

Mayer, Tamar. (Ed.). (2000). *Gender ironies of nationalism: Sexing the nation.* London: Routledge.

Mayers, Lester B., & Chiffriller, Sheila H. (2008). Body art (body piercings and tattooing) among undergraduate university students: "Then and now." *Journal of Adolescent Health, 42,* 201–203.

McAndrew, Francis T. (2009). The interacting roles of testosterone and challenges to status in human male aggression. *Agression and Violent Behavior, 14,* 330–335. doi:10.1016/j.avb.2009.04.006

McCabe, Janice, Fairchild, Emily, Grauerholz, Liz, Pescosolido, Bernice A., & Tope, Daniel. (2011). Twentieth-century children's books: Patterns of disparity in title and central characters. *Gender & Society, 25*(2), 197–226. doi:10.1177/0891243211398358

McCall, Leslie. (2005). The complexity of intersectionality. *Signs, 30,* 1771–1800.

McConnell, Allen R., & Fazio, Russell H. (1996). Women as men and people: Effects of gender-marked language. *Personality and Social Psychology Bulletin, 22*(10), 1004–1013.

McConnell, Allen R., & Gavanski, I. (1994, May). *Women as men and people: Occupation title suffixes as primes.* Paper presented at the 66th Annual Meeting of the Midwestern Psychological Association, Chicago.

McCormick, Maggie. (2011, May 12). *Origins of boys in blue & girls in pink.* eHow.com. Retrieved from www.ehow.com/info_8406183_origins-boys-blue-girls-pink.html#ixzz1k9CNhVM5

McDonald, Paula. (2012). Workplace sexual harassment 30 years on: A review of the literature. *International Journal of Management Reviews, 14*(1), 1–17.

McElhinny, Bonnie S. (2003). Theorizing gender in sociolinguist and linguist anthropology. In Janet Holmes & Miriam Meyerhoff (Eds.), *The handbook of language and gender* (pp. 21–42). Oxford, England: Blackwell.

McGilvery, Keith. (2012, September 20). *Investigation: UVM frat not responsible for rape survey.* Retrieved from www.wcax.com/story/19598271/investigation-uvm-frat-not-responsible-for-rape-survey

McGrath, Mary Jo. (2007). *The early faces of violence: From schoolyard bullying and ridicule to sexual harassment.* McGrath Training Systems. Retrieved from www.mcgrathinc .com/Articles/articles-021.html

McGuffy, C. Shawn, & Rich, B. Lindsay. (2003). Playing in the gender transgression zone: Race, class, and hegemonic masculinity in middle childhood. In Joan Z. Spade & Catherine Valentine (Eds.), *The kaleidoscope of gender: Prisms, patterns, and possibilities* (pp. 172–183). Belmont, CA: Wadsworth.

McKee, Stacy (Writer), & Verica, Tom (Director). (2011, October 6). What is it about men [Television series episode]. In Shonda Rhimes (Executive producer), *Grey's Anatomy.* New York: ABC Broadcasting. Retrieved from http://abc.go.com/watch/greys-anatomy/SH559058/VD55146633/what-is-it-about-men

McKeown, Eamonn, Nelson, Simon, Anderson, Jane, Low, Nicola, & Elford, Jonathan. (2010). Disclosure, discrimination and desire: Experiences of Black and South Asian gay men in Britain. *Culture, Health & Sexuality: An International Journal for Research, Intervention and Care, 12*(7), 843–856.

McNair Barnett, Bernice. (1993). Invisible Southern Black women leaders in the movement: The triple constraints of gender, race, and class. *Gender & Society, 7*(2), 162–182.

Meritor Savings Bank v. Vinson, 477 U.S. 57 (1986).

Messner, Michael S. (2004). *The gendered society* (2nd ed.). New York: Oxford University Press.

Metts, Sandra. (2006). Gendered communication in dating relationships. In Bonnie J. Dow & Julia T. Wood (Eds.), *The Sage handbook of gender in communication* (pp. 25–40). Thousand Oaks, CA: Sage.

Michaud, Shari L., & Warner, Rebecca M. (1997). Gender differences in self-reported response in troubles talk. *Sex Roles: A Journal of Research, 37*(7–8), 527–541.

Miedzian, Myriam. (1993). How rape is encouraged in American boys and what we can do to stop it. In Emilie Buchwald, Pamela R. Fletcher, & Martha Roth (Eds.), *Transforming a rape culture* (pp. 153–164). Minneapolis, MN: Milkweed Editions.

Millenium Campaign. (2004). *About the goals. Goal 3.* Retrieved from www.millenniumcampaign.org/site/pp.asp?c=grKVL2NLE&b=186382

Miller, Casey, & Swift, Kate. (1993). Foreword. In Jane Mills, *Womanwords: A dictionary of words about women* (pp. ix–xii). New York: Henry Holt.

Mills, Jane. (1993). *Womanwords: A dictionary of words about women.* New York: Henry Holt.

Mills, Sara. (2003). *Gender and politeness.* Cambridge, England: Cambridge University Press.

Mink, Gwendolyn. (1995). *The wages of motherhood: Inequality in the welfare state, 1917–1942.* Ithaca, NY: Cornell University Press.

Minnich, Elizabeth Komarck. (1998). Education. In Wilma Mankiller, Gwendolyn Mink, Marysa Navarrao, Barbara Smith, & Gloria Steinem (Eds.), *The reader's companion to U.S. women's history* (pp. 163–167). New York: Houghton Mifflin.

Minsky, Rosalind. (1998). *Psychoanalysis and culture: Contemporary states of mind.* New Brunswick, NJ: Rutgers University Press.

Mischel, Walter. (1966). A social learning view of sex differences in behavior. In Eleanor E. Maccoby (Ed.), *The development of sex differences* (pp. 93–106). Stanford, CA: Stanford University Press.

Moghadam, Valentine. (1994). *Gender and national identity: Women and politics in Muslim societies.* London: Oxford University Press.

Mohanty, Chandra Talpade. (2003). *Feminism without borders*. Durham, NC: Duke University Press.

Monsour, Michael. (2006). Communication and gender among adult friends. In Bonnie J. Dow & Julia T. Wood (Eds.), *The Sage handbook of gender in communication* (pp. 57–70). Thousand Oaks, CA: Sage.

Moradi, Bonnie, & Huang, Yu-Ping. (2008). Objectification theory and psychology of women: A decade of advances and future directions. *Psychology of Women Quarterly, 32*, 377–398.

Morman, Mark T., & Floyd, Kory. (2006a). The good son: Men's perceptions of the characteristics of sonhood. In Kory Floyd & Mark T. Morman (Eds.), *Widening the family circle: New research on family communication* (pp. 37–55). Thousand Oaks, CA: Sage.

Morman, Mark T., & Floyd, Kory. (2006b). Good fathering: Father and son perceptions of what it means to be a good father. *Fathering, 4*(2), 113–136.

Morrell, Carolyn M. (1994). *Unwomanly conduct. The challenges of intentional childlessness*. New York: Routledge.

Morris, Charles E. III (2009). Hard evidence: The vexations of Lincoln's queer corpus. In Barbara Biesecker & John Lucaites (Eds.), *Rhetoric, materiality, and politics* (pp. 185–214). New York: Peter Lang.

Moss, Peter, & Deven, Fred. (Eds.). (1999). *Parental leave: Progress or pitfall?* The Hague: Netherlands. Interdisciplinary Demographic Institute.

Moya, Paula M. L. (1997). Postmodernism, "realism," and the politics of identity: Cherríe Moraga and Chicana feminism. In M. Jacqui Alexander & Chandra Talpade Mohanty (Eds.), *Feminist genealogies, colonial legacies, democratic futures* (pp. 125–150). New York: Routledge.

Muehlenhard, Charlene L., Goggins, Mary F., Jones, Jayne M., & Satterfield, Arthur T. (1991). Sexual violence and coercion in close relationships. In Kathleen McKinney & Susan Spreecher (Eds.), *Sexuality in close relationships* (pp. 155–176). Hillsdale, NJ: Erlbaum.

Muehlenhard, Charlene L., & Peterson, Zoë D. (2005). Wanting and not wanting sex: The missing discourse of ambivalence. *Feminism & Psychology, 15*(1), 15–20.

Muehlenhard, Charlene L., & Peterson, Zoë D. (2011). Distinguishing between sex and gender: History, current conceptualizations, and implications. *Sex Roles, 64*, 791–803. doi:10.1007/s11199-011-9932-5

Mulac, Anthony. (2006). The gender-linked language effect: Do language differences really make a difference? In Katherine Dindia & Dan Canary, (Eds.), *Sex differences and similarities in communication: Critical essays and empirical investigations of sex and gender in interaction* (2nd ed., pp. 219–239). Mahwah, NJ: Erlbaum.

Mullany, Louise. (2007). *Gendered discourse in the professional workplace*. Basingstoke, NY: Palgrave Macmillan.

Mullen, A. L. (2010). *Degrees of inequality: Culture, class, and gender in American higher education*. Baltimore: The John Hopkins University Press.

Mulvey, Laura. (1975). Visual pleasure and narrative cinema. *Screen, 16*(3), 6–18.

Mumby, Dennis K. (2001). Power and politics. In Fredric M. Jablin & Linda L. Putnam (Eds.), *The new handbook of organizational communication: Advances in theory, research, and methods* (pp. 585–623). Newbury Park, CA: Sage.

Murphy, Bren Ortega. (1994). Greeting cards & gender messages. *Women & Language, 17*(1), 25–29.

Murray, Samantha. (2008). Pathologizing "fatness": Medical authority and popular culture. *Sociology of Sport Journal, 25*, 7–21.

Muscanell, Nichole L., & Guardagno, Roseanna, E. (2011). Make new friends or keep the old: Gender and personality differences in social networking use. *Computers in Human Behavior, 28*(1), 107–112.

Muscio, Inga. (2002). *Cunt: A declaration of independence.* New York: Seal Press.

Myers, David G. (2004). *Psychology* (7th ed.). New York: Worth.

Nadasen, Premil. (2005). *Welfare warriors: The welfare rights movement in the United States.* New York: Routledge.

Nadeau, Barbie Latza. (2012, April 20). *Nuns gone wild! Vatican chastises American sisters.* The Daily Beast. Retrieved from www.thedailybeast.com/articles/2012/04/20/nuns-gone-wild-vatican-chastises-american-sisters.html

Nakamura, Lisa. (2005). Head-hunting on the Internet: Identity tourism, avatars, and racial passing in textual and graphic chat spaces. In Raiford Guins & Omayra Zaragoza Cruz (Eds.), *Popular culture: A reader* (pp. 520–533). Thousand Oaks, CA: Sage.

Nakamura, Lisa. (2008). *Digitalizing race and visual cultures on the Internet.* Minneapolis, MN: University of Minnesota Press.

Nakayama, Thomas K., & Krizek, Robert L. (1999). Whiteness as a strategic rhetoric: In Thomas K. Nakayama & Judith N. Martin (Eds.), *Whiteness: The communication of social identity* (pp. 87–106). Thousand Oaks, CA: Sage.

Narayanan, Vasudha. (2003). Hinduism. In Arvind Sharma & Katherine K. Young (Eds.), *Her voice, her faith: Women speak on world religions* (pp. 11–58). Boulder, CO: Westview Press.

National Association for Single Sex Public Education. (2006a). *Advantages for girls.* Retrieved from www.singlesexschools.org/advantages-forgirls.htm

National Association for Single Sex Public Education. (2006b). Learning style differences. *Why gender matters* (2005). Retrieved from www.singlesexschools.org/research-learning.htm

National Campaign to Prevent Teen and Unplanned Pregnancy. (2008). *Sex and tech: Results from a survey of teens and young adults.* Retrieved from www.thenationalcampaign.org/sextech/PDF/SexTech_Summary.pdf

National Center for Education Statistics. (2010). *Student victimization in U.S. schools: Results from the 2007 school crime supplement to the National Crime Victimization Survey.* Retrieved from http://nces.ed.gov/pubs2010/2010319.pdf

National Eating Disorder Association. (n.d.). *Factors that may contribute to eating disorders & Get the facts on eating disorders.* Retrieved from www.nationaleatingdisorders.org

Newcombe, Nora S., Mathason, Lisa, & Terlecki, Melissa. (2002). Maximizing of special competence: More important than finding the cause of sex differences. In Ann McGillicuddy-De Lisi & Richard De Lisi (Eds.), *Biology & behavior: The development of sex differences in cognition* (pp. 183–204). Westport, CT: Ablex.

Newman, Michael. (1992). Pronominal disagreements: The stubborn problem of singular epicene antecedents. *Language in Society, 21,* 447–475.

Ng, Sik Hung. (1990). Androcentric coding of *man* and *his* in memory by language users. *Journal of Experimental Social Psychology, 26,* 455–464.

Norén, Laura. (2012, September 4). *Race and gender in higher education—Who gets degrees?* Graphic Sociology. Retrieved from http://thesocietypages.org/graphicsociology/2012/09/04/race-and-gender-in-higher-education

Norton, Robert. (1983). *Communication style: Theory, applications, and measures.* Beverly Hills, CA: Sage.

Norwood, Kristen. (2006). *Women in conflict: An exploratory study of conflict between women in initial interactions.* Unpublished master's thesis, University of Arkansas, OCLC's Experimental Thesis Catalog.

Norwood, Kristen. (2012). Transitioning meanings? Family members' communicative struggles surrounding transgender identity. *Journal of Family Communication, 12,* 75–92.

Nunberg, Geoff. (2012, March 13). *Slut: The other four letter s-word.* Fresh Air. Retrieved from www.npr.org/2012/03/13/148295582/slut-the-other-four-letter-s-word

Nuns on the Bus. (2012). *The Ryan budget.* Retrieved from http://nunsonthebus.com/ryan-budget

Oakland School Board approves Black English program and sparks national debate [Electronic version]. (1997, January 13). *Jet, 91,* 12.

Oishi, Eve. (2006). Visual perversions: Race, sex, and cinematic pleasure. *Signs, 31*(3), 641–674.

Olasky, Susan. (2008, June 28). Gender wars: A new survey traces the divide between elementary boys' and girls' reading tastes. *World Magazine.* Retrieved from www.worldmag.com/2008/06/gender_wars

Olivardia, Roberto. (2000). Body image and masculinity in college males. Unpublished doctoral dissertation, University of Massachusetts, Boston.

Olivardia, Roberto. (2001). Why now? How male body image is closely tied to masculinity and changing gender roles. *Society for the Psychological Study of Men and Masculinity Bulletin, 6*(4), 11–12.

Olivardia, Roberto, & Pope, Harrison, G., Jr. (1997). Eating disorders in men: Prevalence, recognition, and treatment. *Directions in Psychiatry, 17,* 41–51.

Olivardia, Roberto, Pope, Harrison, G., Jr., Borowiecki, John J. III, & Cohane, Geoffrey. (2004). Biceps and body image: The relationship between muscularity and self-esteem and eating disorder symptoms. *Psychology of Men and Masculinity, 5*(2), 112–120.

Olopade, Dayo. (2010, February 8). Could male unemployment explain the Dodge Charger Super Bowl ad [Blog post]. *Slate.* Retrieved from www.slate.com/blogs/xx_factor/2010/02/08/could_male_unemployment_explain_the_dodge_charger_super_bowl_ad.html

Olson, Loreen. (2002, Winter). Exploring "common couple violence" in heterosexual romantic relationships. *Western Journal of Communication, 66*(1), 104–129.

Orbe, Mark P. (1998, February). From the standpoint(s) of traditionally muted groups: Explicating a co-cultural communication theoretical model. *Communication Theory, 8*(1), 1–26.

Palczewski, Catherine Helen. (1995). Voltairine de Cleyre: Sexual pleasure and sexual slavery in the 19th century. *National Women's Studies Association Journal, 7,* 54–68.

Palczewski, Catherine Helen. (1996). Bodies, borders and letters: Gloria Anzaldúa's "Speaking in tongues: A letter to 3rd world women writers." *The Southern Communication Journal, 62,* 1–16.

Palczewski, Catherine Helen. (1998). "Tak[e] the helm," man the ship . . . and I forgot my bikini! Unraveling why women is not considered a verb. *Women and Language, 21*(2), 1–8.

Palczewski, Catherine Helen. (2001, Summer). Contesting pornography: Terministic catharsis and definitional argument. *Argumentation and Advocacy, 38,* 1–17.

Palczewski, Cathereine Helen, Ice, Richard, & Fritch, John. (2012). *Rhetoric in civic life.* State College, PA: Strata.

Panagopoulos, Costas. (2004) Boy talk/girl talk: Gender differences in campaign communications practices. *Women & Politics, 26*(3/4), 131–155.

Paoletti, Jo B. (2012). *Pink and blue: Telling the boys from the girls in America.* Bloomington: Indiana University Press.

Papp, Lauren M., Kouros, Chrystyna D., & Cummings, Mark E. (2009). Demand-withdraw patterns in marital conflict in the home. *Personal Relationships, 16,* 285–300.

Parker, Patricia S. (2003). Control, resistance, and empowerment in raced, gendered, and classed work contexts: The case of African American women. *Communication Yearbook, 27,* 257–291.

Pascoe, C. J. (2011). *Dude, you're a fag: Masculinity and sexuality in high school.* Berkeley: University of California Press.

Pasterski, V., Prentice, P., & Hughes, J. (2010). Consequences of the Chicago consensus on disorders of sex development (DSD): Current practices in Europe. *Archives of Disease in Childhood, 95*(8), 618–623.

Patterson, Charlotte J. (2000). Family relationships of lesbian and gay men. *Journal of Marriage and the Family, 62,* 1052–1069.

Patton, Tracey Owens. (2006). "Hey girl, am I more than my hair?" African American women and their struggles with beauty, body image, and hair. *NWSA, 18*(2), 24–51.

Penelope, Julia. (1990). *Speaking freely.* New York: Pergamon Press.

Pennington, Dorothy L. (2003). The discourse of African American women: A case for extended paradigms. In Ronald L. Jackson & Elaine B. Richardson (Eds.), *Understanding African American rhetoric* (pp. 293–307). New York: Routledge.

Peplau, Letitia Anne, & Beals, Kristin P. (2004). The family lives of lesbians and gay men. In Anita L. Vangelisti (Ed.), *Handbook of family communication* (pp. 233–248). Mahwah, NJ: Erlbaum.

Petchesky, Rosalind P. (1997). Spiraling discourses of reproductive and sexual rights: A post-Beijing assessment of international feminist politics. In Cathy J. Cohen, Kathleen B. Jones, & Joan C. Tronto (Eds.), *Women transforming politics* (pp. 569–587). New York: New York University Press.

Peters, Michael. (1995). Does brain size matter? A reply to Rushton and Ankney. *Canadian Journal of Experimental Psychology, 49*(4), 570–576.

Petersen, Jennifer L., & Hyde, Janet Shibley. (2010). A meta-analytic review of research on gender differences in sexuality, 1993–2007. *Psychological Bulletin, 136*(1), 21–38.

Peterson, Lori West, & Albrecht, Terrance L. (1999). Where gender/power/politics collide: Deconstructing organizational maternity leave policy. *Journal of Management Inquiry, 8,* 168–181.

Petrecca, Laura. (2012, July 19). Pregnant CEO tests glass ceiling. *USA Today,* A1.

Pew Forum on Religion and Public Life. (2008, Feburary). *U.S. Religious Landscape Survey.* Washington, DC. Retrieved from http://religions.pewforum.org/reports#

Pew Research. (2010). *Support for same-sex marriage edges upward.* Pew Research Center for the People & the Press. Retrieved from www.people-press.org/2010/10/06/support-for-same-sex-marriage-edges-upward

Pheterson, Gail. (Ed.). (1989). *A vindication of the rights of whores.* Seattle, WA: Seal Press.

Phillips, Katherine A., Menard, William, & Fay, Christina. (2006). Gender similarities and differences in 200 individuals with body dysmorphic disorder. *Comprehensive Psychiatry, 47,* 77–87.

Piaget, Jean. (1965). *The moral judgment of the child.* New York: Free Press.

Pickert, Nils. (2012, August 20). *Sometimes fathers just have to be role models.* EMMA Online. Retrieved from www.emma.de/ressorts/artikel/kinder-jugendliche/vater-im-rock

Pike, Kathleen M., & Mizushima, Hiroko. (2005). The clinical presentation of Japanese women with anorexia nervosa and bulimia nervosa: A study of the eating disorders inventory-2. *International Journal of Eating Disorders, 37*(1), 26–31.

Pilkington, Jane. (1998). Don't try and make out that I'm nice! The different strategies women and men use when gossiping. In Jennifer Coates (Ed.), *Language and gender: A reader* (pp. 254–269). Oxford, England: Basil Blackwell.

Pollard, Kevin. (2011, April). *The gender gap in college enrollment and graduation.* Population Reference Bureau. Retrieved from www.prb.org/Articles/2011/gender-gap-in-education.aspx

Pope, Harrison G., Jr., Gruber, Amanda J., Choi, Precilla, Olivardia, Roberto, & Phillips, Katharine A. (1997). Muscle dysphoria: An underrecognized form of body dysmorphic disorder. *Psychosomatics, 38,* 548–557.

Pope, Harrison G., Jr., Olivardia, Roberto, Gruber, Amanda, & Borowiecki, John. (1999). Evolving ideals of male body image as seen through action toys. *International Journal of Eating Disorders, 26,* 65–72.

Pope, Harrison G., Jr., Phillips, Katharine A., & Olivardia, Roberto. (2000). *The Adonis complex: The secret crisis of male body obsession.* New York: Simon & Schuster.

Pope, McKenna. (2012). *Hasbro: Feature boys in the packaging of the Easy-Bake Oven* [Petition]. Retrieved from www.change.org/petitions/hasbro-feature-boys-in-the-packaging-of-the-easy-bake-oven

Popenoe, Rebecca. (2004). *Feeding desire: Fatness, beauty and sexuality among a Saharan people.* London: Routledge.

Potter, Ellen F., & Rosser, Sue V. (2006). Factors in life science textbooks that may deter girls' interest in science. *Journal of Research in Science Teaching, 29*(7), 669–686.

Presiding bishop. (2012). *The Episcopal Church.* Retrieved from www.episcopalchurch.org/page/presiding-bishop

Preston, Cheryl B. (2003, Spring). Women in traditional religions: Refusing to let patriarchy (or feminism) separate us from the source of our liberation. *Mississippi College Law Review, 22,* 185–214.

Price, Janet, & Shildrick, Margrit. (Eds.). (1999). *Feminist theory and the body: A reader.* New York: Routledge.

Purity Ball. (2012). *Welcome to the 2012 Purity Ball.* Retrieved from www.purityball.com

Putney, Clifford. (2001). *Muscular Christianity: Manhood and sports in Protestant America, 1880–1920.* Cambridge, MA: Harvard University Press.

Quinn, Beth A. (2002, June). Sexual harassment and masculinity: The power and meaning of "girl watching." *Gender & Society, 16*(3), 386–402.

Race: Are we so different? (2011). American Anthropological Association. Retrieved from www.understandingrace.org/home.html

Rakow, Lana. (1986). Rethinking gender research in communication. *Journal of Communication, 36,* 11–26.

Ratzinger, Cardinal Joseph (2004). *Letter to the bishops of the Catholic Church on the collaboration of men and women in the church and in the world.* Retrieved from www.wf-f.org/BenedictXVI.html

Rayner, Ju-Anne, Pyett, Priscilla, & Astbury, Jill. (2010). The medicalisation of "tall" girls: A discourse analysis of medical literature on the use of synthetic oestrogen to reduce female height. *Social Science & Medicine, 71,* 1076–1083.

Reis, Elizabeth. (2009). *Bodies in doubt.* Baltimore: John Hopkins University Press.

Reiss, David. (2000). *The relational code: Deciphering genetic and social influences on adolescent development.* Cambridge, MA: Harvard University Press.

Renaissance Learning. (2012). *What kids are reading: The book-reading habits of students in American schools* (2012 edition). Retrieved from *www.renlearn.com*

Rich, Adrienne. (1977/2005). Claiming an education. In Chris Anderson & Lex Runciman (Eds.), *Open questions* (pp. 608–613). Boston: Bedford/St. Martin's.

Rich, Adrienne. (1980). Compulsory heterosexuality and lesbian existence. *Signs, 5,* 631–660.

Richardson, Brian K., & Taylor, Juandalynn. (2009). Sexual harassment at the intersection of race and gender: A theoretical model of the sexual harassment experiences of women of color. *Western Journal of Communication, 73*(3), 248–272.

Risman, Barbara J. (1998). *Gender vertigo: American families in transition.* New Haven, CT: Yale University Press.

Rivers, Caryl, & Barnett, Rosalind. (2011). *The truth about girls and boys: Challenging toxic stereotypes about our children.* New York: Columbia University Press.

Robnett, Belinda. (1996). African-American women in the civil rights movement, 1954–1965: Gender, leadership, and micromobilization. *American Journal of Sociology, 101*(6), 1661–1693.

Romanowski, Perry. (2010). (2010, January 5). *A cosmetic industry overview for cosmetic chemists* [Blog post]. Retrieved from http://chemistscorner.com/a-cosmetic-market-overview-for-cosmetic-chemists

Roof, Judith, & Weigman, Robyn. (Eds.). (1995). *Who can speak? Authority and critical identity.* Urbana: University of Illinois Press.

Rothschild, Joyce, & Davies, Celia. (1994). Organizations through the lens of gender: Introduction to the special issue. *Human Relations, 47,* 583–590.

Ruane, Janet M., & Cerulo, Karen M. (2008). *Second thoughts: Seeing conventional wisdom through the sociological eye* (4th ed.). Thousand Oaks, CA: Pine Forge Press.

Rubin, Gayle. (1984). Thinking sex: Notes for a radical theory of the politics of sexuality. In Carole Vance (Ed.), *Pleasure and danger: Exploring female sexuality* (pp. 267–319). London: Victor Gollancz.

Rubinstein, Ruth P. (2001). *Dress code: Meaning and messages in American culture* (2nd ed.). Boulder, CO: Westview Press.

Rushton, J. Philippe, & Ankney, C. Davison. (2009). Whole brain size and general mental ability: A review. *International Journal of Neuroscience, 119*(5), 692–732.

Ryle, Robyn. (2012). *Questioning gender: A sociological exploration.* Los Angeles: Sage.

Sacks, Harvey, Schegloff, Emanuel, & Jefferson, Gail. (1974). A simplest systematic for the organization of turn-taking for conversation, *Language, 50,* 696–735.

Sadker, David. (2002). An educator's primer on the gender war. *Phi Delta Kappan, 84*(3), 235–244. (Reprinted, 2011). *Kappan Classic, 92*(5), 81–89.

Sadker, David, & Sadker, Myra. (1994). *Failing at fairness: How America's schools cheat girls.* New York: Simon & Schuster.

Sadker, David, & Silber, Ellen S. (Eds). (2007). *Gender in the classroom: Foundations, skills, methods and strategies across the curriculum.* Mahwah, NJ: Erlbaum.

Sadker, David, & Zittleman, Karen. (2005). Closing the gender gap—again! Just when educators thought it was no longer an issue, gender bias is back in a new context. *Principal, 84*(4), 18–22.

Sampson, Rana. (2011, August). *Acquaintance rape of college students.* U.S. Department of Justice. Retrieved from www.cops.usdoj.gov/pdf/e03021472.pdf

Sanger, Kerran L. (1995). Slave resistance and rhetorical self-definition: Spirituals as strategy. *Western Journal of Communication, 59*(3), 177–192.

Santos, Xuan. (2009). The Chicana canvas: Doing class, gender, race and sexuality through tattooing in East Los Angeles. *NEWS Journal, 21*(3), 91–120.

Schegloff, Emanuel A. (1997). Whose text? Whose context? *Discourse & Society, 8*(2) 165–187.

Schilt, Kristen. (2011). *Just one of the guys? Transgender men and the persistence of gender inequality.* Chicago: University of Chicago Press.

Schleff, Erik. (2008). Gender and academic discourse: Global restrictions and local possibilities. *Language in Society, 37,* 515–538.

Schram, Sanford F. (1995). *Words of welfare: The poverty of social science and the social science of poverty.* Minneapolis: University of Minnesota Press.

Schulz, Muriel R. (1975). The semantic derogation of woman. In Barrie Thorne & Nancy Henley (Eds.), *Language and sex: Difference and dominance* (pp. 64–75). Chicago: Newbury House.

Scott, James C. (1992). *Domination and the arts of resistance: Hidden transcripts.* New Haven: Yale University Press.

Segrin, Chris, & Flora, Jeanne. (2011). *Family communication* (2nd ed.). New York: Routledge.

Sellers, Patricia. (2012, July 16). *New Yahoo CEO Mayer is pregnant* [Blog post]. CNNMoney. Retrieved from www.theatlantic.com/business/archive/2012/06/single-people-deserve-work-life-balance-too/259071

Sellnow, Deanne D., & Treinen, Kristen P. (2004). The role of gender in perceived speaker competence: An analysis of student peer critiques. *Communication Education, 53*(3), 286–296.

Sells, Laura R. (1993). Maria W. Miller Stewart. In Karlyn Kohrs Campbell (Ed.), *Women public speakers in the United States, 1800–1925* (pp. 339–349). Westport, CT: Greenwood Press.

Selwyn, Neil. (2004). Reconsidering political and popular understandings of the digital divide. *New Media & Society, 6,* 341–362.

Separa, Matt. (2012, April 16). *Infographic: The gender pay gap.* Center for American Progress. Retrieved from www.americanprogress.org/issues/women/news/2012/04/16/11435/infographic-the-gender-pay-gap

Shapiro, Eve. (2010). *Gender circuits: Bodies and identities in a technological age.* New York: Routledge.

Shelton, Beth Anne, & John, Daphne. (1996). The division of household labor. *Annual Review of Sociology, 22,* 299–322.

Shome, Raka. (1996, February). Postcolonial interventions in the rhetorical canon: An "other" view. *Communication Theory, 6*(1), 40–59.

Shome, Raka, & Hegde, Radha S. (2002, June). Culture, communication, and the challenge of globalization. *Critical Studies in Media Communication, 19*(2), 72–189.

Signorielli, Nancy. (2009). Minorities representation in prime time: 2000–2008. *Communication Research Reports, 26*(4), 323–336.

Simone de Beauvoir. (2010). *Stanford encyclopedia of philosophy. Retrieved from* http://plato.stanford.edu/entries/beauvoir/#SecSexWomOth

Sipe, Stephanie, Johnson, C. Douglas, & Fisher, Donna K. (2009). University students' perceptions of gender discrimination in the workplace: Reality versus fiction. *Journal of Education for Business, 84*(6), 339–349.

Slaughter, Anne-Marie. (2012, July/August). Why women still can't have it all. *The Atlantic, 310*(1), 84–102.

Slesaransky-Poe, Graciela, & García, Ana María. (2009). Boys with gender-variant behaviors and interests: From theory to practice. *Sex Education, 9*(2), 201–210.

Sloop, John M. (2004). *Disciplining gender: Rhetorics of sex identity in contemporary U.S. culture.* Amherst: University of Massachusetts Press.

Sloop, John M. (2005, August). In a queer time and place and race: Intersectionality comes of age. *Quarterly Journal of Speech, 91*(3), 312–326.

Sloop, John M. (2012). "This is not natural": Caster Semenya's gender threats. *Critical Studies in Media Communication, 29*(2), 81–96.

Smith, Jason K. (2002). *Counter-hegemonic masculinity in hip hop music: An analysis of The Roots' construction of masculinity in their music and in the media culture.* Unpublished master's thesis, University of Hartford, West Hartford, CT.

Solomon, Martha. (1987). *Emma Goldman*. Boston: Twayne.

Spencer, Renee, Porche, Michelle, & Tolman, Deborah L. (2003). We've come a long way—maybe: New challenges for gender equity in education. *Teachers College Record, 105*(9), 1774–1807.

Spender, Dale. (1985). *Man made language* (2nd ed.). London: Routledge & Kegan Paul.

Spivak, Gayatri Chakravorty. (1988). Can the subaltern speak? In Cary Nelson & Lawrence Grossberg (Eds.), *Marxism and the interpretation of culture* (pp. 271–313). Urbana: University of Illinois Press.

Spivak, Gayatri Chakravorty. (1993). *Outside in the teaching machine*. New York: Routledge.

Spivak, Gayatri Chakravorty. (1996). *The Spivak reader* (Donna Landry & Gerald MacLean, Eds.). New York: Routledge.

Spivak, Gayatri Chakravorty. (2004). Terror: A speech after 9-11. *Boundary, 2*(31), 81–111.

Starr, Christine R., & Ferguson, Gail M. (2012). Sexy dolls, sexy grade-schoolers? Media & maternal influences on young girls' self-sexualization. *Sex Roles, 67*(7–8), 463–476.

Stelter, Brian. (2011, May 3). Ownership of TV sets falls in U.S. *New York Times*. Retrieved from www.nytimes.com/2011/05/03/business/media/03television.html?_r=0

Stephens, Mitchell. (1998). *The rise of the image, the fall of the word*. New York: Oxford University Press.

Sterk, Helen M. (1989, September). How rhetoric becomes real: Religious sources of gender identity. *The Journal of Communication and Religion, 12,* 24–33.

Sterk, Helen M. (2010, November). Faith, feminism and scholarship: *The Journal of Communication and Religion*, 1999–2009. *The Journal of Communication and Religion, 33*(2), 206–216.

Stokoe, Elizabeth, & Smithson, Janet. (2001). Making gender relevant: Conversation analysis and gender categories in interaction. *Discourse & Society, 12*(2), 217–244.

Stop Street Harassment. (2011, March 1). *Activist interviews: Lani Shotlow-Rincon*. Retrieved from www.stopstreetharassment.org/2011/03/the-dont-call-me-baby-project

Straus, Erwin W. (1966). *Phenomenological psychology*. New York: Basic Books.

Striegel-Moore, Ruth H., Rosselli, Francine, Holtzman, Niki, Dierker, Lisa, Becker, Anne E., & Swaney, Gyda. (2011). Behavioral symptoms of eating disorders in Native Americans: Results from the Add Health survey wave III. *International Journal of Eating disorders, 44*(6), 561–566.

Stringer, Jeffrey L., & Hopper, Robert. (1998, May). Generic *he* in conversation. *Quarterly Journal of Speech, 84,* 209–221.

Strong, Bryan, DeVault, Christine, & Sayad, Barbara W. (1999). *Human sexuality: Diversity in contemporary America*. Mountain View, CA: Mayfield.

Stuart, Gregory L., Moore, Todd M., Hellmuth, Julianne C., Ransey, Susan E., & Kahler, Christopher W. (2006). Reasons for intimate partner violence perpetration among arrested women. *Violence Against Women, 12*(7), 609–621.

Subrahmanian, Ramya. (2005). *Promising practices and implications for scaling up girls' education: Report of the UN girls' education initiative South Asia workshop help in Chandigarh, India, 20–22 September 2004*. London: Commonwealth Secretariat.

Summers, Lawrence H. (2005, January 14). *Remarks at NBER conference on diversifying the science & engineering workforce*. Cambridge, MA. Retrieved from www.harvard.edu/president/speeches/summers_2005/nber.php

Suzette Haden Elgin. (2004). Retrieved from www.sfwa.org/members/elgin

Swain, Jon. (2005). Masculinities in education. In Michael S. Kimmel, Jeff Hearn, & R. W. Connell (Eds.), *Handbook of studies on men and masculinities* (pp. 213–229). Thousand Oaks, CA: Sage.

Swann, Joan. (2003). Schooled language: Language and gender in educational settings. In Janet Holmes & Miriam Meyerhoff (Eds.), *The handbook of language and gender* (pp. 624–644). Malden, MA: Basil Blackwell.

Tanenbaum, Leora. (2000). *Slut! Growing up female with a bad reputation.* New York: HarperCollins.

Tannen, Deborah. (1990). *You just don't understand: Women and men in conversation.* New York: William Morrow.

Tannen, Deborah. (1994a). *Gender and discourse.* New York: Oxford University Press.

Tannen, Deborah. (1994b). *Talking from 9 to 5.* New York: Avon Books.

Tavris, Carol. (1992). *The mismeasure of woman.* New York: Simon & Schuster.

Temple, Jeff R., Paul, Jonathan A., van den Berg, Patricia, Le, ViDonna, McElhany, Amy, & Temple, Brian W. (2012). Teen sexting and its association with sexual behaviors. *Archieves Pediatric Adolescent Medicine.* doi:10.1001/archpediatrics.2012.835

Tesene, Megan. (2012). Book review: Just one of the guys? Transgender men and the persistence of gender inequality. *Gender & Society, 26,* 676–678.

Teunis, Niels. (2007). Sexual objectification and the construction of whiteness in the gay male community. *Culture, Health & Sexuality: An International Journal for Research, Intervention and Care, 9*(3), 263–275.

Texas Board adopts conservative curriculum: New social studies guidelines have made state a lightening rod for ideological debate. (2010, May 21). CBS News. Retrieved from www.cbsnews.com

Thie, Marilyn. (1994, Fall). Epilogue: Prolegomenon to future feminist philosophies of religions. *Hypatia, 9*(4), 229–240.

Thompson, Christie. (2011, Summer). Taking *slut* for a walk. *Ms., 21*(3), 14.

Tobin, Allen J., & Dusheck, Jennie. (1998). *Asking about life.* Ft. Worth, TX: Saunders College.

Tonn, Mari Boor. (1996, February). Militant motherhood: Labor's Mary Harris "Mother" Jones. *Quarterly Journal of Speech, 82,* 1–21.

Tracy, Karen. (2002). *Everyday talk: Building and reflecting identities.* New York: Guilford Press.

Trans 101: Cicgender. (2011, October 9). Basic Rights Oregon. Retrieved from www.basicrights.org/uncategorized/trans-101-cisgender

Travis, Cheryl Brown, Meginnis, Kayce L., & Bardari, Kristin M. (2000). Beauty, sexuality and identity: The social control of women. In Cheryl Brown Travis & Jacquelyn W. White (Eds.), *Sexuality, society, and feminism* (pp. 237–272). Washington, DC: American Psychological Association.

Trethewey, Angela. (2001, November). Reproducing and resisting the master narrative of decline: Midlife professional women's experiences of aging. *Management Communication Quarterly, 15*(2), 183–226.

Trimberger, E. Kay. (2005). *The new single woman.* Boston: Beacon Press.

Trujillo, Nick. (1991). Hegemonic masculinity on the mound: Media representations of Nolan Ryan and American sports culture. *Critical Studies in Mass Communication, 8,* 290–308.

Truth, Sojourner. (1851). *Aren't I a woman?* Retrieved from http://people.sunyulster.edu/voughth/sojourner_truth.htm

Turner, Caroline S. (2003). Incorporation and marginalization in the academy: From border toward center for faculty of color? *Journal of Black Studies, 34,* 112–125.

Turner, Terisa E., & Brownhill, Leigh S. (2004, January-March). Why women are at war with Chevron: Nigerian subsistence struggles against the international oil industry. *Journal of Asian and African Studies, 39*(1-2), 63–94.

Understanding Islam and the Muslims. (n.d.). *USC-MSA compendium of Muslim texts.* Retrieved from www.usc.edu/dept/MSA/introduction/understandingislam.html

Unger, Rhoda. (1979). Toward a redefinition of sex and gender. *American Psychologist, 34,* 1085–1094.

Unger, Rhoda, & Crawford, Mary. (1992). *Women and gender: A feminist psychology.* Philadelphia: Temple University Press.

United Nations Fourth World Conference on Women. (1995). *Beijing declaration and platform for action.* Violence against women. Retrieved from www.un.org/womenwatch/daw/beijing/platform/violence.htm

University of Maryland Medical Center. (2011). *Eating disorders—Introduction.* Retrieved from www.umm.edu/patiented/articles/what_eating_disorders_000049_1.htm#ixzz2BSe4JifE

University of Northern Iowa. (2011). *Student sexual misconduct policy.* Retrieved from www.uni.edu/policies/315

UN Women. (n.d.). *Women, poverty & economics.* Retrieved from www.unifem.org/gender_issues/women_poverty_economics

UN trust fund to end violence against women. (2011). United Nations Entity for Gender Equality and the Empowerment of Women. Retrieved from www.unwomen.org/how-we-work/un-trust-fund

Urban Dictionary. (n.d.). *Man-up.* Retrieved from www.urbandictionary.com/define.php?term=man%20up)

U.S. Bureau of Labor Statistics. (2011). *Median weekly earnings of full-time wage and salary workers by detailed occupation and sex* [Data file]. Retrieved from www.bls.gov/cps/cpsaat39.pdf

U.S. Bureau of Labor Statistics. (2012, June 22). *American time use survey—2011 results* [Press release]. U.S. Department of Labor. Retrieved from www.bls.gov/news.release/atus.nr0.htm

U.S. Census Bureau. (2010, January 15). *Press release.* Retrieved from www.census.gov/Pres-release/www/releases/archives/families_households/01450.html.

U.S. Census Bureau. (2012a, May 2). *Facts for features: Father's day.* Retrieved from www.census.gov/newsroom/releases/archives/facts_for_features_special_editions/cb12-ff11.html

U.S. Census Bureau. (2012b). *Presence and type of computer for households, by selected householder characteristics: 2010* [Data file]. Retrieved from www.census.gov/hhes/computer/publications/2010.html

U.S. Census Bureau. (2012c). *Employed civilians by occupation, sex, race, and Hispanic origin: 2010* [Data file]. Retrieved from www.census.gov/compendia/statab/2012/tables/12s0616.pdf

U.S. Equal Opportunity Employment Commission. (2012). *Sexual harassment charges EEOC & FEPAs combined: FY 1997–FY2011.* Retrieved from www.eeoc.gov/eeoc/statistics/enforcement/sexual_harassment.cfm

U.S. General Accounting Office. (2010, September 20). *Women in management: Analysis of female manager's representation, characteristics, and pay.* Washington, DC: Author.

Vacek, Edward. (2005, March). Feminism and the Vatican [Electronic version]. *Theological Studies, 66*(1), 159–177.

Vaid, Urvashi. (1995). *Virtual equality.* New York: Anchor Books.

Valdes, Francisco. (1995, January). Queers, sissies, dykes, and tomboys: Deconstructing the conflation of "sex," "gender," and "sexual orientation" in Euro-American law and society. *California Law Review, 83*(1), 3–377.

Vandenbosch, Laura, & Eggermont, Steven. (2012). Understanding sexual objectification: A comprehensive approach toward media exposure and girls' internalization of beauty ideals, self-objectification, and body surveillance. *Journal of Communication, 62*(5), 869–887.

Vannoy, Dana. (Ed.). (2001). *Gender stratification: Social interaction and structural accounts.* Los Angeles: Roxbury.

Vidal, Catherine. (2011). The sexed brain: Between science and ideology. *Neuroethics.* doi:10.1007/s12152-011-9121-9

Vince, Emma, & Walker, Ian. (2008). A set of meta-analytic studies on the factors associated with disordered eating. *Internet Journal of Mental Health, 5*(1), 2.

Voss, Linda D., & Mulligan, Jean. (2000, March 4). Bullying in school: Are short pupils at risk? Questionnaire study in a cohort. *British Medical Journal, 320*(7235), 612–613.

Vuola, Elina. (2002). Remaking universals? Transnational feminism(s) challenging fundamentalist ecumenism. *Theory, Culture and Society, 19*(1–2), 175–195.

Vygotsky, Lev S. (1978). *Mind and society: The development of higher mental processes.* Cambridge, MA: Harvard University Press.

Wainright, Jennifer L., & Patterson, Charlotte J. (2008). Peer relations among adolescents with female same-sex parents. *Developmental Psychology, 44*(1), 117–126.

Walker, Alexis J. (1999). Gender and family relationships. In Marvin Sussman, Suzanne K. Steinmetz, & Gary W. Peterson (Eds.), *Handbook of marriage and the family* (2nd ed., pp. 439–474). New York: Plenum Press.

Walsh, Froma. (2012). The new normal: Diversity and complexity in 21st-century families. In Froma Walsh (Ed.), *Normal family processes: Growing diversity and complexity* (4th ed, pp. 3–27). New York: Guilford Press.

Walters, Suzanna Danuta. (1995). *Material girls: Making sense of feminist cultural theory.* Berkeley: University of California Press.

Warner, Michael. (2002). *Publics and counterpublics.* New York: Zone.

Weber, Max. (1947). *The theory of social and economic organizations* (A. M. Henderson & Talcott Parsons, Trans.). New York: Oxford University Press.

Welsh, Sandy, Carr, Jacquie, MacQuarrie, Barbara, & Huntley, Audrey. (2006, February). "I'm not thinking of it as sexual harassment": Understanding harassment across race and citizenship. *Gender & Society, 20*(1), 87–107.

Welter, Barbara. (1976). *Dimity convictions: The American woman in the nineteenth century.* Athens: Ohio University Press.

West, Candice, & Fenstermaker, Sarah. (1995). Doing difference. *Gender & Society, 9*(1), 8–37.

West, Candice, & Zimmerman, Don H. (1983). Small insults: A study of interruptions in cross-sex conversations between unacquainted persons. In Barrie Thorne, Cheris Kramarae, & Nancy Henley (Eds.), *Language, gender, and society* (pp. 103–119). Rowley, MA: Newbury House.

West, Candice, & Zimmerman, Don H. (1987). Doing gender. *Gender & Society, 1,* 125–151.

West, Candace, & Zimmerman, Don H. (2009). Accounting for doing gender. *Gender & Society, 23,* 112–122.

West, Richard, & Turner, Lynn H. (2010). *Introducing communication theory: Analysis and application.* Boston: McGraw-Hill.

Westerfelhaus, Robert, & Brookey, Robert Alan. (2004, July/October). At the unlikely confluence of conservative religion and popular culture: *Fight Club* as heteronormative ritual. *Text and Performance Quarterly, 24*(3–4), 302–326.

Whitam, Frederick L., Daskalos, Christopher, Sobolewski, Curt G., & Padilla, Peter. (1998). The emergence of lesbian sexuality and identity cross-culturally: Brazil, Peru, the Philippines, and the United States. *Archives of Sexual Behavior, 27*(1), 31–57.

Whitam, Fredrick L., Diamond, Milton, & Martin, James. (1993). Homosexual orientation in twins: A report on 61 pairs and three triplet sets. *Archives of Sexual Behavior, 22*(3), 187–207.

White, Mark B., & Tyson-Rawson, Kristen J. (1996, March/April; last reviewed 2012, June 15). Gender wars: A peace plan. *Psychology Today,* 50–54, 74–81. Retrieved from www.psycho logytoday.com/pring/21455

Whitehead, Stephen M. (2002). *Men and masculinities: Key themes and new directions.* Cambridge, England: Basil Blackwell.

Whiteside, Kelly. (2012, July 11). Women majority on Team USA. *USA Today,* A1.

Wiehl, Lis. (2002, Spring). "Sounding Black" in the courtroom: Court-sanctioned racial stereotyping. *Harvard Blackletter Journal, 18,* 185–210.

Wilkes, David. (2012, January 20). *Boy or girl? The parents who refused to say for five years finally reveal sex of their "gender-neutral" child.* Retrieved from www.dailymail.co.uk/news/article-2089474/Beck-Laxton-Kieran-Cooper-reveal-sex-gender-neutral-child-Sasha.html

Williams, Dmitri, Martins, Nicole, Consalvo, Mia, & Ivory, James D. (2009). The virtual census: Representations of gender, race and age in video games. *New Media & Society, 11,* 815–834. doi:10.1177/1461444809105354

Wilson, Elizabeth, & Ng, Sik Hung. (1988). Sex bias in visual images evoked by generics: A New Zealand study. *Sex Roles, 18,* 159–168.

Wilson, G. Terrance, Grilo, Carlos M., Vitousek, Kelly M. (2007). Psychological treatment of eating disorders. *American Psychologist, 62*(3), 199–216.

Wilson, Robin. (2004, December 3). Women in higher education [Special report]. *Chronicle of Higher Education, 51*(15), A8.

Winfield, Nicole. (2012, June 12). Vatican says U.S. nuns must promote church teachings. *San Francisco Chronicle.* Retrieved from www.sfgate.com/cgi-bin/article.cgi?f=/n/a/2012/06/12/international/i071351D11.DTL

Wing, Adrien Katherine. (1997). Brief reflections toward a multiplicative theory of praxis and being. In Adrien Katherine Wing (Ed.), *Critical race feminism: A reader* (pp. 27–34). New York: New York University Press.

Wodak, Ruth. (2008). Feminist post-structural discourse analysis: A new theoretical and methodological approach? In Kate Harrington, Lia Litosseliti, Helen Sauntson, & Jane Sunderland (Eds.), *Gender and language research methodologies* (pp. 243–255). New York: Palgrave MacMillan.

Wohn, Donghee Yvette. (2011). Gender and race representation in casual games. *Sex Roles, 65,* 198–207.

Wood, Jessica L., Heitmiller, Dwayne, Andreasen, Nancy C., & Nopoulos, Peg. (2008). Morphology of the ventral frontal cortex: Relationship to femininity and social cognition. *Cerebral Cortex, 18*(3), 534–540. doi:10.1093/cercor/bhm079

Wood, Jessica L., Murko, Vesna, & Nopoulos, Peg. (2008). Ventral frontal cortex in children: Morphology, social cognition and femininity/masculinity. *Social Cognitive and Affective Neuroscience, 3*(2), 168–176.

Wood, Julia. (2001). The normalization of violence in heterosexual romantic relationships: Women's narratives of love and violence. *Journal of Social and Personal Relationships, 18*(2), 239–261.

Wood, Julia. (2002). A critical response to John Gray's Mars and Venus portrayals of men and women. *Southern Communication Journal, 67*(2), 201–210.

Wood, Julia. (2013). *Gendered lives: Communication, gender and culture* (10th ed.). Boston: Wadsworth.

Wurtzel, Elizabeth. (1998). *Bitch: In praise of difficult women.* New York: Doubleday.

Wysham, Daphne. (2002, October). Women take on oil companies in Nigeria. *Economic Justice News Online, 5*(3). Retrieved from www.50years.org/cms/ ejn/story/82

Yang, Li-Shou, Thornton, Arland, & Fricke, Thomas. (2000). Religion and family formation in Taiwan: The decline of ancestral authority. In Sharon K. Houseknecht & Jerry G. Pankhurst (Eds.), *Family, religion, and social change in diverse societies* (pp. 121–146). Cambridge, England: Oxford University Press.

Yanowitz, Karen L., & Weathers, Kevin J. (2004). Do boys and girls act differently in the classroom? A content analysis of student characters in educational psychology textbooks. *Sex Roles, 51*(1–2), 101–107.

Yi, Robin H. Pugh, & Dearfield, Craig T. (2012). *The status of women in the U.S. media 2012.* Women's Media Center. Retrieved from www.womensmediacenter.com

Young, Iris Marion. (1990). *Throwing like a girl and other essays in feminist philosophy and social theory.* Bloomington: Indiana University Press.

Yousman, Bill. (2003, November). Blackophilia and blackophobia: White youth, the consumption of rap music, and white supremacy. *Communication Theory, 13*(4), 366–391.

Yuval-Davis, Nira. (1997). *Gender and nation.* London: Sage.

Yuval-Davis, Nira. (1999). The "multi-layered citizen": Citizenship in the age of "globalization." *International Feminist Journal of Politics, 1*(1), 119–136.

Yuval-Davis, Nira. (2003). Nationalist projects and gender relations. *Narodna Umjetnost, 40*(1), 9–36.

Zack, Naomi. (1998). *Thinking about race.* Belmont, CA: Wadsworth.

Zhao, Shanyang, Grasmuck, Sherri, & Martin, Jason. (2008). Identity construction on Facebook: Digital empowerment in anchored relationships. *Computers in Human Behavior, 24*(5), 1816–1836.

Zimmerman, Toni Schindler, Haddock, Shelley A., & McGeorge, Christine R. (2001). Mars and Venus: Unequal planets. *Journal of Marital and Family Therapy, 27*(1), 55–68.

Zompetti, Joseph P. (1997). Toward a Gramscian critical rhetoric. *Western Journal of Communication, 61*(1), 66–86.

Zosuls, Kristina M., Miller, Cindy Faith, Ruble, Diane N., Martin, Carol Lynn, & Fabes, Richard A. (2011). Gender development research in sex roles: Historical trends and future directions. *Sex Roles, 64*(11–12), 826–842.

Index

Figures and tables are indicated by f or t following the page number.

About the Authors

Victoria Pruin DeFrancisco, PhD, is a professor of communication studies and affiliate faculty in women's and gender studies at the University of Northern Iowa. She studies and teaches courses in gender, intercultural, and interpersonal communication. She is coordinator of the university's Diversity Inclusion program. Victoria is married and has stepchildren and grandchildren who call her Nana and remind her every day why she wrote this book.

Catherine Helen Palczewski, PhD, is a professor of communication studies, past director of debate, and affiliate faculty in women's and gender studies at the University of Northern Iowa. She teaches courses in the rhetoric of social protest, argumentation, gender, and political communication. She is a past coeditor of *Argumentation and Advocacy* and director of the 2013 AFA/NCA Biennial Conference on Argumentation held in Alta, Utah.

Danielle Dick McGeough, PhD, is an assistant professor of communication studies at the University of Northern Iowa. Her teaching and research interests explore how performance is and can be used for collaborative problem solving, community building, and social justice work. Her father taught her compassion, and her mom taught her to believe in people's ability to change.

This book was a truly coauthored endeavor. The fun, sweat, work, and joy were shared.

CPSIA information can be obtained
at www.ICGtesting.com
Printed in the USA
FFOW04n0604020218
44815650-44980FF

9 781452 220093